FROMMER'S
Easy
TO
NEW ORLEANS

By
Diane K. Schwam

EasyGuides are ✦ Quick To Read ✦ Light To Carry
✦ For Expert Advice ✦ In All Price Ranges

FrommerMedia LLC

Published by
FROMMER MEDIA LLC

ISBN 978-1-62887-013-8 (paper), 978-62887-043-5 (e-book)

Editorial Director: Pauline Frommer
Editor: Alexis Lipsitz Flippin
Production Editor: Donna Wright
Cover Photo: Cheryl Gerber
Cartographer: Andrew Murphy
Cover Design: Howard Grossman

For information on our other products or services, see www.frommers.com.

Frommer Media LLC also publishes its books in a variety of electronic formats. Some content that appears in print may not be available in electronic formats.

Manufactured in the United States of America

5　4　3　2　1

CONTENTS

ABOUT THE AUTHOR

Diana K. Schwam, writer and strategic marketing consultant, has authored four books and numerous articles about New Orleans. She followed a familiar path to the city: vacation; enrapture; homeownership; weight gain. Ms. Schwam has a high tolerance level for fleur de lis iconography and rejects those who reject the accordion.

ABOUT THE FROMMER TRAVEL GUIDES

For most of the past 50 years, Frommer's has been the leading series of travel guides in North America, accounting for as many as 24% of all guidebooks sold. I think I know why.

Though we hope our books are entertaining, we nevertheless deal with travel in a serious fashion. Our guidebooks have never looked on such journeys as a mere recreation, but as a far more important human function, a time of learning and introspection, an essential part of a civilized life. We stress the culture, lifestyle, history and beliefs of the destinations we cover, and urge our readers to seek out people and new ideas as the chief rewards of travel.

We have never shied from controversy. We have, from the beginning, encouraged our authors to be intensely judgmental, critical—both pro and con—in their comments, and wholly independent. Our only clients are our readers, and we have triggered the ire of countless prominent sorts, from a tourist newspaper we called "practically worthless" (it unsuccessfully sued us) to the many rip-offs we've condemned.

And because we believe that travel should be available to everyone regardless of their incomes, we have always been cost-conscious at every level of expenditure. Though we have broadened our recommendations beyond the budget category, we insist that every lodging we include be sensibly priced. We use every form of media to assist our readers, and are particularly proud of our feisty daily website, the award-winning Frommers.com.

I have high hopes for the future of Frommer's. May these guidebooks, in all the years ahead, continue to reflect the joy of travel and the freedom that travel represents. May they always pursue a cost-conscious path, so that people of all incomes can enjoy the rewards of travel. And may they create, for both the traveler and the persons among whom we travel, a community of friends, where all human beings live in harmony and peace.

Arthur Frommer

THE BEST OF NEW ORLEANS

N ew Orleans should come with a warning label. No, no, not about hurricanes. Forget that. That's like solely identifying Hawaii with erupting volcanoes. No, this is about the city itself. See, there's this group of residents known as the "never lefts." They are the people who come to New Orleans as tourists, and the city worked its magic on them.

They become spellbound by the beauty of the French Quarter and the Garden District, and marvel that history is alive right beneath their feet. They listen to music flowing from random doorways and street corners— jazz, Cajun, blues, whatever—and find themselves moving to a languorous rhythm. They kiss beneath flickering gas lamps, and groove to a brass band in a crowded club long past their usual bedtime. They eat sumptuous, indulgent meals, and scandalously indulge yet again hours later, with 3am beignets at Café du Monde, where they watch the passing human parade. They'll catch the scent of jasmine and sweet olive (with a whiff of the Caribbean, and a garlic topnote, perhaps) wafting through the moist, honeyed air.

The air . . . aah the New Orleans air. People say romance is in the air here. It's true, of course, because the air is dreamy. It's the dewy ingénue who grows up fast in the first act, softly whispering your name. And if you're meant to be together, you'll feel that undeniable flutter, the high-voltage spark that says *I'm in your heart forever.*

That's what happens to the never lefts. They came for Mardi Gras, for a festival, a conference, a tryst, a reunion—just came—and fell hard. New Orleans does that to people.

What is it about this place? Well for one thing, New Orleans is where centuries commingle, perhaps not effortlessly but nowhere more fruitfully, as if nothing essential has passed between them. It's where a barstool or a park bench becomes the opening salvo in a conversation you may never forget—for raconteurship thrives here. It's where a masquerade party of old masters, modernists, and bohemian street artists fill the city's stunning mélange of museums and galleries. It's in a state that actually has an *official cocktail*—which speaks volumes to its state of mind. It's where gumbo—the savory Creole stew that is often (over) used in describing the city's multicultural tableau—is actually an apt metaphor: It speaks of a place that's deep and mysterious, rich with flavor and plenty spicy, and so much more than the sum of its many disparate parts.

New Orleans, the most unique city in the United States, works its charms like a spell. But don't take our word for it. Go. See, hear, and taste for yourself. The best way to get inside New Orleans is to plunge right in. Don't just go for the obvious. Sure, we've met people who never left

Bourbon Street and had a terrific time, but the city has so much more to offer. Look over the advice that follows, and see if New Orleans finds you and works its seductive spell. See if you come to understand the never lefts. And maybe even become one.

THE most AUTHENTIC NEW ORLEANS EXPERIENCES

- **Do Festivals, Big or Small:** Yes to Jazz Fest, Mardi Gras, or French Quarter Fest, but also the smaller fests in New Orleans and nearby towns. If one is on while you're visiting, seek it out. See p. 39.
- **Dress for Dinner:** At better restaurants, men wear jackets—including seersucker when in season—and un-ironic hats. Women can and do wear dresses (LBDs and others) and heels. It's required at the finest spots, optional but frequently done at the more moderate bistros (where jeans are also okay).
- **Frequent Dive Bars,** if that's your thang. For those whose thang it is, this town is siiick with good ones. See p 182.
- **Tour the Swamps:** Don't discount this because you think it's too touristy (New Yorkers still go to Broadway, right?). It's an absolutely authentic, historically and ecologically fascinating, unique-to-the-region experience. See p. 154.
- **Ride a Bike:** New Orleans is flat and compact, and you can see a lot on two wheels. See p. 233 for rentals and p. 158 for tours.
- **Cheer the Saints:** In the Dome, if possible—ain't nothing like it, nowhere. Or at least from a barstool, like everyone else who ain't in the Dome. See p. 163.
- **Eat Take-out from Verti Marte:** Traditionally done while leaning against a building or sitting on the curb (or on someone's stoop, which we probably shouldn't encourage). See p. 87.
- **Argue about the Best Po'Boy:** Which requires trying a few. See p. 74.
- **Go to Church:** Despite the reputation for decadence, this is a pretty pious city. Going to church is a wonderful way to get some faith on, hear some astounding gospel, and mingle with the welcoming locals. See p. 134.
- **Check Out Concerts in the Parks:** Free shows (with food and drink booths, natch) bring the locals to Armstrong Park across from the French Quarter (spring and fall Thusdays; www.pufap.org); City Park in Mid-City (spring–summer Thursdays; p. 139); and Lafayette Square in the CBD (Wednesday at the Square; http://wednesday atthesquare.com).
- **Stroll the Galleries:** There are openings with wine and low-key revelry the first Saturday of each month on Julia Street and on second Saturdays on St. Claude Avenue (http://scadnola.com), but any time will do. See p. 186.
- **Eat Indulgent, Unhurried, Fancy Lunches:** Especially on Friday.
- **Chat:** Discuss. Debate. Banter. In restaurants, bars, or shops. With people you've just met. I'll give you topics: football, and city politics/ineptitude. Barring your expertise in those arenas, trading anecdotes about your observations as a tourist, discussing a recent meal, or asking for recommendations about your next meal (or other activity) gets the convo started.
- **Eat with Your Hands:** Specifically, slurp oysters, best done standing at a bar and jiving with the shucker. Also, peel shrimp and crawfish, best taken to go and eaten outdoors (i.e., in Woldenberg Park in the French Quarter, or the Fly in Audubon Park). Bring drinks and plenty of napkins.

○ **Join the Street Spontaneity:** If a wailing trumpet catches your ear, follow the sound till you find it. If the swing band playing in the middle of Royal Street moves you, give your partner a whirl (and drop a few bucks in their hat). And if you're lucky enough to happen upon a second-line parade passing by, don't dare watch from the sidewalk. Jump in and high-step it down the street. It's New Orleans—it's what you do.

THE best PLACES TO EAT IN NEW ORLEANS

○ **Best All-around Dining Experience You Can Have in New Orleans:** No surprises here, they're world-famous for good reason: **Commander's Palace** (p. 103), hands down. At the other end of the spectrum, **Café du Monde** (p. 112). In the middle: **Brigtsen's** (p. 103).

○ **Best Classic New Orleans Restaurant:** Of the three old-line, fine-dining mainstays that have been enjoyed for generations (the others being **Galatoire's** and **Antoine's**; p. 75 and 80), **Arnaud's** (p. 81) is our choice.

○ **Best Contemporary Creole:** We're awfully fond of **Coquette** (p. 104), **Herbsaint** (p. 98), and the lovely **Iris** (p. 83).

○ **Best Contemporary Cajun:** Pork-centric **Cochon** (p. 100), where you won't find yo mama's Cajun, and **K-Paul's** (p. 78), the originator and still a standard-bearer.

○ **Best Italian: Irene's Cuisine** (p. 82) represents New Orleans's traditional Italian; **Domenica** (p. 101) is carrying the banner for contemporary Italian.

○ **Best Neighborhood Restaurants:** New Orleans tucks away some shockingly good restaurants on unassuming residential streets. **Clancy's** (p. 102), **Elizabeth's** (p. 91), **Gautreau's** (p. 105), and **Liuzza's by the Track** show the range.

○ **Best Neighbahood Restaurants:** In contrast to those above, these are old-school *neighbahood* joints, where locals still ask, "Hey, dahwlin', wheah y'at?" We've gotta go wit da Italian and Creole oldies at **Mandina's** (p. 94) and **Liuzza's** (p. 93).

○ **Most Innovative Restaurants: Root** (p. 99) is the clear standout in this category, with **Maurepas Foods** (p. 91) right up there; on the high end, stalwart **Stella!** (p. 80) is still pushing boundaries.

○ **Best Expense or Savings Account Blowouts: Restaurant R'evolution** (p. 78), **Emeril's** (p. 96), and **August** (p. 97).

○ **Best Bistro:** Tough choice, given the richness of this category, but **La Petite Grocery** (p. 106), **Lilette** (p. 106), and **Sylvain** (p. 86) figure highly.

○ **Best Outdoor Dining:** The pretty courtyards at **Bayona** (p. 81), **Martinique** (p. 106), and **Café Amelie** (p. 85) are delightful on starry nights or balmy afternoons. And the balcony at **Tableau** (p. 84).

○ **Best for Kids:** The no-brainers are **Café du Monde** (p. 112), for powdered sugar mess and mania; the counter at **Camellia Grill** (p. 88); and a **snoball** outing (p. 114). **American Sector** (p. 100) fits the bill, and **Antoine's** (p. 80) offers a good fine-dining introduction.

○ **Best Slightly Offbest but Utterly New Orleans Restaurants:** Definitely **Jacque-Imo's** (p. 105) and **Bacchanal** (p. 90). **Cochon Butcher** (p. 101) and the even fancier **Upperline** (p. 107) might fit the category.

- **Best Seafood: GW Fins** sets a high bar (p. 82); **Peche** (p. 99) and **Borgne** (p. 97) are strong contenders; **Big Fisherman** (p. 109) covers the boiled seafood angle.

- **Best Desserts:** A meal at **Emeril's** (p. 96) is incomplete without its banana cream pie; ditto **Commander's Palace's** (p. 103) bread pudding soufflé. **Palace Café** (p. 99), **Lilette** (p. 106), and **Coquette** (p. 104) excel at dessert. Or head to a specialist at **Sucré** (p. 115) or **Angelo Brocato's** (p. 111).

- **Best Brunch: Ralph's on the Park** (p. 92) or **Dante's Kitchen** (p. 108) can't miss. The jazz brunch at **Antoine's** (p. 80), **Arnaud's** (p. 81), and **Commander's Palace** (p. 103) are also good fun.

- **Restaurants with the Best Cocktail Programs:** This could be a very long list, but we'll go with **Kingfish** (p. 83), **Iris** (p. 83), and **Café Adelaide** (p. 98).

- **Best Wine Lists:** The extensive collection at **Emeril's** (p. 96), **Commander's Palace** (p. 103), and **Antoine's** (p. 80) cover every base. The lists at **Bayona** (p. 81) and **Gautreau's** (p. 105) are smaller but well-curated.

- **Best for Late-Night Eats:** Get 24-hour satisfaction at **Clover Grill** (p. 88), **Camellia Grill** (p. 88), and **Verti Marte** (p. 87). For heartier, sit-down fare, **La Boca** (p. 98) and **Root** (p. 99) serve late. And there's always beignets from **Café du Monde** (p. 112).

THE best PLACES TO STAY IN NEW ORLEANS

Selecting one place to stay in New Orleans is a little like deciding on a scoop of ice cream—there are many tasty options to choose from, and different people like different flavors. But since you must choose, we've tried to narrow down some selections based on the following various criteria.

- **Best Moderately Priced Lodging:** In general, you'll get the biggest bang in the **off-season** (including the heat of summer), when even luxury properties drop their rates to levels that are hard to pass up. In the Central Business District, The **Drury Inn** (p. 64) is surprisingly reasonable and an easy hop to the Quarter. In the B&B category, the **Chimes** (p. 66) is a delightful family-owned guesthouse in the Garden District. The charming owners have been operating the B&B for more than 20 years, generating loyal return guests.

- **Best Luxury Hotel:** At the **Audubon Cottages** (p. 50), the luxury commences when your 24-hour butler greets you at the private, unmarked entrance. For sheer opulence, amenities, and vast expanses of room, our vote goes to the **Windsor Court** (p. 63). Go for a suite, of course.

- **Best Service:** All those in the "Luxury" category above excel in the service category. We're also continually impressed by the attentive **Loews** (p. 63). Of the most modest accommodations, the Campo family make you feel at home at the **Villa Convento** (p. 57). Uptown, the **Maison Perrier** (p. 66) and **Maison de Macarty** (p. 59) in the Bywater both go over and above to ensure guest comfort.

- **Most Romantic:** Romance is wherever you make it, but **Ashtons** (p. 61) encourages long, languid mornings. The pricy, private **Audubon Cottages** (p. 50) win for intimacy; and the sleek **International House** (p. 63) oozes pure sex appeal.

- **Best for Families:** It's not fancy, but we like the **Homewood Suites** (p. 64) for the spacious two-room suites, location, and freebie meals. The **Richelieu** (p. 57) and **Maison Dupuy** (p. 56) also offer easy comfort and swimming pools.
- **Best Faaabulous B&B:** A lot of B&Bs are crammed with over-the-top antiques, but at the **Antebellum** (p. 61), they all come with a story.
- **Best for Hipness:** The innovative minimalist style, myriad comforts, and Loa Bar at the **International House** (p. 63) will fit the bill; while the elaborate **Melrose Mansion** (p. 61) is a Victorian mansion on the outside, but an oasis of upscale cool inside.
- **Best Funky Little Spot:** We're also fond of the sweetly oddball **B&W Courtyards,** the Frenchmen-adjacent **Royal Street Inn,** and the hodge-podgey but well-located **Dauphine Orleans.**
- **Best Hidden Gem:** Just beyond the French Quarter and veiled behind high walls is an enchanting cluster of old plantation buildings, the stunning **Jazz Quarters Bed & Breakfast** (p. 54). Hidden in Bywater is a friendly oasis called the **B&W Courtyards** (p. 59).

THE best TRIP MEMENTOS

Nothing wrong with T-shirts, caps, Mardi Gras beads, and snow globes (except that you can get those anywhere). We offer some alternate ideas.

- **A Book from Faulkner House:** Pick up some reading material from this charming jewel on little Pirate's Alley, crammed with Louisiana-related tomes. Many an author has tried, with varying success, to capture New Orleans on the page. Their efforts may help you know what it means to miss New Orleans. Check out our favorite New Orleans–related fiction and nonfiction in chapter 3. For more on the Faulkner House, see p. 188.
- **A Photo or Art Book from A Gallery for Fine Photography:** The owner calls his impressive shop "the only museum where you can buy the art." A fine photograph from one of the many famous photographers represented here is a souvenir you can relish every day—not to mention a wise investment. If an original isn't feasible, it also carries fine photo books. See p. 187.
- **A Southern Scent from Hovè:** This classic perfumery creates its own perfumes and soaps. We got hooked on sachet-favorite vetiver, described as "smelling like the South." Locals also adore the scents made from the indigenous sweet olive, and the fine gentlemanly scents. See p. 193.
- **A Razor from Aidan Gill:** Manly and mannerly, the selection of hand-sculpted razors (and other accessories) will charm even the most diehard disposable dude and up his style quotient in a single stroke. Or just take home some smooth cheeks courtesy of an ultraluxe straight-razor shave. See p. 192.
- **A CD from Louisiana Music Factory:** New Orleans's soundtrack is as essential to your experience as her sights and tastes. A few CDs will keep the good times rolling back at home. Check out our recorded-music recommendations in chapter 3; for details on the Louisiana Music Factory, see p. 193.
- **A Hat from Meyer:** We're mad about **Meyer the Hatter,** for the selection, the service, and the 100-year-plus history. You're in the South, *chère,* you can rock some class headgear—and these hat whisperers know just how to top every head. See p. 190.

- **A "Be Nice or Leave" Sign:** Dr. Bob's colorful, bottle-cap-edged signs may have proliferated around the city, but they're still true, local works of folk art, handmade with found materials. Available in a variety of sizes, materials, and sentiments at **Pop City,** 940 Decatur St. (✆ **504/528-8559**); **Funrock'n,** 3109 Magazine St. (✆ **504/895-4102**); or at Bob's **Bywater studio,** 3027 Chartres St. (✆ **504/945-2225**), the latter open "by chance or appointment."

- **Fleur-del-lis Jewelry:** Gold, silver, glass, cufflink, nose ring, pendant: The selection is unending. Wear it with pride; give it with joy. Consider something from **Mignon Faget** (p. 193) or an inexpensive bauble from the flea-market stands at the **French Market** (p. 121).

- **Sazerac Glasses:** If you've taken a shine to the city's official cocktail, the gift shop at the **Roosevelt Hotel** (p. 62) has perfect reproductions of their original glasses. Don't forget a bottle of Sazerac rye from **Martin Wine Cellar** (p. 192) or **Vieux Carré Wine and Spirits** (p. 192).

- **Pralines:** The choice for office gifts. And for home. Maybe one for the plane or road trip. See p. 189.

THE best OF OUTDOOR NEW ORLEANS

Yeaaahhh, we know—not exactly what you think of when you think Big Easy. No, it's not Yellowstone, but there are some surprisingly wonderful outdoorsy things to do here that will only enhance the vacation you envisioned. Besides, it can't all be about dark bars and decadent meals. Oh wait, it's New Orleans. Yes, it can. Still . . . these experiences make a fine counterpoint, and you might see things you wouldn't otherwise see.

- **Kayak Bayou St. John:** A guided kayak tour of placid, pretty Bayou St. John is an entrancing way to see this historically significant waterway—and maybe work off a few bites of fried shrimp po'boy. See p. 157.

- **Do City Park:** Whatever your outdoor thing, it's probably doable somewhere in the glorious, 1,300-acre City Park, from pedal-boating to picnicking, birding to bicycling, mini-golfing to art-gazing. It's a great spot for a morning run; so is **Audubon Park** (p. 138) if you're staying Uptown. See p. 139.

- **Tour the Swamps:** The swamps are spooky, serene, and fascinating. The gators are spellbinding, and the guides are knowledgeable naturalists who will open your eyes to every flora and fauna in this unique ecoculture. See p. 154.

- **Ferry Cross the Mississippi:** It's not quite Huck Finn, but a brief "cruise" on the ferry to the historic Algiers neighborhood is an easy way to roll on the river and take in a different view. See p. 183.

- **Take a Bicycle Tour:** Whether you rent a bike (p. 233) or take a guided tour (p. 158), seeing the flat, compact city via two wheels makes for a sweet ride. Or see it by Segway, on a tour with **City Segway Tours** (✆ **504/619-4162**; http://neworleans.citysegwaytours.com).

- **Dine Alfresco:** We didn't say the best of *active* outdoor New Orleans, did we? A languid, courtyard dinner under the Southern stars (or lunch under an umbrella) at **Bayona, Martinique, Café Amelie, Bacchanal, Green Goddess**, or **Tableau** is an experience to be savored. See p. 70.

- **Do Yoga in the Besthoff Sculpture Garden:** In fact, we can't think of a more sublime way to start a Saturday. Especially when it's followed by beignets and coffee (just steps away at **Morning Call** café). A little yin, a little yang. Saturdays at 8am in City Park (p. 133; ℂ **504/456-5000**).

○ **Walk. Walk. And Walk Some More:** This city is made for walking. It's truly the best way to take in the captivating sights, appreciate the silken air, and ogle (or join) the goings-on you will undoubtedly encounter. We won't bring up the c-word benefits. (Calories. Oops, drat . . . sorry).

THE best MUSEUMS IN NEW ORLEANS

New York, Chicago, Paris, Rome . . . great museum cities, all. New Orleans isn't included in that list, but it's a surprisingly excellent museum city. Museums also make stellar retreats when the elements become overbearing.

○ **New Orleans African American Museum:** Located in the historic Faubourg Tremé, the collection recounts the astounding historical and cultural contributions that emanated from this very neighborhood (and beyond). See p. 152.

○ **Backstreet Museum:** To truly appreciate them, you really must see the Mardi Gras Indians' astounding beaded suits up close (if not in action, then in this collection), and learn about this unique tradition. See p. 152.

○ **The Cabildo:** An extensive recollection of Louisiana and New Orleans history, including terrific Mardi Gras exhibits. And Napoleon's death mask. See p. 125.

○ **The Insectarium:** Yes, it is what it sounds like. It's especially good for families, but unexpectedly captivating even for the bug-averse. See p. 120.

○ **Louisiana Children's Museum:** There's so much hands-on, interactive fun to be had here (for all ages) that you don't even realize you're also learning. See p. 162.

○ **New Orleans Museum of Art:** Consistently well-curated exhibits and an excellent collection of all forms of fine art, housed in a stunning, neoclassical building in the heart of beautiful City Park. See p. 132.

○ **Ogden Museum of Southern Art:** A splendid collection of the art of the American South, new and old, in a modern atrium nestled between two historic buildings. See p. 133.

○ **Pharmacy Museum:** Leeches and opium and voodoo spells, oh my. A mightily worthwhile, off-the-wall diversion. See p. 127.

○ **The Presbytère:** The excellent exhibit on hurricanes here captures their impact from all aspects; other rotating exhibits are consistently good. See p. 128.

○ **Southern Food and Beverage Museum:** It's no surprise that this museum recently moved to a much-expanded location, given the importance of food and drink to this area. A great diversion for anyone with an interest beyond the next meal. See p. 133.

○ **World War II Museum:** It's the best museum of its kind, and the world-class collection and interactive displays here are simply not to be missed, period. See p. 132.

SUGGESTED ITINERARIES

It's easy to wander aimlessly through New Orleans with your eyes wide, your mouth agape, your hand holding someone else's (or holding your Frommer's guide . . .). It's truly unlike any place in the United States, so nearly everything you happen upon will be new and wondrous. It's equally easy to duck into a restaurant or watering hole, or take a meditative rest on a bench in Jackson Square or along the Mississippi River . . . and end up there for hours. Nothing wrong with that (we encourage it, in fact). But the city has some serious spots of interest, not to mention curious little nooks you probably shouldn't miss. The following itineraries are designed to help you to navigate the city and make the most of your time in it. If you have the time, take our **walking tours** (p. 196) or sign up for a **guided tour**—see our recommendations for the best on p. 149.

THE ICONIC QUARTER IN 1 DAY

You could spend days, weeks even, in the glorious, historic **French Quarter,** but even if you only have 1 day to explore, you can't go wrong here. We've included all the requisite factors of a New Orleans visit: eating, walking, drinking, soaking in some history, eating more, music, and dancing. *Tip:* As you stroll the neighborhood, check out the building exteriors: apart from the ironwork (mostly slave-made, originally), they're rather plain. The Creoles saved the embellishments for their indoor living quarters. ***Start:*** *Along the riverfront at St. Louis St.*

Hour 1: A Riverfront Stroll in Woldenberg Park ★★

Rise with the riverboats, and take a walk along **Woldenberg Park** (the pedestrian walkway along the river) toward the Moonwalk overlooking **Jackson Square.** Stop to notice some of the curious public art installations and take in the sights of the vessels rounding the curving crescent in Ol' Man River, much like they have for centuries.

Hour 2: Café du Monde ★★★

Downing a cup of chicory coffee and savoring beignets covered in powdered sugar is the ideal way to start a New Orleans day. Watch this city come to lazy life as carriage drivers line up across the street.

If the line for a table is too long at Café du Monde, go around back, get your beignets to go, and walk across to Jackson Square to enjoy them from a park bench. *Hint:* Dark clothes and powdered beignets don't mix. See p. 112.

Hour 3: St. Louis Cathedral ★

It's not the most inspiring ecclesiastical building, but it is the center of spiritual life for a town that is surprisingly devoutly Catholic (it's always a shock to note how many foreheads bear ashes the day after Mardi Gras' frantic antics). Legend has it that the serene garden in the back was a favorite haunt of good Catholic Marie Laveau—better known as the Voodoo Queen. Not even the infamous Pere Antoine, sent to New Orleans by the Office of the Inquisition, could convince Madame Laveau to forsake voodoo. The imposing statue of Jesus lost a thumb to Katrina; at night its stunning shadow is otherworldly. See p. 122.

Hour 4: The Presbytère & The Cabildo ★★★

The former home of the priests who worked at St. Louis Cathedral has been turned into a museum housing a terrific "Living with Hurricanes" exhibit (p. 128). It's well worth an hour. If you still have time, the **Cabildo** museum (on the other side of St. Louis Cathedral; p. 122) is where the Louisiana Purchase was signed. Its exhibits illustrate New Orleans and Louisiana history and culture, including Mardi Gras. Our favorite item? Napoleon Bonaparte's death mask. See p. 125.

Hour 5: Muffuletta at Central Grocery

Ya gotta do it. Gotta get a muffuletta from **Central Grocery,** whose version of the celebrated Italian sandwich—filled with olive salad and Italian cold cuts and cheese—is ginormous; half is more than enough for one person. Eat in the tiny tables in back or thread your way through the buildings across the street to chow down on the banks of the Mississippi (p. 90).

Hour 6: Shops on Royal Street ★★★

Royal Street is lined with swanky antique, art, and clothing shops and has loads of antebellum eye candy, architecturally speaking. Be sure to browse the sublime and ridiculous collection at **M.S. Rau,** at 630 Royal (p. 186); it welcomes gawkers. Royal is closed to vehicles from 11am to 4pm, and street performers dot each block.

Hour 7: Bourbon Street ★

Dusk is the best time to do Bourbon, when it's not too tame and it's not too rowdy. Sure, Bourbon Street is gaudy, loud, and sometimes even gross. But before the obnoxiousness sets in, when music pours out the doors and dancers and barmen hawk their wares, it's also seductive and exhilarating. Everyone has to do it once; some do it often. Have a pre-dinner cocktail at **Galatoire's 33** (p. 78), the new classic on the street, or a legendary Hurricane on the always-lively patio at **Pat O'Brien's** (p. 178).

Hour 8: Bayona Restaurant ★★★

Food is an intensely important part of your time in New Orleans, and you must dine well, several times daily. For your iconic French Quarter dinner, try **Bayona,** Chef Susan Spicer's iconic modern eatery, deservedly so. (p. 81).

New Orleans Itineraries

The Iconic Quarter in 1 Day

1. Woldenberg Park
2. Jackson Square
3. Café du Monde
4. St. Louis Cathedral
5. The Presbytère
6. The Cabildo
7. Central Grocery
8. M.S. Rau
9. Galatoire's 33
10. Pat O'Brien's
11. Bayona Restaurant
12. Preservation Hall
13. Felix's Restaurant & Oyster Bar
14. Irvin Mayfield's Jazz Playhouse

Beyond the Quarter in 1 Day

1. National World War II Museum
2. St. Charles Streetcar stop, Canal Street at Carondelet
3. Garden District Book Shop
4. Lafayette Cemetery No. 1

Culture Vulturing in 5 Days

1. Swamp Tour
2. Maurepas Foods
3. World War II Museum
4. Cochon Butcher
5. Ogden Museum of Southern Art
6. American Sector
7. City Park
8. St. John's Bayou
9. Liuzza's by the Track
10. Plantation Homes
11. Acme Oyster House
12. Commander's Palace
13. Tipitina's
14. Maple Leaf Bar

5. Tracey's
6. Casamento's
7. Magazine Street
8. Coquette
9. Frenchmen Street

Hour 9: Let the Good Times Roll ★★★

Nightlife is essential to your day. Do not miss **Preservation Hall** (p. 169)—it's cheap, and it's the real, traditional jazz McCoy. Late-night munchies? Head for **Felix's Restaurant & Oyster Bar** (p. 88) for a dozen raw. Still going? Slink into swanky **Irvin Mayfield's Jazz Playhouse** (p. 169), where the city's finest play. When you finally must, collapse in your bed. If you're exhausted, full, and smiling, your day is done.

BEYOND THE QUARTER IN 1 DAY

You've had your day of exploring the Quarter. Now get out of the Quarter, *get out of the Quarter*, **get out of the Quarter.** Got it? Today you must explore New Orleans beyond the French Quarter, and we send you to the other side of the city for a completely different perspective. It's a full day, packed with great stuff to see and do, but if you have limited time, just take the St. Charles streetcar ride, stroll through the Garden District, and visit the **National World War II Museum** (p. 132). *Start: St. Charles Streetcar line, Canal Street stop.*

Hour 1: St. Charles Avenue Streetcar ★★★

Hop on the oldest continuously operating wooden streetcar in the country. Expect breezes through open windows, not air-conditioning, so doing this in the cool of the morning is a good idea. Admire the gorgeous homes and sprawling oaks along the way, and remember which side of the car you rode on so that you can sit on the other side for the ride back. (*Tip:* Get a **JazzyPass,** good for a full day of streetcar and bus transportation.) See p. 233.

Hours 2–3: The Garden District ★★★

Aside from its historical significance, this neighborhood of fabulous houses and lush greenery is just plain beautiful. Contrast the plain exteriors of the "French" Quarter with these grand, ornamented "American district" spectacles. Follow our walking tour on p. 204 or take a guided tour from **Historic New Orleans Tours** (p. 149). Start at the **Garden District Book Shop** (p. 189), 2727 Prytania St. at Washington Ave.

Hour 4: Lafayette Cemetery No. 1 ★★

The "little cities of the dead" are part of the iconic landscape of New Orleans. This pretty cemetery catered to Uptown folks, and has more foliage and room than others. Notice the tombs with French or German writing, and the four matching mausoleums in the far left corner. They belong to four boyhood friends (one a Civil War vet) who once played together here. Like many of the city's cemeteries, Lafayette 1 is in great need of maintenance and lacking funds to do so. See p. 143.

Hour 5: Magazine Street Lunch Break

Two surefire lunch options are on nearby Magazine Street. For a cold beer and a very respectable roast beef po'boy, hit up **Tracey's,** just 2 blocks away on 2604 Magazine St. (p. 209). **Casamento's** (p. 111), about a mile up at 4330 Magazine, is about as classic as an oyster bar gets, and theirs are sublime. A cab or the #11 bus will get you there. Call ahead to make sure they'll be open.

Hour 6: Magazine Street Shopping ★★★

Use that JazzyPass to explore the fab boutiques, antiques, and galleries along **Magazine Street** (p. 185). Even non-shoppers can enjoy the fascinating mix of upscale-downscale, old-meets-new here, and you'll surely find better souvenirs than in the T-shirt shops of Bourbon Street. Use that JazzyPass to hop on and off the #11 (it runs about every 20 min.); cabs or feet also work.

Hour 7: Dinner at Coquette ★★★

We're positively smitten with **Coquette,** a bistro about as perfect as they come, in an atmosphere as perfect as you could hope for. See p. 104, and do make a reservation.

Hour 8: Frenchmen Street ★★★

Hit the dozen clubs and bars of **Frenchmen Street** in the Quarter-adjacent Faubourg Marigny. Wander, mingle, people-watch, heed the music pouring forth, and pick a club or two where you can work your mojo. See p. 172.

CULTURE VULTURING IN 5 DAYS

A trip to New Orleans is not just about eating, drinking, dancing, and admiring fancy houses. The city and surrounds have a wealth of cultural offerings that put many other big cities to shame. The following 5-day itinerary lets you fill your cultural plate with a range of activities sure to enlighten, entertain, and educate. Each day involves one big cultural attraction, plus suggestions for nearby dining (and maybe another idea or two that we can't resist planting)—leaving you to discover the city as it's meant to be discovered, in serendipitous fashion. ***Start:*** *Arrange for round-trip transportation from your hotel to a swamp tour. See p. 154.*

Day 1: Swamp Tour ★★★

We scoff at those who scoff at swamp tours because it's too "touristy." Because it's not something you should miss. Everyone knows about the gators, and they're cool enough. But the swamps themselves are mystical and otherworldly, and their ecological, cultural, and economic relevance is fascinating. Get an early start so you have time for afternoon activities. **Dr. Wagner's Honey Island Swamp Tour** (p. 154) can arrange round-trip transportation from your hotel.

After watching gators chowing down on food unlikely to be part of their natural diet, you're probably ready to do the same. Since you're already out exploring farflung waterways, we're sending you to **Maurepas Foods** (p. 91) in the Bywater, a popular, newer spot in this artsy neighborhood with creative (but not experimental), locally focused food and drink (at fair prices to boot).

Day 2: National World War II Museum ★★★

This remarkable historical jewel is sprawling and jam-packed with interest, but make sure to listen to some of the potent, personal oral histories. Veterans often volunteer—say thank you for us, please.

Have lunch at **Cochon Butcher** (p. 101), a tiny, upscale Cajun-inflected deli 2 blocks from the museum. The cured meats stand out, but just about everything is stellar (we've never left without a side of their Brussels sprouts). If you liked the muffuletta from Central Grocery, you can do a comparison test here. It's debatable, but Butcher's might just be the best in town.

You could spend hours here, and you should. But you could also split your time appreciating the premier collection of Southern art in the country, traditional and modern, at the stylish, airy **Ogden Museum of Southern Art,** just a block away (p. 133).

If you're hanging around in the area come happy hour, stop in at the National World War II Museum's **American Sector** (p. 100). It's kicky, American comfort food as prepared through the lens of noted Chef John Besh, with a cocktail program to match: The 3-to-6pm happy hour is one of the best in town (75¢ sliders!). It stays open after the museum closes; use the Magazine St. entrance (at Poeyfarre St.).

Day 3: City Park ★★★

The 1,300 acres here are full of nature's glory and activities, from the Spanish moss–draped giant live oaks to the splendid **New Orleans Museum of Art** (p. 132) to the outstanding **Sculpture Garden.** If you have kids in tow, take a ride in a pedal boat in the lake or visit the kids' amusement park and **Storybook Land.** The lush **Botanical Gardens** include the **Train Gardens,** a sort of melted Dr. Seuss replica of the city in miniature, complete with model trains (not to mention enormous lily pads). See p. 139.

Just outside the main entrance to City Park is **St. John's Bayou,** a former bustling canal turned scenic body of water, and the sight of the city's origins. If you're up for footwork, a stroll here is one of the lesser-known, more peaceful delights of the city. Or, point yourself down Esplanade Avenue and turn left on Lopez, where shivering-cold schooners of Abita and one of the city's best gumbos awaits at **Liuzza's by the Track** (p. 95). Also get the garlic oyster po'boy. You're welcome.

Day 4: River Road Plantation Homes

To see an altogether different, but vitally important, side of the city and its history, visit one or two of the **plantation homes along River Road** (p. 214). You'll need a car or tour company for this outing, a very worthwhile look at the pre– and post–Civil War eras, slavery, and Reconstruction. After this outing, make a beeline for the French Quarter and hit up **Acme Oyster House** (p. 87), home to some of the best bivalves around. Don't neglect the charbroiled ones (gateway oysters for those who don't do them raw), and get some boiled crawfish too, if it's in season (p. 214).

Day 5: Commander's Palace

Your iconic cultural event today is a grand dining adventure at Commander's Palace. Choose a long, luxurious dinner or a languid, martini-laden lunch. It's never rested on their laurels but continues to push Creole cuisine in new and exciting directions while honoring its origins. It's fine dining done the New Orleans way: with fun. Later, check out who's on at **Tipitina's** (p. 175) or the **Maple Leaf Bar** (p. 175), both pillars of stellar NOLA tuneage. This represents our perfect day in New Orleans: mixing high-society dining with down-and-dirty dancing (yes, you can wear your fancypants clothes to the clubs; many people do), going from an elegant manse to an everyman's dive. Great food. Great music. Great time.

Neighborhoods in Brief

"Where y'at?" goes the traditional local greeting. "Where" is straightforward in the French Quarter, a 13-block-long grid between Canal Street and Esplanade Avenue, running from the Mississippi River to North Rampart Street.

After that, fuggedaboutit. Because of the bend in the river, the streets are laid out at angles and curves that render directions useless. Re-adjust your thinking to New Orleans's compass points: *lakeside, riverside, uptown,* and *downtown.* You'll catch on quickly if you keep in mind that North Rampart Street is the *lakeside* boundary of the Quarter and Canal Street is its *uptown* border. And by all means, use the maps provided—you'll need them. Note that street names change when they cross Canal Street: Bourbon Street becomes Carondelet, and Royal becomes St. Charles, for example.

CITY LAYOUT

The French Quarter Made up of about 90 square blocks with Jackson Square at its center, this section is also known as the Vieux Carré (Old Square) and is bordered by Canal Street, North Rampart Street, the Mississippi River, and Esplanade Avenue. The Quarter (or FQ) is full of hotels, restaurants, clubs, bars, stores, residences, and museums. Its major public area is Jackson Square. The most historic and best-preserved area in the city, it's the focal point for most first-time visitors. Explore the neighbhorhood in detail with our French Quarter walking tour (p. 196).

Faubourg Marigny Bordering the eastern edge of the French Quarter, across Esplanade Avenue, the Marigny now boasts the city's premier nightlife center: famed Frenchmen Street. It's a must-visit haunt for music lovers and anyone seeking a scene. This small Creole suburb is populated by many old-time residents, younger urban dwellers who have recently moved in, and a thriving gay and lesbian community.

Bywater This riverside neighborhood is past the Faubourg Marigny and is bounded on the east by an industrial canal. This hotbed of renovation and gentrification still has its share of modest and rundown homes, amid sparkling renovations and artily rehabbed shotgun shacks. Historically, the area was also home to immigrants, free people of color, and artisans, and today many studios still dot the area, along with hip new bars and cafés.

Mid-City/Esplanade Ridge Stretching north from the French Quarter to City Park, Esplanade Ridge hugs either side of Esplanade Avenue (once the grande avenue of New Orleans's Creole society, rivaling St. Charles Avenue). Crossing Esplanade is the historic **Bayou St. John** waterway, adjacent to the lovely **Faubourg St. John** neighborhood. Booming, popular **Mid-City** also encompasses **City Park,** and its residential neighborhoods stretch upward toward Lake Pontchartrain.

Faubourg Tremé Directly across Rampart Street from the French Quarter, this dense 19th-century Creole community is one of the oldest African-American neighborhoods in the country. Home to many of the city's best musicians, it is seeing some post-Katrina gentrification, but remains a dynamic, organic residential community, as highlighted in the HBO series named for the area. Once considered unsafe for tourists, it's much improved and more populated, though as in many parts of the city, it has its share of crime, and it is not advisable to walk through the area at night or solo.

Central Business District In the 19th century **Canal Street** divided the French and American sections of the city, and historically has been New Orleans's main street. It's a far cry from the days of yore when white-gloved ladies and seersuckered men shopped this grand avenue, but signs of renewed glory are afoot in several fine hotels and restaurants and the just-renovated Saenger Theatre. Uptown of Canal Street is the **CBD,** also roughly bounded by the elevated Pontchartrain Expressway (Business Rte. U.S. I-90) between Loyola Avenue and the Mississippi River. This current hotbed of hip houses New Orleans's

New Orleans: The City at a Glance

"downtown" business and government sections, with some of the city's most elegant hotels and best restaurants, as well as the Mercedes-Benz Superdome. Within the CBD is the **Warehouse District.** More than 20 years ago, this area was nothing more than abandoned warehouses. With the efforts of some dedicated individuals and institutions, it has evolved into a thriving residential and commercial neighborhood, with cool loft conversions, a plethora of terrific restaurants, and hot music clubs. The area also houses the city's lively **arts district,** with major museums and myriad galleries along **Julia Street** (see p. 186).

Uptown/The Garden District Bounded by St. Charles Avenue (lakeside) and Magazine Street (riverside) between Jackson and Louisiana avenues, the **Garden District (GD)** remains one of the most picturesque areas in the city. Originally the site of a plantation, it was subdivided and developed as a residential neighborhood for wealthy Americans, who built elaborate

homes and gardens, some still existing. See our Garden District walking tour on p. 204. The Garden District is located "uptown"; the neighborhood west of the Garden District is also called **Uptown** (the term is used for the direction and the area). The **Lower Garden District (LGD)** refers to the segment between the Pontchartrain Expressway (I-90) and Jackson Avenue.

The Irish Channel The area bounded by Magazine Street and the Mississippi River, Louisiana Avenue, and the Central Business District got its name during the 1800s when more than 100,000 Irish immigrated to New Orleans and found (mostly blue-collar) work. This quiet residential neighborhood mixes the rundown with the fixed up.

Algiers Point Directly across the Mississippi River and connected by the Algiers Ferry (p. 233), Algiers Point is another original Creole suburb, largely unchanged if a little less than it was during the once-booming days of the railroad and dry-docking industries.

NEW ORLEANS IN CONTEXT

Throughout this book, we talk about the mystique of New Orleans and its ineffable essence. But first, it's time for some stats. The largest city in Louisiana (population 360,000) and one of the chief cities of the South, New Orleans is nearly 100 miles above the mouth of the Mississippi River system and stretches along a strip of land 5 to 8 miles wide between the Mississippi and Lake Pontchartrain. Surrounded by a river and a lake, the city is largely under sea level. The highest natural point is in City Park, a whopping 35 feet above sea level.

New Orleans has always been known for its jazz-infused joie de vivre, a place where antebellum-meets-bohemia in a high-stepping dance of life, lived fully and out loud. Its recent history, however, is marked by two horrific, well-known events: the failure of the levee system following Hurricane Katrina, and the Deepwater Horizon oil spill in the nearby Gulf of Mexico.

In this chapter, we briefly recount the area's rich history, starting with today and then reaching back to its foundation, to help explain how New Orleaneans got their resilient, life-affirming "yatitude" (from "Where y'at?"—the local version of "How ya doin'?").

NEW ORLEANS TODAY

Since Katrina, a new entrepreneurial drive has taken hold. Residency, tourism, and convention numbers have increased. Construction cranes crisscross the airspace (particularly along Tulane Avenue, where an ambitious new biomedical corridor is under way), and cameras and booms are seemingly everywhere as the local film industry is, well, booming. Rebuilding and start-up projects helped protect New Orleans from the depths of the 2008 recession.

The hopping Frenchmen Street club scene shows no sign of stopping, and there are an astounding 500 more restaurants in the city than there were pre-Katrina. The HBO series *Tremé* portrayed authentic New Orleans with a (mostly) spot-on eye and a killer soundtrack, focusing a new fascination with the local culture.

Once untrammeled streets, like Oak, Freret, and St. Claude, have blossomed with business and activity (we'll probably add Oretha Castle Haley to the list soon). The public schools, rebuilt largely as charters, have the test numbers to confirm that the possible is provable.

Still, all is not rosy. While the tourist zones show zero signs of ill wind, those venturing into certain neighborhoods will still find pristine, rebuilt homes next to abandoned blights. Redevelopment in the decimated Lower 9th Ward is creeping along. It's a massive tabula rasa cleared of its upended homes populated by a few pioneering resettlers and the architectural anachronisms of Make It Right homes (Brad Pitt's foundation). Yet amid their stark backdrop, these homes and their owners embrace their in-your-face presence, as if to proclaim, "Damn right we're here. And we've got *solar panels.*"

The grim images that focused the eyes of the world on New Orleans in August, 2005 are not easily erased, nor should they be. The category 5 storm was downgraded to a category 3 when it hit New Orleans, but the surge was too much for the city's federal levee system. Its failure flooded 80% of the city, causing 1,836 recorded deaths and all forms of astounding, horrifying loss. Some 28,000 people took refuge in the Superdome, the ill-prepared refuge of last resort.

Four and a half years later, the Dome's home football team, the New Orleans Saints, at long last came marching in with their first-ever Super Bowl victory. The long-derided 'Aints restored what billions in rebuilding funds couldn't: civic pride.

It may seem trivial, even disrespectful, to cite a football game as a turning point in the city's rebirth—but it isn't. The effects of this real and symbolic victory reached far beyond the ecstatic, extended celebrations—and they cannot be understated. It was one of many high points in 2010: The *prior* week, Mitch Landrieu won the mayoral race with 66% of the vote, marking the end to the prior administration's fumbling, inertia, and corruption. The week *after* the Saints victory, the largest Mardi Gras crowds in 25 years watched the hyper-exultant parades roll. Two months later, a record half-million revelers packed the streets for the French Quarter Fest. The good times were rolling once again, at full speed.

And then, the whammy. One. More. Time. (Eye roll, headshake.)

The BP Deepwater Horizon oil spill hit, with potent imagery again painting New Orleans black with a wide, crude brush. In reality, New Orleans is some 150 miles from the spill, and those images of taint were far worse than the reality (though

DATELINE

1682 La Salle stops near the present site while traveling down the Mississippi River from the Great Lakes region and plants a cross claiming the territory for Louis XIV.

1699 Pierre Le Moyne, Sieur d'Iberville, rediscovers and secures the mouth of the Mississippi—on Mardi Gras day.

1718 The first governor of Louisiana, Iberville's brother, Jean-Baptiste Le Moyne, Sieur de Bienville, founds New Orleans.

1723 New Orleans replaces Biloxi as the capital of Louisiana.

1752 Ursuline Convent completed.

1762 Louis XV secretly cedes New Orleans and all of Louisiana west of the Mississippi to Spain.

1768 French residents in New Orleans banish Spanish commissioner Don Antonio de Ulloa, proclaiming independence from Spain.

1769 The Spanish return.

1783 Treaty of Paris confirms Spanish possession.

state-mates in the affected areas were hard-hit). New Orleans remained utterly unsullied, and the sumptuous Gulf seafood was and is safe and plentiful.

Although locals will forever mark time as B.K. or A.K. (Before Katrina or After Katrina), New Orleans is undoubtedly back: buoyant, secure, galvanized, and optimistic. New Orleaneans just did what they do: tidied up, mixed a cocktail, and exclaimed their undying love for their city. Oh, and throw a few parties for half a million people, and host a Super Bowl, and earn top awards on umpteen "Best of" travel polls.

The indomitable spirit is intact. The oysters are still sweet, the jasmine air still sultry. Kermit Ruffins still plays Vaughan's on Thursdays, and parades erupt at random. New Orleans is still the best city in the United States, and the *bons temps*—like those beloved Saints of field and song—go marching in and on, and we're right there with them.

HISTORY 101

In the Beginning

In 1682, explorer René Robert Cavelier, Sieur de la Salle, claimed the region for France, as he had with lands northward to Canada. His navigational and leadership failures in later explorations resulted in his mutinous murder in Texas in 1687 by his own party, fed up with his life-risking demands. Next, at the turn of the 18th century, two French-Canadian brothers led an expedition from France to rediscover the mouth of the Mississippi. The expedition succeeded, and Pierre Le Moyne, Sieur d'Iberville, and 18-year-old Jean Baptiste Le Moyne, Sieur de Bienville, staked a claim at a dramatic bend in the river, near where La Salle had stopped almost 2 decades earlier. Iberville also established a fort at Biloxi. Brother Bienville stayed on there, becoming commanding officer of the territory while harboring thoughts of returning to the spot up the river to establish a new capital city.

In 1718 Bienville got his chance. The French monarch was eager to develop, populate, and garner the riches that Louisiana promised. Bienville was charged with finding a suitable location for a settlement, one that would also protect France's New World

1788–94	Fires destroy much of the city; new brick buildings replace wood.
1794	Planter Etienne de Boré granulates sugar from cane for the first time, spawning a boom in the industry.
1795	Treaty of Madrid opens port to Americans; trade thrives.
1800	Louisiana again becomes a French possession.
1803	France officially takes possession of the territory. United States then purchases it and takes possession.
1805	New Orleans incorporates as a city; first elections are held.
1812	The *New Orleans*, the first steam vessel to travel the Mississippi, arrives from Pittsburgh. Louisiana admitted as a U.S. state.
1815	Battle of New Orleans.
1831	The first (horse-drawn) railway west of the Alleghenies is completed, linking New Orleans and Milneburg.
1832–33	Yellow fever and cholera epidemic kills 10,000 people in 2 years.
1837	First newspaper coverage of Mardi Gras parade.

continues

holdings from British expansion, and the "property development" was entrusted to John Law's Company of the West.

Bienville chose the easily defended high ground at the bend in the river. Although it was some 100 miles inland along the river from the Gulf of Mexico, the site was near St. John's Bayou, a waterway into Lake Pontchartrain. This "back door" was convenient for a military defense or escape, and as a trade route (as the Choctaw Indians had long known)—allowing relatively easy access to the Gulf while bypassing the perilous Mississippi.

The new town was named New Orleans in honor of the duc d'Orléans, then the regent of France. Following the plan of a late French medieval town, a central square (the Place d'Armes) was laid out with streets forming a grid around it. A church, government office, priest's house, and official residences fronted the square, and earthen ramparts dotted with forts were built around the perimeter. A tiny wooden levee was raised against the river, which still flooded periodically and turned the streets into rivers of mud. Today this area of original settlement is known as the Vieux Carré (Old Square) and the Place d'Armes as Jackson Square.

A Melting Pot

In its first few years, New Orleans was a community of French officials, adventurers, merchants, slaves, soldiers, and convicts from French prisons, all living in rude huts of cypress, moss, and clay. These were the first ingredients of New Orleans's population gumbo. The city's commerce was mainly limited to trade with native tribes and to beginning agricultural production.

To supply people and capital to the colony, John Law's company essentially pulled the first real estate scam in the New World. The territory and the city were marketed on the continent as Heaven on Earth, full of immediate and boundless opportunities for wealth and luxury. The value of real estate soared, and wealthy Europeans, aristocrats, merchants, exiles, soldiers, and a large contingent of German farmers arrived—to find only mosquitoes, a raw frontier existence, and swampy land. The scheme nearly

1840 Antoine Alciatore, founder of Antoine's restaurant, arrives from Marseille. New Orleans is the fourth-largest city in the United States and is second only to New York as a port.

1850 Booming commerce totals $200 million; cotton accounts for 45% of total trade. City becomes largest slave market in the country.

1852 New Orleans annexes Lafayette.

1853–55 Yellow fever epidemic during the summer; 12% of the population killed in 1853 in roughly 2 months.

1861–62 Louisiana secedes from the Union; city captured by Admiral Farragut.

1865–77 Reconstruction; "carpetbaggers" swarm into the city, and tensions climax in clashes between the Crescent White League and government forces.

1884–85 Cotton Centennial Exposition (World's Fair) held at the present site of Audubon Park.

1890 Jelly Roll Morton born.

1890 Creole of color Homer Plessy gets arrested riding a train recently segregated by Jim Crow laws. He sues the state, culminating in bankrupted the French nation, but New Orleans' population grew, and in 1723 it replaced Biloxi as the capital of the Louisiana territory.

The next year, Bienville approved the Code Noir, which set forth the laws under which African slaves were to be treated and established Catholicism as the territory's official religion. While it codified slavery and banished Jews from Louisiana, the code did provide slaves recognition and a degree of protection under the law, unusual in the South at that time.

A lack of potential wives created a significant barrier to population and societal development. In 1727, a small contingent of Ursuline nuns arrived and established a convent. While they weren't exactly eligible, they did provide a temporary home and education to many shiploads of *les filles à la cassette*. The "cassette girls" or "casket girls"—named for the government-issue *cassettes* or casketlike trunks in which they carried their possessions—were young women of appropriate character sent to Louisiana by the French government to be courted and married by the colonists. (If we're to believe the current residents of the city, the plan was remarkably successful: Nearly everyone in New Orleans claims descent from the casket girls or from Spanish or French nobility, which makes one wonder at the rampant infertility of the colony's earlier population of convicts and "fallen women.")

John Law's company relinquished its governance of Louisiana in 1731, and the French monarch regained direct control of the territory. In the following decades, planters established estates up and down the river from New Orleans. In the city, wealthier society began to develop a courtly atmosphere on the French model. Amid their rough-and-tumble existence, families competed to see who could throw the most opulent parties.

During the 18th century, colonization of a different sort was taking place to the west, along the Gulf of Mexico. There, many French colonists, displaced by British rule from Acadia, Nova Scotia, made their way south from Canada and formed a rural outpost. We've Anglicized the name of these Acadians, but many of their descendants still live, farm, trap, and speak their unique brand of French to New Orleans. We know them today as Cajuns.

the landmark U.S. Supreme Court decision *Plessy v. Ferguson*.

1892 First electric streetcar operates along St. Charles Avenue.

1897 Sidney Bechet born. Storyville established.

1901 Louis Armstrong born.

1911 Razzy Dazzy Spasm Band performs in New York; another band takes its name, adjusting it to Razzy Dazzy Jazz Band—first use of "jazz".

1917 Original Dixieland Jazz Band attains height of popularity.

1921 Inner-Harbor Navigational Canal built, connecting Lake Pontchartrain and the Mississippi.

1928 Colorful Huey P. Long elected governor of Louisiana; 4 years later he is elected to U.S. Senate.

1935 Long is shot dead.

1938 Tennessee Williams arrives in New Orleans. Huey P. Long Bridge built over Mississippi River.

1939 French Quarter Residents Association formed as an agent for preservation.

continues

Meanwhile, New Orleans commercial development was stymied by trading restrictions imposed by France: The colony could trade only with the mother country. To subvert the restrictions, smugglers and pirates provided alternative markets and transportation for the local crops, furs, bricks, and tar.

As the French saw it, the colony was costing them development money, and the return on investment wasn't paying off. In 1762, Louis XV traded the city and all of Louisiana west of the Mississippi to his cousin Charles III of Spain in the secret Treaty of Fontainebleau. It took 2 years for the news to reach a shocked New Orleans, and the Spanish took 2 more years to send a governor, Don Antonio de Ulloa. He made few friends among local residents, who eventually demanded Ulloa's removal. Some proposed the formation of a Louisiana republic. Ulloa was sent packing, and for a time, New Orleans and Louisiana were effectively independent of any foreign power. That came to a crashing end in 1769 when the Spanish sent forth Don Alexander ("Bloody") O'Reilly and 3,000 soldiers. Leaders of the relatively peaceful rebellion were executed, and Spanish rule was reimposed. With a Gallic shrug, French aristocracy mingled with Spanish nobility, intermarried, and helped to create a new "Creole" culture.

Devastating fires struck in 1788 (when more than 850 buildings were destroyed) and again in 1794 in the midst of rebuilding. From the ashes emerged a new architecture dominated by the proud Spanish style of brick-and-plaster buildings replete with arches, courtyards, balconies, and, of course, attached slave quarters. Today you'll still see tile markers giving Spanish street names at French Quarter street corners.

The Spanish imposed the same kind of trade restrictions on the city that the French had, with even less success (these were boom years for pirates and buccaneers like the infamous Jean Lafitte and his brother Pierre). Still, this was a period of intense imperial conflict and maneuvering between the Spanish, French, English, and Americans. Spain allowed some American revolutionaries to trade through the city in support of the colonists' fight against Britain, but France rallied and regained possession of the territory in 1800 with a surprisingly quiet transfer of ownership. They held on for 3 years while Napoleon negotiated the Louisiana Purchase with the United States for the paltry (as it turned out) sum of $15 million. For Creole society, the return to French

1956 Lake Pontchartrain Causeway, world's longest bridge, completed.

1960 The city's public schools integrated.

1973 Parades banned in the Vieux Carré, changing the character of the city's observance of Mardi Gras.

1975 Superdome opens.

1976 Anne Rice publishes best-selling "Interview with Vampire," set in New Orleans.

1977 Ernest N. "Dutch" Morial becomes first African-American mayor.

1984 Louisiana World Expo draws disappointing crowds but spurs redevelopment of the riverside area.

1988 Anne Rice moves back to New Orleans, with major cultural impact.

1999 Harrah's opens new casino.

2000 The National World War II Museum. Mardi Gras 2000 draws record crowds.

rule was unpleasant enough because France had long been facing serious financial troubles, but a sale to uncouth America was anathema. To their minds, it meant the end of a European lifestyle in the Vieux Carré.

Thus, when Americans arrived in the city, the upper classes made it known that they were welcome to settle—away from the old city and Creole society across Canal Street (so named because a drainage canal was once planned along its route).

And so it was that New Orleans came to be two parallel cities. The American section spread outward from Canal Street along St. Charles Avenue; business and cultural institutions centered in the Central Business District, and mansions rose in what is now the Garden District, which was a separate, incorporated city until 1852. French and Creole society dominated the Quarter for the rest of the 19th century, extending toward Lake Pontchartrain along Esplanade Avenue. Soon, however, the Americans (crass though they may have seemed) brought commercial success to the city, which quickly warmed relations—the Americans sought the vitality of downtown society, and the Creoles sought the profit of American business. They also had occasion to join forces against hurricanes, yellow-fever epidemics, and floods.

From the Battle of New Orleans to the Civil War

Perhaps nothing helped to cement a sense of community more than the Battle of New Orleans, during the War of 1812. The great turning point in Creole-American relations was the cooperation of Andrew Jackson and Jean Lafitte. To save the city, Jackson set aside his disdain for the pirate, and Lafitte turned down offers to fight for the British, instead supplying the Americans with cannons and ammunition that helped swing the battle in their favor. When Jackson called for volunteers, some 5,000 citizens from both sides of Canal Street responded. In the battle on January 8, 1815, in a field a few miles downstream from the city, approximately 2,000 British troops and 20 Americans were killed or wounded. Jackson became a hero, though ironically neither he nor the British had been aware that a treaty concluding the war had been signed a full 2 weeks before, on December 24, 1814.

2005 City floods when levees fail following Hurricane Katrina.

2010 "Who Dat" frenzy: underdog Saints win NFL Super Bowl championship for first time in the team's 43-year history.

2010 HBO's Tremé TV series debuts.

2010 Worst offshore spill in U.S. history—BP Deepwater Horizon despoils Gulf of Mexico.

2012 Census shows city has reached 75% of its pre-Katrina population.

From then until the Civil War, New Orleans was a boomtown. Colonial trade restrictions had evaporated with the Louisiana Purchase, and steam-powered river travel arrived in 1812. River commerce exploded, and by the 1840s New Orleans's port was on par with New York's. Cotton and sugar made many local fortunes; wealthy planters joined the city merchants in building luxurious town houses and attending festivals, opera, theater, banquets, parades, and spectacular balls (including "Quadroon Balls," where beautiful mulatto girls were displayed to the male gentry as possible mistresses). As always, politics and gambling were dominant pastimes of these citizens and visitors.

By the middle of the century, cotton-related business was responsible for nearly half of the total commerce in New Orleans, so it's no surprise that the city housed a large and ruthless slave market. Paradoxically, New Orleans also had an extensive, established population of "free men (and women) of color" in the American South. Furthermore, racial distinctions within the city increasingly became difficult to determine; people could often trace their ancestry back to two or even three different continents. Adding to the diversity, waves of Irish and German immigrants arrived in New Orleans during this period, supplying important sources of labor to support the city's growth.

The only major impediments to the development of the city in these decades were occasional yellow-fever epidemics, which killed thousands of residents and visitors. Despite the clearing of swampland, the mosquito-borne disease persisted until the final decades of the 19th century.

Reconstruction & Beyond

The boom era ended rather abruptly with the Civil War and Louisiana's secession from the United States in 1861. Federal troops marched into the city in 1862 and stayed until 1877, through the bitter Reconstruction period. As was the case elsewhere in the South, this period saw violent clashes between armed white groups and the state's Reconstruction forces.

After the war, the city went about the business of rebuilding its economic life— without slavery. By 1880, annexations had fleshed out the city limits, port activity had picked up, and railroads were establishing their economic importance. A new group of immigrants, Italians, came to put their unique mark on the city. Through it all, an undiminished enthusiasm for fun survived. Gambling thrived; there were hundreds of saloons and scores of "bawdy houses" engaged in prostitution (illegal, but uncontrolled). New Orleans was earning an international reputation for open vice, much to the chagrin of the city's polite society.

In 1897, Alderman Sidney Story moved all illegal (but highly profitable) activities into a restricted district along Basin Street next to the French Quarter, in an effort to improve the city's tarnishing image. Quickly nicknamed Storyville, the district boasted fancy "sporting palaces" with elaborate decor, musical entertainment, and a wide variety of ladies of pleasure. The *Blue Book* directory listed the names, addresses, and races of more than 700 prostitutes, working the swanky "palaces" down to the decrepit "cribs." Black musicians such as Jelly Roll Morton played in the more ornate bordellos, bringing popularity to early forms of jazz. When the secretary of the Navy decreed in 1917 that armed forces should not be exposed to so much open vice, Storyville closed down and disappeared without a trace beyond its great cultural impact.

The 20th Century

The 20th century found the city's port becoming the largest in the United States and the second-busiest in the world (after Amsterdam), with goods coming in by barge and rail. Drainage problems were conquered by means of high levees, canals, pumping stations, and great spillways, which direct floodwater away from the city. Bridges were built across the Mississippi River, including the Huey P. Long Bridge, named after Louisiana's famous politician and demagogue. New Orleans's emergence as a regional financial center, with more than 50 commercial banks, led to the construction of soaring office buildings, mostly in the Central Business District.

Like most other American cities, the city's population spread outward, filling suburbs and nearby municipalities. A thriving community in New Orleans East was developed by Vietnamese refugees, who immigrated in the 1970s. Unlike other cities, however, New Orleans has been able to preserve its original town center and much of its historic architecture.

NEW ORLEANS IN POPULAR CULTURE

Books

You can fill many bookcases with New Orleans literature and authors, so consider the following list as just a starter kit. Get more recommendations at the fine bookshops listed in chapter 9.

GENERAL FICTION

There are many examples of early fiction that give a good taste of old-time New Orleans life. George Washington Cable's stories are revealing and colorful, as in *Old Creole Days* (1879). Perhaps the best writer to touch on the lives of the earliest Creoles is Kate Chopin, whose late-1800s works, including the revered *The Awakening,* are set in Louisiana.

Frances Parkinson Keyes lived on Chartres Street for more than 25 years. Her most famous works are *Dinner at Antoine's* and *Madame Castel's Lodger*, each with curious descriptions of life in the city at that time, along with excellent descriptions of food.

Ellen Gilchrist's contemporary fiction, including the short-story collection *In the Land of Dreamy Dreams,* portrays life in wealthy uptown New Orleans. Sheila Bosworth's wonderful tragicomedies perfectly sum up the city and its collection of characters—check out our all-time favorites *Almost Innocent* or *Slow Poison.* Other possibilities are Nancy Lemann's delightful *Lives of the Saints* and Michael Ondaatje's controversial *Coming Through Slaughter,* a fictionalized account of Buddy Bolden and the early New Orleans jazz era.

New Orleans native Poppy Z. Brite's comic novels set in the New Orleans restaurant world are stuffed full of NOLA (and the chef biz) verisimilitude, starting with *Liquor.* Misfit detective Dave Roubicheaux solves crime in a small Cajun town in the popular series by James Lee Burke.

And then there is the cottage industry known as Anne Rice, who undeniably ignited the current era of pop vampire culture (bow to the master, *True Blood, Twilight,* and *Vampire Diaries*). Her *Vampire Chronicles* captures the city's spooky, elegant essence.

HISTORY

Lyle Saxon's *Fabulous New Orleans* is the most charming place to start learning about the city's past. (Saxon was director of the writer's program under the WPA.) From there, move on to his coauthored folk-tale collection, *Gumbo Ya-Ya.* Roark Bradford's Civil War novel, *Kingdom Coming,* contains a lot of information about voodoo. Mark Twain visited the city often in his riverboat days, and his *Life on the Mississippi* has a good number of tales about New Orleans and its riverfront life. *The WPA Guide to New Orleans* also contains excellent social and historical background and provides a fascinating picture of the city in 1938. *Beautiful Crescent,* by Joan Garvey and Mary Lou Widmer, is a solid reference book on the history of New Orleans. Those who loved *Gangs of New York* will be pleased to learn Herbert Asbury gave the same highly entertaining, not terribly factual treatment to New Orleans in *The French Quarter: An Informal History of the New Orleans Underworld.* New Orleans's favorite patroness, the Baroness de Pontalba, gets the biography treatment in Christina Vella's *Intimate Enemies.* In *The Last Madam: A Life in the New Orleans Underworld,* Christine Wiltz reveals a bawdy bygone era, conveyed through the words of Norma Wallace. The brothel owner recorded her memoirs before her 1974 suicide.

Two newer, eminently readable histories are Ned Sublette's *The World That Made New Orleans*, which focuses on the cultural influences of European, African, and Caribbean settlers, and Lawrence Powell's *Accidental City*, a definitive look back at the city's scrappy evolution.

Of the many guides to Mardi Gras, Henri Schindler's *Mardi Gras New Orleans* account is that of a historian and a long-term producer of balls and parades. *Mardi Gras in New Orleans: An Illustrated History* is a concise history of the celebration from ancient times to 2001, produced by *Mardi Gras Guide* publisher Arthur Hardy.

Lovers of the lurid will enjoy *Madame LaLaurie*, a well-researched biography of the notorious, high-society murderess. Sara Roahen's charming *Gumbo Tales: Finding My Place at the New Orleans Table* left us hungering for more of her uproarious outsider's insights, as the recent transplant to New Orleans discovers the culture through its distinctive food and drink.

Speaking of which, in *The Fish That Ate the Whale: The Life and Times of America's Banana King,* Rich Cohen recounts the rags-to-riches-to-revolution tale of fruit magnate Sam Zemurray.

LITERATURE

William Faulkner came to New Orleans, lived on Pirate's Alley, and penned *Soldiers' Pay.* Several other Faulkner novels and short stories are set in New Orleans. Tennessee Williams became a devoted New Orleans fan, living in the city on and off for many years. It inspired him to write *A Streetcar Named Desire,* one of the best-known New Orleans tales. He also set *The Rose Tattoo* in the city.

Other notable New Orleans writers include Walker Percy and Shirley Ann Grau. Percy's novels, including *The Moviegoer* and *Love in the Ruins,* are classic portrayals of the idiosyncrasies of New Orleans and its residents. Grau's most famous novel, *The Keepers of the House,* won the Pulitzer Prize in 1964. John Kennedy Toole also received a Pulitzer, but he wasn't around to know about it, having committed suicide years before. At the time of his death, none of his works had even been published. Toole's *A Confederacy of Dunces* is a timeless New Orleans tragicomedy that'll have you laughing out loud.

Robert Penn Warren's classic novel *All the King's Men,* an exceedingly loose telling of the story of Huey P. Long, makes the list because it's so good—and because it gives a portrait of the performance art known as Louisiana politics.

A further notable modern writer is Robert Olen Butler, who won the Pulitzer in 1993 for his collection of stories, *A Good Scent from a Strange Mountain,* set primarily in New Orleans's Vietnamese community.

POST-KATRINA LITERATURE

It's true that from great tragedy comes great art, and the following help give a picture of pre- and post-flood New Orleans. Tom Piazza's *Why New Orleans Matters* is a love letter to and about the city and our number one choice for people trying to "get" New Orleans. His novel, *City of Refuge,* bisects Katrina through the experiences of two families. Rosemary James, of Faulkner House Books, edited *My New Orleans,* a collection of essays by locals ranging from writers to restaurateurs and raconteurs, attempting to pin down just what it is about this place that keeps them here, come hell or high water. Local historian Douglas Brinkley's meticulous *The Great Deluge* may not end up the definitive postmortem examination of Katrina, but it will be hard to top. *Times-Picayune* columnist Chris Rose collected his heartbreaking personal essays, written as he and his colleagues covered their flooded city, in *1 Dead in Attic.*

Zeitoun, Dave Eggers' gripping narrative nonfiction, recounts the tale of one man's horror and a nation's injustice (Google Zeitoun's even more shocking post-publication story for a completely different perspective), while *New Yorker* columnist Dan Baum weaves together differing perspectives to illustrate how the multihued city unifies nine diverse narratives in *Nine Lives.*

Finally, fans of football and motivational memoirs may enjoy *Home Team* by Saints coach Sean Payton or Drew Brees' *Coming Back Stronger.*

BOOKS ABOUT MUSIC

We highly recommend Ann Allen Savoy's *Cajun Music Vol. 1,* a combination songbook and oral history. It features previously untranscribed Cajun music with lyrics in French (including a pronunciation guide) and English. A labor of many years, it's an invaluable resource.

For a look at specific time periods, people, and places in the history of New Orleans jazz, you have a number of choices. They include William Carter's *Preservation Hall*; John Chilton's *Sidney Bechet: The Wizard of Jazz*; Gunther Schuller's *Early Jazz: Its Roots and Musical Development*; *A Trumpet Around the Corner: The Story of New Orleans Jazz* , by Samuel Charters; *New Orleans Jazz: A Revised History,* by R. Collins; and *New Orleans Style,* by Bill Russell. Al Rose's *Storyville, New Orleans* is an excellent source of information about the very beginnings of jazz; while *Up From the Cradle of Jazz* tells its story post-WWII. We quite enjoyed *Songs of My Fathers,* Tom Sancton's retelling of his boyhood at the feet of the great Preservation Hall musicians.

If you prefer primary sources, read Louis Armstrong's *Satchmo: My Life in New Orleans,* or *Satchmo: The Wonderful World and Art of Louis Armstrong,* a bio by way of his own artworks. Two other suggestions are Sidney Bechet's *Treat It Gentle,* and the story of Mac Rebennack's (aka Dr. John) wild life as reflected in *Under a Hoodoo Moon.*

Film & Television

With atmosphere and mystery to spare, all forms of water and roadways, new and old architecture, and attractive tax incentives, there's a veritable production boom here in "Hollywood South." The city isn't a character in all of them, but it's the heart of the highly authentic HBO series *Tremé*. If you come across the stellar, little-seen series *Frank's Place* (1987–88), don't miss it. *True Blood* is filmed mostly in Baton Rouge, but that's okay.

Consider these for some pre- or post-visit flavor: classics like Brando in *A Streetcar Named Desire* (1951); Betty Davis in *Jezebel* (1938); the kitschy but decent Elvis vehicle *King Creole* (1958); and counterculture Mardi Gras freakout *Easy Rider*. *Belizaire the Cajun* (1986) tells of the violence between 19th-century Cajuns and English speakers; Tom Waits bums around the city, the countryside, and jail in the indie *Down by Law* (1986); and a young Brooke Shields navigates a Storyville childhood in Louis Malle's *Pretty Baby* (1978). Then there's the steamy but flawed *The Big Easy*. Brad Pitt ages backwards in *The Curious Case of Benjamin Button* (2008) and goes fang to fang with Tom Cruise in *Interview with the Vampire* (1994). Lastly, for kids of any age, when *Abbott & Costello Go to Mars* (1953), they end up at Mardi Gras—an altogether different universe.

Documentaries about the Katrina experience cover every angle, notably in Spike Lee's *When the Levees Broke;* the remarkable, Oscar-nominated *Trouble the Water;* the superb prize-winning *Faubourg Tremé: The Untold Story of Black New Orleans;* and Harry Shearer's exposé *The Big Uneasy*.

Recordings

The selections listed below should give you a good start, though we could fill pages more (and we're barely even touching on the many fine pop, rock, or folk contributions). Also see the names we list in the nightlife section (p. 165), and for more advice or recommendations, consult the über-helpful know-it-alls at **Louisiana Music Factory,** 210 Decatur St. (© **504/586-1094**).

CROSS-GENRE ANTHOLOGIES

There are many collections and anthologies of New Orleans and Louisiana music available, including the 1990s Alligator Stomp series by Rhino Records. The most comprehensive, critically acclaimed *Doctors, Professors, Kings & Queens: The Big Ol' Box of New Orleans* is a four-disc package released in 2004 by Shout! Factory and the one collection that touches all the bases of the diverse musical gumbo that is the Crescent City. For a more modest taste, order up the *Tremé, Season 1* soundtrack, which covers a bit of the same fertile, funky ground, albeit just from recent years.

JAZZ

A classic New Orleans jazz collection starts with the originators: King Oliver, Kid Ory, Sidney Bechet, Original Dixieland Jazz Band, and Jellyroll Morton, say. Add some early Louis Armstrong, with his Hot Five and Hot Seven bands.

Ken Burns' Jazz box covers them and more from New Orleans and beyond), and the anthologies *New Orleans* (Atlantic Jazz), *Recorded in New Orleans Volumes 1 and 2* (Good Time Jazz), and *New Orleans Jazz* (Arhoolie) are good choices. Preservation Hall's *Preservation* covers the classics; Pete Fountain, Al Hirt (try *Honey in the Horn*), and Louis Prima (*The Wildest*) all swing things in a new direction.

Leaping forward, Wynton Marsalis and Harry Connick, Jr., build on those traditions, as do trumpeter Irvin Mayfield and clarinetist Tim Laughlin. Old-time revivalists like the New Orleans Jazz Vipers, Cottonmouth Kings, Meschiya Lake (we like *Lucky Devil*), the Smoking Time Jazz Band, and Aurora Nealand are local phenoms—well worth the cost of a disc or a download. Legendary Allen Toussaint doesn't dabble, he delves—as demonstrated by *The Bright Mississippi*, his fine jazz foray.

BRASS BANDS

The age-old tradition of brass-oriented street bands underwent a spectacular revival in the 1980s and 1990s with the revitalization of such long-term presences as the Olympia Brass Band and the arrival of newcomers like the Dirty Dozen Brass Band (try their monster anthology *This Is the Dirty Dozen Brass Band*). They inspired a younger and funkier generation, with the Rebirth Brass Band, the New Birth Brass Band, the Hot 8, up-and-comers TCB, and the Soul Rebels, the best of the crowd. It's all better live, so try *The Main Event: Live at the Maple Leaf*. The loose, bumping *Rock with the Hot 8*, New Birth's moving tribute to late co-founder Tuba Fats *New Birth Family*, and the Tremé Brass Band's *Gimme My Money Back* are all irresistible. And go see them live.

RHYTHM, BLUES & SOUL

First things first: Get your Fats on with *My Blue Heaven* or any "Best of" compilation. Then get Dr. John's *Gumbo* or *Mos Scocious: The Dr. John Anthology*. Round out your legends collection with Professor Longhair's *'Fess: The Professor Longhair Anthology* and fellow key wizard James Booker's *Classified*. Go down funk road with the Meters' classic *Cissy Strut* and *The Wild Tchoupitoulas* for Mardi Gras Indian funk. Ivan Neville's Dumpstaphunk is keeping the funk alive, while Galactic might be funk, might be jazz, could be rock or jam—but is never uninteresting. Start with *Ruckus*. Troy "Trombone Shorty" Andrews rocked jazz, R&B, funk, and hip hop into his own thang on monster hits *Backatown* and *For True*. We're true to hometown heroes the Neville Brothers' *Yellow Moon* and *Treacherous: A History of the Neville Brothers, 1955–1985*. *The Complete 'Tousan' Sessions* shows why producer/writer Allen Toussaint is a legend. Also get some soul crooners in, like Irma Thomas' *Time is On My Side* and Johnny Adams' *Heart & Soul*. Worthwhile anthologies include *The Best of New Orleans Rhythm & Blues Volumes 1 and 2*; *Sehorn's Soul Farm*; and *The Mardi Gras Indians Super Sunday Showdown*.

HIP-HOP & BOUNCE

New Orleans is home to several noted hip-hop and rap artists and a homegrown sub-genre: booty-dropping, second-line-influenced, twerk-propagating bounce. It began with Big Freedia's *Hitz Vol. 1*. Breakout dirty Southerner Juvenile's *400* is a classic, while hip-hop star Lil Wayne came back strong with *I Am Not a Human Being*. Mystikal's risqué rhymes broke musical ground before legal troubles sidelined his career; the comeback release and one from protégé Lil Cali were pending at press time.

EATING & DRINKING

Where oh where to start? Is there any other American city so revered, so identified with the glory of gluttony and the joy of the juice than New Orleans? Perhaps, but none with a truly indigenous cuisine (or two), none that lay claim (rightly or not) to inventing the cocktail, and surely none that does it with such unbridled gusto. As the oft-repeated homily goes: In most places, people eat to live; in New Orleans, people live to eat. Seriously, you're only visiting, so convince your tortured psyche that you can resume a sensible diet when you get home and immerse yourself in the local culture. In other words, *indulge*. It's so very worth it. We've known very strident vegans who give it up for a few days while here (yes, really), though most chefs, and certainly those in the better restaurants, are adept at adapting to any specified "isms" or dietary restriction. Of course those who must can seek out the usual, benign ethnic restaurants. The single most important thing to know? *Make reservations.*

Chapter 11 has much more about Cajun and Creole food. Chapter 8 has cocktailing info. And Chapter 6, "Where to Dine in New Orleans," points you to the top troughs.

WHEN TO GO

With the possible exception of July and August (unless you thrive on heat and humidity), just about any time is the right time to go to New Orleans. We love the warm, jasmine-infused nights and warmer days of mid-fall and spring best, and even relish the occasional high drama of a good summer thunderstorm.

It's important to know what's going on when, since the city's landscape, and hotel availability and rates, can change dramatically depending on what events or conventions are on. Mardi Gras is, of course, the hardest time of year to get a hotel room, but it can also be difficult during major festivals (French Quarter Fest, Jazz & Heritage Festival) and sporting events (BCS, Sugar Bowl, Saints and LSU Superdome games). New Orleans isn't recognized as a holiday destination, but in December it's gussied up with decorations, there are all kinds of holiday special events, and the weather is quite fine. Eager hotels often have good deals, and many restaurants offer special prix fixe "Reveillon" deals. Take advantage of it.

The Weather

The average mean temperature in New Orleans is an inviting 70°F (21°C), but it can drop or rise considerably in a single day. (We've experienced 40°F/4°C and rain one day, 80°F/27°C and humidity the next.) Conditions depend primarily on whether it rains and whether there is direct sunlight or cloud cover. Rain can provide slight and temporary relief on a hot day; it tends to hit in sudden (and sometimes dramatically heavy) showers, which disappear as quickly as they arrive. In unimpeded sun it gets much warmer. The high humidity can intensify even mild warms and colds. Still, the semitropical climate is part of New Orleans's appeal—the slight moistness makes for lush, sensual air.

New Orleans should be pleasant most of the year. During the muggy, bargain summer months, follow the natives' example: stay out of the midday sun and duck from one air-conditioned locale to another. June and September can still be humid and warm; early spring and mid-fall are glorious. Winter is mild by

New Orleans Average Temperatures & Rainfall

	JAN	FEB	MAR	APR	MAY	JUNE	JULY	AUG	SEPT	OCT	NOV	DEC
High (°F)	62	65	71	78	85	89	91	90	87	80	71	65
High (°C)	17	18	22	26	29	32	33	32	31	27	22	18
Low (°F)	43	46	52	58	66	71	73	73	70	60	50	45
Low (°C)	6	8	11	14	19	22	23	23	21	16	10	7
Days of Rainfall	10	9	9	7	8	11	14	13	10	6	7	10

hot time IN THE CITY

If you can stand it, do consider braving the city in summer; the tourist business is often slow, which produces hotel bargains. On a recent July visit, high-end hotels were offering rooms from $99 to $129 (way, *way* below their regular rates), sometimes with additional perks thrown in. Plus, you can often get upgrades to fancy suites for a song—ask when you check in. In August (and sometimes July or Sept), local restaurants run "Coolinary" specials, three-course prix-fixe meals at bargain prices. Yeah, it's hot and humid, but bearable for all but the most sensitive, and there are plenty of air-conditioned respites to duck into.

American standards—don't expect Florida warmth—and punctuated by an occasional freeze-level cold snap. But *unpredictable* and flexible are the watchwords. The whims of the weather gods are at play, so be ready to adjust accordingly.

Hurricane season runs June 1 to mid-November. Obviously, there are no guarantees, but despite their unpredictability and the high drama of recent years, hurricanes actually don't happen too terribly often. In the height of summer, T-shirts, shorts, and tissue-weight fabrics are acceptable everywhere except the finest restaurants. In the spring and fall, something a little warmer is in order; in the winter, carry a lightweight coat or jacket and pack a folding umbrella (though they're available everywhere, as are cheap rain ponchos, for that unexpected downpour). The biggest summertime climate problem can be the air-conditioning overcompensation that chills rooms—especially restaurants—to meat-locker-like temps, so bring those light wraps along even on warm nights.

New Orleans Calendar of Events

For more information on **Mardi Gras, Jazz Fest, Festivals Internationale,** and other major area events, see chapter 4, "Mardi Gras & Jazz Fest." For general information, contact the **New Orleans Metropolitan Convention and Visitors Bureau,** 2020 St. Charles Ave., New Orleans, LA 70130 (✆ **800/672-6124** or 504/566-5011; www.neworleanscvb.com). For a list of other Louisiana festivals, visit www.laffnet.org.

JANUARY

Allstate Sugar Bowl Classic. First held in 1934, this is New Orleans's oldest yearly sporting occasion. The football game in the Superdome is the main event, but there are other activities. ✆ **504/828-2440;** www.allstatesugarbowl.org. January 2, 2014.

FEBRUARY

NBA All-Star Game. The hometown Pelicans host the best of the best of the hardwood at the New Orleans Arena on Sunday, February 16, 2014. www.nba.com.

Lundi Gras. This tradition brings a free, outdoor music and food celebration to Spanish Plaza (Poydras St. at the river), with the big event at 6pm: the ceremonial, waterfront arrival of the Kings of Rex and Zulu, marking the beginning of Mardi Gras. They're welcomed by the mayor, fireworks, and much whoop-de-doo. ✆ **504/522-1555.** See also p. 41. Monday before Mardi Gras (March 3, 2014; February 16, 2015).

Mardi Gras. The culmination of the 2-month-long carnival season, Mardi Gras is the centuries-old annual blowout. Each year the eyes of the world are on New Orleans, as the entire city stops working and starts partying, and the streets are taken over by awe-inspiring parades. See chapter 4. Day before Ash Wednesday (March 4, 2014; February 17, 2015).

St. Patrick's Day Parades. There are several, with dates (like the paraders) usually staggered. Instead of Mardi Gras beads, watchers are pelted with veggies, including the coveted cabbages. In 2014, a funky French Quarter parade kicks off at Molly's at the Market (1107 Decatur St.) on Friday, March 14, at 6pm (© **504/525-5169**). On St. Patrick's Day (Monday, March 17, 2014), the downtown parade begins at 6pm at Burgundy and Piety in the Bywater and stumbles along a route to Bourbon Street (© **504/525-5169**). www.stpatricksdaynew orleans.com).

St. Joseph's Day Parade. Another fascinating, little-known festivity. Italians venerate St. Joseph, patron saint of families and working men, on his saint's day (March 19) with a parade (usually the weekend before) and the creation of devotional altars. These moving, elaborate works of art feature food, candles, and statues and can be viewed at various churches and private homes (where you might also get fed), and at the American Italian Museum, 537 St. Peters St. Locations are listed in the *Times-Picayune* classifieds and on www.nola.com prior to the event. © **504/522-7294.**

Super Sunday. This annual Mardi Gras Indians showdown takes place on the Sunday nearest St. Joseph's Day (March 16, 2014). The more organized "uptown" event is in A. L. Davis Park, Washington Avenue and LaSalle Street, from noon till late afternoon. Indian tribes garbed in full, feathered regalia gather to preen, parade, and engage in ritualized showdowns with traditional chants (with food booths and music, of course). The "downtown" Indians have a much looser street meeting, determined by weather or whim. The unique gathering can happen a few weeks or even months after St. Joseph's Day, usually on Bayou St. John at Orleans Avenue. It is intentionally underannounced, but check with the Backstreet Museum (p. 131) or the Community Events listings at www.wwoz.org. Mid-March. More on p. 42.

Tennessee Williams New Orleans Literary Festival. This 5-day series celebrates New Orleans's rich literary heritage with theatrical performances, readings, discussions, master classes, musical events, walking tours, and the ever-popular Stella Shouting Contest. It's not exclusive to Williams, and the roster of writers and publishers participating is impressive. Info at © **504/581-1144** or go to www.tennesseewilliams.net. March 19 to 23, 2014.

APRIL

French Quarter Festival. The 3½-day French Quarter Festival celebrates local music of the traditional jazz, brass band, Cajun/zydeco, or funk variety. The free event has become wildly popular: in 2013, more than half a million attended. There are scores of outdoor concerts, food booths, art shows, children's activities, tours, and seminars set throughout the Quarter (making it easy to return to your hotel room for a rest, though some stages are at far-flung ends of the Quarter). Book travel early; this good time is becoming a victim of its own success. © **800/673-5725** or 504/522-5730; www.fqfi.org. April 10 to 14, 2014.

The Crescent City Classic. This 10k race from Jackson Square to Audubon Park brings an international field of top (and lesser) runners to the city. © **504/861-8686;** www.ccc10k.com. Saturday before Easter. April 19, 2014.

New Orleans Jazz & Heritage Festival presented by Shell (Jazz Fest). A 10-day event that draws musicians, cooks, and craftspeople and their fans to celebrate music and life, Jazz Fest rivals Mardi Gras in popularity. For much more information, go to chapter 4. © **504/410-4100;** www.nojazzfest.com. April 25 to May 4, 2014.

Festival International de Louisiane. Some people split their festing between Jazz Fest and the popular (read: big) Festival International in Lafayette. The free, 5-day street fair, which focuses on French music and culture, overlaps with the first weekend of Jazz Fest so it dovetails nicely. See p. 39. © **337/232-8086;** www.festivalinternational.com. April 23 to 27, 2014.

MAY

New Orleans Wine & Food Experience. Some 10,000 people attend this 4-day gourmandistic pleasure, at which 150 vintners, 75 restaurants, and myriad chefs feature their wines and wares via tastings, seminars, and vintner dinners. The culmination is a grand, 2-day tasting held in the Superdome, but the party might really hit its stride with the Royal Street Stroll, where revelers indulge their way from one tasting station to the next along the closed street. ✆ **504/529-9463;** www.nowfe.com. May 21 to 24, 2014.

Mid-City Bayou Boogaloo. Another weekend, another laid-back New Orleans music, art, and food fest. This one's themeless, with the pretty location along Bayou St. John (and the rubber-ducky derby) being the draw for the largely local crowd. Bring a blanket, a parasol, and cash for snacks and brews, and go now before it gets huge. ✆ **504/488-3865;** www.thebayouboogaloo.com. May 16 to 18, 2014.

JUNE

Vieux-to-Do Creole Tomato and Cajun Zydeco Festivals. Two sweet, smallish (but growing) fests, the Creole Tomato Festival with the Jazz Fest–sponsored Cajun-Zydeco Festival, meld into one for 2 days of music, food, cooking demos, arts markets, and kids' activities. Music stages and booths stretch from the U.S. Mint on Esplanade to the French Market. ✆ **504/522-2621;** www. frenchmarket.org and http://www.jazzandheritage.org/cajun-zydeco. June 7 to 8, 2014.

JULY

Go Fourth on the River. The annual Fourth of July celebration begins in the morning along the French Quarter riverfront and culminates with a spectacular fireworks display at 9pm. For details, go to www.go4thontheriver.com or ✆ **800/672-6124.** July 4th.

Essence Music Festival. This massive, 3-day event sponsored by *Essence* magazine consistently presents a stellar lineup of R&B, soul, and hip-hop musicians (like Beyoncé, Kanye West, Mary J. Blige, Jill Scott, Chaka Khan, and George Clinton) in evening concerts on main stage and club-like "Super Lounges." During the day, this "party with a purpose" offers educational and empowerment seminars featuring A-list (Cosby! Oprah!) speakers and celebs, crafts and trade fairs. 2013 ticket prices started at $58 for a single day; $1,000 for VIP. www.essencemusicfestival.com. July 4 to 7, 2014.

Tales of the Cocktail. This 5-day mixtravaganza celebrates all things liquor. Based at the Monteleone Hotel but pouring over into other venues, it's a scholarly gathering of 20,000 hospitality professionals, serious mixologists, and admirers of the cocktail culture (read: If you make your own bitters and take 10 minutes to mix a drink, this might be for you. If your drink of choice is a Cosmo or PBR, pass). The popular events, including "Spirited Dinners" (food and cocktail pairings at local restaurants), fill up fast. Go to www.talesofthecocktail.com. July 16 to 20, 2014.

AUGUST

Satchmo Summerfest. Louis Armstrong, hometown boy made very good, is celebrated with his own festival, held around his real birthday (he claimed to be born on July 4th, but records prove otherwise). There's food, music, kids' activities, and seminars, with the emphasis on jazz entertainment and education to ensure that Satchmo lives on. ✆ **504/522-5730** or www.fqfi.org. August 1 to 3, 2014.

The Rayne Frog Festival. Cajuns can always find an excuse to hold a party, and here the humble frog begets a *fais-do-do* (dance), waltz competition, and frog-racing, -jumping and -eating contests. For the amphibian-deprived, there's even a Rent-a-Frog service. Gotta love it. ✆ **800/346-1958** in the U.S., 800/543-5340 in Canada, or 337/232-3808; www.raynefrogfestival.com. Mid-August.

SEPTEMBER

Southern Decadence. This multiday, multi-night dance/party/raunchfest attracts more than 100,000 gay men (and some women) from around the world. The frenzied peak is during the bar-studded parade route. Book rooms early or get a weekend ticket package in advance to save line time; and even if *you're* not too hot for leather, September in New Orleans is. www.southerndecadence.net (✆ **504/522-8047**). Labor Day weekend, August 28 to September 1, 2014.

OCTOBER

Festivals Acadiens & Creoles. Much smaller than the nearby, Francophone-focused **Festival International** (see April), this Lafayette event doesn't conflict with Jazz Fest. It combines the **Bayou Food Festival,** the **Festival de Musique Acadienne,** and the **Louisiana Native Crafts Festival.** Players, bring your instruments—there's a jam tent. It's fun, easygoing, tasty, and free, so spend freely to help keep it going. (✆ **800/346-1958** in the U.S., 800/543-5340 in Canada, or 337/232-3737; www.festivalsacadiens.com). October 2014; call or check website for exact dates.

Halloween. Halloween is celebrated especially grandly here in the ghosty city, rivaling Mardi Gras for costume outrageousness. The French Quarter is Halloween central (especially for the LGBT crowd), but ghoulish action around the city includes Boo-at-the-Zoo (last 2 weekends in October) for kids; the spooky Mortuary Haunted House in Mid-City (www.themortuary.net); and the truly terrifying House of Shock on the outskirts of town (www.houseofshock.com). October 31 and surrounding dates.

Ponderosa Stomp. This weekend celebration of early American rock is a mecca for fans and students of all things roots—blues, twang, swamp, thrash, or beyond—who attend scholarly daytime conferences and nighttime concerts by seminal, but largely unheralded performers. ✆ **504/810-9116;** http://ponderosastompfoundation.org. October 2014; call for check website for exact dates.

Voodoo Music + Arts Experience. The monstrous 3-day Voodoo Fest draws 150,000 youngish people to the City Park festival grounds, where 100+ acts fill six stages and a huge dance space. The diverse lineup features major stars from Metallica to Macklemore and Skrillex to Snoop Dogg, plus up-and-comers and a solid crop of locals. Eclectic art and exotic performances, Halloween-costumed people-watching, and food and drink round out the available diversions. www.worshipthemusic.com. October 31 to November 2, 2014.

NOVEMBER

Words & Music: A Literary Fest in New Orleans. This highly ambitious literary and music conference offers round-table discussions with eminent authors with varying connections to the city; original drama; poetry readings; master classes; and writing competitions. ✆ **504/586-1609** or visit www.wordsandmusic.org. Mid-November.

DECEMBER

Christmas, New Orleans Style. It's no surprise that the ever-celebratory New Orleaneans do Christmas really well. The town is decorated to a fare-thee-well and there are nightly concerts in St. Louis Cathedral and candlelit caroling in Jackson Square (Dec 21, 2014). Bonfires line the levees along the River Road on Christmas Eve (to guide Papa Noël, in his alligator-drawn sled), and house tours offer glimpses of stunningly turned-out residences. Lowered room rates and discounted "Réveillon" restaurant dinners also make this an economically attractive time to visit. ✆ **504/522-5730;** www.neworleansonline.com/christmas.

Celebration in the Oaks. Hundreds of thousands of lights illustrating holiday themes bedeck sections of City Park, and a walking and miniature-train tour lets you take in the charm and grandeur at your leisure. It's simple, affordable, nostalgic winter wonderment for the whole family. Plus there's ice skating and carousel and amusement park rides. ✆ **544/482-4888;** www.neworleanscitypark.com. Late November to early January.

New Year's Eve. The countdown party takes place in Jackson Square and, in the Southern equivalent of Times Square, revelers watch a lighted fleur de lis drop from the top of Jackson Brewery. Fireworks ensue. December 31.

Greater New Orleans

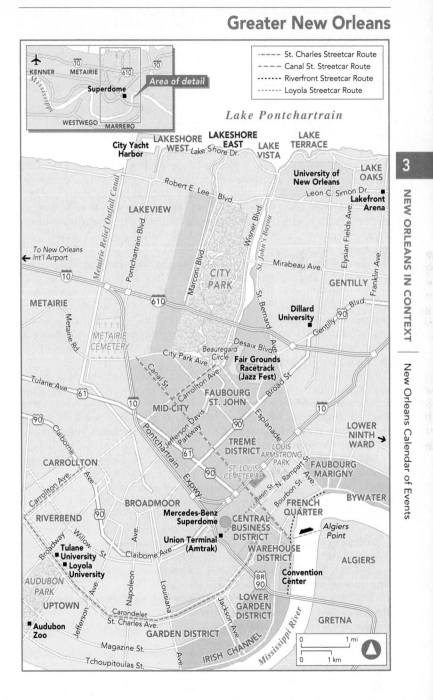

St. Charles Streetcar Route
Canal St. Streetcar Route
Riverfront Streetcar Route
Loyola Streetcar Route

Lake Pontchartrain

RESPONSIBLE TOURISM

Responsible tourism in New Orleans may start as you leave the airport, since many airport shuttle vans are propane-powered hybrids. Mardi Gras revelers will probably watch biodiesel-powered floats and catch beads on biodegradable string to help the strands fall from the tree branches.

Still, ecotourism isn't a major movement in New Orleans (like, say, drinking). But it helps that many attractions are easily accessed by foot, streetcar, or tour bus. Bike paths, bike tours, and bike rentals (p. 233) have become more prevalent, and drivers are becoming more cyclist-aware.

In terms of caloric intake, a visit to New Orleans can be decidedly *ir*responsible. You certainly won't find many vegetarian or vegan options in the tourist areas. But nearly every restaurant will accommodate diners' dietary preferences, and standard Middle Eastern and Asian restaurants are readily available. Further, almost every fine and contemporary dining establishment (and many simpler ones as well) have long embraced the lake-, river-, ocean-, and farm-to-table movement, sourcing local ingredients and purveyors, and in some cases planting their own farms and gardens. Given the bounteous supply of produce and seafood (and that industry's hardships), it's no surprise that "buy local" and support sustainability are long-standing practices.

A structure's age, plus regulations that protect historic buildings, can make green improvements difficult or even prohibitive (especially in the French Quarter). New or recently rebuilt properties including the Hyatt Regency and the Roosevelt (p. 62) have incorporated significant allowable smart-energy features. Still, most have instituted modest sustainability programs like recycling and on-demand linen replacement. Larger hotels and chains with corporate-wide programs, like the Ritz-Carlton (p. 51) and Harrah's (p. 162), are further along.

Ironically, Hurricane Katrina and the Deepwater oil spill actually had some environmental upsides: Locals and tourists alike became more aware of the need to support locally owned businesses as a means of rebuilding the local economy and maintaining the city's unique culture. The Urban Conservancy's **Stay Local** program (www.stay local.org) has a searchable directory of locally owned businesses to patronize—a superb, still relevant resource.

Voluntourism is still popular, especially with groups. **Habitat for Humanity** accepts volunteers for a day, a year, or any term. The respected organization has created the Musicians Village for artists who lost their homes in the flood (© **504/861-2077**; www.habitat-nola.org). Or try **Common Ground**, © **504/218-1729**; www. commongroundrelief.org) and the **United Saints Recovery Project**; © **504/895-2922**, ext. 108; www.unitedsaints.org), which has also done remarkable rebuilding work.

Americans Wetlands Conservation Corps focuses on vitally important wetlands restoration and sometimes has volunteer activities (© **504/293-2610**; www.americas wetland.org), as does **Groundwork New Orleans,** which builds rain gardens and other ecological improvements (www.groundworkNOLA.org).

Larger groups can also work through the **New Orleans Convention and Visitors Bureau** (p. 243) or **Projects with a Purpose** (© **504/934-1000**; www.projectswitha purpose.org). All potential volunteers should plan at least 1 to 2 weeks ahead, to complete applications and paperwork before beginning. In some cases, volunteers may be responsible for certain expenses and accommodations. Make sure the type of work you'll be doing is a good fit for you. **Volunteer International** (www.volunteerinter national.org) has a helpful list of questions to ask.

MARDI GRAS & JAZZ FEST

For many people, what they know about New Orleans begins and ends with its parties: Mardi Gras—the biggest street party in America—or Jazz Fest, the grandpère of all other music fests and the best music event in the country. In the place where anything here is an excuse for a party (festivals center on swamps, gumbo, crawfish, frogs, tomatoes, daiquiris, pork, and on it goes), the first thing you need to bring is a rollicking, party-ready attitude. New Orleans pretty much does the rest.

Still, this chapter gives you some background, foreground, and tips to help you get on your good foot for Mardi Gras or Jazz Fest.

4

MARDI GRAS

The granddaddy of all New Orleans celebrations is Mardi Gras. Thanks to sensational media accounts that zero in on the salacious aspects of this Carnival, its rep as a "Girls Gone Wild"–style spring break persists, drawing masses of wannabes for decadent, X-rated action rather than tradition. If that's your thang, by all means go forth and par-tay (just remember, Facebook is *forever*).

But there is so much more to Carnival than the media-hyped wanton action. Truth is, Mardi Gras remains one of the most exciting times to visit New Orleans, for people from all walks. Yes, you can hang in the Bourbon Street fratmosphere till you're thoroughly, wholly hung, but you can also spend days admiring and reveling in the city's rich traditions or have a fun family vacation beyond anything any mouse could offer.

Knowing some of its long and fascinating history helps put matters in perspective. First of all, Mardi Gras is both a day and a time period: French for "Fat Tuesday," Mardi Gras is the day before Ash Wednesday, when Lent begins. Carnival refers to the 5- to 8-week stretch from Twelfth Night (Jan 6) to Mardi Gras Day. The idea was that good Christians would eat as much as they could in preparation for their impending self-denial and fasting during Lent.

The party's origins can be traced to the Roman **Lupercalia** festival: 2 days when all sexual and social order disappeared, cross-dressing was mandatory, and the population ran riot (sound familiar?). The early Christian church was naturally appalled by this but was unable to stop it. So Lupercalia was grafted to the beginning of Lent, as a compromise to bribe everyone into being observant.

Carnival (from a Latin word roughly meaning "farewell to flesh") and its lavish masked balls and other revels became popular in Italy and France, and the tradition followed the Creoles to New Orleans. The first Carnival balls occurred in 1743. By the mid-1800s, Mardi Gras mischief had grown so ugly (the habit of tossing flour on revelers gradually turned into throwing bricks at them) that everyone predicted the end of the tradition.

THE BIRTH OF THE KREWES   Everything changed in 1856. Tired of being left out of the Creoles' Mardi Gras, a group of Americans who belonged to a secret society called Cowbellians formed the Mystick Krewe of Comus (named after the hero of a John Milton poem). On Mardi Gras evening, they presented a breathtakingly imaginative torchlit parade.

A new tradition was born, with new rituals and standards set. Mardi Gras marked the height of the social season for **"krewes,"** comprised of prominent society and business types.

After the Civil War put a temporary halt to things, two new enduring customs were added. Members threw trinkets to onlookers, and a "queen" reigned over their lavish balls.

As an elite Old South institution, Mardi Gras eschewed racial equality or harmony. African Americans participated in parades only by carrying torches to illuminate the route (the atmospheric if controversial *flambeaux,* as the torches are known). In 1909, a black man named William Storey mocked the elaborately garbed Rex by prancing after his float wearing a lard can for a crown. Storey was promptly dubbed "King Zulu." Thus begat the Krewe of Zulu, which parodied Rex and mocked racial stereotypes. The Zulu parade quickly became one of the most popular aspects of Mardi Gras, famously crowning Louis Armstrong as King Zulu in 1949.

Unfortunately, most krewes still excluded blacks, Jews, and women even as late as the 1990s when anti-discrimination sentiment and laws (tied to parade permits) finally forced the issue. The mighty Comus, in a move that many old-liners still feel marked the beginning of the end of classic Mardi Gras, canceled its parade rather than integrate. Proteus and Momus followed.

Then as now, the krewes and traditions of Mardi Gras change. Today there are dozens of unofficial krewes and "sub-krewe" spinoffs, and more crop up with some regularity.

SPECTACLE & BEAUTY   Parades were always things of spectacle and beauty, but they grew bigger than the narrow Quarter streets could accommodate—and bigger yet. New "superkrewes" emerged, like Orpheus (founded by musician and lifelong Mardi Gras enthusiast Harry Connick, Jr.), Bacchus, and Endymion, with nonexclusive memberships and block-long floats. The largest parades can have dozens of floats, celebrity guests, marching bands, dancing groups, motorcycle squads, and thousands of participants.

The trinkets known as **throws** fly thick and fast from the floats, to the traditional cry of "Throw me something, Mister!" The ubiquitous plastic beads were originally glass, often from Czechoslovakia. **Doubloons,** the oversize aluminum coins stamped with the year and the krewe's coat of arms, are collector's items for natives. Other throws include **stuffed animals, plastic krewe cups,** and especially the cherished **Zulu coconuts.**

Kickin' Up Your Heels: Mardi Gras Activities

Mardi Gras can be whatever you want. The entire city shuts down (including schools and many businesses) so that every citizen can join in the celebrations. Families and friends gather on the streets, on their stoops, or on balconies. They barbecue in the neutral ground along the route, and throw elaborate house parties. Bourbon Street is a parade of exhibitionism and drunkenness. Canal Street is a hotbed of bead lust. Frenchmen Street is a dance of free spirits and costume fantasies made real.

THE SEASON   The date of Fat Tuesday is different each year, but Carnival season always starts on **Twelfth Night,** January 6, when the Phunny Phorty Phellows kick off the season with a streetcar party cruise.

Over the following weeks, the city celebrates, often with round, purple, green, and gold **king cakes.** Each has a plastic baby baked right in. Getting the piece with the baby can be a good omen, and traditionally means you have to throw the next King Cake party. For the high-society crowd, the season brings dozens of ritualized parties and **masked balls,** where krewes introduce their royal courts.

Two or three weeks before Mardi Gras itself, the parading (and parodying) begins. Adorable canines parade in the **Mystick Krewe of Barkus,** often with their humans in matching costumes, and the hilarious **Krewe du Vieux** outrages with un-family-friendly decadence. For a slightly mellower Mardi Gras experience, consider coming for the weekend 10 days before Fat Tuesday. You can count on 10 to 15 small to mid-size parades, and easily manageable crowds.

The following weekend the parades (15 of 'em) and the crowds are *way* bigger—the massive party is *on.*

LUNDI GRAS   In a tradition going back to 1874, King Zulu arrives by boat to meet King Rex on the Monday before Fat Tuesday (it's March 3, 2014). With the mayor presiding, this officially welcomes Mardi Gras day. Nowadays, an all-day music and food fest along the riverfront celebrates the grand event (unsurprisingly). Events start by noon; the kings meet around 5pm; major fireworks follow. That night, **Proteus** and the **Krewe of Orpheus** hold their parades, and a good portion of the city pulls an all-nighter.

MARDI GRAS DAY   The two biggest parades, **Zulu** and **Rex,** run back to back to kick things off. Zulu starts near the Central Business District at 8:30am; Rex starts uptown at 10am. Across town, the bohemian **Societé of St. Anne** musters around 9am near Burgundy and Peity streets in the Bywater area. The walking club (no floats) is known for its madcap, au courant, and sometimes risqué costumes.

In between the parades, you can see other elaborately costumed Mardi Gras **walking or marching clubs,** such as the Jefferson City Buzzards, the Pete Fountain Half Fast, and Mondo Kayo (identifiable by their tropical/banana theme). They walk (or stumble), accompanied by marching bands. Catch the "marchers" anywhere along St. Charles Avenue between Poydras Street and Washington Avenue.

Also keep a watch out for unofficial and rogue krewes and marching clubs like the **Julus,** which includes members of the New Orleans Klezmer All-Stars and throws painted bagels; the sci-fi **Krewe of Chewbacchus;** or the legume-adorned **Krewe of Red Beans.** They're sometimes announced on WWOZ.org or in Gambit (www.bestof neworleans.com). These groups form among friends or neighbors or along any random theme.

By early afternoon, Rex spills into the Central Business District. Nearby, you may be able to find some of the elusive **Mardi Gras Indians.** The "tribes" are small communities of African Americans and black Creoles (some of whom have Native American ancestors), mostly from the inner city. The tribes have an established hierarchy and deep-seated traditions, including enormous, elaborate beaded and feathered costumes. They're entirely made by hand, and a great source of pride, each attempting to out-outlandish the next. The men work on them all year in preparation for Mardi Gras and St. Joseph's Day.

The timing is loose, but traditionally tribes converge throughout the day at main intersections along the Claiborne Avenue median (underneath the interstate), and at St. Augustine's church in the Tremé. Crowds of locals mill around to see the spectacle: When two tribes meet, they'll stage a mock confrontation, resettling their territory. After marching in various parades, they reconvene around mid-afternoon on Claiborne, where a party gets going. Play it cool, however—this is not your neighborhood, nor a sideshow act. It is a ritual deserving of respect. Also, Indian suits are copyrighted works of art; photos of them can't be sold without permission. For times and locations, ask locals, tune into WWOZ 90.7 FM, and listen for drums. You can also try to catch these confrontations during St. Joseph's Day, at parties, and at Jazz Fest.

As you make your way through the streets, keep your eyes peeled for members of the legendary **Krewe of Comus,** men dressed in tuxes with brooms over their shoulders, holding cowbells. Ask them if they are Comus, and they will deny it, insisting they are Cowbellians. But if they hand you a vintage Comus doubloon, the truth will be out.

The last parade each day (on both weekends) is usually scheduled to end around 9:30pm but can run way later. Expect exhaustion. If you're in the Quarter at midnight, you'll see another traditional marvel: The police come en masse, on foot and horseback, and efficiently, effectively, shoo the crowds off—officially ending Mardi Gras. If you're tucked in, tune in to WYES (Channel 12) for live coverage of the Rex Ball—it's serious pomp.

Doing Mardi Gras

LODGING   During Mardi Gras, accommodations in the city and the nearby suburbs are booked solid, *so make your plans well ahead and book a room as early as possible*— a year or more in advance is quite common. Prices spike and minimum-stay requirements apply. Some hotels along the parade routes offer packages including bleacher or balcony seats. They're popular but pricey.

CLOTHING   For the parades before Mardi Gras day, dress comfortably and prepare for whatever weather is forecast (which can vary widely). You'll see some wigs and masks, but most don't dress up. Fat Tuesday is a different story. A **costume** and **mask** automatically makes you a participant, which is absolutely the way to go. You needn't do anything fancy; scan the thrift stores for something loud and it's all good. Anything goes, so fly your freak flag if you're so inclined.

If you've come unprepared, see p. 190 for costume shops, or try the secondhand stores along Magazine Street and in the Bywater.

> ### Save the Date
>
> **Mardi Gras** falls exactly 47 days before Easter: That's March 4, 2014; February 17, 2015; and February 9, 2016.

DINING For restaurant dining during Mardi Gras, make reservations as early as possible. Pay attention to **parade routes** (see map on p. 45), because if there is one between you and your restaurant, you may not be able to drive or park nearby, or even cross the street, and you can kiss your dinner goodbye. Thus, restaurants often have a high no-show rate during Mardi Gras, so a well-timed drop-in may work to the non-planner's advantage.

DRIVING & PARKING Don't. Traffic and navigating during Mardi Gras is horrendous. Take a cab, walk, or pedal (call well in advance for a bike reservation). Parking along parade routes is not allowed 2 hours before and after the parade. Parking on the neutral ground (median strip) is illegal (despite what you may see), and you'll likely be towed. *Note:* Taxis are very busy, and streetcar and bus schedules will be radically altered (none run on St. Charles Ave.). Contact the **Regional Transit Authority** (RTA; *©* **504/248-3900;** www.norta.com) for more information.

FACILITIES Restrooms are notoriously scant along the parade routes. Take advantage of the facilities when you come across them. Otherwise it's the ever-popular porta-potty. Bring tissues.

THE DAY PLAN It's not necessary to make a plan for the big day, but it might help. Get your hands on the latest edition of *Arthur Hardy's Mardi Gras Guide,* through www.mardigrasguide.com or at nearly any store around town. Download the app, since schedules and routes occasionally change at the last minute. Also download the real-time parade-tracker app from WWLTV.com. Resolve that you'll probably adjust the plan, or throw it out altogether—and that you'll chill and go with it. The fun is everywhere—but with limited transportation and facilities available (and until you've done it enough to determine a satisfying routine), you'll have to make some choices about what to do, and adjust accordingly. Read the rest of this section and check the route maps. Then decide if you want to head uptown, downtown, to the Quarter, the Bywater, Claiborne Avenue, or some combination of the above, as your stamina dictates.

SAFETY Many, many cops are out, making the walk from uptown to downtown safer than at other times of year, but pickpockets enjoy Mardi Gras too. Take precautions.

SEATING A limited number of bleachers are erected along the downtown parade route. Most are reserved for private use, but some are sold to the public—you'll pay dearly for the convenience. Start checking Ticketmaster and www.neworleansparade tickets.com in December. Some folks buy cheap folding chairs at local drug stores, which typically don't make it home; others just bring a blanket or tarp. You might find a spot to use them on the Uptown routes; downtown, you'll probably be standing. The longest parades can last 3-plus hours, so plan in accordance with your staying power.

KIDS Though it may seem contrarian, you can bring the kids to Mardi Gras if you stick to the Uptown locales (you'll see hundreds of local kids seated atop custom-rigged ladders, the better to catch throws). It's a long day so make sure to bring supplies and diversions for between parades. There may be some schlepping involved, but their delight increases everyone's enjoyment considerably.

WHAT ELSE TO BRING The usual dilemma applies: You'll want to stay unencumbered, but well-supplied. Much depends on whether you plan to stay in one place or make tracks. A starter set of beverages and snacks is called for, or a full picnic if you desire (food carts and trucks, not to mention enterprising homeowners-turned-delis, are usually available along the routes). Toilet tissue and hand sanitizer are good ideas, and don't forget a bag or backpack for those beads.

How to Spend the Big Day

Despite the popular impression of Mardi Gras, the parades don't even go down Bourbon Street. Your Carnival experience will depend on where you go and whom you hang out with. Here are three ways of doing it: nice, naughty, and nasty. Us? We prefer the first two, traversed on two wheels.

NICE   Hang out exclusively Uptown with the families. Find a spot on St. Charles Avenue (which is closed that day) between Napoleon Avenue and Lee Circle, and set up camp with a blanket and a picnic lunch for **Rex,** the truck parades, and walking clubs. Dressed-up families are all around. One side of St. Charles is for the parades and the other is open only to foot traffic, so you can wander about, admire the scene, and angle for an invitation to a barbecue or balcony party. New Orleans kids assure us that Mardi Gras is more fun than Halloween, and we can see why.

Zulu's route starts at Jackson and goes downriver, so those further uptown will miss out. Staking out a spot downtown is another option; the crowds are a bit thicker and rowdier.

For an utterly different experience, head out around 9am-ish and look for the **Mardi Gras Indian** tribes' meeting. It's a hit-or-miss proposition; the Indians themselves never know in advance when or where the gatherings occur. But running across them on their own turf is one of the great sights and experiences of Mardi Gras.

NAUGHTY   Around mid-morning, track down the **Krewe of Kosmic Debris** and the **Societé of St. Anne:** no floats, just wildly creative, costumed revelers. At noon, try to be near the corner of Burgundy and St. Ann streets for the **Bourbon Street** awards. You may not get close enough to actually see the judging, but the participants are all around you so that you can gawk up at their sometimes R- and X-rated costumes. It's boisterous and enthusiastic, but not (for the most part) obnoxious. Afterward, head to Frenchmen Street, where dancing and drum circles celebrate Carnival well into the night.

NASTY   Stay on **Bourbon Street.** Yep, it's every bit as crowded, booze-soaked, and vulgar as you've heard (and there are no fabulous floats). Every square of the street and every overhanging balcony is packed with partiers. Those balcony dwellers pack piles of beads (some with X-rated anatomical features) ready to toss down in exchange for a glimpse of flesh (by the way, flashing is technically illegal). It's anything goes and wildly fun—but it can grow old fast.

Parade Watch

A Mardi Gras parade works a spell on people. There's no other way to explain why thousands of otherwise rational men and women scream, plead, and sometimes expose themselves for a plastic trinket. Nobody goes home empty-handed (even the trees end up laden with glittery goods), so don't forget to actually look at the amazing floats. When the nighttime floats are lit by flambeaux torch bearers, it is easy to envision a time when Mardi Gras meant mystery and magic.

These are just a few of the major parades of the last days of Carnival. Also see the route map on the next page.

o **Muses** (founded 2000): This popular all-gals krewe honors New Orleans's artistic community—and shoes. Their glittery, decorated pumps are highly sought throws. Thursday evening before Mardi Gras.

Major Mardi Gras Parade Routes

- **Krewe d'Etat** (founded 1996): Social satire is their specialty. No current event is left unscathed, and their hilarious float designs can be the topic of discussion for weeks. Friday evening before Mardi Gras.
- **Iris** (founded 1917): This women's krewe follows traditional Carnival rules of costume and behavior. Saturday afternoon before Mardi Gras.
- **Endymion** (founded 1967): One of the early 1970s "superkrewes," they feature a glut of floats and celebrity guests such as Alice Cooper, Tom Jones, Dolly Parton, and John Goodman. It runs in Mid-City, concluding with a big party in the Superdome. Saturday evening.
- **Bacchus** (founded 1968): The original "superkrewe," it was the first to host international celebrities. Bacchus runs from Uptown to the Convention Center. Sunday before Mardi Gras.
- **Orpheus** (founded 1994): Another youngish krewe, it was founded by a group that includes Harry Connick, Jr., and adheres to classic krewe traditions. Popular for its many stunning floats and generous throws. Follows the Bacchus route on Lundi Gras evening.
- **Zulu** (founded 1916): Lively Zulu has float riders decked out in woolly wigs and blackface. They carry the most prized of Mardi Gras souvenirs: glittery hand-painted coconuts. These status symbols must be placed in your hands, not tossed, so go right up to the float and do your best begging. The parade runs on Mardi Gras morning.
- **Rex** (founded 1872): Rex follows Zulu and various independent walking clubs down St. Charles. It features the King of Carnival and some classic floats. Mardi Gras day.

CAJUN MARDI GRAS

For an entirely different experience, take the 2 ½- to 3-hour drive out to Cajun Country, where Mardi Gras traditions are just as strong but considerably more, er, traditional. **Lafayette** celebrates Carnival in a manner that reflects the Cajun heritage and spirit. The 3-day event is second in size only to New Orleans's celebration with parades and floats and beads a-plenty, but their final pageant and ball are open to the general public. Don your formal wear and join right in!

MASKED MEN & A BIG GUMBO In towns like Eunice and Mamou in the Cajun countryside, the Courir de Mardi Gras celebration is tied to the traditional rural lifestyle. Bands of masked men dressed in raggedy patchwork costumes and peaked *capichon* hats set off on Mardi Gras morning on horseback, led by their *capitaine.* They ride from farm to farm, asking at each, *"Voulez-vous reçevoir le Mardi Gras?"* ("Will you receive the Mardi Gras?"). *"Oui,"* comes the invariable reply. Each farmyard then becomes a miniature festival of song, dance, antics, and much beer. As payment for their pageantry, they get "a fat little chicken to make a big gumbo" (or sometimes a bag of rice or other ingredients).

All meet back in town where cooking, dancing, games, storytelling, and general merriment continue into the wee hours, and yes, there is indeed a very big pot of gumbo. Get particulars from the **Lafayette Parish Convention and Visitors Commission** (© **800/346-1958** in the U.S., 800/543-5340 in Canada, or 337/232-3737; www.lafayettetravel.com).

NEW ORLEANS JAZZ & HERITAGE FESTIVAL

What began in 1969 as a small gathering in Congo Square to celebrate the music of New Orleans now ranks as one of the best attended, most respected, and most musically comprehensive festivals in the world. Although people call it Jazz Fest (of just "Fest") the full name is **New Orleans Jazz & Heritage Festival,** and the "heritage" part is broadly interpreted. Each of the 12 stages showcases a musical genre or three.

Jazz Fest encompasses everything the city has to offer, in terms of music, food, and culture. That, and it's a hell of a party. After Shell Oil sponsored Jazz Fest's uncertain return after Katrina, Bruce Springsteen's triumphant, emotionally stunning set sealed its eternal resurrection. Such musical and emotional epiphanies abound at Fest. While such headliners as Arcade Fire, Pearl Jam, Stevie Wonder, Van Morrison, Dave Matthews, My Morning Jacket, Maroon 5, and The Roots have drawn record-setting crowds in recent years, serious Festers savor the lesser-known acts. They range from the avant-garde to old-time Delta bluesmen, from African artists making rare U.S. appearances to bohemian street folkies, and from the top zydeco players to gospel mass choirs. And, of course, jazz.

Filling the infield of the Fair Grounds horse-racing track up near City Park, the festival covers two long weekends, the last in April and the first in May (for 2014, that's Apr 25–27 and May 1–4). It's set up about as well as a large event can be. When the crowds get thick, though—especially the popular second Saturday—it can be tough to move around, more so if the grounds are muddy from rain. Lines at the most popular of the several dozen food booths can be frighteningly long, but it's all quite civil and most move quickly (and they're invariably worth the wait).

Attending Jazz Fest means making some tough decisions. Hotels, restaurants, and flights fill up months (if not a year) in advance, but the schedule is not announced until a couple of months before the event. So reserving travel requires a leap of faith in the talent bookings. But truth be told, just about every day at Jazz Fest is a good day regardless of who is playing (avoid the dilemma by going for both weekends). The Thursday before the second weekend traditionally has more locals, on stage and in the audience, and smaller crowds. It's a great time to hit the best food booths and check out the crafts areas.

Jazz Fest Pointers

"It's a marathon, not a sprint" as the saying goes. With music in every direction, you can plot out your day or just wander from stage to stage, catching a few songs by various acts—some of the best Jazz Fest experiences come from stumbling across an undiscovered musical gem. Or you can set up camp at one stage—from the big ones with famous headliners to the gospel tent, where musical miracles are pretty much a given. It's akin to sit-down dining versus a buffet: Both have advantages.

At your hotel or as you're walking to Fest, grab a free *Offbeat* magazine (they're everywhere). You'll need the schedule "grids" and performer descriptions. Also download the Jazz Fest and Offbeat apps. For $5, the official Fest program also has the schedule, plus food coupons (available onsite).

On a typical Jazz Fest day, you'll arrive sometime after the gates open at 11am and stay until you are pooped or they close at 7pm. The whole thing usually runs as efficiently as a Swiss train. After you leave, get some dinner, and hit the clubs. Every club in the city has top-notch bookings (of note are Piano Night at the House of Blues, Tipitina's' Instruments a Comin' benefit, and the jam-heavy shows produced by Super-fly—check out www.superflypresents.com). Alternatively, sleep.

The excellent nonmusical aspects of Jazz Fest are plentiful. Local craftspeople and juried artisans fill a sizable area with artwork and products for show, for demonstration, or for purchase. Most vendors will pack and ship goods to your home (and there's a U.S. Post Office on site, too).

And as always in New Orleans, there is food. There are local standbys—not burgers and dogs but red beans and rice, jambalaya, étouffée, gumbo. More interesting choices include *cochon de lait* (a mouthwatering roast-pig sandwich), a fried soft-shell crab po' boy, quail and pheasant gumbo, and all manner of oyster and crawfish. And that's not even discussing the various ethnic or vegetarian dishes available, or the desserts . . . oooh, the desserts. The terrific kids' area has PB&J, mac and cheese, and other easy-pleasing faves. We recommend trying at least one new thing daily, and also sharing, so you can sample more variety and decide which booths to revisit. *Tip:* There's copious cold beer, but the lines can get long. Smaller stages = shorter lines, and it's often worth it to trek there.

Experienced Fest-goers also know to duck into the air-conditioned Grandstand for art and folklore exhibits, cooking demonstrations, and real bathrooms. The upstairs Heritage Stage features interviews and short performances by some of the top acts in a much more intimate setting.

Wear and bring as little as possible; you'll want to be comfy and unencumbered. But do bring sun protection, something that tells time, a poncho if rain is forecast (they sell them there, but for double what you'll pay at a souvenir store), and moola (cash only for food; credit okay for crafts). Wear comfy, supportive, well-broken-in shoes.

Note: No outside beverages (apart from 1 liter of water) are allowed in. There are seats in the tented stages. Outside, people sit on the ground, stand, or bring blankets or folding chairs. When left vacant, these become annoying space hogs. Kind Fest-goers invite others to use their space when they leave temporarily, but don't be shy about asking.

JAZZ FEST TICKETS Purchase tickets when they go on sale in late fall or early winter, when they are the cheapest. They're available through **Ticketmaster** (© 800/745-3000; www.ticketmaster.com). Daily admission for adults in 2013 was $50 in advance, $65 at the gate, $5 for children (plus Ticketmaster's ample handling fees). There are also various VIP packages with a range of swanky seating, access, and amenities, topping out at $1,275 for one weekend (and they do sell out). Tickets are also available at the gate For more information, contact **New Orleans Jazz & Heritage Festival** (© 504/410-4100; www.nojazzfest.com).

JAZZ FEST PARKING & TRANSPORTATION The only parking at the Fair Grounds is for people with disabilities at $50 a day, first-come, first-served. Take public transportation or one of the available shuttles. The **Regional Transit Authority** operates bus routes to the Fair Grounds from various pickup points. For schedules, contact © 504/248-3900 (www.norta.com). Taxis, though busy, charge a special-event rate of $5 per person or the meter reading if it's higher (see p. 230). Gray Line's **Jazz Fest Express** (© 800/535-7786 or 504/569-1401; www.graylineneworleans.com) operates shuttles from the steamboat *Natchez* dock in the French Quarter; the Sheraton at 500 Canal Street; and City Park. It's $18 round-trip and you must have a Jazz Fest ticket to ride (purchase shuttle tickets with your Ticketmaster ticket order). *Note:* The

Canal Street streetcar line will be packed, but it's an option from the Quarter. Take it to the Carrollton line, which then gets you close to the Fair Grounds' City Park entrance. Fare is $1.25.

PACKAGE DEALS   **Festival Tours International** (© **310/454-4080;** www.gumbo pages.com/festivaltours) offers a tour that includes accommodations and tickets for Jazz Fest, plus a midweek visit to Cajun Country for unique personal encounters with local musicians. If you're flying to New Orleans specifically for the Jazz & Heritage Festival, visit **www.nojazzfest.com** to get a Jazz Fest promotional code from a list of airlines that offer special Fest fares.

WHERE TO STAY IN NEW ORLEANS

Accommodations in New Orleans range from your basic lodger to over-the-top luxurious, so like the city itself, there's something for every preference. Rates also vary widely. Those shown don't reflect spikes during high season or discounts during low season. Parking rates for oversized vehicles can also be higher than those shown. Also, although many properties are entirely nonsmoking, most of those provide an outdoor smoking area. Verify your preferences when you reserve your room.

5

FRENCH QUARTER & FAUBOURG TREMÉ

The Vieux Carré (Old Quarter), as it is called, is the picturesque soul of the city that most people envision. Comprised of a two-thirds-square-mile grid, the architecture looks much like it did when it was built in the late 17th and early 18th centuries, enabling visitors to walk out of their hotel and feel wholly transported. When you stay in the French Quarter, you are ensconced in the total N.O. experience—from the serene to the sybaritic.

Best for: First-time visitors; short-term visitors; historians; architecture buffs; partiers; everyone.

Drawbacks: During high season it can be bustling with tourists and goings-on. Parking is scarce and expensive.

Very Expensive

Audubon Cottages ★★★   La Liz Taylor stayed here, but it feels like you're staying at her place (if she lived in a sublime warren of 18th-century apartments). An unmarked gate and leaf-canopied pathway lead to seven ultra-private one- and two-bedroom cottages with a large courtyard with seating and a trickling fountain (some private, some shared). Each is gracefully but not overly antiqued; a 2012 renovation kept the gorgeous brick walls and gleaming hardwood floors and added needed freshening. The cottages surround a brick-lined, heated pool, and it's all attended to by a 24-hour butler. It's easy to imagine naturalist John James Audubon watching birds alight from his studio here (he did), inspiring him to capture their images in his historic paintings. If you have the means, by all means, stay here.

509 Dauphine St. www.auduboncottages.com. ℂ **504/586-1516.** 7 units. $279–$799 room. Rates include welcome beverage, breakfast, bottled water. Valet parking $30. **Amenities:** Butler service; pool; fitness room; Wi-Fi (free).

Ritz-Carlton New Orleans ★★★
It may not be the ritziest of all Ritz-Carltons, but do expect Ritz-level luxury, service, and amenities, including a stellar spa and the soignée Davenport Lounge. It's all quite gracious and stately (as was its previous tenant, legendary Maison Blanche department store), though the hotel is a bit confusing to navigate. Room decor leans very traditional; even the smaller rooms have superb bedding. Try for a larger room on the 12th, 14th, or 15th floor, unless you can muster a suite. Better yet, the Maison Orleans club level, with concierge service and food and beverages served throughout the day, is hard to surpass. Check for construction updates—renovations are afoot for 2014.

921 Canal St. www.ritzcarlton.com/neworleans. ℂ **800/522-8780** or 504/524-1331. 452 units. $199–$329 double; executive suites start at $299–$499. Valet parking $40. Pets welcome. **Amenities:** Restaurant; bar; concierge; complimentary access to spa and fitness center; room service; shops; Wi-Fi (free in public areas; $13/day in rooms).

Soniat House ★★
Inside these unassuming Creole townhouse exteriors lies an oasis of indulgent calm. The staff spoils guests, and the sweet courtyards, candlelit at night, soothe them. Every room is different, sizes and furnishings vary. Most in the main house have high ceilings; some have balconies (a room with both helps justify the high rates). Bathrooms are small though some have Jacuzzi tubs. But the experience is all gracious, romantic, and adult. It's more about ambiance than amenities here (well, except the $12.50 charge for continental breakfast, even if it is fresh baked and squeezed).

1133 Chartres St. www.soniathouse.com. ℂ **800/544-8808** or 504/522-0570. 30 units. $195–$375 queen or king room; $400–$795 and up, suites. Valet parking $35. No children under 10. **Amenities:** Concierge; complimentary access to nearby New Orleans Athletic Club; Wi-Fi (free).

Expensive

Bourbon Orleans Hotel ★★
Location location location. And a big pool. This large property has that, plus good service, and even better history. The formal lobby makes an impressive impression right off the bat, and rooms are fully renovated (as of early 2013), so the decor is fresh (though still standard nouveau hotel) and bathrooms have been sexed up in black marble. The smallest rooms are a tad tight; the bi-level loft suites with balcony are ideal for party people (participants *and* spectators) but too noisy for others. Long hallways mean you might be walking your muffuletta off—for some that's a plus (otherwise, request something close to the elevators). We're quite happy about the updates to the **Bourbon O** bar; it's now a definite cocktail destination.

717 Orleans St. www.bourbonorleans.com. ℂ **866/513-9744** or 504/523-2222. 218 units. $110–$379 double; $279–$579 suites; includes welcome beverage. Valet parking $34. **Amenities:** Restaurant (breakfast and dinner only); bar; concierge; fitness room; outdoor pool; room service (breakfast and dinner only); Wi-Fi (free).

New Orleans Hotels

1896 O'Malley House **15**

Antebellum Guest House **18**

Ashtons Bed & Breakfast **16**

Auld Sweet Olive
Bed & Breakfast **25**

B&W Courtyards
Bed & Breakfast **24**

Chimes Bed & Breakfast **2**

Drury Inn & Suites **7**

Homewood Suites **6**

Hotel Storyville **19**

India House Hostel **15**

International House **10**

Le Pavillon Hotel **5**

Loews New
  Orleans Hotel **14**
Maison de Macarty **23**
Royal Street Inn & R Bar **21**
Maison Dubois **20**
Maison Perrier **1**
Melrose Mansion **20**

Prytania Park Hotel **4**
Queen & Crescent **11**
Renaissance Arts Hotel **8**
St. Charles Guest House **3**
St. James Hotel **12**
The Roosevelt **9**
Windsor Court **13**

Dauphine Orleans Hotel ★★ This warren of vintage rooms, some with private courtyards, others surrounding the popular pool, is quite charming. Avoid those overlooking the dour parking lot. Atmosphere and rooms are both friendly and relaxed—the former welcoming, the latter showing some age. Inclusive breakfast and beverages are a bonus (the bar displays authentication of its history as a former brothel). Easy access to—but a quiet respite—from Bourbon Street.

415 Dauphine St. www.dauphineorleans.com. ℂ **800/521-7111** or 504/586-1800. 111 units. $119–$269 doubles; $199–$399 suite. Rates include continental breakfast and welcome wine or beer coupon. Extra person $20. Children 17 and under stay free in parent's room. Valet parking $34. **Amenities:** Bar; coffee lounge; small fitness room; outdoor pool; Wi-Fi (free).

Hotel Monteleone ★★ There is almost nothing modest about the venerable Monteleone, family-owned since 1886. Not the ornate lobby, not the hallowed literary tradition (Faulkner, Hemingway, Capote, Tennessee Williams, and Eudora Welty slept, drank, and/or wrote here, among others), not the happy hour scene at the rooftop pool or those stellar views. And certainly not the sublime, silly **Carousel Bar** (p. 177). The larger suites here offer roomy, classic gentility, but standard rooms can be, well, on the modest side. Some are quite petite, and those ending in #27 have no windows (though #56 and #59 are bigger and high-ceilinged). The family ownership is reflected in gracious, accommodating service throughout (gentlemen should spring for a proper hot-towel, straight-razor shave in the barbershop here; everyone should spring for something from the pricy but very soothing full-service spa). The new **Criollo Restaurant** is a big step up from standard hotel fare, and the fitness room doesn't skimp on the equipment.

214 Royal St. www.hotelmonteleone.com. ℂ **800/535-9595** or 504/523-3341. 570 units, including 55 suites. $189–$399 double; $579 and up suites. Extra person $25. Children 17 and under stay free in parent's room. Valet parking $35. Pets allowed on the 3rd floor, for a fee and deposit. **Amenities:** Restaurant; 2 bars; concierge; fitness center; heated rooftop pool; room service; spa; Wi-Fi (free in lobby; $10 in-room; $15 for hi-speed).

Jazz Quarters Bed & Breakfast ★★★ An unexpected and unassuming enclave of entrancing private cottages (part of the original Tremé plantation) lies hidden behind greenery and gates next to Armstrong Park. Most are two-room suites, each decorated for comfort with smart, contemporary wares, a nod to the birthplace of jazz across the street, and a smattering antiques (no more is needed—history seeps out from the very brick walls here). The unobtrusive but obliging hosts serve a stellar, Southern-style breakfast (sweet potato pancakes, oh my) at pretty communal tables indoors or out. Lots of nice little touches here—chilled towels are available any time you return from a humid outing, and help yourself to a glass of complimentary champagne, wine, and beer whenever you like—but not many other amenities to speak of. No matter: If you're not out exploring the French Quarter (half a block away), you'll want to relax in your plush bed, or lounge languidly in the tropical gardens. It's all awfully inviting, for small groups, families, or romantics.

1129 St. Philip St. www.jazzquarters.com. ℂ **800/523-1372** or 504/523-1060. 9 units. $125–$450. Rates include breakfast. **Amenities:** Free secured parking; Wi-Fi (free).

French Quarter Hotels

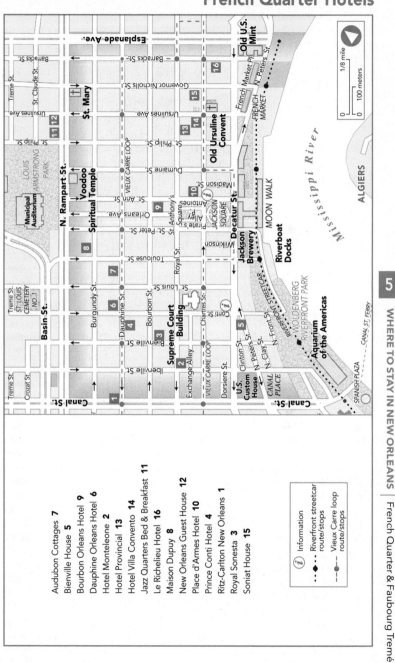

Audubon Cottages **7**
Bienville House **5**
Bourbon Orleans Hotel **9**
Dauphine Orleans Hotel **6**
Hotel Monteleone **2**
Hotel Provincial **13**
Hotel Villa Convento **14**
Jazz Quarters Bed & Breakfast **11**
Le Richelieu Hotel **16**
Maison Dupuy **8**
New Orleans Guest House **12**
Place d'Armes Hotel **10**
Prince Conti Hotel **4**
Ritz-Carlton New Orleans **1**
Royal Sonesta **3**
Soniat House **15**

Information
Riverfront streetcar route/stops
Vieux Carre loop route/stops

Maison Dupuy ★★★   We're fond of this midrange, architecturally picturesque hotel with very good service, set in a quiet part of the Quarter but within walking distance of Bourbon Street. The building surrounds a large courtyard (popular for weddings) with a heated pool. Courtyard-side balconies are extra pleasant; streetside ones are noisier, but it's a fun view of the action. Rooms aren't anything special, though a mid-2014 renovation promises a full refresh with a mix of antiques and hipster furnishings. This might mean construction, ergo discounts and/or annoyances, so double-check the status you reserve.

1001 Toulouse St. www.maisondupuy.com. (C) **800/535-9177** or 504/586-8000. 200 units. $169–$369double; $329–$1,200 suite. Valet parking $32. **Amenities:** Restaurant; bar; exercise room (24 hr.); heated outdoor saltwater pool; room service. Wi-Fi (free).

Royal Sonesta ★★   You might forget you're right on Bourbon Street, what with all the graciousness inside. The Sonesta is large, bustling, and classy, with outstanding service for the mix of tourists and business patrons. Rooms and bathrooms are among the more handsomely decorated of those that go for French reproductions (get one facing the inside courtyard to avoid the Bourbon Street racket—or facing Bourbon if that's what you're here for). The large courtyard pool is wonderfully welcoming but can get pretty crowded. All the amenity bases are covered; indeed, almost everything you could need is here, including the so-so **Desire Oyster Bar,** the terrific **Restaurant R'evolution** (p. 78), and **Irvin Mayfield's Jazz Playhouse** (p. 169)—which definitely adds to the luster and liveliness.

300 Bourbon St. www.sonesta.com/royalneworleans. (C) **800/766-3782** or 504/586-0300 483 units. $149–$629 double; $400–$2,500 suite. Parking $39. **Amenities:** 3 restaurants; coffee shop; 3 bars; concierge; exercise room; outdoor pool/terrace; room service, Wi-Fi (free).

Moderate

Bienville House ★★   This boutique hotel, owned by the Monteleone (see above), injects a touch of class here and there: in the hand-painted murals on the small, classically elegant lobby walls, and in the intimacy of the pool area (you'd never know you're right off a major street, and not in a European mansion). Rooms have high ceilings and French reproduction furnishings, nothing particularly pizazz-y; size and brightness vary—a lot—the lowest-priced ones are windowless. Swing one with a balcony if you can—what a difference. Rooms are showing their age a bit, but some sprucing up (scheduled for 2014) may be completed by the time you arrive. The staff here is truly welcoming, even to pets. Take your continental breakfast around the pool rather than in the blah breakfast room, and absolutely do dine at the excellent restaurant **Iris.** (And a cocktail—theirs are superb.)

320 Decatur St. www.bienvillehouse.com. (C) **800/535-9603** or 504/529-2345. 83 units. $169–$369 double; $499 and up for suites. Rates include continental breakfast and afternoon reception with cookies and punch. Parking $32. **Amenities:** Restaurant; outdoor saltwater pool; room service; Wi-Fi (free in lobby; $10 in-room).

Hotel Provincial ★★   On the whole, this family-run hotel has plenty of character, from the flickering gas lamps to the rumored ghosts (it's a former Civil War hospital) to the quiet, high-ceilinged rooms (those facing the street still get some noise). The better ones have fireplaces (nonworking) or huge windows; the best (on the upper floors) even have a little view of the river—but with no elevators, be willing to climb for that view. We're also fond of those on the first floor that open onto the small courtyard (though they're all a bit of an antique mish-mosh). Another courtyard is mostly pool. The complimentary breakfast is basic; dinner restaurant **Stella!** (p. 80) is one of the city's finest.

1024 Chartres St. www.hotelprovincial.com. ℂ **800/535-7922** or 504/581-4995. 92 units. $89–$289 double including continental breakfast. Valet parking $25. **Amenities:** Restaurant; bar; pool; Wi-Fi (free).

Hotel Villa Convento ★
It's not luxurious and the decor is on the fusty side, but the family-owned, Creole townhouse boasts balconies with views, guesthouse warmth, and captivating history—all of which nonetheless infuse it with a bit of a sexy vibe. Maybe it's because it's the original House of the Rising Sun, and the spot where a young Jimmy Buffett first, ahem, saw the sun rise as a man (both rumors, but we choose to believe). Free parking (a few blocks away, but still in the FQ) is a big bonus for drive-in visitors; so are the small, hard-to-find single rooms for solo travelers on a budget. Some rooms are pretty dark. Ask for one with brick walls, the better to feel the history. If Wi-Fi is crucial, make it known when you book, since some rooms get a stronger signal than others.

616 Ursulines Ave. www.villaconvento.com. ℂ **504/522-1793.** 25 units. $89–$185 double; $125–$205 suite. No children 9 or under **Amenities:** Computer station; shared fridge and microwave; complimentary coffee in lobby; Wi-Fi (free).

Le Richelieu Hotel ★
Nothing here to knock your socks off, but this former row house (and macaroni factory) in the quiet, residential end of the French Quarter has clean rooms and fair prices. The public spaces feel sorta like a Daddy-cave, additions he'd build on to his suburban home to entertain all the cousins, aunts, and uncles: a small wood-paneled bar; a glassed-in, poolside cafa; and a dunking pool. It's all oddly cozy and welcoming, and a perfectly okay choice. It was for Sir Paul McCartney and family, who stayed here while he was recording in town.

1234 Chartres St. www.lerichelieuhotel.com. ℂ **800/535-9653** or 504/529-2492. 87 units. $95–$190 double; $200–$550 suite. Extra person, including children, $15. Self-parking $20. **Amenities:** Restaurant (breakfast and lunch only); bar; concierge; saltwater pool; room service; Wi-Fi (free).

Place d'Armes Hotel ★
If you're planning to spend a lot of time sightseeing, this is a good choice for French Quarter lodging, especially given the relatively good rates (with basic continental breakfast included). You're a hop-skip from both Jackson Square and Café du Monde, and it's hard to have a care when you're lounging around an amoeba-shaped pool shaded by palm trees. But if your vacation includes much lolling in plush rooms and you live for light-filled mornings, this may not be for you. Several buildings are knitted together by brick hallways and awfully pretty courtyards (that feel truly vieux), and the rooms and decor, while perfectly serviceable, are showing their age a bit (bathrooms too). Some rooms are dark or windowless, even, but a few splendid ones have terraces with a Jackson Square corner view.

625 St. Ann St. www.placedarmes.com. ℂ **800/626-5917** or 504/524-4531. 80 units. $99–$499. Rates include continental breakfast. Children under 12 free. Valet parking $28. **Amenities:** Pool; Wi-Fi (free).

Prince Conti Hotel ★
The highlights here are Bourbon Street proximity and a very good martini bar/jazz club. Rooms facing Conti may get Bourbon noise; others are set back from the street, which provides a nice sense of seclusion but doesn't help with light (some rooms are windowless or overlook parking). It's got the French

French Quarter & Faubourg Tremé

There are no lack of lodging options in New Orleans listed on Craigslist, AirBnB, Couchsurfing, HomeAway, and the like. But it's a city with plenty of not so straight-and-narrow characters, and we really can't recommend using these options at this point. We've heard too many horror stories of bait-and-switch, or pay-and-ditch, with visitors left high and dry and homeless. Not to mention legit landlords whose lodgers turn out to be not so legit. We're not against "sharing economy" options in theory, but we'll give it another couple of years to let the model and its security features mature, let the scammers get flushed out, and let things equalize a bit more fairly with the tax-paying, insurance-buying, license-getting businesses.

Quarter feel, and rooms are clean if a bit shopworn and thin-walled. Nonetheless the small cafe is convenient for breakfast, the staff is helpful, and given the location and non-Princely rates, it's a good value.

830 Conti St. www.princecontihotel.com. © **800/626-4319** or 504/529-4172. 76 units. $69–$349 double; $129–$499 suite, depending on season. Children under 12 free; others in room $20. Valet parking $28. **Amenities:** Restaurant; piano bar; Wi-Fi (free).

5 | Inexpensive

New Orleans Guest House ★   Fear not, bold crossers of Rampart. The Quarter-adjacent Tremé has some downright deals and is no longer downright scary. Don't let the Pepto-pink exterior scare you either. It hints at the oddballness here but belies the sweetness: There's a certain camaraderie amongst the guests, with the long-time owners setting the tone. The lobby is fussy, the whole place is somewhat musty, the room furnishings mix 1890s and 1970s, and yet the Sisterhood of the Bright Pink Lodgers lends it charisma. At the heart of that charm is the pretty-in-pink, plant-laden courtyard and breakfast room. Rooms that open onto it share the garden feel (though lose some privacy). Rooms with terraces bring the freshness in. All in all a great deal if you don't demand perfection or sparkling newness.

1118 Ursulines Ave. www.neworleans.com/nogh. © **800/562-1177** or 504/566-1177. 14 units. $99–$109 double; $119–$129 queen or twin; $129–$139 king or 2 full beds. Rates include continental breakfast. Extra person $25. Free off-street parking for passenger cars. **Amenities:** Wi-Fi (free).

FAUBOURG MARIGNY & BYWATER

A few inns and a slew of B&Bs (mostly newly minted) dot this gentrified-meets-working-class area. A smattering of artists' workshops, galleries, and a fresh crop of darn good restaurants are scattered throughout the area.

Best for: Artists, bohemians, and regular folks who prefer staying among like-minded residents. GLBTQ. Music lovers making the Frenchmen Street scene who seek a bed within stumbling distance.

Drawbacks: While parts of the Marigny are within walking distance of the French Quarter, others are too far from the action or from public transportation, so a car or bike is warranted. Expect dicey, rundown homes commingling with renovated shotgun houses.

Moderate

Auld Sweet Olive Bed & Breakfast ★★
Sweet is the operative word for this B&B, from the backyard hammock to the yummydelish breakfast muffins to the custom-painted walls in airy rooms in a butter-yellow Creole cottage. But it's genuine rather than syrupy—in fact it's about as close as it gets to having a true residential experience. Owner Nancy's hints and hospitality will help that along (also see recommendations for doing the St. Claude Avenue clubs on p. 175). The unfussy furnishings and wicker porch chairs are just what one wants to curl up in for a few lazy hours.

2460 N. Rampart St. www.sweetolive.net. ✆ **877/470-5323** or 504/947-4332. 5 units. $110–$300. Rates include full breakfast. Street parking. **Amenities:** Wi-Fi (free).

B&W Courtyards Bed & Breakfast ★★
The simple exterior masks a serene courtyard, a soothing hot tub, and a six-room B&B—4 blocks and a world away from the madding Frenchmen crowd. They've had some mix-and-match fun here, blending tropical West Indies hues with French antiques and Oriental touches, and each clever room is unique (sometimes even strange—you enter one through the bathroom; saloon-style swinging doors lead from the bathroom to the bedroom). The charming and hilarious hosts (Rob and Kevin—newlyweds after 21 years!) hold court over breakfast (light, but homemade and beautiful plated) with witty banter and insider sightseeing tips.

2425 Chartres St. www.bandwcourtyards.com. ✆ **800/585-5731** or 504/267-5007. 6 units. $119–$250 double. Rates include continental breakfast. Street parking. **Amenities:** Hot tub; Wi-Fi (free).

Maison Dubois ★★
The spacious, raised building dates to the 1920s, so it's decidedly different from the city's 18th-century European and Caribbean influences. That's part of its interest, but non-architecture buffs will be more taken by the pretty (if petite) pool and spa, the quiet residential feel, the ever-helpful host, and the proximity to the French Quarter and Frenchmen Street. Nothing's too fancy here: the midsize rooms; the small, clean bathrooms; the continental breakfast. But for location and the comfy indoor and outdoor places to chill, it's a perfectly good choice. The room with a queen and two twin beds is a good family option; the balcony rooms' French doors open to a pretty, sweet-scented courtyard.

1419 Dauphine St. www.maisondubois.net. ✆ **866/948-1619.** 5 units. $149–$259 double including continental breakfast. Limited street parking (free). **Amenities:** Saltwater pool; spa; Wi-Fi (free).

Maison de Macarty ★★
Tucked away in the backwaters of the Bywater neighborhood is a Victorian treasure that comes complete with a chocolatier (in one of your hosts). Six rooms are in the high-ceilinged main house, and two are in separate private cottages; all were smartly decorated (not overly so) with old and new pieces in 2013. Room sizes vary, and bathrooms fluctuate between shower-only style and those with deep Jacuzzi tub. The Storyville room works well with its loft space but is not for the claustrophobic; the others are well-sized, and some open over the courtyard for added airiness. Add a pool (with cabana bar!), plush bedding, a generous breakfast, and the

inherently neighborly ambience and you're nearly a local. Not all rooms have TVs; some allow pets. You'll definitely want a car or bike (loaner bikes are available).

3820 Burgundy St. www.maisonmacarty.com. *©* **504/267-1564.** 8 units. $129–$189 including breakfast. Street parking. **Amenities:** Pool; Wi-Fi.

Royal Street Inn & R Bar ★★ Do pay attention to the fact that the name of this guesthouse also includes the name of the attached bar. You're welcomed with complimentary drink tokens, and you should count on participating in the bar action (here at **R Bar** or elsewhere) late into the night—lest you become its victim. As long as you're aware that this is part of the experience here (music, cigarette smoke, and all), it's all good—including the actual rooms. They're a hip, clever mix of leather seating, mood lighting, pops of color with the existing wood-and-brick vibe. It's the free-spirited Marigny attitude at play—which also describes the service and the clientele. Punk-intellectuals and urban artist/gentrifiers populate the bar, and like-minded visitors stay at the inn. It's decidedly Marigny but also Quarter- and Frenchmen-close; location and atmosphere help you feel a bit like a local (on Mon, dudes can even get a $10 shot and a haircut).

1431 Royal St. www.royalstreetinn.com. *©* **504/948-7499.** 5 units. $150–$380 double including bar beverage. Street parking available. **Amenities:** Bar; Wi-Fi (free).

MID-CITY/ESPLANADE

This thriving, mostly residential area encompasses diverse socioeconomies and architectural styles amid quiet neighborhood streets and busy commercial corridors. It's near the Jazz Fest Fairgrounds, City Park, and not far from the French Quarter. There are a number of B&Bs along Esplanade Avenue, still grand along some stretches and shabby along others.

Best for: Repeat visitors seeking to experience the city more like a resident; those who prefer B&Bs; Jazz & Heritage and Voodoo goers.

Drawbacks: You'll probably want to rent a car or will need to rely on taxis and public transportation to get you where you're going. It's a large area with some altogether lovely sections; others not at all.

Expensive

1896 O'Malley House ★★★ For those who want to be amongst the regular folk, you'd never expect this nondescript Mid-City neighborhood to house such a grand B&B. But it offers a splendid experience, antiqued but not frilly, far from the madding crowds but steps from the Canal Street streetcar line. Fine art, stunning woodwork, and gorgeous fireplace surrounds add architectural interest. Breakfast is served in the formal dining room, or you can take your homemade muffin to the unexceptional but pleasant outdoor space. The largest rooms are on the second floor; most of the dull bathrooms have Jacuzzi tubs. The smaller, garret-like rooms on the third floor make clever use of their odd shapes and bleached wood. Ghost hunters should request the haunted room. Rooms come with a preprogrammed iPad to use for exploring neighborhood restaurants and local attractions, but host Larry and two lazy golden retrievers provide a pleasantly personal touch.

120 S. Pierce St. www.1896omalleyhouse.com. *©* **866/226-1896** or 504/488-5896. 8 units. $180–$210 including breakfast, snacks, complimentary beverages. Limited free off-street parking. **Amenities:** Wi-Fi (free).

Ashtons Bed & Breakfast ★★★   Ashtons stops just short of lavish, which is ideal for a bed-and-breakfast since it remains comfortable rather than over the top. We might even call it homey—if home was a genteel, Esplanade Avenue antebellum mansion—in that once you sink into your comfy bed, you may not want to leave your romantic, pastel-walled, antiques-filled room. But you will for stellar breakfasts like eggs *cochon de lait*. The main-house rooms are plenty spacious; ceilings are ridiculously high, sheets equally silky. Room #4 has a half-tester bed and an extravagant rain-shower showerhead; #7 has a clawfoot whirlpool tub. It's all light and bright, from the wide front gallery to the huge, oak-shaded backyard, and the on-site hosts are most congenial. Excellence is in the details, and the owners have carefully covered every base here.

2023 Esplanade Ave. www.ashtonsbb.com. ✆ **800/725-4131** or 504/942-7048. 8 units. $179–$209 double. Rates include full breakfast and complimentary beverages. **Amenities:** Secure parking (free); Wi-Fi (free).

Melrose Mansion ★★★   The glamorous Melrose Mansion stands out even on an avenue of eye-popping manses (well, Esplanade has some lesser properties too). But looks can be deceiving. Enter the grandly columned 1854 Victorian Gothic, and rather than antiques and brocades, you're met with ultramodern, atonal leather furnishings set against stark white 21-foot-high walls. The architectural bones and original embellishments of the house have been retained, including stunning carved cornices, moldings, and chandelier medallions, but have been accented with abstract art and a pop of green. The overall effect is a sexy shock to the system. The well-appointed guest rooms in the main house and a bungalow building range from large to enormous and follow the vibe: low-slung king beds in super-soft sheets, with marble and glass bathrooms (some with Jacuzzi tubs). Similarly chic condo-style suites in a third building have full kitchens and living rooms. Between them is the heated pool, where generations of sleek bodies have swum (this is, after all, a former Storyville "party house"). There's a generous continental breakfast, evening wine and cheese, and complimentary snacks round the clock. The 24-hour staff is equally smooth and solicitous, but not at all cold; they'll gladly help with arrangements or share recommendations and anecdotes. Like which perfume the ghost of Miss Kitty wears—it's said to waft through her old room. No worries; it's a storage room now. A well-scented storage room.

937 Esplanade Ave. www.melrosegroup.com. ✆ **800/650-3323** or 504/944-2255. 21 units. $160–$300. Rates include continental breakfast and nightly wine and cheese. Street parking or limited off-street parking at $26 and up. **Amenities:** Heated outdoor pool; concierge; Wi-Fi.

Moderate

Antebellum Guest House ★★★   Grandiosity, check. Dripping with antiques. High ceilings. Elaborate breakfast. Check, check, all here. The real difference is in the experience, and the hosts. You could spend your entire visit chatting with them, about New Orleans, art, travel, history, and whatever far-flung topics arise. They're interesting and interested, which describes much of New Orleans's population, but now you're at home with them (home being an 1830s Esplanade Avenue glamour gal, the former "party home" to a wealthy plantation family, now tarted up to the nines). Quibblers (those who post Instagram photos of scuffed baseboards—who should just not come to a 300-year-old city) will find things to complain about. The anachronistic, 1970s bathrooms are boring, for starters. But there are loaner bikes to get you to the nearby

French Quarter or City Park. And when you step into the dreamy, moss-hung backyard, complete with hot tub and a secret garden, magic begins.

1333 Esplanade Ave. www.antebellumguesthouse.com. *C* **504/943-1900.** 3 units. Around $145 including full breakfast. Street parking. **Amenities:** Hot tub; bicycles; Wi-Fi (free).

Hotel Storyville ★   Great location (especially for Jazz Fest goers), friendly host, clean, unfussy rooms with kitchenettes, and good rates. We're okay with all that. The exterior looks fittingly New Orleanean, with tall columns and wide double galleries, and the mint-green color hints at the hotel's beachy tone (aquas, and laid-back). Rooms vary in size and configuration, from a tiny single to a multi-bedroom. The huge back yard is event-ready, which may or may not work to your benefit (if a crawfish boil is on, you're probably invited; if a wedding is on, there's a party in your yard). Other amenities and services are scant, so don't expect to be doted on, but the price is surely right.

1261 Esplanade Ave. www.storyville.net. *C* **504/948-4800.** 9 suites. $119–$199. Secured offstreet parking $5, or limited free off-street parking. **Amenities:** Wi-Fi (free).

Inexpensive

India House Hostel ★   Foreign travelers and students (passport or student ID required) looking for budget lodging and an instant party, welcome home. The four buildings comprising India House have private rooms (some with their own bathrooms) and bunk-bed dorms; a usable kitchen (which also serves cheap meals); aboveground pool; outdoor bar; and a ready-made social scene. There's a den with TV, and events are frequent—the small stage next to the pool is well-used by local and visiting bands. It's very close to the Canal Street streetcar and bus lines, and tour companies pick up here regularly. It's funky but not filthy, and friendly, and backpacker-ready. Book directly for the best rates.

124 S. Lopez St. www.indiahousehostel.com. *C* **504/821-1904.** 140 beds. $20–$55. Limited off-street parking; street parking. **Amenities:** Pool; kitchen privileges; Wi-Fi (free).

CENTRAL BUSINESS DISTRICT

The "CBD" abuts the French Quarter along Canal Street and extends west to include the Warehouse District, with loft-conversion hotels and a thriving restaurant scene. As the city's commerce center, modernity and history mix—as do tourists and businesspeople. Some of the city's finest restaurants and hotels are here, as are some good deals (especially on weekends and off-season), and most of it is still walking distance to the French Quarter action.

Best for: Conventioneers; Superdome attendees; museum-goers; the budget-minded; hipsters; foodies; families (a number of suite and chain hotels are here, which suit both business folk and families).

Drawbacks: It's New Orleans, not New York, but you *are* in a city center. There are office buildings and people around you who may actually be working. Parking is pricey.

Very Expensive

The Roosevelt ★★★   This grandiose Waldorf property is fairly regal throughout, but the movie-star glamorous, block-long lobby is positively stunning, and the history and pedigree equally impressive. Sizes and views in the well-appointed, traditional rooms vary: luxury suites are more than ample, but the smallest rooms are simply too small for what you're probably paying (though check for package deals and great season specials). Some have tubs (even claw-foots!); some on the upper floors overlook the city or the fourth-floor pool—so make your preferences known. All have luscious beds. But guest rooms really take a back seat to the exceptional lobby and other common areas: the sumptuous Guerlain Spa, **Domenica** restaurant (p. 101), **Sazerac Bar** (p. 180), and the historic **Blue Room** club. Holiday season here is magical.

123 Baronne St. www.therooseveltneworleans.com. © **877/887-1006** or 504/648-1200. 504 units, including 125 suites. $199–$499 double; $$299–$999 suites. Valet parking $42. Pets less than 20 lbs. allowed ($175 fee). **Amenities:** 2 restaurants; coffee shop; bar; Blue Room club; concierge; fitness room; gift shop; Jacuzzi; pool; room service; spa; Wi-Fi (free in lobby; $14/day in room).

Windsor Court ★★★ There's a kind of hush at this ultra-fine hotel, for decades the center of New Orleans high society. Everything is serene and mannerly, from the proper high tea to hallway galleries of original 17th- to 19th-century art to the restaurant—the highest-end **Grill Room.** A massive 2012 overhaul refreshed all the fabrics and finery (service ought to be next—it's still spottier than it should be). The spacious accommodations are traditional if not particularly distinctive; suites are enormous—all are large-windowed and full of light. Those with balconies and river views are exceptional (though some "view" rooms are only partial views), and a club level adds 24/7 concierge service. The terrific rooftop pool is one of several superb places to enjoy a smart beverage here; the cool **Cocktail Bar** and chichi **Polo Club** are also on that list (p. 177).

300 Gravier St. www.windsorcourthotel.com. © **888/596-0955** or 504/523-6000. 316 units. $195–$450 standard double; $215–$550 suites; $320–$620 club-level. Children 16 and under stay free in parent's room. Valet parking $32. **Amenities:** Restaurant; 2 lounges; concierge; fitness center; pool; Jacuzzi; room service; spa; Wi-Fi (free).

Expensive

International House ★★ Rooms in this boutique sanctuary are minimalist chic in grays and pale gold tones, with comfy beds and fab bathrooms (request one with a tub if you so desire)—a nice contrast to all the Victoriana around (though the building's beautiful old bones still honor its history). Black-and-white photos of local musicians give a nod to the locale. With all that cool (including craft cocktail bar **Loa**), the fashionably uniformed staff is still warm, making this popular with business types and film crews. But it's more about appearances than amenities, so when rates are at their higher end it may not be merited (conversely, it runs some good online specials). We're anxiously awaiting the new (opening early 2014) restaurant here, and expect a concurrent renewal of room service.

221 Camp St. www.ihhotel.com. © **800/633-5770** or 504/553-9550. 117 units. $119–$379 double; $369–$1,799 suite. Valet parking $32. **Amenities:** Restaurant; bar; fitness room; Wi-Fi (free).

Loews New Orleans Hotel ★★★ We're fans of the crisply contemporary Loews, with its judicious sprinkles of New Orleans flavor, and the consistently genteel, professional service. The bright, expansive rooms come with local photography and sophisticated finishes (upholstered goods will be updated in mid-2014); some have terrif river views (others face surrounding buildings). Even the smallest are on the large size (though the handsome wood and granite bathrooms are not too large). All get access to the steamy indoor pool and well-equipped fitness room, not to mention the persistently fine **Café Adelaide** restaurant (a member of the Commander's Palace family, literally) and the **Swizzle Stick Bar** (p. 180).

300 Poydras St. www.loewshotels.com/neworleans. ✆ **866/211-6511** or 504/595-3300. 285 units. Rooms $149–$289; suites start at $400. Valet parking $39. Pets allowed ($100 nonrefundable fee, plus $25 daily cleaning fee). **Amenities:** Restaurant; bar; concierge; exercise room; pool; room service; spa. Wi-Fi (free in lobby; $13/day in room).

Renaissance Arts Hotel ★★ A film-crew favorite for its loft-conversion style, the proximity to the Howlin' Wolf (p. 174) and other Warehouse area attractions, and especially the modern art throughout the hotel. Nothing's outstanding, but everything is clean-lined and well done—and the staff is particularly efficient. The large rooftop pool makes up for a lot, with spectacular views and a jumping social scene. Rooms are good-sized (bigger on the concierge floor); the streetside ones have large, original windows, and interior rooms overlook the '70s-era atrium and courtyard or neighboring buildings. **Rene Bistrot** is still finding its footing after a 2013 restart here.

700 Tchoupitoulas St. www.renaissanceartshotel.com. ✆ **800/431-8634** or 504/613-2330. 217 units. $229–$299 double. Valet parking $38. **Amenities:** Restaurant; bar; concierge; sundries shop; fitness center; newspaper deliver on request; pool; room service; Wi-Fi (free in public spaces; $13/day in-room).

Moderate

Drury Inn & Suites ★★★ The looming, generic exterior hides a grander-than-expected interior and a ton of amenities—made even better through a major 2013 expansion. Most rooms have high ceilings and decent square footage (avoid the darker ones on the lower floors and shorter ones on floors four and five). It's not too pricey and well worth it to upgrade to one of the downright large suites here, but everyone gets the free breakfast buffet and afternoon "kick-back" snacks (hot dogs, nothing fancy, but a nice touch). Staff is invariably friendly, and the serviceable pool and hot tub will move to the roof of the new building, where we're assured they'll also be gussied up. All that, a good location, and surprisingly good rates make this one of the best deals in town.

820 Poydras St. www.druryhotels.com. ✆ **800/DRURY-INN** (378-7946) or 504/529-7800. 214 units. $119–$139 regular room; $149–$249 suite. Rates include full breakfast plus weekday evening snacks and beverages. Valet parking $25. **Amenities:** Fitness room; heated rooftop & hot tub; Wi-Fi (free).

Homewood Suites ★★ Don't come for the irrelevant room decor; do come for the free breakfast and weeknight dinners (perfunctory, but hey you'll save a few bucks), indoor pool and whirlpool, and the rooms, which are all two-room suites with kitchenettes—and you'll be pretty dazzled in a cookie-cutter way. Yes, it's a Hilton chain, but the location is convenient, and the exterior has plenty of historical appeal so you don't feel completely ensconced in dullness. When it's at the bottom or mid-range of its rates, it's a great value, especially for families and extended stays. Check online travel sites for frequent discounts.

901 Poydras St. http://homewoodsuitesneworleans.com. ✆ **800/225-5466** or 504/581-5599. 166 units. Suites $149–$249. Rates include full breakfast plus basic dinner Mon–Thurs. Valet parking

$29; self-parking $21. **Amenities:** Fitness room; indoor pool and whirlpool; kitchenettes; coin laundry; fitness center; Wi-Fi (free).

Le Pavillon Hotel ★★   One's chin may rise a centimeter or two when entering Le Pavillion's soaring lobby, with crystal chandeliers overhead, plush Oriental rugs underfoot, enormous marble pillars, and ornate carved ceilings. It's a Historic Hotel of America dating to 1907, and the first in New Orleans to have an elevator. It's also famous for late-night peanut butter and jelly service (silver platter and all), with a hot chocolate nightcap; we're equally amused by the classical statuary around the heated rooftop pool. The heavily draped rooms are fine, but pale in contrast to all that gleaming luxe, though some have painted ceilings and glam black-granite bathrooms with gold fixtures. Suites, with original art and antiques, are a different story—would that a wee bit of their elegance was extended to the standard rooms. Service and amenities are all topnotch: The Crystal Room restaurant is a little touch of Versailles. Discounted rates do pop up on travel websites.

833 Poydras St. www.lepavillon.com. ⓒ **800/535-9095** or 504/581-3111. 226 units. $129–$699 queen; $595–$1,695 suite. Valet parking $35. **Amenities:** Restaurant; bar; concierge; fitness center; whirlpool spa; heated outdoor pool; room service; Wi-Fi (free).

St. James Hotel ★   It's not next to anything in particular, but it's close to so many things, which metaphorically describes the property's quality as well as its geography. The old sugar and coffee trading company pays homage to its roots with a quasi-Caribbean motif, so look for subtle decorative touches of parrots and palm trees. Rooms are on the small side; it's less noticeable in those with private or shared terrace space or high ceilings (the rooms in the back building). Top-floor rooms still have some original brick or wood, and most have marble-floored bathrooms. A courtyard pool is sweet if miniscule, but complimentary morning coffee and fresh-baked croissants, feather beds, in-room fridge and microwave, and good online discounts make up for a lot.

330 Magazine St. www.saintjameshotel.com. ⓒ **888/211-3447** or 504/304-4000. 86 units. $109–$299 double. Valet parking $30. **Amenities:** Restaurant; concierge; pool; free passes to nearby gym; Wi-Fi (free).

Inexpensive

Queen & Crescent ★   Expect bare-bones accommodations, and you won't be disappointed. Let's just say princesses need not apply—there's not a lot of attention to detail or hop-to-it staff. This Quarter-close, budget hotel has smallish rooms and bathrooms. On the upside, it's a historic building and some rooms have exposed brick; those on the upper floors might even have good views. There's a very simple continental breakfast buffet and a few older machines in the fitness room. There's a $10-a-day charge for access to that and the Wi-Fi, whether you use it or not—but rumor is that the charge is being discontinued when new ownership takes over in early 2014. They'll also be giving the place a major going-over, so check for construction updates. But we're told it will still be an affordable option, and you can't change that Bourbon-close location.

344 Camp St. www.queenandcrescentneworleans.com. ⓒ **800/247-7936** or 504/587-9700. 250 units. $99–$139 double. Valet parking $32. **Amenities:** Restaurant; bar; fitness center; Wi-Fi (free).

UPTOWN/THE GARDEN DISTRICT

The Garden District offers iconic Old South charm, complete with moss-laden greenery and palatial, columned homes (as well as many more modest, no less charming properties). Not all of Uptown is as grandiose as the name might suggest, but it's mostly residential, and the best sections are both spacious and gracious.

Best for: Repeat visitors, romantics, history buffs, claustrophobes, garden lovers, lollers-about, style-seeking shoppers (for nearby Magazine Street).

Drawbacks: Allow extra time and expense to get around. You'll likely be near public transportation, but you're not in the thick of the action or the city's top attractions. A car is helpful but not necessary.

Expensive

Grand Victorian Bed & Breakfast ★★   This magazine-gorgeous 1893 Victorian home on St. Charles Ave is what we picture when we think of a sumptuous, antiques-filled Southern B&B. All of the elegantly furnished rooms vary; several have antique beds that are small by today's standards, and some have Jacuzzi tubs or balconies. If you can snag one of those balcony rooms or any room, really, during Carnival season, you've scored: you're right on the parade route (and convenient to the St. Charles streetcar year-round; the rumble might bother some people, but we love it). Friendly owner Bonnie sees to it that feather mattresses are fluffy, coffee and snacks are available round-the-clock, and all your needs are met.

2727 St. Charles Ave. www.gvbb.com. © **800/977-0008** or 504/895-1104. 8 units. $165–$325 double. Rates include continental breakfast. Street parking. **Amenities:** Wi-Fi (free).

Maison Perrier Bed & Breakfast ★★   The impressive exterior of this former house of ill repute is frillier than inside, which isn't to say that there isn't plenty to impress here. Antiques abound, but they're not overdone, and a smattering of country touches help create genuine, unstuffy comfort. The beds are deep and piled with soft linens, and room configurations are amenable to couples, families, and friends (including four-legged friends). Nearly all the well-appointed bathrooms have whirlpool tubs—some big enough for two. A full breakfast with Southern specialties like puffed pancakes, an ample supply of snacks and beverages, and weekend wine and cheese parties round out the pleasing experience here. Check the website for excellent seasonal deals.

4117 Perrier St. (2 blocks riverside from St. Charles Ave., 3 blocks downtown from Napoleon Ave.). www.maisonperrier.com. © **888/610-1807** or 504/897-1807. 16 units. $130–$265 double. Rates include tax and breakfast. Parking available on street; free limited on-site parking as well. **Amenities:** Complimentary concierge; Wi-Fi (free).

Moderate

The Chimes Bed & Breakfast ★★★   This gem has no grand airs, just pure charm and contentment in a true neighborhood setting. Rooms vary in size, but all are a tasteful, unfussy unpretentious mix of antiques, creature comforts, and thoughtful amenities. The helpful hosts bring in breakfast pastries daily from the beloved Le

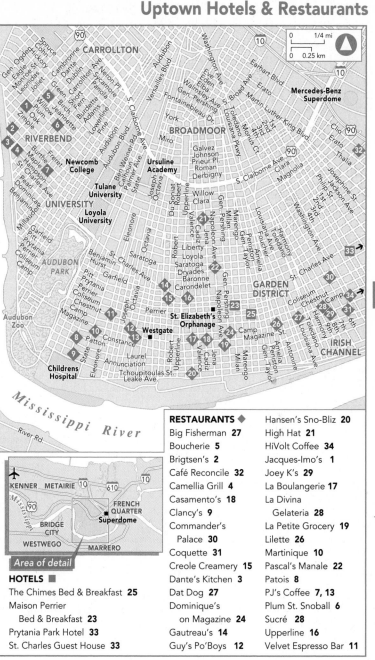

RESTAURANTS ◆

Big Fisherman **27**
Boucherie **5**
Brigtsen's **2**
Café Reconcile **32**
Camellia Grill **4**
Casamento's **18**
Clancy's **9**
Commander's
  Palace **30**
Coquette **31**
Creole Creamery **15**
Dante's Kitchen **3**
Dat Dog **27**
Dominique's
  on Magazine **24**
Gautreau's **14**
Guy's Po'Boys **12**

Hansen's Sno-Bliz **20**
High Hat **21**
HiVolt Coffee **34**
Jacques-Imo's **1**
Joey K's **29**
La Boulangerie **17**
La Divina
  Gelateria **28**
La Petite Grocery **19**
Lilette **26**
Martinique **10**
Pascal's Manale **22**
Patois **8**
PJ's Coffee **7, 13**
Plum St. Snoball **6**
Sucré **28**
Upperline **16**
Velvet Espresso Bar **11**

HOTELS ■

The Chimes Bed & Breakfast **25**
Maison Perrier
  Bed & Breakfast **23**
Prytania Park Hotel **33**
St. Charles Guest House **33**

NOT YOUR MOTHER'S room & board

It goes without saying that wherever you stay in New Orleans, good food is close by. But if that's just not close enough—if you're one of those who selects your accommodations based on its culinary offerings—here's a guide to hotels with outstanding restaurants (page links are shown for restaurants we've reviewed):

- **Café Adelaide** in Lowe's New Orleans (CBD)
- **Domenica** (p. 101) in the Roosevelt Hotel (CBD)
- **The Grill Room** in the Windsor Court (CBD)

- **Iris** (p. 83) in the Bienville House (FQ)
- **Lüke** in the Hilton St. Charles (CBD)
- **MiLA** (p. 98) in the Renaissance Pere Marquette (CBD)
- **Restaurant R'evolution** (p. 78) in the Royal Sonesta (FQ)
- **The Rib Room** in the Omni (FQ)
- **Stella!** (p. 80) in the Hotel Richelieu (FQ)
- **Vacherie** (p. 87) in the Hotel St. Marie (FQ)

Boulangerie bakery—tastier yet in the pretty courtyard. They also bring 25+ years of hospitality experience, and it shows in the caring details. Rooms got a thorough renewal in 2013, with fresh furnishings and an impressive gallery wall displaying striking black-and-white photographs of local musicians—the work of one of their many repeat guests.

1146 Constantinople St. www.chimesneworleans.com. © **504/899-2621** or 504/453-2183. 5 units. $125–$180 double. Rates include breakfast, tax, parking. Look for featured specials online. Limited free off-street parking. Well-behaved pets accepted with prior approval; call to discuss. **Amenities:** Wi-Fi (free).

Inexpensive

Prytania Park Hotel ★   Most rooms in this Lower Garden District budget property are decorated in standard motel contemporary, but a few have hardwood floors and brick walls. Go for those, to feel like you're actually in New Orleans. Part of the hotel dates to the 1840s; other sections are in newer, added-on buildings, and in between is a small courtyard. Prytania is a major through street, so light sleepers should request an off-street room, but it's also conveniently situated between St. Charles Avenue and Magazine Street, and not too far from the Warehouse District. Amenities are basic, but continental breakfast, parkingm and Wi-Fi are all free; plus, summer and off-season rates can be downright cheap.

1525 Prytania St. (enter off Terpsichore St.). www.prytaniaparkhotel.com. © **800/862-1984** or 504/524-0427. 62 units. $89–$119 doubles. Children free in parents' room; extra adult $10. Must be 21 to check in. Rates include continental breakfast. Free off-street parking. **Amenities:** Fridge; microwave; vending machines; Wi-Fi (free).

St. Charles Guest House ★   It's humble, funky, old, slightly crumbling, and not for everyone. But if you're a budget traveler and don't demand spick-and-span, you'll appreciate the location and the value, and even the offbeat charm. Some rooms are downright spartan (no A/C); others are larger and even furnished with antiques.

There's a pool with a deck area and a tented seating section. Don't expect much of the continental breakfast (or anything else), and you won't be disappointed, but overpaying for accommodations during a festival will only leave you bitter.

1748 Prytania St. www.stcharlesguesthouse.com. ℰ **504/523-6556.** 26 units, 22 with private bathroom. $65–$105 double. Rates include continental breakfast. No credit cards; PayPal accepted. No in-room phones. Street parking. **Amenities:** Pool; Wi-Fi (free).

WHERE TO DINE IN NEW ORLEANS

New Orleans restaurant matriarch Miss Ella Brennan says that whereas in other places, one eats to live, "In New Orleans, we live to eat." It's hard to spoil such a big appetite.

Here, we don't call a friend and ask, "How are you?" Instead, it's the colloquial "Where y'at?" or, more likely, "What're you eatin'?" Here, cuisine is community, cuisine is culture, cuisine is practically church (except for the fact that Church is church). Food forms the crucial threads of the city's multicolored fabric: It weaves through the people, the music, the history, the parties, the traditions. A style of gumbo can define a neighborhood. A roux technique can unite (or divide) generations of families.

At last count New Orleans had more than 1,350 restaurants, so there's goodness in every direction and on every level: in the centuries-old grande-dame restaurants and the corner po'boy shops; in a gas station with shockingly good steam-table food; and in the sleek bistro of a brash, upstart culinary-school grad fusing Grandma's recipes with unpronounceable techniques and ingredients.

There are culinary training grounds like the recently renovated **Café Reconcile** (1631 Oretha Castle Haley Blvd.; © **504/568-1157;** www.cafe reconcile.org) and **Liberty's Kitchen,** 422½ S. Broad St.; © **504/822-4011;** www.libertyskitchen.org), serving sturdy meals while training young men and women for careers in food service. And there are fourth-generation chefs working backstreet dives whose menus and ingredients haven't varied in, well, ever.

You are going to want to eat a lot here. And you are going to want to eat here, a lot. And then you are going to talk about it. You'll probably adopt the local custom of talking about dinner while you're at lunch (and lunch while you're breakfasting). The food here is utterly, unashamedly regional, which isn't to say that (in some cases) it's not also utterly of the moment and sophisticated. But it's ingredient- and chef-driven, which makes it uniquely New Orleanean: It will never be Copenhagen or Bilbao, nor does it want (or need) to.

In many restaurants, certainly in the more traditional ones, dishes are based largely on variations of Creole recipes. Others, the innovators, take Creole as a cue and go wildly afield. Creole food was originally based on recipes brought by the French settlers, the herbs and filé (ground sassafras leaves) used by the Native Americans, and saffron and peppers introduced by the Spanish. From the West Indies came new vegetables, spices, and sugarcane, and when slave boats arrived, an African influence was added.

Today, the Italian influence runs deep, and even Vietnamese flavors are now finding their way onto the plate, brought by a newer wave of immigrants. And while nearly all restaurateurs source fresh ingredients from local purveyors, the ban on butter never took hold here (thankfully). Flavor comes first.

So indulge and enjoy. It's what you do here. Try some of everything. We're particularly big on lunching, since many of the best restaurants have terrific prix-fixe lunch deals that include dishes you'd pay twice as much for during dinner. Then start planning the next trip, so you can do it again.

Please keep in mind that all prices, hours, and menu items in the following listings are subject to change according to season, availability, or whim. You should call in advance to ensure the accuracy of anything significant to you.

Make sure to check out our "**Best of**" recommendations in chapter 1.

OF BEIGNETS, BOUDIN & DIRTY RICE

Many of the foods in New Orleans are unique to the region and consequently may be unfamiliar to first-time visitors. Here's a list that will help you navigate any New Orleans menu:

andouille (ahn-doo-*we*) A spicy Cajun sausage made with pork.

bananas Foster Bananas sautéed in liqueur, brown sugar, cinnamon, and butter, drenched in rum, set ablaze, served over vanilla ice cream.

barbequed shrimp Not actually grilled nor BBQ-sauced, but a butter-soaked, garlicky, pepper-shot peel-and-eat gulf local specialty.

beignet (bin-*yay*) A big, puffy, deep-fried, hole-free doughnut, liberally sprinkled with powdered sugar—the more sugar, the better.

boudin (boo-*dan*) Cajun pork and rice sausage of varying spice levels.

café brûlot (cah-*fay* brew-*low*) Coffee, spices, and liqueurs, served flaming.

crawfish A tiny, lobsterlike creature commonly local and eaten in every conceivable way, including boiled whole with spices and peeled by hand.

debris The rich, juicy bits of meat that fall off when beef or pork is roasted meat and carved.

dressed A "dressed" po'boy comes with lettuce, tomato, mayonnaise, and sometimes pickles.

étouffée (ay-too-*fay*) A Cajun stew (usually containing crawfish or shrimp) served with rice.

filé (*fee*-lay) G round sassafras leaves, frequently used to thicken gumbo.

gumbo A thick, spicy soup of poultry, seafood, and/or sausage, with okra in a roux base, served with rice. Gumbo z'herbes, a Good Friday tradition, eschews meat for greens.

holy trinity   Onions, bell peppers, and celery: the base of much Creole and Cajun cooking.

Hurricane   A local drink of rum and passion-fruit punch.

jambalaya (jum-ba-*lie*-ya)   A stew of yellow rice, sausage, seafood, poultry, vegetables, and spices.

lagniappe (lan-*yap*)   A little something extra: a bonus freebie.

mirliton (*mur*-li-tone)   A pear-shaped squash also called chayote.

muffuletta   A mountainous sandwich made with Italian deli meats, cheese, and olive salad, piled onto a specially-made round bread.

oysters Rockefeller   Oysters on the half shell in a creamy spinach sauce, so called because Rockefeller was the only name rich enough to match the taste.

po'boy, po-boy, poor boy   A sandwich on long French bread, similar to submarines and grinders. Often filled with fried seafood or roast beef, or famously with French fries and gravy, they can include most anything. Originally, free sustenance for striking transit workers, those "poor boys."

pralines (*praw*-leens)   A sweet confection of brown sugar and pecans.

rémoulade   A spicy sauce, usually over shrimp, concocted of mayonnaise, boiled egg yolks, horseradish, Creole mustard, and lemon juice.

roux   A mixture of flour and fat that's slowly cooked over low heat, used to thicken stews, soups, and sauces.

Sazerac   The official cocktail of New Orleans, consisting of rye whiskey with sugar and bitters.

shrimp Creole   Shrimp in a tomato sauce seasoned with what's known around town as the "holy trinity:" onions, bell peppers, and celery.

RESTAURANTS BY CUISINE

AMERICAN, NEW AMERICAN & REGIONAL AMERICAN
American Sector ★★★ ($$, p. 100)
Iris ★★ ($$$, p. 83)
Emeril's ★★★ ($$$$, p. 96)
Root ★★, ($$$, p. 99)
Stanley ★★ ($, p. 89)

ASIAN
Dong Phuong ★★ ($, p. 110)
Yuki ★ ($$, p. 92)

BAKERY (ALSO SEE DESSERTS)
Buttermilk Drop Bakery and Cafe ★★ ($, p. 111)
Café Beignet ★ ($, p. 88)
Café EnVie ($, p. 113)
Cake Café & Bakery ★ ($, p. 92)
Croissant D'Or ★★ ($, p. 113)
La Boulangerie ★★★ ($, p. 113)
Mr. Gregory's ★★★, ($, p. 89)

BARBECUE
The Joint BBQ ★★★ ($, p. 91)
Walker's ★★ ($, p. 110)

BARS & CLUBS WITH FOOD
Bacchanal ★★★ ($$, p. 90)
Bombay Club ★ ($$, p. 176)
Borracho's & Pidgin ★★ ($, p. 175)
Erin Rose & Killer Po'Boys ★★★ ($, p. 178)
Kermit's Tremé Speakeasy ★ ($, p. 174)
Little Gem ★★★ ($$, p. 174)

KEY TO ABBREVIATIONS:
$$$$** = Very Expensive   **$$$** = Expensive   **$$** = Moderate   **$ = Inexpensive

Molly's at the Market & Dis Tacos ★★ ($, p. 178)

Napoleon House ★★ ($, p. 179)

SoBou ★★ ($$, p. 179)

Snug Harbor ★★★ ($$, p. 172)

Three Muses ★★★ ($$, p. 172)

Tico Tolteca ★★ ($, p. 179)

BISTRO

Café Degas ★★★ ($$, p. 93)

Coquette ★★★ ($$$, p. 104)

Dominique's on Magazine ★ ($$, p. 104)

Herbsaint ★★★ ($$$, p. 98)

La Petite Grocery ★★★ ($$, p. 106)

Lilette ★★ ($$, p. 106)

Martinique ★★ ($$$, p. 106)

Meauxbar ★★★ ($$, p. 84)

Patois ★★★ ($$$, p. 107)

Sylvain ★★★ ($$, p. 86)

CAFES/COFFEEHOUSES

Café Beignet ★ ($, p. 88)

Café du Monde ★★★ ($, p. 112)

Café EnVie ★ ($, p. 113)

Croissant D'Or ★★ ($, p. 113)

Hi Volt ★★ ($, p. 112)

Merchant ★★★ ($, p. 112)

Morning Call ★★ ($, p. 112)

Mr. Gregory's ★★★, ($, p. 89)

P.J.'s Coffee & Tea Company ★ ($, p. 114)

Royal Blend Coffee & Tea House ★ ($, p. 114)

Somethin' Else Café ★ ($, p. 89)

Spitfire ★★ ($, p. 112)

Velvet ★★ ($, p. 112)

CAJUN/CONTEMPORARY CAJUN

Brigtsen's ★★★ ($$$, p. 103)

Cochon ★★ ($$, p. 100)

Cochon Butcher ★★★ ($, p. 101)

K-Paul's Louisiana Kitchen ★ ($$$$, p. 78)

Toup's Meatery ★★ ($$, p. 94)

CREOLE/CONTEMPORARY CREOLE/NEW LOUISIANA

Antoine's ★★ ($$$, p. 80)

Arnaud's ★★★ ($$$, p. 81)

Brigtsen's ★★★ ($$$, p. 103)

Broussard's ($$$$, p. 75)

Café Adelaide ★★★ ($$$, p. 98)

Clancy's ★★★ ($$$$, p. 102)

Commander's Palace ★★★ ($$$$, p. 103)

Court of Two Sisters ★ ($$$, p. 82)

Dante's Kitchen ★★ ($$, p. 108)

Dooky Chase ★ ($$, p. 93)

EAT ★★ ($$, p. 85)

Elizabeth's ★★★ ($$, p. 91)

Emeril's ★★★ ($$$$, p. 96)

Felix's Restaurant & Oyster Bar ★★ ($, p. 88)

Iris ★★ ($$$, p. 83)

Jacques-Imo's ★★ ($$$, p. 105)

Joey K's ★ ($, p. 111)

K-Paul's Louisiana Kitchen ★ ($$$$, p. 78)

Lil' Dizzy's ★★ ($, p. 95)

Liuzza's ★★ ($$, p. 93)

Liuzza's by the Track ★★★ ($, p. 95)

Louisiana Bistro ★★ ($$, p. 83)

Mandina's ★★ ($$, p. 94)

Mother's ★ ($, p. 102)

Mr. B's Bistro ★ ($$$, p. 84)

Muriel's ★ ($$$, p. 84)

Napoleon House ★★ ($, p. 179)

Palace Café ★★ ($$$, p. 99)

Patois ★★★ ($$$, p. 107)

Praline Connection ★ ($$, p. 91)

Ralph's on the Park ★★★ ($$$, p. 92)

Restaurant August ★★★ ($$$$, p. 97)

Tujague's ★ ($$$, p. 85)

Upperline ★★★ ($$$, p. 107)

Tableau ★★ ($$$, p. 84)

Vacherie ★★ ($$, p. 87)

Ye Olde College Inn ★★★ ($$, p. 94)

DESSERT/ICE CREAM/ SNOBALL

Angelo Brocato's Ice Cream & Confectionery ★★★ ($, p. 111)

Buttermilk Drop Bakery and Cafe ★★ ($, p. 111)

Café du Monde ★★★ ($, p. 112)

Creole Creamery ★★★ ($, p. 113)

Hansen's SnoBliz ★★★ ($, p. 114)

La Divina Gelateria ★★ ($, p. 113)

Meltdown Ice Pops ★★ ($, p. 113)
Pandora's SnoBalls ★★★ ($, p. 114)
Peity St. SnoBalls ★★★ ($, p. 114)
Plum St. SnoBalls ★★★ ($, p. 114)
Sucré ★★★ ($, p. 115)

DINER

Camellia Grill ★★★ ($, p. 88 and
  p. 109)
Clover Grill ★ ($, p. 88)
Joey K's ★ ($, p. 111)
Port of Call ★★ ($$, p. 86)

FRENCH/CLASSIC CREOLE

Antoine's ★★ ($$$, p. 80)
Arnaud's ★★★ ($$$, p. 81)
Café Degas ★★★ ($$, p. 93)
Galatoire's ★★ ($$$$, p. 75)
Gautreau's ★★ ($$$, p. 105)
Meauxbar ★★★ ($$$, p. 84)
Restaurant August ★★★ ($$$$,
  p. 97)
Tableau ★★ ($$$, p. 84)
Tujague's ★ ($$$, p. 85)

HAMBURGERS (SEE DINER)

ICE CREAM (SEE DESSERT)

INTERNATIONAL

Bacchanal ★★★ ($$, p. 90)
Bayona ★★★ ($$$, p. 81)
Dominique's on Magazine ★ ($$,
  p. 104)
Green Goddess ★ ($$, p. 86)
Lola's ★★ ($$, p. 94)
Mondo ★★ ($$, p. 110)
Stella! ★★ ($$$$, p. 80)

ITALIAN

Domenica ★★★ ($$, p. 101)
Irene's Cuisine ★★★ ($$$, p. 82)
Liuzza's ★★ ($$, p. 93)
Mandina's ★★ ($$, p. 94)
Mariza ★★ ($, p. 83)
Mosca's ★★★ ($$$, p. 110)
Napoleon House ★★ ($, p. 179)
Nor-Joe's Importing ★★ ($, p. 90)
Pascal's Manale ★★ ($$, p. 108)
R&O's ★★ ($$, p. 110)

LIGHT FARE

Acme Oyster House ★★★ ($, p. 87)
Café Amelie ★★ ($$, p. 85)
Café Maspero ★ ($, p. 88)
Cake Café & Bakery ★ ($, p. 92)
Camellia Grill ★★★ ($, p. 88 and
  p. 109)
Café EnVie ($, p. 113)
Central Grocery ★★★ ($, p. 90)
Cochon Butcher ★★★ ($, p. 101)
Coop's ★ ($, p. 88)
Dat Dog ★ ($, p. 109)
EAT ★★ ($$, p. 85)
Gene's Po'Boys ★★ ($, p. 92)
Guy's Po'Boys ★★ ($, p. 111)
Jimmy Buffett's Margaritaville ★ ($$,
  p. 86)
Johnny's Po-Boys ★ ($, p. 89)
Liuzza's by the Track ★★★ ($, p. 95)
Morning Call ★★ ($, p. 112)
Mr. Gregory's ★★★, ($, p. 89)
Mother's ★ ($, p. 102)
Old Coffee Pot ★ ($, p. 89)
Parkway Bakery and Tavern ★★★ ($,
  p. 95)
Quarter Grocery ★ ($, p. 87)
QuarterMaster ★ ($, p. 87)
Royal Blend Coffee & Tea House ★
  ($, p. 114)
Sammy's ★★ ($, p. 110)
Somethin' Else Café ★ ($, p. 89)
Sucré ★★★ ($, p. 115)
Verti Marte ★★ ($, p. 87)
Ye Olde College Inn ★★★ ($$, p. 94)

PO'BOYS (SEE LIGHT FARE)

SEAFOOD

Acme Oyster House ★★★ ($, p. 87)
Big Fisherman ★★ ($, p. 109)
Borgne ★★★ ($$$, p. 97)
Café Maspero ★ ($, p. 88)
Cajun Seafood ★★ ($, p. 109)
Casamento's ★★★ ($, p. 111)
Deanie's ★★ ($$, p. 110)
Dickie Brennan's Bourbon House
  Seafood ★★ ($$$, p. 82)
Drago's ★★ ($$, p. 101)

THE FRENCH QUARTER

Very Expensive

Broussard's NEW LOUISIANA   This iconic, circa-1920 grand dame turned tourist trap got a complete makeover in 2013. The French chef, menu, and owners are all sparkling new, and the glorious old mansion has been renewed, inside and out. Broussard's was about to reopen at press time, and advance word and menu previews were very promising.

819 Conti St. ℰ **504/581-3866.** www.broussards.com. Main courses $28–$42. Daily 5:30–10pm.

Galatoire's ★★ CLASSIC CREOLE/FRENCH   Considered New Orleans's consummate old-line Creole French restaurant, Galatoire's is a time-honored, fine-dining classic beloved by generations—perhaps because their families are beloved by Galatoire's. Or perhaps because Tennessee Williams supped here, as did his characters Stella and Blanche in *A Streetcar Named Desire.* It oozes tradition: Ceiling fans whir, bentwood chairs strain, mirrored walls reflect the civilized frivolity. But the jovial obsequiousness that the tuxedoed waiters lavish upon their regulars isn't always bestowed upon moi et toi. Things are a tad more somber in the (lesser—but perfectly fine) upstairs dining room. Either way, the drinking commences upon arrival, and doesn't (and shouldn't) let up for a few hours.

No one comes here for great gastronomy, but Galatoire's does know fish. Go with a classic shrimp rémoulade, crab maison, or the eggplant fingers. Ask the waiter which fish is best today, get it a la meunière and topped with crabmeat; or order the soft-shell crab if available and some creamed spinach. We're not fond of the heavy sauces they ladle on the fine fish, but don't scoff at asparagus with spot-on hollandaise. The puffy

soufflé potatoes are legally required. Skip the meh desserts; order a glass of port instead. Reservations accepted for upstairs only; reserve well in advance.

209 Bourbon St. © **504/525-2021.** www.galatoires.com. Jackets required after 5pm and all day Sun. Main courses $19–$42. Tues–Sat 11:30am–10pm; Sun noon–10pm. Fri lunch: Recommend lining up 45–60 min. before opening.

Galatoire's 33 ★★★ STEAK   Galatoire's regulars have known for years that the seafood specialists grill a mean steak. In 2013, venerable Galatoire's, dowager Queen of the New Orleans restaurant scene for 100+ years, spawned a steakhouse offshoot. The fun starts with starters. We love the high-styled deviled eggs, the burly bone marrow—generous, filthy rich, and a bargain at $8—and the unskimping lobster maison. Six prime cuts, from a single-source ranch that raises the cattle to G33's exacting specifications, comprise the crux of the menu—and each is done to perfection. The bone-in tenderloin is just a meat marvel. Add the sauces and sides, including many favorites from Big G next door (like Brabant potatoes, with garlic here), and you're in the carnivore Olympics. It doesn't have the high-society-playground feel of the original Galatoire's (give it a few decades), but that actually makes it more approachable for visitors. The bar here, a great hang, unsurprisingly took about 30 seconds to become a happening scene.

215 Bourbon St. © **504/335-3932.** http://galatoires33barandsteak.com. Appetizers $11–$21; steaks $29–$49. Sun–Thurs 5–10pm; Friday lunch 11:30am–3pm. Bar: Mon 5pm–close; Tues–Sun 11am–close.

K-Paul's Louisiana Kitchen ★★ CAJUN/CREOLE   Paul Prudhomme started the Cajun cooking craze in the 1980s and is responsible for introducing the term "blackened" to our culinary vocabulary. His sauce and spice empire still thrives, and the restaurant remains a standard-bearer for American regional food—but it's difficult to justify the sky-high prices. We're partial to the blackened beef tenders with debris from the rotating menu, and the classic blackened drum is always available. Now that it's also served (albeit on a po'boy) during the "deli lunch" service, that might be the way to go—lunch offers a limited menu, counter service, paper plates, and entrees about $25 less than dinner. Reserve in advance for dinner.

416 Chartres St. © **504/524-7394.** www.kpauls.com. Business casual. Gentlemen asked to remove hats and caps inside. Main courses $28–$38 dinner; $12–$14 lunch. Thurs–Sat 11am–2pm; Mon–Sat 5:30–10pm.

Restaurant R'evolution ★★ NEW LOUISIANA   Two years (and $6 million) in the making, two food-world icons at the helm (John Folse and Rick Tramonto), and two tons of hype—and it nearly lives up to the brash name claim. Taking Creole cuisine in globe-hopping directions keyed to New Orleans's past and present influences, this is big-league, big-idea, big-ticket dining in a fanciful but refined setting. The most r'evolutionary aspect may be that this restaurant is 2 years old, not 102—this much grandness is rarely launched any more. It's Event Dining, and making it memorable is the best way to approach it. Set aside the time. Tour each elegant but disparate room (ask to see the private rooms if they're available—better yet, book one, or request the stunning Storyville Parlor). Indulge in something marvelous from the wine list, so enormous that only an iPad can contain it (dessert options are also delivered via device). Augment your order with sides, sauces, and toppings—the menu is flush with them. Then, having saved your paychecks for a month or two, hope for the best—experiences here have been inconsistent and service is a bit casual for a restaurant of this

Acme Oyster House **2**
Antoine's **20**
Arnaud's **8**
Bayona **18**
Broussard's **19**
Café Amelie **43**
Café Beignet **11, 13**
Café du Monde **34**
Café Envie **52**
Café Maspero **29**
Camellia Grill **24**
Central Grocery **44**
Clover Grill **42**
Coop's **49**
Court of Two Sisters **26**
Croissant D'Or **48**
Dickie Brennan's Bourbon House Seafood **3**
EAT **39**

Felix's Restaurant & Oyster Bar **7**
Galatoire's **5**
Galatoire's 33 **6**
Green Goddess **14**
GW Fins **4**
Irene's Cuisine **45**
Iris **17**
Jimmy Buffett's Margaritaville **50**
Johnny's Po-Boys **23**
Kingfish **15**
K-Paul's Louisiana Kitchen **21**
La Divina **32**
Louisiana Bistro **10**
Meauxbar **41**
Mr. B's Bistro **9**
Mr. Gregory's **37**

Muriel's **35**
Napoleon House **22**
Palace Café **1**
Port of Call **53**
Quarter Grocery **38**
QuarterMaster **47**
Restaurant R'evolution **12**
Royal Blend Coffee & Tea House **27**
Somethin' Else Café **16**
Spitfire **33**
Stanley **36**
Stella! **46**
Sylvain **30**
Tableau **31**
The Old Coffee Pot **28**
Three Muses **54**
Tujague's **40**
Vacherie **25**
Verti Marte **51**

YOU GOT YOUR cajun IN MY CREOLE!

The difference between Cajun and Creole cuisine lies chiefly in distance between city and countryside. Cajun cooking came from the Acadians who settled in the swamps and bayous of rural Louisiana and adapted the recipes of French heritage to their new location. Their cuisine is like their music: spicy and robust. They used available ingredients like sausage, seafood, poultry, and rice in single-pot stews that fed large families and farms. Creole dishes, on the other hand, were developed by French and Spanish city dwellers and feature fancier sauces and ingredients. Today, the two cuisines have a happy marriage, blurring the distinctions and inviting other influences. Our advice? Disregard the classifications, try it all, and decide what *you* prefer.

caliber and cost. But the plating is unconditionally beautiful. A dark pool of "Death by Gumbo," rich as your surroundings, surrounds a baby quail, and it's terrific. The gently crisped crab beignets, each in a different rémoulade dollop, are also a hit. The terrines, including a lustrous duck liver moose and a more rugged country pâté, are the best bang. We couldn't justify the pastas, but the shrimp and grits, with its chili and ginger Asian kick, were a favorite; the considerable veal chop was temperature-perfect and bursting with flavor. The jewelry box with tiny cookies tucked into its drawers is a nice dessert lagniappe. Other desserts were almost an afterthought after all this excess, but we fell for the "beignets with coffee," a mocha pot de crème. Reserve well in advance during special events.

777 Bienville St. (in the Royal Sonesta Hotel). ℂ **504/553-2277.** http://revolutionnola.com. Entrees $18–$62. Reserve well in advance for dinner. Wed–Thurs 11:30am–2:30pm; Mon–Thurs 5:30–10pm; Fri–Sat 5:30–11pm; Sun 10:30m–2pm and 5–10pm.

Stella! ★★★ INTERNATIONAL   The graceful, adult room is aglow with the soft light of chandeliers and the anticipation of something special, which Stella! presents, in five or seven courses (plus a caviar menu). Even if the bloom is off a bit since the days when Chef Boswell won James Beard nominations, his globe-hopping culinary explorations are displayed with every course. The daily prix-fixe menus (a la carte available only upon arrangement) indicate that diners are in for a luxurious long run, so opt for the very well-selected wine pairings. The food is stunningly presented, often fresh from their own farm across the street, and many dishes are inventive updates of classics, a boon for the food-shy. Crisped veal sweetbreads with stuffed morels were enriched by black truffles and braised black carrots; delectable charcoal-grilled octopus was served with a tomatillo sauce, almonds, and pea shoots. Dishes are simpler than the lengthy list of fine ingredients would have them appear. Isn't that the definition of elegance? Reserve in advance during peak periods.

1032 Chartres St. (in the Hôtel Provincial). ℂ **504/587-0091.** www.restaurantstella.com. No shorts or tank tops; business casual okay. 4-course prix fixe $85; 7 courses $125; vegetarian menu available. Daily 5:30–10:30pm.

Expensive

Antoine's ★★ CLASSIC CREOLE   We're sentimental about Antoine's, it being one of the first fine-dining restaurants in the New World. It's been owned and operated by the same family (and serving generations of patrons' families) for an astonishing 170 years. It's as classic as New Orleans dining gets, but truth be told, there's better food (and presentation) elsewhere. Still the experience can be well worth it. The best strategy: Go for conviviality, classics, and drama. Request Johnny or Charles as your server. Befriend neighboring guests. Order the spinach-soaked baked oysters Rockefeller (invented here); buttery, crab-topped trout Pontchartrain; and a side or two of the hollowed soufflé potato puffs; finish with a *café brûlot* (see "Anythin' Flamin'," p. 105) and the frivolous, football-size (and -shaped) baked Alaska. Get one or two of the daily featured 25¢ cocktail. Then tour some of the 15(!) memorabilia-packed rooms, peek at the astounding wine alley, and catch some good local music in the **Hermes Bar.** The three-course, prix-fixe Friday lunch at $20.13 is worth every penny. Make dinner reservations well in advance during peak periods.

713 St. Louis St. ℭ **504/581-4422.** No shorts, sandals, or T-shirts; collared shirts for gentlemen (jackets welcome, not required). Main courses $25–$45. Mon–Sat 5:30–9pm; Mon–Sat 11:30am–2pm; Sun 11am–2pm.

Arnaud's ★★★ CLASSIC CREOLE   Arnaud's isn't the best known of the old New Orleans restaurants, but it tops them in quality, and far exceeds them in the cocktail arena. It's classically atmospheric, with white tile floors and dark wood accents, and the recipes are classics as well. Thus, it's not wildly creative, but the quality and attention to detail are there. Have the signature shrimp Arnaud appetizer (topped with a spicy rémoulade sauce), and the spicy pompano Duarte or the definitive *filet au poivre.* We also love the quail Elzey—petite, elegant fowl stuffed with foie-gras mousse, wrapped with bacon, and ensconced in a truffle-wine sauce, and no one should leave without ordering some poufy soufflé potatoes and bananas Foster, flamed tableside (see the Anythin' Flamin' counsel, p. 105), although our resident crème brûlée expert rates theirs very high. Allow time to visit the impressive Mardi Gras museum upstairs. A more casual jazz bistro room features nighttime entertainment (a $4 cover covers the band)—all of which makes Arnaud's a good fine-dining introduction for well-behaved children. Make dinner reservations well in advance during peak periods.

813 Bienville St. ℭ **866/230-8895** or 504/523-5433. www.arnaudsrestaurant.com. Reservations suggested. Business casual. Main courses $23–$40. Dinner nightly 6–10pm; Sun brunch 10am–2:30pm.

Bayona ★★★ INTERNATIONAL   After 23 years, chef-owner Susan Spicer's modern classic restaurant still tops many "Best of" lists, with good reason. The food, cocktails, and wine list continue to be thoughtful and inspired. The ambience inside and out is positively lovely, and if service occasionally suffers a tad, that is the exception. Begin with the signature cream of garlic soup; and select among extremes of sweetbreads with lemon caper butter (another signature), any rabbit preparation, or whatever vegetarian dish is on—ever-changing preparations of the latter options are consistently superb. At lunch, the famed smoked duck with cashew butter and pepper jelly is a knockout, but the ever-clever specials may sway you. Desserts center on seasonal fruits, like the divine mango cheesecake flan with pistachio crust and blackberries. Saturday's $25 light lunch features three small-plate options. Reservations required for dinner; book early.

430 Dauphine St. ℭ **504/525-4455.** www.bayona.com. Main courses $14–$16 lunch, $28–$38 dinner. Wed–Sat 11:30am–1:30pm; Mon–Sat 6–10pm.

Court of Two Sisters ★ CLASSIC CREOLE   No doubt about it, this is one of the prettiest places around, thanks to the huge, wisteria-shaded courtyard and the 200-year-old building, and you should soak up that ambience by enjoying a smart cocktail or two. And then you should go out to eat. Sadly, the food is just mediocre, and let's face it, even supermodels eventually need some personality. The daily jazz brunch buffet is nonetheless popular, and we do get the attraction, so you'd do best to stick with the basics (like simple eggs Benedict) and enjoy the company. Make brunch reservations well in advance.

613 Royal St. © **504/522-7261.** www.courtoftwosisters.com. Main courses $25–$35; brunch $29. Daily 9am–3pm jazz brunch buffet and 5:30–10pm.

Dickie Brennan's Bourbon House Seafood ★★ SEAFOOD   Although it looks a bit sprawling and formulaic from the street, this modern version of a classic New Orleans fish house has much to recommend it. Hang out at the raw bar, or order the head-turning *fruits du mer* platter. A simple grilled redfish is fresh and perfect (top it with fresh lump crabmeat for $12 more, a worthy addition). In a city of good BBQ shrimp dishes (shrimp sautéed in a buttery, garlicky spicy sauce, heaven to sop up with bread), we love their version, finished with bourbon. Leave room for a frozen bourbon milk punch, a dreamy booze-shake. Naturally they're committed to, and knowledgeable about, all things bourbon. Happy hour features $5 small plates and $1 oysters (and a good shucker show); the three-course lunch for $26 is also a good deal.

144 Bourbon St. © **504/522-0111.** www.bourbonhouse.com. Main courses $11–$16 breakfast, $12–$32 lunch, $20–$34 dinner. Daily 6:30–10:30am; Sun–Thurs 11am–10pm; Fri–Sat 11am–11pm.

GW Fins ★★★ SEAFOOD   Here's the city's best modern seafood restaurant, and one of its best restaurants, period. It is polished from the top down, with the owner prowling the floor like a tiger mama assuring that no imperfection makes it to the table, or even enters into diners' consciousness. It's clear that GW Fins takes the same care in sourcing its fish, which comes from the Gulf and far beyond, and is just bratty fresh. Preparations are stylish enough but don't dare upstage the star—as evident in the perfectly seared yellowfin tuna. The signature "scalibut" (thin sliced scallop "scales" atop grilled halibut) on lobster risotto is worthy of its fame. A diverting starter of watermelon and pork belly is also to be savored, as are the lobster dumplings with a light brush of fennel. The wine list thoughtfully complements the cuisine, with a good range of midpriced bottles and a much-appreciated, extensive array of finer pours by the glass. Order the pretzel-crusted salty malty ice cream pie, even if you only have room for a bite. The large, tiered dining room is handsome and high-ceilinged, while also managing to be conversation conducive. We love the high-backed gangsta booths along the back wall. Check the website for excellent seasonal multicourse deals. Make dinner reservations well in advance.

808 Bienville St. © **504/581-3467.** www.gwfins.com. Collared shirts for men; better jeans. No shorts or flip-flops. Main courses $21–$38. Sun–Thurs 5–10pm; Fri–Sat 5–10:30pm (open 5:30 in summer).

Irene's Cuisine ★★★ ITALIAN   If you detect the scent of simmering garlic from blocks away and aren't lured to its source, Irene's may not interest you. No worry— that leaves more of the French Provincial and Creole-Italian cooking for the rest of us. Irene—herself a Quarter institution—and her friendly crew create delectable house-made pastas and sauces, but the *secondi* are the real standouts. Locals come on

Thursdays for the ginormous osso buco flavor bomb, and someone at the table needs to order Duck St. Phillip (with raspberry-pancetta demi-glace) so that everyone can taste it and wish they had ordered it. The seemingly simple *pollo rosemarino*—marinated, par-cooked, remarinated, and roasted—is nearly

perfect. The cramped, low-ceilinged little rooms have a strange, mob-headquarters sort of appeal. Would that the desserts were a little bit better, but the cheesecake will do. Irene's is notorious for long waits, even with reservations, and alas, it can be true. Just figure it into your plans. Limited reservations accepted if space is available; it's worth it to try.

539 St. Philip St. ℂ **504/529-8811.** Main courses $18–$38. Mon–Sat 5:30–10pm. Closed major holidays and the week of Labor Day.

Iris ★★★ CONTEMPORARY CREOLE   This exceedingly pretty little spot serves cuisine that is so well sourced and prepared that it barely needs the chef's subtle Asian, French, and tropical dashes, but they elevate it to unforeseen heights. It's delicate yet utterly approachable, a welcome respite from the heavier Creole fare around town, with dishes like the herb-scented sweetbreads starter, and local shrimp in a light broth hinting of the region's strong Vietnamese influence. Servers glide in and out pleasantly if a bit automatically, and the cocktail program is notable on its own. *Note:* The restaurateurs also debuted the more casual, Italian-focused **Mariza** in 2013 in the Bywater neighborhood—also well worth a visit (2900 Chartres St.; ℂ **504/598-5700;** http://marizaneworleans.com; Tues–Sat 5–10pm).

321 N. Peters St. (in the Bienville House Hotel). ℂ **504/299-3944.** www.irisneworleans.com. Main courses $18–$34. Mon & Wed–Sat 6pm–closing; Fri 11:30am–2pm.

Kingfish ★★ CONTEMPORARY SOUTHERN   This 2013 newbie opened with a high-profile bang, bringing craft-cocktail guru Chris McMillan out of retirement and landing veteran local chef Greg Sonnier. For now, the ample bar space has the edge over the kitchen, which may have tried to gun the engines before it was fully warmed up. We like what they're doing, though, and the elongated, brick and tin-paneled dining room, which wraps around the swarming bar, is easygoing for casual walk-ups. The slightly strange ramen with duck turned out to be a favorite, and while the signature "King" pompano, seared and served on a salt brick, didn't live up to expectations, the gooey/crunchy oysters thermidor and crab-stuffed, prosciutto-wrapped shrimp salad—and those drinks—will keep us coming back to see where their clearly creative impulses take them.

337 Chartres St. ℂ **504/598-5005.** www.cocktailbarneworleans.com. Main courses $18–$39. Mon–Sun 11am–2:30pm; Sun–Thurs 5:30–10pm; Fri & Sat 5:30–11pm. Bar 5–12am.

Louisiana Bistro ★★ CONTEMPORARY CREOLE   You've seen the movie. On a ramble through Paris, you stumble into *une petite cafe*, just 11 tables, with a nutty chef at the helm. You can hear him shouting at someone from behind the kitchen doors; waiters roll their eyes conspiratorially, and shrug. Then Chef Mars appears at your side, flashing a charming smile, saying "Trust me, you'll like it." So you do, and you do. The a la carte menu here is just a concession to the three-, four-, and five-course

"Feed Me" tasting menus, made to order based on market availability and Chef Mars' whim. Call it Louisiana *omakase*. You might get dreamy crawfish beignets in brown beurre, or maybe a cast-iron-bronzed Louisiana swordfish with a shocking drizzle of jalapeño hollandaise. It's good. It's fun. It's good fun. Skip dessert. Not wine.

337 Dauphine. ✆ **504/525-3335.** www.louisianabistro.net. Entrees $22–$34; "Feed Me" tasting menu, 3 courses $39, 5 courses $59. Wed–Sun 6–10pm.

Meauxbar Bistro ★★★ BISTRO/FRENCH   Locals know that the checkerboard floors and honey-hued walls in this sweet, sophisticated upper Quarter bistro make it an easy spot for relaxing over a few bottles of well-chosen Cote du Rhône and the evening's special. Meauxbar leans toward traditional French fare, with the occasional unexpected flavor creeping in (a la the ginger-perfumed seabass in parchment). But you can't go wrong with the classic steak frites au poivre or frog legs Provençal. Like any good French bistro, Meauxbar's soups also stand out—like chilled asparagus with crabmeat in summer or soul-warming l'onion in summer. To close, just say oui to the tarte tartin.

942 N. Rampart St. ✆ **504/569-9979.** www.meauxbar.com. Reservations suggested. Main courses $18–$29. Tues–Sat 6–10pm.

Mr. B's Bistro ★★ CONTEMPORARY CREOLE   The "B is for Butter" BBQ shrimp is the claim to fame here, and that's what you should get. Not that anything else is bad, but the plump, peppery house special is the standout and indeed the distinguishing feature here. In fact, we'll take a seat at the bar and place an order right now, please. The hunt-club motif draws a businessmen's lunch crowd for the strong drinks and attentive service.

201 Royal St. ✆ **504/523-2078.** www.mrbsbistro.com. No shorts or tank tops; business casual. Main courses $14–$23 lunch, $26–$38 dinner; jazz brunch entrees $19–$35. Mon–Sat 11:30am–2pm; bar menu 2–5:30pm; dinner 5:30–9pm; Sun jazz brunch 10:30am–2pm.

Muriel's ★ CONTEMPORARY CREOLE   The dreaded "fine." That's how we feel about perennially popular Muriel's. We want to fall in love with, or at least in, their romantic, red-walled dining rooms, and pose on the elegant balconies overlooking Jackson Square. We want to *ooh* over the crawfish and goat-cheese crêpes, like others seem to do. But there's just nothing especially inspired or inspiring here, on the plate or working the floor. So we opt for the safety of the pan-roasted half-chicken or the three-course table d'hôte menu (value priced at $30). We visit the ghost's table, have our palms read in Jackson Square, and the night is still a good one. Lunch here is a waste of atmosphere. Reserve well in advance during peak periods.

801 Chartres St. (at St. Ann). ✆ **504/568-1885.** www.muriels.com. Main courses $11–$19 lunch, $16–$21 brunch, $17–$35 dinner. Mon–Sat 11:30am–2:30pm; Sun jazz brunch 11am–2pm; Mon–Fri 5:30–10pm; Sat–Sun 5–10pm.

Tableau ★★ CLASSIC CREOLE   The pristine white space betrays the fact that Tableau, with its soaring staircase and impressive, high-arched entries, is brand new. And it's a local hero, for having financially rescued its famous neighbor, Le Petit Theatre (see p. 183). Its other notable neighbor is Jackson Square, which the second-floor balcony overlooks—scoring a spot on the list of New Orleans's most scenic dining spots. We relish an afternoon here with a well-balanced classic cocktail, slices of the addictive, tart bread, and a "Grand Royal" quartet of seafood starters—including sublime bacon-wrapped, rosemary-skewered oysters. Or, in cooler climes, we'll opt for a hearty red and the heartier, hopped-up onion soup. The airy main dining room looks onto the gleaming open kitchen and brick courtyard; the genteel upstairs room features gold-flocked, vaulted ceilings. Like the cuisine, the overall Tableau experience is classic New Orleans, tuned up—not to racing speed, but enough to honor gastronomy in 1880 as well as 2013. Things we like: servings in full or demi portions, aiding those who want less *and* those who want more. Chicken Tableau's juicy dark and white portions in a rich Bearnaise sauce. Time-honored poached-egg dishes on the dinner menu. Rare tournedos of steak, with a buttery red-wine reduction and a seared foie-gras souvenir. The logo-branded crème brûlée, served in a shallow, wide bowl (as at other Brennan's restaurants), masterfully maximizing the crispy-crust-to-silken-custard ratio. Service is still ramping up and needs a little smoothing out. But Tableau is just a baby grand. Welcome (back) to the neighborhood.

675 St. Peter St. ℘ **504/934-3463.** www.tableaufrenchquarter.com. Dinner main courses $18–$42. Mon–Thurs 11:30am–10pm; Fri–Sat 11:30am–11pm; Sun 10am–10pm. Brunch Sat & Sun.

Tujague's ★ CLASSIC CREOLE   Spared the wrecking ball in 2013 (it almost succumbed a T-shirt-shop takeover), this 1856 landmark is more precious than ever. Its perfect Sazerac and anti-nouvelle, fork-tender brisket are blessings to be cherished. The threat of closure also kickstarted some needed changes to the menu and decor (style-wise, you'd never know from looking; it's just fresher). There's an a la carte menu now, but being traditionalists, we still say opt for the six-course prix-fixe menu with a choice of entrées. Choose the veal chop or the soft-shell crab meunière when in season, or go off-menu for the baked garlic chicken Bonne Femme. It's solid, authentic Creole cooking, from the sinus-clearing shrimp rémoulade appetizer to the last bread pudding bite, and while the experience is priceless, the menu prices are more than right. Do visit their famous **bar** (p. 179) before or after dinner. Reserve in advance during peak periods.

823 Decatur St. ℘ **504/525-8676.** www.tujagues.com. 6-course dinner $36–$45. Daily 5pm–closing; Sat–Sun 11am–3pm.

Moderate

Café Amelie ★★ CONTEMPORARY SOUTHERN   The pretty-as-a-chocolate-box courtyard and fresh, straightforward local cuisine are Amelie's calling cards. Amelie's serves cafe standards with something for everyone to enjoy, like crab cakes or a goat cheese and beet salad, and local faves like *a cochon de lait* pork sandwich or grilled catfish with a kick. It's an awfully nice, relaxing spot, calling loudly for a lemonade or mint julep, which might even entice the ladies (and men) who lunch to indulge in a slice of lemon doberge cake. We concur with that decision. (All that lovely old slate, brick, and greenery make this a popular wedding spot; they're frequently closed for events). Reserve in advance for Sunday brunch.

912 Royal St. ℘ **504/412-8965.** www.cafeamelie.com. Main courses $13–$29, brunch $10–$15. Wed–Sat 11am–9pm; Sun 6–8pm; Sat & Sun brunch 11am–3pm. Closed occasionally for special events; call ahead to check.

EAT new orleans ★★ CONTEMPORARY CREOLE/LIGHT FARE   This charming bi-level corner spot in a tucked-away French Quarter section attracts plenty of locals. The chatty, efficient servers will make you feel like one of them. Trust them when they suggest the hearty, down-to-earth chicken and dumplings or the surf-and-turf stuffed red pepper. At brunch, eggs Dumaine are just what the hangover ordered.

Note: Proximity to a nearby school means no liquor license, but they will gladly serve whatever you bring from nearby **Matassa's** (1001 Dauphine St.).

900 Dumaine St. ℰ **504/522-7222.** http://eatnola.com. Lunch $11–$18; dinner $12–$24. Lunch Tues–Fri 11am–2pm. Dinner Tues–Sat 5:30–10pm. Brunch Sat–Sun 9am–2pm.

Green Goddess ★★ INTERNATIONAL   The masses of international attention and praise heaped upon Green Goddess when it opened in 2009 were well-deserved. People waited hours for the few alleyway tables, to taste the groundbreaking, "globe-trotting cuisine" and cocktails inspired by Spanish, Indian, Hawaiian, and Middle Eastern cuisines (for starters). Five years hence, one of the original chefs is gone (the partner remains), the seating has quadrupled, and there's even an indoor dining room. The Bohemia-in-a-bowl concept (tamped down a bit) remains, including a few of the original recipes. The service, never stellar, hasn't changed. It's no longer groundbreaking or even great, but it's a good choice for a taste of the unusual, the offbeat atmosphere, and a vegetarian-friendly menu. Top choices include the shrimp-and-pork-belly banh mi; the Cuban sandwich with collard greens (better than it sounds); and Father Pat's grilled cheese, made with Guinness and pear butter. Skip the over-lauded bacon sundae and get the sultan's nest. In fact, if you've just come for that dessert and the still-superb cocktails, you'll be in good stead. Reservations not accepted.

307 Exchange Place. ℰ **504/301-3347.** Main courses $7–$16. Wed–Sun 11am–9pm.

Jimmy Buffett's Margaritaville ★ LIGHT FARE   The focus here is on margaritas and cheeseburgers, naturally, and merchandise (is it a gift store with a cafe or vice versa?). But it's parrothead heaven, there's usually some benign, "trop rock" band playing predictable singalong tunes in the tavern (is that an actual genre?), and the upstairs balcony is good spot for Decatur Street people-watching, come Monday or any other day.

1104 Decatur St. ℰ **504/592-2565.** www.margaritavilleneworleans.com. Daily 11am–10pm.

Port of Call ★★ HAMBURGERS   For a decade or two before the great gourmet burger tsunami of 2012 overtook New Orleans, Port of Call was putting out a product that drew hordes. Still does. This is not a burger for teeny-patty people. It's a dripping, half-pound monster, served with a loaded baked potato. You're probably going to wait a while for it (get the fruity signature Monsoon cocktail to bide the time), and you probably won't even be able to see it inside the dark den of a dining room. They have steaks, but they're irrelevant. Sometimes you just need a good burger. No reservations.

838 Esplanade Ave. ℰ **504/523-0120.** http://portofcallnola.com. Main courses $10–$27. Sun–Thurs 11am–midnight; Fri–Sat 11am–1am.

Sylvain ★★★ BISTRO   Little-known fact: Until recently, the French Quarter was a cool-restaurant desert. Sylvain changed that. With its side-alley entrance, speckled flooring reclaimed from an old church, and Civil-War-meets-Soho vibe, it's almost hip overkill. It even has a resident ghost (with a literary backstory, no less) and requisite craft cocktails. But dang if the service isn't downright friendly and the food straight-up delicious. For the ultimate gastropub, it's shockingly unpretentious. Thus it's often packed to the gills . . . ergo waits, noise, and service slowdowns. No place is perfect. But the absurdly tender beef cheeks are, and the lightly dressed shaved-apple and Brussels sprout salad is awfully close. Both bruschettas are worthy: the lush chicken

BACK-ROOM bites

Long before there were pop-up restaurants, there were back-room deli counters in unassuming corner stores. It's how a lot of French Quarter residents still eat, because it's fast, cheap, diverse, available 'round the clock, and often surprisingly good. Take it out or have it delivered, and be sure to ask for utensils. True locals eat while leaning against a wall or seated on someone's front stoop.

○ **Quarter Grocery** (836 Burgundy St. ℂ **504/529-2702;** daily 9am–9pm). Best for: anything fried. Chicken, potatoes, catfish.

○ **QuarterMaster** (1110 Bourbon St.; ℂ **504/529-1416;** daily 24 hr.). Best choice: Basic po'boys, especially the French-fry po'boy, and greasy burgers.

○ **Verti Marte** (1201 Royal St.; ℂ **504/525-4757;** daily 24 hr.). Best choice: anything in the deli case or from the mother lode of a menu, especially the day's specials, like Grandma's Boardinghouse Meat Loaf or catfish Bienville. Salads, specialty sandwiches, and loads of veggies.

liver and the tangy goat cheese and roast beet. At brunch (and after) you'll want the fried chicken and biscuits. The menu doesn't skew light, so you might be forced to share the chocolate pot du crème. On a nice evening, the discreet back-alley tables have their own cool vibe: a quieter one.

625 Chartres St. ℂ **504/265-8123.** www.sylvainnola.com. Main courses $16–$24. Fri–Sat 11:30am–2:30pm and 5:30pm–midnight; Mon–Thurs 5:30–11pm; Sun 10:30am–2:30pm and 5:30–10pm.

Vacherie ★★ CONTEMPORARY CREOLE What a surprising little find. They've clearly taken some care with both the food and the look of the small, attractive room at this 2013 newbie. Ask about the stunning pastoral oil painting and the intriguing sepia-toned photographs, and their connection to the philosophy of Vacherie's Cajun Louisiana–driven cooking. For breakfast, try the Andouille hash or some fried keques with cane syrup (they also poach eggs perfectly); at dinner, have some yam chips and the boudin-stuffed fried hen with greens—a delicious, rustic surprise. You don't need to cross town for it, but if you're in the neighborhood of the Hotel St. Marie, Vacherie is huge step up from your average hotel dining room.

827 Toulouse St. ℂ **504/207-4532.** www.vacherierestaurant.com. Breakfast $8–$17; dinner entrees $13–$30. Breakfast Mon–Fri 7am–2pm; brunch Sat–Sun 7am–2pm; dinner Mon–Sat 6pm–10pm (closed for lunch).

Inexpensive

Acme Oyster House ★★★ SEAFOOD/LIGHT FARE Is it worth the wait, you ask? They're Gulf oysters, people, and this is the oldest oyster bar in the French Quarter. In other words, yes (unless you're famished—then just go across the street to Felix's). The oysters are tastiest when you're standing at the bar, talking tourist trash with the shucker, piling up shells that they tally when you're done, knocking back some oyster shooters (chilled vodka, cocktail sauce, erster, gullet). But if you sit at a checked-cloth-covered table, you can also order a dozen or two of the garlicky char-broiled oysters, which may change your life. There are po'boys and other Creole stand-bys (jambalaya, gumbo, red beans and sausage, etc.), good enough for those who do not partake of the pearlmaker. It's boisterous and there's much scurrying about of waiters, so things do move fast once you're inside. No reservations.

724 Iberville St. ☏ **504/522-5973.** www.acmeoyster.com. Oysters $14 per dozen raw or $19 charbroiled; po' boys $8–$17; entrees $9–$24. Sun–Thurs 11am–10pm; Fri–Sat 11am–11pm.

Café Beignet ★ CAFE/BAKERY Some swear the beignets here are better than those at Café du Monde, and we can attest that they're usually fresh out of the deep fryer, but we're true to the CdM for just the right chewiness and puffiness of its beignets. Still, you won't find lines here, and it also serves waffles, brioche French toast, gumbo, and simple sandwiches and salads. Both locations have nice patios; there's live jazz Thursday through Sunday afternoons and evenings at the Bourbon Street location.

334B Royal St. ☏ **504/524-5530.** www.cafebeignet.com. Most items under $10. Daily 7am–5pm. Also at 311 Bourbon St. ☏ **504/525-2611.** Mon–Wed 8am–3pm; Thurs & Sun 8am–10pm; Fri–Sat 8am–midnight.

Café Maspero ★ CAFE/SEAFOOD/LIGHT FARE Why is it always so crowded here? We'll give you five good reasons: It's got a big menu, it's inexpensive, the food is decent, the portions are large, and you can watch the Decatur action go by. It may not merit a Facebook posting, but it's easy enough to duck in here for a burger, club sandwich, or a muffuletta (regular or veggie).

601 Decatur St. ☏ **504/523-6250.** Main courses $4–$14. No credit cards. Sun–Thurs 11am–10pm; Fri–Sat 11am–11pm.

Camellia Grill ★★★ DINER/LIGHT FARE The French Quarter branch is a near-perfect replica (in style, service, and menu) of the original Uptown diner. See on p. 109.

540 Chartres St. ☏ **504/522-1800.** www.camelliagrill.net. All entrees under $10. Sun–Thurs 8am–midnight; Fri–Sat 8am–2am.

Clover Grill ★ DINER The burger here is just a frozen patty thrown on the grill, but it's cooked under a hubcap (the better to seal in the juices), available at 4am, and served by a sassy queen in a "Clever Girl" T-shirt, making it so very worthwhile. Basic egg breakfasts and standard diner fare are also available. Bonus points for: excellent '80s jukebox; Formica counter and red vinyl stools you can spin around on; pie. But mostly for aforementioned sass, which they have in spades here, 24/7.

900 Bourbon St. ☏ **504/598-1010.** www.clovergrill.com. All items under $8. Daily 24 hr.

Coop's ★ CREOLE/LIGHT FARE This divey, locals-only hangout has long since been discovered by tourists too, which may mean a sometimes unjustifiably long wait: It's good, but not OMG so awesome. Except for the well-known rabbit and sausage jambalaya, and the fried chicken, both of which really are pretty awesome. Decent food, friendly prices, late hours, and a menu that covers all the bases make this a good fallback if the line isn't crazy prohibitive.

1109 Decatur St. ☏ **504/525-9053.** www.coopsplace.net. Entrees $8–$18. Daily 11am–close (usually at least 10pm; later on weekends).

Felix's Restaurant & Oyster Bar ★★ SEAFOOD/CREOLE Seventy-year-old Felix's got new owners and a thorough, much-needed housecleaning in 2013, and we're happy to say they left most everything else alone. Like Acme, its across-the-street friendly rival, it's just a down-home, nuthin'-fancy oyster bar, but the dozens come out fresh and bitterly chilled, needing nothing more than a squeeze of lemon. You can also have them in stews, soups, pastas, or omelets broiled, fried, or baked. And if it's crawfish season, order up a spicy pile. It's not nearly as much of a scene as Acme (a big plus), and the shuckers have fast hands and quick wit.

739 Iberville St. ✆ **504/522-4440.** www.felixs.com. Dozen raw oysters $13; po'boys under $15; other main courses $11–$20. Sun–Thurs 11am–10pm; Fri–Sat 11am–11pm.

Johnny's Po-Boys ★ LIGHT FARE   Johnny's is the standard-bearer for po'boys in the French Quarter—in fact it's the only proper po'boy shop in the area. Little known insider fact: It's also a good, cheap, quick breakfast spot. Other little known fact: They deliver to French Quarter hotels. They'll put almost anything on that crunchy, fluffy Leidenheimer bread, but they're best known for their roast beef po'boy. We have a soft spot for the fried pork chop po'boy, just 'cause it's hard to find one elsewhere. The line moves fast; don't be discouraged.

511 St. Louis St. ✆ **504/524-8129.** www.johnnyspoboys.com. Most items under $10; specials may be more. No credit cards. Daily 8am–4:30pm.

Mr. Gregory's ★★★ CAFE/BAKERY/LIGHT FARE   Bienvenue! A welcome 2013 addition to the upper Quarter, Mr. Gregory's brings much-needed coffee, breakfast, and lunch options to this area. Pastries are baked on-site, including the elusive proper croissant. Soups, salads, quiches, and *croque* sandwiches (with gruyére! and house-cured tuna!) round out the lunch menu. There's simple goodness here. Best of all? You can get brewed-to-order French-press coffee for $2.50.

806 N. Rampart St. ✆ **504/407-3780.** www.mistergregorys.com. Everything under $8. Mon–Sun 10am–6pm.

The Old Coffee Pot ★ LIGHT FARE   Known for being one of the few places that serve calas, sweetened fried rice cakes that date to the mid-1800s. The egg dishes are okay, but it's the calas you want (and we can't recommend lunch or dinner entrees). The high-ceilinged room and outdoor courtyard will immerse you in the French Quarter aura, and the service is full of hons and dahlins, though no one's moving too fast.

714 St. Peter St. ✆ **504/524-3500.** www.theoldcoffeepot.com. Breakfast $9–$13. Mon, Thurs, Sun 8am–10:30pm; Tues–Wed 8am–2:30pm; 5:30–10:30pm; Fri–Sat 8–11:30am.

Somethin' Else Café ★★ CAFE/LIGHT FARE   This is an above-average sidewalk cafe with indoor and outdoor seating, and some well-done nods to local cuisine. It's also a good stop for salads—not that easy to find in these parts—and you can design your own here (or just get the mighty good Popeye, with avocado, crab and grilled shrimp). But enough about healthy things—let's talk carbs. Biscuits of unusual size, specifically. Large, homemade and served with pulled pork, or boudin balls, which you should get with a side of sweet potato hash. House-ground burgers and oddly textured but tasty shrimp burgers come on fluffy egg buns—good even if they don't hold up well. It's often a wait on weekend mornings, and service isn't exactly speedy. Open late weekend nights, usually till 2ish.

620 Conti St. ✆ **504/373-6439.** www.somethinelsecafe.com. Omelets, burgers, sandwiches $6–$14. Sun–Wed 7am–10pm; Thurs 7am–midnight; Fri–Sat 7am–3am.

Stanley ★★ AMERICAN   It's cute and convenient (right on the corner of Jackson Square) and serves well-prepared, "regular" food that kids and grown-ups will like (pancakes, good burgers, and an old-fashioned soda fountain serving homemade ice

WHOLE LOTTA muffuletta GOIN' ON

Muffulettas are sandwiches of (pardon the expression) heroic proportions, enormous concoctions of round Italian bread, Italian cold cuts and cheeses, and olive salad. One person cannot (or should not) eat a whole one—at least not in one sitting. A half makes a good meal; a quarter is a filling snack. They may not sound like much on paper, but once you try one, you'll be hooked. Vegetarians swear they're delicious done meatless.

Several places in town claim to have invented the muffuletta and also claim to make the best one. You decide: Comparison-shopping can be a rewarding pastime.

The lunchtime line can be daunting but moves fast at world-famous **Central Grocery** ★★★, 923 Decatur St. (© **504/523-1620**). There are a few seats at the back of this crowded, garlic-scented Italian grocery, or you can order to go. Best of all, they ship, so you can satisfy your craving or throw an envy-inducing party. Eat it across the street on the banks of the Mississippi for an inexpensive, romantic meal (about $14 for a whole). The staff at Central Grocery makes up their sandwiches early in the day, so they're ready for the rush. Don't worry about freshness; it actually helps when the olive flavors soak through the layers.

Are the heated muffulettas at **Napoleon House** ★ (p. 179) better or blasphemy? It's a different taste sensation, and a heated debate. Feeling experimental? Drive to **Nor-Joe's Importing Co.** ★★, 505 Friscoe, in Metairie (© **504/833-9240**), where the ginormous, outstanding muffulettas, constructed with iconoclastic ingredients like prosciutto and mortadella, have their own cult following. Then there's **Cochon Butcher** ★★★ (p. 101), whose house-cured meats form the basis of what may be our new favorite 'letta.

cream). So naturally it's popular as all get-out; try to go during off-peak hours. Their take-out shop next door has coffee, ice cream, and ready-made sandwiches to go, which is awfully convenient. But if you choose the sit-down restaurant, the cornmeal-crusted oyster po'boy is a good way to go. For breakfast (served all day), those oysters come Benedict style, with poached eggs and hollandaise. Yum.

547 St. Ann St. (corner of Jackson Sq. and St. Ann). © **504/587-0093.** www.stanleyrestaurant.com. Everything under $15. Daily 7am–10pm.

THE FAUBOURG MARIGNY & BYWATER

For the restaurants in this section, see the "French Quarter Restaurants" map on p. 79.

Moderate

Bacchanal ★★★ INTERNATIONAL   It's a broken-down, ramshackle old building. It's a wine store. It's a bar. It's a jazz club. And now, it's an actual restaurant. Sorta. Whatever it is, it epitomizes New Orleans, and it's one of our favorite spots anywhere. The unusual, European-leaning wine selection and funky, twinkle-lit outdoor garden with the corner jazz combo attracts locals kicking back in plastic chairs, steampunk wine snobs deep in discussion, maybe a smattering of out-of-towners enlightening to the "real" New Orleans . . . all tantalized by the ambience and Spanish-inspired small plates. You order at a window and grab your own utensils, and a starter of grilled corn with cotija cheese, crema, and spices (or pork rillettes with mustard sauce and figs) shows up. After the 2013 conversion of an attic to an actual dining room, it's accessible even on rainy days, but ahh, that garden. Never boring, frequently tasty, perpetually affordable—it all seems thrown together, but it melds into something much greater than the sum of its parts.

600 Poland Ave. ⓒ **504/948-9111.** www.bacchanalwine.com. Tapas & small plates $6–$16. Daily 11am–midnight; kitchen closes at 11pm Sun–Mon.

Elizabeth's ★★★ CREOLE   It's rightly famous for its brown-sugar-coated praline bacon (they were driving the bacon truck long before the bandwagon hooked on), but the rest of the menu is pretty great too. Thusly, be warned: Breakfast is often crowded, with waits on weekend. But it's worth it. You just don't see a chicken-liver omelet too often, so get it (add onions and a side of creamy grits), unless you get the indulgent bananas Foster *pain perdu*. Or both—we don't judge. We're working our way through the dinner menu since they expanded a few years back, but so far we're stuck at their osso bucco with grit cakes. Dessert? More praline bacon, of course.

601 Gallier St. ⓒ **504/944-9272.** www.elizabethsrestaurantnola.com. Breakfast and lunch everything under $15; dinner $11–$22, specials higher. Mon–Sun 8am–2:30pm; Mon–Sat 6–10pm.

The Joint ★★★ BARBECUE   When you think of barbecue, you might think Memphis, St. Louis, Texas . . . now think Bywater. When that smoked-meat hankering hits, the Joint stands up to the best of them. Its newish (2012) location is less joint-like and more modern roadhouse than their old one. Picnic tables inside and out are a fitting complement to the luscious baby-backs and smoldering brisket. For something truly local, try the Cajun sausage, made around these parts. The sides are fine, but save room for the peanut butter pie.

701 Mazant St. ⓒ **504/949-3232.** www.alwayssmokin.com. Main courses $7–$27. Mon–Sat 11:30am–10pm.

Maurepas Foods ★★★ MODERN SOUTHERN   These Bywater brainiacs are having fun with food and drink, and you're the beneficiary. Creative, affordable combinations on the plate and in the glass make for a line out the door. We actually like fashioning a meal of the sides here; the veggies are spot-on. Add a Swan Song (vodka lemongrass cocktail) and a fruity panna cotta, and call it a day. Unless you get the signature chicken leg with grits and a poached egg—for the quality, it's one of the best deals around at $12. No reservations.

3200 Burgundy St. ⓒ **504/267-0072.** www.maurepasfoods.com. Main courses $8–$16. Thurs–Tues 11am–midnight. Closed Wed.

Praline Connection ★ CREOLE/SOUL FOOD   The servers in their cute hats and skinny ties are undeniably adorable, but the food and service aren't as adorable as they used to be. The fried chicken is still dependably juicy, though, and our top choice, with some fried pickles. The rest of the menu is only okay, too much something (sweet, in the yams), not enough of something else (flavor, in the greens). But we've had good luck with the nightly specials; they seem to get a more care, and it's conveniently Frenchmen Street close.

542 Frenchmen St. ⓒ **504/943-3934.** www.pralineconnection.com. Main courses $12–$24. Mon–Sat 11am–10pm; Sun 11am–9pm.

Yuki Izakaya ★ ASIAN   You could easily miss this nook in the midst of the Frenchmen frenzy, but don't. Yuki Yamaguchi's a-traditional Japanese *izakaya* (neighborhood pub/noshery) offers an impressive array of imported sakes, beer, *shochu,* and Japanese bar snacks—many from family recipes. We go for octopus *shumai* dumplings, the carbo-reloading udon soup, crispy, lemony beef tongue, and karaage fried chicken. It's tiny and hip and sometimes smells of fish (there's some sashimi, but it's not a sushi house), which we put up with because it screens vintage Japanese films above the bar while accordionist **Norbert Slama** plays mournful Piaf tunes on the accordion (sometimes with guitarist **Raphael Bas**). This earns our love.

525 Frenchmen St. ✆ **504/943-1122.** Small plates $4–$15. Mon–Thurs 6–11:30pm; Fri–Sat 6pm–2am (or later); Sun 6–10:30pm.

Inexpensive

Cake Café & Bakery ★ LIGHT FARE/DESSERT   About a 10-minute walk from Esplanade is this humble but yummy spot—a bakery and then some. House-baked pastries, bagels and biscuits are on top, and of course delectable cupcakes in standard and exotic flavors (Sazerac!). It serves fine omelettes and a simple poached salmon salad, and it's worth the walk just for the crab, brie, spinach, and bacon sandwich (and you'll need the walk back). Best buck you'll spend today: dollar cupcake with lunch.

2440 Chartres St. ✆ **504/943-0010.** www.nolacakes.com. Everything under $11. Daily 7am–3pm.

Gene's Po'Boys ★★ LIGHT FARE   Just outside the tourist zone is a serious po'boy for people who are serious about po'boys: Gene's homemade hot sausage patty with American cheese. (And we mean hot—the building is Pepto-pink for a reason.) No chips, no dessert, no atmosphere, comes with a soda, open 24 hours. That's all she wrote and all you need to know. Caution: If you love it like we do, you might be nearing a down payment.

1040 Elysian Fields Ave. ✆ **504/943-3861.** Everything under $10. Cash only. Daily 24 hr.

McHardy's Chicken and Fixins ★★ SOUL FOOD   Popeye's will do when we're far from New Orleans, but if we're in town it's gotta be family-owned McHardy's for take-out fried chicken. It's moist, tender, slightly crispy-skinned, perfectly seasoned, and cheap. Stellar. We never have a party without it, and we often *make* a party *just* to have it. The other "fixins" are fine, but the bird is the word here. Cheap, hot to-go breakfasts, too.

1458 N. Broad St. ✆ **504/949-0000.** www.facebook.com/pages/McHardys-Chicken-Fixin/176427879083461. $5 and up. Mon–Thurs 11am–6:30pm; Fri–Sat 11am–7:30pm; Sun 11am–3pm. Breakfast Mon–Fri 6:30–9:30am.

MID-CITY/ESPLANADE

For the restaurants in this section, see the "French Quarter Restaurants" map on p. 79.

Expensive

Ralph's on the Park ★★★ BISTRO   Huge picture windows look out on Spanish moss–draped oaks in City Park. Music from Joe Krown's stylish stride piano seeps from the lounge and across the cream-upholstered dining room. You're sipping a French 75, eagerly anticipating the turtle soup and prosciutto-wrapped, seared scallops you've just ordered, gazing out upon the setting sun, the glistening rain, or into your sweetheart's baby blues. Whatevs—it's dreamy here. The fare, if not dreamy, is quite good—straightforward continental with a pinch of Creole. Desserts are playful and crowd-pleasing (just say chocolate crème brûlée). The whole experience is the epitome of Southern elegance—a vacation within a vacation (the daylight view is best, whether brunch, lunch, or early supper), and it's easily reachable by cab or the City Park street-car. Check the website for terrific multi-course specials (especially for lunch), and allow time to hear Mr. Krown at happy hour or brunch. Reserve well in advance for brunch.

900 City Park Ave. ℂ **504/488-1000.** www.ralphsonthepark.com. Main courses $12–$22 lunch, $21–$42 dinner, $15–$23 brunch. Daily 5:30–9pm; Tues–Fri 11:30am–2pm; Sun 10:30am–2pm.

Moderate

Café Degas ★★★ BISTRO/FRENCH   Every neighborhood in every city should have a charming, casual French bistro that serves a perfect salad Niçoise and has a tree growing in the middle of the indoor/outdoor dining room. But only Faubourg St. John has it. It's darling, perfectly suited to a romantic dinner or a gals' lunch. Traditional favorites like escargot, hanger steak, and rack of lamb are straightforward, flavorful, and generous; a delicate roast quail starter was tempting to double as an entrée. It's a popular spot, particularly for brunch, so reserve ahead. Check www.restaurant.com and the cafe website for coupons. Make reservations well in advance during peak periods.

3127 Esplanade Ave. ℂ **504/945-5635.** www.cafedegas.com. Main courses lunch/brunch $11–$17, dinner $18–$30. Wed–Sat 11am–3pm; Wed–Sat 6–10pm; Sun 6–9:30pm; Sun 10:30am–3pm.

Dooky Chase ★ SOUL FOOD/CREOLE   First, the important Dooky trivia: Ray Charles (among other musicians) hung out here after shows here and wrote "Early in the Morning" about it. Leah Chase, the nonagenarian chef and Dooky's wife, was the model for Tiana in Disney's delightful film *The Princess and the Frog* (the "Queen of Creole Cuisine" has also won just about every culinary award in existence). In the '60s, Dooky Chase was an important meeting place for civil rights leaders. Dooky and Leah are still important civic figures. After Hurricane Katrina, the couple lived in a FEMA trailer across the street for 2 years while they were rebuilding the restaurant. Oh, and Presidents Obama and Bush I both dined at Dooky's (not together). Today it's not quite what it was in the glory days, but us lesser folk can partake of the weekday lunch buffet with traditional Creole standards in the art-filled dining room. A better choice is the Friday dinner, because the fried chicken here is a serious contender for the city's best. It certainly gives Willie Mae's (p. 96), its much-touted neighbor, a run for the title. Come for the hallowed history; stay for the fried chicken.

2301 Orleans Ave. ℂ **504/821-0600.** www.dookychaserestaurant.com. Main courses $9–$20. Tues–Fri 11am–3pm dine-in or take-out. Fri 5–9pm.

Liuzza's ★★ CREOLE/ITALIAN   Actual Liuzza's moment: Crusty waitress hands customer a menu ("Here you go, Bay-bee"), then abruptly closes it. "Bay-bee," she instructs, gesticulating with intent, "Numba One, or Numba Two—but *definitely* Numba One." Naturally, the Number One special was ordered (a seafood lasagna, drip-ping with a white cream sauce) and promptly devoured, in all its enormity. If you've been wondering what Creole Italian is all about, come here. This is a true, humble neighborhood institution, and we're pretty sure that the same regulars that were there before it took on 8 feet of Katrina waters are still going. So when the waitress talks, you betta listen. There's nothing subtle about the hearty, saucy comfort food and po'boys; it's solid and rib-sticking. Do get a massive frosted mug of Abita Amber and the famous deep-fried dill pickles. "You people will batter and deep-fry anything that isn't nailed down!" said yet another astonished visitor. Good times.

3636 Bienville St. (C) **504/482-9120.** www.liuzzas.com. Main courses $10–$20. No credit cards. Sun–Mon 11am–4pm; Tues–Sat 11am–10pm.

Lola's ★★ INTERNATIONAL/SPANISH   For something completely different and very local (that feels very European), try Spanish fare at teeny Lola's. Start with the garlic soup (one of several good vegetarian options; another is refreshing gazpacho). Then get paella—we prefer the mussel-loaded combination. If there's a wait, relax with a carafe of red or white sangria; if there isn't, relax with a carafe of red or white sangria. Once you're seated, service is prompt, though paellas are cooked to order. Close with the silky homemade flan.

3312 Esplanade Ave. (C) **504/488-6946.** www.lolasneworleans.com. Main courses $16–$28. Sun–Thurs 5:30–9:30pm; Fri–Sat 5:30–10:30pm.

Mandina's ★★ CREOLE/ITALIAN   Dis is da ultimate neighbahood N'Awlins restaurant, owned by the same family since the late 1800s—and largely unchanged— as it should be. Nothing innovative here, just comfort food the way Maw Maw made it, served by someone who looks like her. If the daily specials aren't to your liking, get some butter-soaked garlic bread to share and the right and true seafood gumbo or turtle soup au sherry. Then go for the sweet Italian sausage and spaghetti combo or red beans and rice with Italian sausage. Then again, the brown-buttery trout meunière is hard to pass up. The cocktails are strong here; so is the A/C. Bring a sweater.

3800 Canal St. (C) **504/482-9179.** www.mandinasrestaurant.com. Main courses $10–$25. No credit cards. Mon–Thurs 11am–9:30pm; Fri–Sat 11am–10pm; Sun noon–9pm.

Toup's Meatery ★★ CONTEMPORARY CAJUN   Just another neighborhood spot with killer food, mostly of the porky variety. Talking our language. As you are being seated, order some crunchy porkalicious cracklins to munch on while you're deciding what to eat. As the name implies, one should order the charcuterie plate here. Another should get the cheese plate, just to even things out. We're actually more a fan of lunch here than dinner, but we'll still eat the short ribs if they're on the oft-changing menu. And despite our red-meat-centric advice, the mussels and the sky-high chicken sandwich are both worthy. Absolutely get whatever variety of multi-layered doberge cake is available.

845 N. Carrollton Ave. (C) **504/252-4999.** www.toupsmeatery.com. Lunch $11–$20; dinner large plates $15–$28. Tues–Sat 11am–2pm and 5–9pm. Fri & Sat 11am–10pm.

Ye Olde College Inn ★★★ CREOLE/LIGHT FARE   If you're headed to Rock 'n' Bowl (p. 175), your dinner destination is next door. Even if you're not, it's a very worthy choice. It's a high-ceilinged 1930s hangout, well-renovated with an inviting bar, murals, and store signs reminiscent of ye olde New Orleans. The cuisine is more refined than that implies, in the inventive daily specials, and they take the farm-to-table commitment seriously (even walkig from the restaurant to their farm, complete with chickens). A succulent, perfectly grilled lamb loin comes topped with sun-dried tomato and shiitake mushrooms in a red-wine reduction. Even the old-school options are crafted with a deft touch. The platter-size breaded veal cutlet is so much better than the memory; the familiar bleu cheese and pecan salad is elevated with aromatic roast duck. For sheer decadence, the award-winning oyster, Havarti cheese, and bacon po'boy is hard to top; but if that's your goal, order the fried bread pudding po'boy. A tower of onion rings for the table is legally mandated. You get $5 per-person off admission to Rock 'n' Bowl (same owners)—ask your server for the deets.

3000 S. Carrollton Ave. ℰ **504/866-3683.** www.collegeinn1933.com. Main courses $12–$36. Tues–Sat 4–11pm.

Inexpensive

Lil' Dizzy's ★★ CREOLE/SOUL FOOD   This is another quintessential, family-owned, neighborhood restaurant—this time the family is from the Tremé and the menu has soul food and Creole specialties. It's lively with locals at breakfast (mostly average, the homemade hot sausages slightly above that) and for the lunch buffet. If you're a light eater it might be a bit high-priced, so come hungry and dig into the terrific fried chicken, okay gumbo and red beans, and a few other items (also come early, they do run out). Better yet, order a la carte—the aforementioned chicken or our favorite, the standout trout Baquet: fish topped with garlic-butter sauce and sometimes fresh crabmeat.

1500 Esplanade Ave. ℰ **504/569-8997.** Lunch buffet $16 ($7 kids under 9); a la carte lunch items under $12; Sun brunch buffet $18; dinner entrees under $22. Lunch daily 8am–2pm; dinner Thurs–Sat 4–8pm; Sun brunch menu 9am–2pm.

Liuzza's by the Track ★★★ CREOLE/LIGHT FARE   Is it gumbo or is it heroin? Well, heroin doesn't start with a deep, rich roux, so it must be Liuzza's gumbo that we're addicted to. When we fly in from out of town, we stop here the way home, just for the gumbo fix. The BBQ-shrimp po'boy is their signature, overstuffed with peppery, butter-soaked shrimp, but we're partial to the garlic oyster sammie. When we're feeling feisty we switch to the drippy garlic-stuffed roast beef, with its pinch of horseradish in the mayo (you can get a cup of gumbo and half a po'boy, except for that BBQ shrimp). Specials can be pretty special, so check the board. The veggie-deprived should opt for the Portobello salad, and everyone here should strike up a conversation with whoever's nearby. It's that sort of place. Avoid prime weekday lunch hours if you can.

1518 N. Lopez St. ℰ **504/218-7888.** www.facebook.com/liuzzas. Everything under $17. Mon–Sat 11am–7pm.

Parkway Bakery and Tavern ★★★ LIGHT FARE   It's hard to believe that this corner shop began life as a bakery more than 100 years ago. Or that it was shuttered for years in between then and now. Or that it was essentially under water after Katrina. Now, after getting love from umpteen magazines and travel- and food-channel shows and a visit from the Obama family, people literally come by the busload. Try to sit inside or on the original deck, which have more charm than the massive outside picnic area, thrown up to accommodate their popularity. But don't be put off—all that matters is that the po'boys still hold up terrifically. Claims to fame are the fried shrimp and juicy roast beef—our favorite in the city, even if (maybe because) it's among the sloppiest. We're fond of the Reuben or lighter caprese, too. The homemade potato salad is killer, and the banana pudding is old skool. We round it all out with a bottled Barq's and a stroll along nearby Bayou St. John. They promise that after the 2014 kitchen expansion, oysters will be back on the menu full time (Mon only till then—but now available with bacon!). The line can be daunting but moves pretty fast (more so with a beer in hand, so hit up the bar), or try for off-peak hours.

538 Hagan Ave. ✆ **504/482-3047.** www.parkwaypoorboys.com. Everything under $13. Wed–Mon 11am–10pm. Closed Tues.

Willie Mae's Scotch House ★★ SOUL FOOD   In 2004, this was a humble chicken shack in a not great neighborhood, known to locals, the budding foodie community, and a few enterprising tourists. In 2005, octogenarian Willie Mae and her secret-recipe fried chicken were designated "American classics" by the James Beard Foundation, and the world came knocking. Weeks later, her home and restaurant were 8 feet under water. The remarkable, volunteer-driven recovery began quickly, with hands-on support from local restaurateurs—a testament to New Orleans' food community. Nowadays, with the matriarch's family helming the fryers, the chicken is still beautifully spiced and crisped—on a good day. Which is much more common than a bad (dry overcooked) day, but we've had them. For safety, we also order the fried pork chops and catfish, and we always get the creamy butterbeans (which don't get near the attention the chicken does, but should). Plan for a wait—first in line, then for the fried-to-order bird. Cab recommended.

2401 St. Ann St. ✆ **504/822-9503.** Everything under $15. Mon–Sat 11am–5pm.

CENTRAL BUSINESS DISTRICT & WAREHOUSE DISTRICT

For the restaurants in this section, see the "French Quarter Restaurants" map on p. 79.

Very Expensive

Emeril's ★★★ CREOLE/NEW AMERICAN   Yes, Emeril heads an empire, but he's wisely seen to it that his flagship, namesake restaurant has not flagged in reverse proportion to his empire's expansion. It's still remarkably high-quality (and high-priced), interesting, and exciting dining. The wine list is intelligent and broad; service is professional and helpful. The room is buoyant with energy, the noise is tolerable. The plate shows clear commitment to first-rate, locally sourced ingredients: A salad of local tomatoes and melon is dotted with tiny, crispy duck hearts, a wisp of herb in the vinaigrette.

The menu builds on tradition in small but significant ways. Grilled pork chops, done perfectly despite their girth, are artfully glazed with tamarind and tomatillo molé sauces. Seared scallops are bathed in garlicky, anchovy-infused bagna cauda butter, accompanied by sweet mashed yams and spicy toast points. Submit your chocolate soufflé request when you order your entrées. Then you won't have to decide what to get at dessert time, because you should also get the banana cream pie (it has its own Facebook page, or at least should). As with so many other fine New Orleans restaurants, the bargain three-course lunch is a serious steal ($22.50 here). It's also one of many places

> **Impressions**
>
> *New Orleans is one place you can eat and drink the most, and suffer the least.*
> —William Makepeace Thackeray

where the open-kitchen bar seating is perfect for single diners (or anyone). Reserve well in advance.

800 Tchoupitoulas St. ℂ **504/528-9393.** www.emerils.com. 3-course lunch $23; main courses $15–$18 lunch, $25–$44 dinner; degustation by advance arrangement. Daily 6–10pm; Mon–Fri 11:30am–2pm.

Restaurant August ★★★ CONTEMPORARY SOUTHERN/FRENCH   If you live under a rock (aka, don't watch cable TV), you may not know about Chef John Besh's meteoric rise in culinary circles. But he's not just about blue eyes and back-lighting: His local-boy-made-good routine is real. He's won a James Beard Best Chef award, and all of his New Orleans area restaurants (8 at last count) range from very good to excellent. August, his fine dining flagship, is a marvel of Creole and Cajun creativity. It is a rare mishit here, when a boundary-pushing dish goes one ingredient over the limit, say, or a molecular gimmick interferes rather than enhances. On the whole your experience will be memorable—decorous, cultured, and stunningly plated—and mostly spectacular.

These are masters of foie gras. It's unfailingly off the charts, done "Three Ways" or in any incarnation. The sweet, tart pork belly with peach mustard met the palate with a quick crunch before introducing a velvet mouthfeel: divine. In braised short ribs, days of simmering produce a soaring orchestra of flavors: apples, wine, root vegetables, and tender, beefy sweetness; it's a triumph of earthy richness. But a calabaza squash ravioli was overpowered by its oxtail and bone marrow brew. The sweets themselves are urbane yet slightly exotic. The deconstructed banana pudding has a following; we're more taken with a summery Meyer lemon soufflé tart. The service is professional and unhurried, whether in the sedate main dining room, where chandeliers glint off the tall windows, or in the warm, wood-paneled wine room with the clever overhead cellar. If the $$$$ prices are off-putting, the Friday prix-fixe lunch, at $20.13, makes August indisputably doable.

301 Tchoupitoulas St. ℂ**504/299-9777.** www.restaurantaugust.com. Reservations recommended. 3-course lunch $20; main courses $25–$38; 3-hr. degustation menu $97 per person, $147 with wine (whole table must participate). Daily 5:30–10pm; Fri 11am–2pm.

Expensive

Borgne ★★★ SEAFOOD   We like Borgne, the fish-focused John Besh property helmed by Chef Brian Landry, formerly of Galatoire's. We like its easy-going vibe and the well-versed servers who show up when you want them to and don't when you don't. We like most of the items we've tried here, with their interesting Spanish accents. We love that they serve a $10-plate lunch every day, especially Tuesday's ropa vieja. We like the loooong bar and the friendly service there. In fact we quite like dining in the bar, separated from the main room by a low wall that provides a bit of a sound buffer. Which brings us to the thing we like least about Borgne: The shell-crusted columns and cement floor look cool, but the expansive, slightly sterile, hard-surfaced room incites a cross-table shouting match. Shame that you can't talk about how good the soothing oyster spaghetti is, or ask your friend if she's going to eat that last duck popper—a bacon-jalapeno rillette that we're still thinking about. The server may push the Hummingbird cake on you; stick with the chocolate hazelnut puddin'. Make dinner reservations well in advance during peak periods.

601 Loyola Ave. (in the Hyatt Regency). ℂ **504/613-3860.** www.borgnerestaurant.com. Entrees $19–$30 lunch; $19–$32 dinner. Sun–Thurs 11am–10pm; Fri–Sat 11am–11pm.

Café Adelaide ★★★ CONTEMPORARY CREOLE   This undersung hotel restaurant from the Commander's Palace branch of the Brennan family borrows some of their time-tested aspects, including 25¢ martinis at lunch. They're even cheaper—as in free—if you wear a hat to Sunday brunch, and optional prix-fixe lunch and dinner menus are such good value that they're hard to pass up. The regular menu covers the people-pleaser requisites, then goes offscript with some winning, whimsical culinary curveballs—starting with the must-have shrimp-and-tasso corndog starter—sweet, spicy, and addictive. There's a wacky crab po'boy with brie cheese and babaganoush. The shrimp and creamy grits is treated with garlic and fresh herbs, and it's a winner. Their signature dessert, a white chocolate biscuit pudding, is worth whatever it does to your thighs. Adelaide also benefits greatly from being next to the splendid **Swizzle Stick** (p. 180), one of the better bars in town.

300 Poydras St. (in the Loews Hotel). ℂ **504/595-3305.** www.cafeadelaide.com. Main courses $15–$18 lunch; $22–$38 dinner. 3-course prix fixe $16 lunch; $28 brunch; $34–$38 dinner. Mon–Fri 6:30–10:30am; Sat–Sun 7am–1:30pm; Mon–Thurs 11:30am–2pm; Fri 11:30am–2:30pm; Sun–Thurs 5:30–9pm; Fri–Sat 5:30–10pm. "Off hours" menu available at bar 11:30am–10:30pm.

Herbsaint ★★★ BISTRO   Donald Link may not be a Food Channel staple like Emeril and John Besh, but he's right up there in terms of modern New Orleans restaurant royalty. His sweet, window-lined bistro, one of New Orleans's best restaurants, is usually packed and always lacks elbow room. It's uphill from there. As if to prove his mettle, the James Beard Best Southern Chef winner creates one of the city's best gumbos, including a meatless, herb-based gumbo z'herbes version that we crave. The winning signature starter of homemade spaghetti with a creamy, guanciale-spiked sauce is topped with a batter-fried poached egg (yes, you can double it as an entrée); a watermelon gazpacho with lump crab is a simple little cup of summer. For heartier fare, a slow-cooked lamb neck is astoundingly sized, equally tender, and rich with flavor and arrives on a well-paired bed of saffron fideo. Desserts here are terrific—try whatever they put in a tart shell. A bistro menu served from 1:30 to 5:30pm features light entrees from both the lunch and dinner menus. Reserve well in advance.

701 St. Charles Ave. ℂ **504/524-4114.** www.herbsaint.com. Main courses $15–$20 lunch, $27–$36 dinner. Mon–Fri 11:30am–1:30pm; Mon–Sat 5:30–10pm.

La Boca ★★ STEAK   One might not think of New Orleans as a steak town, but it's yet another tradition that runs deep here (one friend calls it the Big Meaty—it's the city that gave us Ruth's Chris, after all). At this cavern-like Argentinean steakhouse, you choose your cut and your knife, and you should get the transcendent 3-day fries regardless of what else you order. But for the best-flavored beefiness we suggest the *entraña fina* skirt steak (which can also be had skin-on, interesting but unnecessary) or the *centro de entraña* hanger steak. Temperatures are proper; the trio of chimichurri sauces add zip. Servers know their meats and are helpful about the (accordingly Argentinian) wines, but aren't particularly sociable. We do love the atmosphere here; it seems made for sharing secrets.

857 Fulton St. ℂ **504/525-8205.** www.labocasteaks.com. Appetizers $8–$20; main courses $15–$38. Mon–Wed 6–10pm; Thurs–Sat 6pm–midnight.

MiLa ★★ NOUVEAU SOUTHERN   We're not sure why MiLa doesn't get more buzz. The married co-chefs (one from Mississippi, one from Louisiana, thus MiLa) are skillful kitchen explorers and source from their own farm. It's refined, ultra-fresh, and dependably delectable (not so for the service—it's been excellent, and it's been disinterested). A sweet-potato pappardelle with shiitake mushrooms in a brown butter sauce could be heavy, but isn't at all; the peppery barbeque lobster is balanced with lemon confit and punched up with a hit of thyme—a stunner. At lunch, the fresh fish filet (we've had both trout and salmon) is just crisped; sauteed baby bok choy lends extra lightness. The wine list and desserts show equal consideration; the root beer float even adds a welcome touch of quirk. At lunch, local business people energize the contemporary room, its marine blue ceiling hung with cylindrical lampshades.

817 Common St. (in the Renaissance Pere Marquette hotel). ℂ **504/412-2580.** www.milanew orleans.com. Main courses $17–$20 lunch, $19–$38 dinner; seasonal tasting menu $75, $110 with wine pairings. Mon–Fri 11:30am–2pm; Mon–Sat 5:30–10pm.

Peche ★★ SEAFOOD   In a shocking departure from his pork-centric reputation and surname, noted chef Donald Link opened Peche in 2013, showcasing wood-fired seafood. We've eaten our way through this menu, and we've yet to find a dud. It's just . . . loud. We cannot explain the acoustics, we can only shake our heads. Or nod. Point. Anything to convey information, since voices are futile. We'd say Peche is best done with a group, so you can order lots of small plates, plus a whole grilled fish (ours was buttery, fire-crusted redfish with aptly low-profile salsa verde; you debone it). Except that it's also the worst way to do Peche if you intend to socialize. That said, this is seafood that should not be missed, especially the beer-battered fish sticks (really) and hearty crawfish gratinée. Okay, you can skip the shrimp toast and Betty Crockery tuna dip (it's good, but we can make it at home). So go by yourself. Go early or late. Sit in a corner or at the raw bar (also excellent, though grilled is why you're here). Practice your ASL communication skills. Order something from the great craft beer, cocktail, and European wine menus. For your dessert, the chocolate peanut butter banana pie (duh). For your after-dinner drink, Chloraseptic. Reserve in advance during peak periods.

800 Magazine St. ℂ **504/522-1744.** www.pecherestaurant.com. Snacks & small plates $7–$14; grilled entrees $14–$25. Whole grilled fish $37–$69. Mon–Thurs 11am–10pm; Fri–Sat 11am–11pm.

Palace Café ★★ CONTEMPORARY CREOLE   This is a good standby for low-key, non-intimidating Creole dining, and the setting is just right—a historic, two-story building (the former Werlein's music store) with sidewalk seating—fun for people-watching and lovely on a balmy eve. It comes with the stamp of New Orleans authenticity that Brennan-family ownership conveys, and its oft-practiced multi-server attention. The crabmeat cheesecake appetizer is what makes people pound the table, and it's truly delish. The andouille-crusted fish is a winner, and a simple rotisserie chicken with truffle mashed potatoes may be available nationwide, but it's done right, and many people will be happy to see something familiar. Then there's the white chocolate bread pudding, which they invented. Pay homage. In fact, weather permitting, we enjoy just desserts at one of those streetside tables (also the "$5 after 5:00pm" happy-hour small plates, one of their frequent good deals, including summer specials).

605 Canal St. ℂ **504/523-1661.** www.palacecafe.com. Main courses $12–$28 lunch, $19–$35 dinner, $14–$21 brunch; 3-course meal before 7pm $28. Mon–Sat 11:30am–2:30pm and 5:30–10pm; Sun brunch 10:30am–2:30pm.

Root ★★ NEW AMERICAN   The gleaming wood beams, painted cement floors, and leaf-green molded chairs immediately telegraph the high-hip, downscale tone. But the dining-room-as-chemistry-set trend sends our antenna up. So we were primed for disappointment in this critics' darling. We're still not sycophants, but our appreciation has definitely taken, uh, root (sorry). The Root folks are reaching for new culinary targets, and even if they don't always hit dead center, we're curious, and we admire the wit and ambition. Other than sourcing locally, Root's modern American cooking makes no concession to Louisiana. House-cured charcuterie and sausage are front and center. We enjoy the former (and loved the condiments and pickled garni) more than the latter (which tended toward tough). Our faves: the lardo, pâté de champagne, rosemary guanciale, and Moroccan pork & duck rillettes. The foie-gras cotton candy is adorable, but we'd rather just have a hunk of the stuff (for the record, we also prefer shaved truffles over anything truffle-oiled). The signature cohiba-smoked scallops, served in a fume-filled cigar box, are quite good despite our scoffing. Ditto the Korean short ribs in their little clay pot. But the pork belly went one flavor over the line (echoes of Tim Gunn: edit, edit, edit). Desserts have fun with gimmicks and florals; the fruit-based ones fared best, including a peach crumble with Middle Eastern undertones. The drinks list is equally out there, but they're quite helpful in pairing beer and wine, much appreciated given the food's complexity. Reserve well in advance. A tasting-menu-only offshoot, **Square Root,** is opening in late 2013 at 1800 Magazine Street.

200 Julia St. © **504/252-9480.** www.rootnola.com. Entrees $ $13–$15 lunch; $22–$32 dinner. Mon–Fri 11am–2pm; Sun–Thurs 5–11pm; Fri–Sat 5pm–2am.

Moderate

American Sector ★★★ AMERICAN   This Chef John Besh project inside the National WWII Museum (p. 132) puts a globalized, 21st-century riff on retro American comfort food. Kick it off with duck wings, done with Korean BBQ sauce, and a spritzer bottle of house-made soda for the table, mixed to order from homemade syrups (there are fine classic adult beverages, too). An appetizer of half-moon shrimp or crab-meat pies are tasty treats. Wagyu beef short ribs are peachy, accompanied by mac n' cheese at lunch and squash blossoms at dinner. Kids young and old can enjoy the foot-long hot dog, made in house, done corndog style on the kids' menu, and served in a tin lunch box; crispy fries come in a tin can, and other items come in Mason jars and mini cast-iron kettles. It's a swell choice, right down to the yummy mini cupcakes, and one of the better happy hours in town (3–6pm daily).

945 Magazine St. (in the National WWII Museum). © **504/528-1940.** http://nationalww2museum. org/american-sector. Sandwiches $8–$14; main courses $15–$34; sides and desserts $3–$7. Sun–Sat 11am–9pm. Museum admission not required for restaurant access.

Cochon ★★ CONTEMPORARY CAJUN   We must admit we're not fully on board with the heaps of praise Cochon gets, and we speak fluent pork. We think it's good, sometimes very good, and it is one of the few games in town for Cajun food—the rustic, country cousin to big-city Creole cooking (see p. 101). The Cochon version, of course, is amped up several notches: This is Donald Link and Steve Stryjewski Cajun, after all. But the things they do well, they do very well, so we'll point you in that direction, and if you end up with one of the good servers, it can be altogether enjoyable. All visits to Cajun country should kick off with some cracklins and a good local beer, maybe the Lazy Magnolia Pecan Ale. Follow with the boudin balls—crunchy outside, savory and porky inside. For a hog break, the briny bite of wood-fired oysters or the chicken livers with pepper jelly will do. Moving on, the fork-tender pork cheeks are disappointing only in terms of serving size (get two orders) and the skillet-baked rabbit and dumplings is a soul-warming dish that, if you skip everything else, should not be missed. The ambrosia cake is a potluck-perfect finish (not like any potluck we go to)—a creamy fruity happy ending. Reserve well in advance.

930 Tchoupitoulas St. ✆ **504/588-2123.** www.cochonrestaurant.com. Reservations strongly recommended. Small plates $7–$11; main courses $15–$24. Mon–Thurs 11am–10pm; Fri–Sat 11am–11pm.

Domenica ★★★ ITALIAN   Bittersweet chocolate walls, soaring ceilings, great art, glossy surfaces, small bar, large crowd, cacophony. Which all sets the scene for perfectly bubble-edged Neapolitan pizzas, arguably the best salumi in the city, and a man in the kitchen (Chef Alon Shaya) who knows his way around a vegetable. We rarely make it to the *secondi* here because it's so easy, and such a pleasure, to load up on antipasti and *primi* (and a pizza or two). Buttery sautéed chanterelle mushrooms are flavored with marrow and cut through with parsley—decadently rich. A whole roasted cauliflower makes an impressive presentation and is delicious addition to the table. Fresh tagliatelle is sauced with rabbit and porcini mushrooms, hearty and divine, and we'd never leave home if Mom could make a *stracci* with oxtail and fried chicken livers. All this assumes that you've already enjoyed their notable cocktails, worked through a salumi and cheese board, and selected some pizzas from the broad array of toppings (yes, you can do it all—the wisp of a crust makes for easy eating). The better to end with the satiny chocolate hazelnut *budino*. Did we mention that Domenica, like all of John Besh's restaurants, has a superb happy hour from 3 to 6pm, when select pizzas are half-price? No wonder it's cacophonous. The bar pours well-priced boutique Italian wines and popular homemade cellos. Okay, service is inconsistent, ranging from prompt and knowledgeable to perfunctory to disorderly. And still it's worth it. Reserve well in advance.

123 Baronne St. (in the Roosevelt Hotel). ✆ **504/648-6020.** www.domenicarestaurant.com. Reservations recommended. Pizza $13; antipasti $10–$18; lunch panini $12–$15; main courses $12–$34 dinner, $12–$26 lunch. Daily 11am–11pm.

Drago's ★★ SEAFOOD   The booming Hilton lobby isn't too conducive to an atmospheric experience. Fortunately that's irrelevant, because you're here for one thing and one thing only (okay, two): Drago's buttery, garlicky, Parmesan-y, charbroiled oysters—your new paramour, the one you can't get enough of. Other places do them, but none so well. They become like a home renovation project: However many you think you want to order, double it. The bargain-priced Maine lobsters are also worth mentioning. Not much else matters. Sports-minded folks can sit at the bar, order oysters, and watch what's on—there are worse ways to take in a game. Be mindful that the sprawling dining room can fill up, and they don't take reservations, so a wait is possible.

2 Poydras St. (in the Hilton Riverside). ✆ **504/584-3911.** Also 3232 N. Arnoult Rd., Metairie. ✆ **504/888-9254.** www.dragosrestaurant.com. Charbroiled oysters $18 per dozen; dinner appetizers $8–$15; main courses $20–$29; Maine lobster $20–$52. Mon–Sat 11am–10pm.

Inexpensive

Cochon Butcher ★★★ CONTEMPORARY CAJUN   If Donald Link and Stephen Stryjewski's Cochon is the head cheerleader of updated Cajun cuisine, Butcher is its cooler little sister with the punk haircut. And we're its bestie. The deli-style storefront with about six bar-height tables has a more extensive menu than one might expect from its limited space (it's mostly take-out; great for a picnic in the park or room). And honestly, it's all good. The excellent house-smoked meats and sausages, in small plates or on a sandwich, are sure hits; their muffuletta rivals (and might surpass) Central Grocery's, and the pork belly with cucumber and mint is wondrous. Get the vinegary Brussels sprouts or rue the day you didn't. The boudin sausage link is the best within the city confines (but not outside them), A few choice wines by the glass are offered.

930 Tchoupitoulas St. ✆ **504/588-PORK** (588-7675). www.cochonbutcher.com. Sandwiches $8–$12; charcuterie plate $14; sides and bar food $3–$6. Mon–Thurs 10am–10pm; Fri–Sat 10am–11pm; Sun 10am–4pm.

Mother's ★ CREOLE/LIGHT FARE   Mother's gets the haters who accuse it of being touristy, but hey, Paris is touristy. And if it's good enough for Beyoncé and Jay Z (who posted photos of themselves lunching there in 2013), it's . . . actually that has no bearing on anything. Mother's worth is in direct proportion to the line of people waiting to get in. If it extends past the second window (say, more than 3 to 4 parties ahead of you), it's not worth waiting. It's good, not great. If you can waltz right in, fine: You'll get solid Creole cooking in an easy-access location, good for an introduction to the cuisine and family-friendly. The traditional Creole hot plates (jambalaya, shrimp Creole) are serviceable; mild or hot homemade sausage elevates the red beans (go hot). Po'boys are the safer bet, especially anything that revolves around Mother's signature baked ham. The Ferdi (ham, roast beef debris) is the top seller, but we think the ham gets lost in all that. We prefer it solo with cheese, or combo'd with turkey, which stands up better. We'll also have the ham with biscuits at the unsurprising breakfast. The bread pudding needs to be experienced, if only to post about the retro use of canned fruit cocktail, maraschinos and all (it's also freakishly good). Make no never mind, there are rules here: 1) Get in the cafeteria line to order food and get steam-table items. 2) Order and receive drinks. 3) Pay. 4). Then and only then find a table—don't send a scout to save one. 5). A server delivers the rest of the food. Follow these rules lest you get some hostess lip.

401 Poydras St. ✆ **504/523-9656.** www.mothersrestaurant.net. Menu items $4–$25. Mon–Sun 7am–10pm.

UPTOWN/THE GARDEN DISTRICT

For a map of restaurants in this section, see "Uptown Hotels & Restaurants," on p. 67.

Very Expensive

Clancy's ★★★ CONTEMPORARY CREOLE   Clancy's epitomizes the New Orleans tradition of fine neighborhood dining. Although it's been at this location for 70 years, it's been reenergized and popularized since a late-1900s renaissance, and a favorite ever since. It's got the look: tuxedoes on the waiters, linen on the tables, white on the beadboard walls. It's got the attitude: It's fun, fine dining, aspirational for some; a weekly ritual for others. It's got a menu full of new Creole classics: flash-fried oysters topped with brie; creamy, succulent shrimp and grits; a colossal smoked duck leg that stands on its own with the simplest of sides. When softshell crab is in season, it's de rigueur on every menu in town, but here it's smoked—and it's a wonder. We've had success with veal here, lighter than it sounds despite the Bernaise and crabmeat. We'd order more starters if they weren't so pricey; the ample wine list is also short on lower-end options. But once you give in to the kind of evening that can be had here, you may choose to give in to all that too, and commune over conversation and cognac. Reserve in advance.

6100 Annunciation St. © **504/895-1111.** www.clancysneworleans.com. Main courses $26–$38. Mon–Sat 5:30–10:30pm; Thurs–Fri 11:30am–2pm.

Commander's Palace ★★★ CONTEMPORARY CREOLE The Commander's Palace miracle is that they are meal (and mood) mentalists. It's as if there is a sliding scale of formality, and they have an uncanny ability to serve up just the amount your mood requires (and a room to match it). An elegant, "event" evening? Got it. Rollicking (civilized) good time? Jaded foodie who wants a wow? They're on it. Marriage proposal in the offing? Just tell them when to serve the ring. They understand the ultimate New Orleanean experience: that stately needn't be stuffy; formal can still be fun; and that sometimes, innovation is the best way to honor tradition—and they immerse you in it. They're also leaders in mentoring and fostering the city's culinary scene: A who's who of New Orleans restaurant owners, chefs, and front-of-house managers resembles a Commander's family tree. Yet regardless of how many "best of" lists and awards Commander's racks up, they never rest on their laurels (we'll just mention the James Beard "Best Chef" award that Tory McPhail picked up in 2013).

The continually changing menu reflects Chef McPhail's commitment to local ingredients and fervent imagination, on best display in the seven-course "Chef's Playground." The a la carte menu mixes their classics (spicy-sweet shrimp & tasso henican, the gateway drug of Commander's Palace dishes; consistently perfect pecan-crusted Gulf fish) with seasonal newbies (a sublime quail, with Creole cream cheese, bacon, and jalapeño cornbread dressing in an understated blueberry and hisbiscus tea reduction). The gumbo can be a tad salty for our palate; we opt for the robust turtle soup instead. For enders, the famed bread pudding soufflé is a puff of gladness with whiskey sauce. The wine list is one of the finest in this or any city, with a good selection offered by the glass in half or full pours. Everyone should eat at Commander's, and everyone can. It's unintimidating finery, and multicourse lunch and happy-hour deals start under $20 (less than some po'boys); $36 at dinner. So worth it. Reserve well in advance.

1403 Washington Ave. © **504/899-8221.** www.commanderspalace.com. No shorts or T-shirts; jackets preferred for men at dinner. Main courses $26–$40. Tasting menu $90, $147 with wine. 3-course dinner $36–$42. 25¢ martinis Mon–Fri lunch only. Mon–Fri 11:30am–2pm; daily 6–10pm; brunch Sat 11:30am–1pm and Sun 10:30am–1:30pm. Summer hours June 1–Sept 1: dinner from 6:30pm; brunch ends at 1pm.

Expensive

Brigtsen's ★★★ CONTEMPORARY CAJUN Brigtsen's was one of the early modern Creole revolutionaries, and one of the first to convert a beautiful, 19th-century house into an upscale neighborhood restaurant way back in 1986. The perennial favorite still maintains a warm, romantic intimacy, with the hostess circulating amiably though the sweet little mural-decorated rooms. The service and cuisine—which shows homey, Cajun country roots—have been polished to consistent excellence. The "Shell

Beach Diet," their famously grand seafood platter, changes seasonally but includes five to six sauced, baked, or otherwise unfried seafood items. It's an impressive extravagance for sharing or for a hungry, indecisive diner. Chef Brigtsen has a special touch with game and rabbit. His panéed sesame-crusted version in a tangy Creole mustard sauce, as well as his crispy, moist roast duck are known far and wide; his pecan pie with its perfect, copious crust is actually famous. A modest wine list satisfies, but could be improved. Reserve well in advance during peak periods.

723 Dante St. ℰ **504/861-7610.** www.brigtsens.com. Reservations highly recommended. Main courses $26–$38. Tues–Sat 5:30–10pm.

Coquette ★★★ BISTRO   It's hard to believe Coquette is just 4 years old. It feels like it's occupied its tin-ceilinged, chandeliered, bistro-chic space for much longer. We mean this in the best way—it's smart and polished, and altogether comfortable in its skin, even if that skin changes daily. We're sure that somewhere in an attic Chef/Owner Michael Stoltzfus has a menu that's aging—because his well of culinary creativity seems to keep Coquette eternally fresh. That, plus dedication to ingredient perfectionism, and top talent heading the bar and pastry programs, lands Coquette firmly in the upper echelon of New Orleans's restaurants.

Whatever we suggest will be long gone by the time you get there (and really what you should do if at all possible is spring for the five-course tasting menus). Tuna crudo interspersed with compressed cantaloupe and garnished with herb-dusted popcorn had us chuckling with delight. Chicken-fried sweetbreads on a blueberry puree are a miracle in the mouth; baby eggplant paired with ricotta gnocchi over a chilled peach-tomato sauce weren't a beautiful sight—but were altogether divine on the palate. If any version of cheesecake is on the menu, make that your choice, unless you're a chocolate lover. Then get the pudding. If all this sounds a bit daunting, the $20 three-course lunch menu might be one of the best deals in town.

2800 Magazine St. ℰ **504/265-0421.** www.coquettenola.com. Reservations highly recommended. 3-course lunch $20; lunch entrees $14–$19; 5-course blind tasting $70 (wine pairing $30); dinner entrees $24–$32. Wed–Sat 11:30am–3pm; Wed–Mon 5:30–10pm; Sun 10:30am–2pm.

Dominique's on Magazine ★ BISTRO/INTERNATIONAL   Chef Dominique Maquet's cuisine is mature yet adventurous, reflecting his experience in some of the city's finest restaurants; his Mauritian roots explain the French-African influences that seep into the gently surprising flavor profiles. His sense of style is clearly evident in this sleek, bleached-out room, with enough accent mirrors to ensure that you don't miss seeing yourself (hearing is a different story). Service, like the room, also tends toward the cool—and occasionally confused, but we're hoping time will heal (the restaurant, the second under this name, opened in spring 2013). Chef Macquet's food aims high and hits the target or just below. Ceviche with gorgeous shrimp was punched up by fresh jalapeños and herbs from the backyard garden. Grilled lamb with basil, mint, and harissa jus is spot-on. But housemade spaghetti with wagyu meatballs in veal jus is anachronistic and avoidable. There's no bar to speak of—too bad since the drinks are terrific—but the white-on-white courtyard is pleasant and more sedate than the main dining room, a good choice, weather permitting. The handsome upstairs room is mostly used for events.

4213 Magazine St. ℰ **504/891-9282.** www.dominiquesonmag.com. Main courses $23–$26. Mon–Thurs 5:30–9:30pm; Fri–Sat 5:30–10:30pm.

Once upon a time, while waiting for Casamento's doors to open and just moments from an oyster loaf, three youngish tourist gals struck up a chat (as happens nearly automatically in New Orleans) with three Uptown ladies-of-a-certain-age ahead of them. They were St. Charles–born and –bred, dined at Casamento's weekly, and offered us NOLA newbies some well-tested tips. This one still sticks (and sounds best when read with a high-pitched, breathy lilt): "You simply *must* go to any of the fine, old French restaurants, and when you do, why you just order anythin' flamin'." Meaning, go to Antoine's, Arnaud's, Commander's Palace, or Galatoire's, and get bananas Foster, baked Alaska, *café brûlot*, or anything prepared tableside and involving conflagration. Naturally we bought the ladies a round, and to this day we're still following their fine advice and living by the "anythin' flamin' " creed: Indulge a bit, relish fun, and while one needn't embrace drama in all aspects of life, when it comes to dessert, by all means *bring it on.*

Gautreau's ★★ CONTEMPORARY SOUTHERN   Tucked away in a residential Uptown neighborhood, with no signage to speak of, is a reclusive spot that pretty much every major food magazine has managed to find. Chef Sue Zemanick has been lavished with their praise, garnered umpteen awards, and by the time you read this may be a Top Chef Masters winner. There's a finery to the food here that hews close to that at classic French treatments, but steps forward with an added degree of modernity. A dewy foie-gras torchon adds a reduction of stone fruit and huckleberries, with bits of macadamia for crunch. A bright starter marries jicama and watercress with roast pineapple. Moist, sautéed snapper shares a basil bath with tiny fregola pasta, roasted kale, and baby onions. The grown-up wine list matches the low-ceilinged room, with its trompe l'oeil linen walls and warm lighting. We're excited to see where the talented pair heading Gautreau's takes us with their next ventures, **Ivy** and **Marti's,** both scheduled to open in late 2013, but we'll surely return to the original. Reserve in advance.

1728 Soniat St. ⓒ **504/899-7397.** http://gautreausrestaurant.com. Main courses $27–$42. Mon–Sat 6–10pm.

Jacques-Imo's ★★ CREOLE/SOUL FOOD   Speaking of food trucks, the gator-painted pickup in front of Jacques-Imo's actually has a table set up in its bed, where some lucky couple can dine. This funky, colorful spot with the long line (longer in proportion to who's playing next door at the Maple Leaf; p. 175) is hugely popular for all that jacked-up fun, not to mention the Creole soul-food stylings. Fortunately, the drinks are well-made, and as soon as you're seated you'll be appeased with righteous cornbread muffins. The signature shrimp and alligator-sausage "cheesecake" (more like a quiche) has fans and detractors (we're on board), but no one doesn't love the legendary fried chicken with the divine hard crunch. The blackened redfish with a crab-chili hollandaise is also a winner, and the lightly batter-fried softshell-crab "Godzilla" is killer. Get there early—it's well worth the wait when there's no line.

8324 Oak St. ⓒ **504/861-0886.** www.jacques-imos.com. Reservations for 5 or more required; smaller parties are first-come, first-served. Main courses $19–$37. Mon–Thurs 5–10pm; Fri–Sat 5–10:30pm.

La Petite Grocery ★★★ BISTRO   Among the many bistros along Magazine Street, this way-Uptown standard-bearer is more traditionally French than some in decor and wine selections. They've eased into a reliably good, comfortably welcoming groove here, and the food is a distinctive mélange of Creole creativity, relying on local ingredients, keen technique, and the adroit palate of Chef/Owner Justin Devillier (a *Top Chef* contestant as we write this). We believe deeply in the steak tartare (though it seems to come and go from the menu), and require the blue crab beignets as well as the ricotta dumplings with lobster and fresh peas. But they're also soup geniuses here, so preliminary courses are a tough choice. For entrees, the smoky shrimp and grits with roasted mushrooms is one of the better treatments we've tried; and the beef tenderloin gets a deep, satisfying sear from the pan roasting. We like the side of fried green beans (good to munch on at the bar, too), and the newish pastry chef is a marvelous addition: Her floral addition to a simple local strawberry shortcake changed our view of that dessert forever. The bar can get pretty lively—good or not so much depending on your goals for the evening—and the generally smart, on-point service suffers a bit during peak periods.

4238 Magazine St. ℭ **504/891-3377.** www.lapetitegrocery.com. Main courses $15–$29 lunch, $16–$32 dinner. Tues–Sat 11:30am–2:30pm; Sun–Thurs 5:30–9:30pm; Fri–Sat 5:30–10:30pm; Sun 10:30am–2:30pm.

Lilette ★★ BISTRO   Lilette's pedigreed chef-owner brings his training in some of New Orleans's finest kitchens and at Michelin-starred restaurants in France to bear here, resulting in an artistic if somewhat serious approach. The NOLA classic space—high-ceilinged, columned, tiles—is made East Village–ready (where a sister restaurant, Exchange Alley, is in fact located) with tobacco-toned walls. Lunch is thick with business people and ladies who lunch; dinner (which gets dear) sees a mixed crowd of tourists, neighbors, and young hipsters, all here for the tasteful, clean lines of the cooking. Start with the truffled Parmigiano toast with wild mushrooms, marrow, and veal glace (you may end with it too; it's divine) and the braised veal cheeks with baby greens in a spiky horseradish vinaigrette (if you stop now, you've done well). A roast chicken breast with Brussels sprouts and balsamic-glazed onions is flawless simplicity. Desserts are worth the indulgence, notably the curious signature of goat-cheese crème fraîche rounds, paired with vanilla-poached pears sprinkled with pistachios and lavender honey (baklava is turning in its grave). And if you're a wine enthusiast trying to decide between the Uptown bistros, Lilette is your choice.

3637 Magazine St. ℭ **504/895-1636.** www.liletterestaurant.com. Main courses $12–$24 lunch, $24–$45 dinner. Tues–Sat 11:30am–2pm; Tues–Thurs 5:30–9:30pm; Fri–Sat 5:30–10:30pm.

Martinique Bistro ★★ BISTRO/FRENCH   Dining on the romantic, jasmine-scented courtyard at this Uptown jewel box, we expect someone, anyone, to propose to us at any moment. It's a favorite among locals for that ambience, as well as the French- and Mediterranean-influenced dishes. A Gulf fish stew done Mediterranean style is just right under the stars. Modern Southern specialties are also on hand, the ubiquitous pork belly done deliciously here with peach preserves and a jalapeño and goat-cheese corncake. The boneless New Zealand lamb loin with pickles, couscous, and a Meyer lemon-watercress aioli and tomato-sherry vinegar sounds like it would be one ingredient over the line, but that wasn't at all the case. We should mention that there is an indoor space, but for best effect, request a courtyard table. If no one proposes, it's also a great spot for a girls' lunch or brunch.

5908 Magazine St. *℃* **504/891-8495.** www.martiniquebistro.com. Main courses $11–$20 lunch; dinner $18–$32. Nov–May Fri–Sun 11am–2:30pm, Tues–Thurs 5:30–9:30pm, Fri–Sat 5:30–10pm, Sun 5:30–9:30pm; June–Oct open for dinner half an hour later.

Patois ★★★ BISTRO/CONTEMPORARY CREOLE   Can we just cut to the chase and say that this is a near-perfect bistro? The tucked-away restaurant is chic but inviting; the locally sourced ingredients are bright with freshness; service is practiced; and the menu is French meets modern Southern bistro and shakes hands with Spain. Your head won't spin round, but you'll likely enjoy every precisely-done option. We sampled an octopus carpaccio made lively with a pepper-and-chorizo citrus vinaigrette, and loved a simple lamb-ribs appetizer—just right with a dollop of marinated eggplant and Creole tomato jam. The grilled hanger steak, in a rich red-wine bone-marrow reduction, is deeply flavored, and local dessert favorites are tweaked in amusing, inviting ways, like sweet potato beignets and king-cake bread pudding with Creole cream-cheese ice cream. All are sweet and worthy. Reserve well in advance during peak periods.

6078 Laurel St. *℃* **504/895-9441.** www.patoisnola.com. Main courses $24–$31 dinner, $12–$22 lunch Wed–Thurs 5:30–10pm; Fri 11:30am–2pm and 5:30–10:30pm; Sat 5:30–10:30pm; Sun 10:30am–2pm.

Upperline ★★ CONTEMPORARY CREOLE   These past few years, our eyebrows were raised by chef turnover here, but it was for naught: Genial owner/host JoAnn Clevenger has maintained the hospitable vibe that has always been a touchstone at this charming little residential spot, and the new chef has kept signature items unmolested while adding a few tricks of his own. Standout appetizers include fried green tomatoes with shrimp rémoulade sauce (an oft-copied dish that was invented here) and a gumbo as rich as Bill Gates (and many shades darker). For entrees, the moist roast duck with a spry ginger-peach sauce is crispy perfection on a plate; a mellow, sautéed drum comes with a shock of spicy shrimp. If you're in town in the summer, the all-garlic menu is great fun. Don't leave without having the warm honey-pecan bread pudding, touring the art-filled restaurant, and thanking JoAnn (though she'll probably get to you first to do the same). Reserve well in advance during peak periods.

1413 Upperline St. *℃* **504/891-9822.** www.upperline.com. Reservations suggested. Main courses $20–$30; 3-course prix-fixe menu $40. Wed–Sun 5:30–9:30pm.

Moderate

Boucherie ★★★ CONTEMPORARY SOUTHERN   To tell or not to tell: That was the moral dilemma we faced when we first tried Boucherie. And we don't just mean *you,* we mean our best friends. But when the food is this good, the diminutive dining room is as cute as can be, and the prices are solidly affordable, word gets out. They parlayed food-truck-turned-bricks-and-mortar success into what Chef/Owner (and *Chopped* alumni) Nathaniel Zimet calls "fine dining for the people." There's so much Cajun-inflected goodness (and dashes of global influences) that you could blindly point at the menu and be happy with whatever wine, drinks, and plates small or large are put in front of you. Especially if it's the duck confit with plantains (with butternut squash and duck-and-tasso "baklava" in another treatment); or the shrimp-and-grits cake with bacon vinaigrette; or the grilled sugarcane-smoked scallops. Oddly, we think the signature house-smoked *boudin* balls *are* skippable. Super-sweet Krispy Kreme bread pudding is no longer the hilarious curiosity that it once was; get the chocolate terrine instead if it's available. We can't wait to see what wonders Chef Zimet's new Frenchmen Street restaurant will bring when it opens in late 2013. Reserve well in advance.

8115 Jeannette St. ⓒ **504/862-5514.** http://boucherie-nola.com. Dinner small plates $6–$13; large plates $13–$18. Tues–Sat 11am–3pm and 5:30–9:30pm.

Dante's Kitchen ★★ BISTRO/CONTEMPORARY CREOLE   Locals give this low-profile spot steady love, and we understand why, given the shrewd use of seasonal and local products, cheerful "This Old House" interior, and obliging staff. And their lively New Orleans cuisine comes with little surprises, alternately simple and refined. At dinner, hope that the herb-suffused redfish "on the half shell" is on the menu, or go for short ribs with housemade kimchi, jalapeños, and pickled carrots. Most everything they do with veggies is wondrous, and you could make a meal of just them (a pea soup with crab butter and bacon counts). Brunch is a strong alternative. We like their reworked Benedict, in which tender rosemary-crusted pork replaces Canadian bacon, honey sweetens the hollandaise, and a caramelized biscuit supports it all. It's a ways from the FQ, but just 2 blocks off the St. Charles streetcar line when it makes the big turn onto Carrollton Avenue (Hampson stop). Reserve well in advance during peak periods.

736 Dante St. ⓒ **504/861-3121.** http://danteskitchen.com. Main courses $10–$14 brunch, $23–$28 dinner. Mon & Wed–Sun 6–10pm; Sat–Sun brunch 10:30am–2pm. Closed Tues.

High Hat ★★★ CONTEMPORARY SOUTHERN   If you make it here (by cab or car), you'll have the fringe benefit of checking out Freret Street, a booming restaurant street and one of the best post-Katrina success stories. This casual neighborhood spot had nothing to go on but an idea and original tile floors, and what a go they've made of it. It's possible this is our favorite new spot in New Orleans's rapidly expanding restaurant scene; it's definitely in our top five. We come for the always interesting drinks, often fashioned with house-made ingredients. We come for the graceful oyster fennel soup, and the Southern comfort foods, like a mound of fork-tender slow roast pork with sublime braised greens. But mostly we come for the crispy, light, piled-high fried catfish with tangy slaw and housemade tartar sauce (everything here save the Delta tamales is made in-house, even the condiments). Then we get whatever freshly made pie is available, and the inane Grillswith—a grilled donut topped with melting ice cream—because it would be equally inane to skip it.

4500 Freret St. ⓒ **504/754-1336.** www.highhatcafe.com. Everything under $18. Sun–Thurs 11am–9pm; Fri–Sat 11am–10pm.

Pascal's Manale ★★ ITALIAN/STEAK/SEAFOOD   We adore the old school neon, and the where-everybody-knows-your-name feel at this definitive neighborhood joint. But more than anything we love the barbecued shrimp—the bowl of colossal, buttery crustaceans that made Manale (mu-*nah*-lee). Make sure you get them (schedule a long workout tomorrow) and some turtle soup, but start the meal at the oyster bar. The bivalves might be frigid (in contrast to their effect, some might say), but if Thomas is shucking, his repartee is hot. Ask him anything, and your party is officially started.

It's crowded and noisy here, but unlike a cozy bistro, it's a welcome intrusion (people wear bibs here, fer Pete's sake).

1838 Napoleon Ave. ℂ **504/895-4877.** www.neworleansrestaurants.com/pascalsmanale. Main courses $18–$35. Mon–Sat 11:30am–10pm.

Inexpensive

Big Fisherman ★★ SEAFOOD This. Is. The. Stuff. If you really want a true local experience, that means eating a sack of boiled seafood—crawfish, shrimp, crab, whatever's in season. Order shellfish by the pound, and potatoes, half cobs of corn, heads of boiled garlic, maybe some sausage by the piece. Make sure to grab a beer or sweet tea to soothe the spice, plenty of paper towels, and a fistful of newspapers by the door. That's to dump your hot seafood onto, often done on a patio table, in a park, or sitting atop a levee watching the river run (there's no seating here). But no reason it can't be done in a hotel room (expect some lingering eau de shellfish). Contrary to logic, go at peak times, even if there's a line. Boiled seafood is best when it's straight out of the pot. They ship or pack for travel, too, so you can take the boil home with you. If you're on the other end of town, **Cajun Seafood** in the 7th Ward provides a similar experience and quality, with table seating and prepared foods too.

3301 Magazine St. ℂ **504/897-9907.** www.bigfishermanseafood.com. Boiled seafood $3–$10 lb. (market price). Sun–Thurs 10am–6pm; Fri till 6:30. Cajun Seafood: 1479 N. Claiborne St. ℂ **504/948-6000.** Mon–Sat 10:30am–9pm; Sun 10:30am–8:30pm.

Dat Dog ★ LIGHT FARE This darling of the gourmet hot-dog boom will pretty much satisfy any dog-related craving, what with 16 types of franks and snausages and umpteen toppings. Success depends on your personal combo selections, and as dog traditionalists, we like the brats and imported German wieners best (our attempt at "server's choice" left us with uninspired toppings on both the dogs but decent fries). And while you might like the gator, turducken, or crawfish dogs better than us, we admit the duck version with blackberry sauce was pretty darn good, and the fluffy buns held up well. The bright blue buildings at all three locations make for an easy, fun hang with a brew and your crew, and while it's an inexpensive dinner, it's still a $7 to $9 hot dog.

5030 Freret St. ℂ **504/899-6883.** http://datdognola.com. All items under $10. Cash only; ATMs on site. Mon–Sat 11am–10pm; Sun 11am–9pm. Also at 3336 Magazine St. ℂ **504/324-2226;** 601 Frenchmen St. (opening spring 2014).

Camellia Grill ★★ DINER/LIGHT FARE Even though it's *only* been a part of the city's food culture since 1946, the Camellia Grill seems to have always been there. That may change soon: A 2013 lawsuit is threatening to force a change to the name or the iconic white-columned building. We hope not, because there's really nowhere else to go for counter service with white linens, Southern hospitality, witty banter dished out by white-jacketed servers, and a classic burger. The omelets manage to be simultaneously heavy and fluffy and come in the standard varieties (if it's been a rough night, we go with chili cheese). Late-night hours make both locations popular after-club spots, but any time is good for the chocolate pecan pie (heated on the grill and a la mode, please). Good prices, true character.

Uptown: 626 S. Carrollton Ave. ℂ **504/309-2679;** French Quarter: 540 Chartres St. ℂ **504/522-1800.** All items under $10. Sun–Thurs 8am–midnight; Fri–Sat 8am–2am.

road trip EATS

You can snag plenty of good eats out in the suburbs and parishes in and around New Orleans. If you have a car (or a friend with one), these local favorites are well worth the 10- to 30-minute drives.

Deanie's. This well-respected seafood joint is the very model of a neighborhood restaurant. There's one in the French Quarter now, but we prefer the original.

1713 Lake Ave., Metairie. ✆ **504/831-4141.** $10–$25 or market price. Tues–Sat 11am–10pm; Sun 11am–9pm.

Dong Phuong. Banh mi, pho, and other Vietnamese specialties are among the many excellent contributions that New Orleans's huge Vietnamese population has made to the city. Head east for the best.

14207 Chef Menteur Hwy., N.O. East. ✆ **504/254-0214.** $3–$10. Mon & Wed–Sun 8am–4pm (bakery only open till 6pm).

The Galley. The folks who do the softshell-crab po' boys at Jazz Fest do other things just as well, and they're nearby in pretty Old Metairie.

2535 Metairie Rd. ✆ **504/832-0955.** $10–$27. Tues–Sat 11am–9pm.

Middendorf's. A classic on-the-water joint that fries up the crispiest, thinnest, freshest catfish imaginable.

30160 Hwy. 51 South, Akers. ✆ **985/386-6666.** $12–$19. Wed–Sun 10:30am–9pm.

Mondo. Bayona chef Susan Spicer's popular, casual place in the suburb of Lakeview.

900 Harrison Ave., Lakeview. ✆ **504/224-2633.** $9–$15 lunch, $12–$27 dinner. Mon–Fri 11:30am–2:30pm, Mon–Thurs 5:30–10pm, Fri–Sat 5:30–10:30pm, Sun brunch 11am–2pm.

Mosca's. Generations of New Orleaneans make the drive and wait the wait for killer old-school Italian.

4137 U.S. Hwy. 90 West, Avondale. ✆ **504/436-8950.** $11–$34. No credit cards. Tues–Sat 5:30–9:30pm.

R&O's. Thoroughly unpretentious old-school neighborhood joint serving the usual classics: po'boys, fried seafood, Italian essentials.

216 Hammond Hwy., Metairie. ✆ **504/831-1248.** Most items under $15, crab $24. Mon–Fri 11am–3pm; Wed–Thurs 5–9pm; Fri 5–9:30pm; Sat 11am–9:30pm; Sun 11am–4pm and 5–9pm.

Sal's Seafood. Many locals cite the fresh, meaty, spiced-just-right boiled crawfish at this hole in the wall as the best around. Worth the half-hour drive across the river into suburban Marrero.

1512 Barataria Blvd., Marerro. ✆ **504/341-8112.** Boiled seafood $3–$9/lb. [market price]. Tues–Sat 9am–9pm; Sun 9am–7:30pm.

Sammy's. Out of the tourist zone but close enough for a cab. The Ray Ray po'boy (fried chicken, grilled ham, Swiss cheese) made one health-conscious skeptic laugh aloud with joy on first bite.

3000 Elysian Fields Ave. ✆ **504/947-0675.** $5–$15. Mon–Thurs 10:45am–5pm; Fri 10:45am–7pm; Sat 10:45am-4pm.

Walker's. Another Fest favorite. The *cochon de lait* po'boy comes from right here, along with really good barbecue.

10828 Hayne Blvd., Lakefront. ✆ **504/241-8227.** $5–$17. Wed–Sat 10:30am 'til sold out.

Casamento's ★★★ SEAFOOD   Probably the best "erster" joint in the city, Casa-mento's takes its oysters so seriously that it simply closes down when they're not in season (well, Gulf oysters are always in season, but we're sure they've got their reasons). The all-tile restaurant has been family owned since 1919. The oysters are scrubbed clean and well selected; the shucker is a hoot (if you dare him, he'll shoot a bivalve into your mouth from across the room). You should also take the plunge and order the oyster loaf: a whole loaf of bread fried in butter, filled with oysters (or shrimp), and fried again to seal it. Seriously.

4330 Magazine St. ✆ **504/895-9761.** www.casamentosrestaurant.com. Main courses $5–$15, market price on some items. No credit cards. Tues–Sat 11am–2pm; Thurs–Sat 5:30–9pm. Closed June, July, Aug & all major holidays.

Guy's Po'boys ★★ LIGHT FARE   This is the Uptown choice for a lowdown po'boy. We hate to be repetitive, but as with all good po'boy joints, the bread is Leiden-heimer's and the best choices are the fried shrimp or the gravy-soaked roast beef—you can't go wrong with either. This lunch-only spot isn't a slick operation; it takes time to fry and slice, so you may wait a few minutes for your sammie. We promise you, it's worth it, so make friends with the locals, sip on your Barq's, and be patient, grasshopper.

5259 Magazine St. (at Tchoupitoulas St.). ✆ **504/891-5025.** All tems under $10. Cash only. Mon–Sat 10am–4pm.

Joey K's ★ CREOLE/SEAFOOD/DINER   This corner hangout gets locals and a few visitors, who know that the trout Tchoupitoulas—a rocking pan-fried trout topped with grilled veggies and shrimp—is worth a stop if you're out for a shop. Nothing else will blow your hair back here, but the daily blackboard specials such as brisket, lamb shank, and white beans with pork chops are just fine, and somehow we often end up around this stretch of Magazine.

3001 Magazine St. ✆ **504/891-0997.** www.joeyksrestaurant.com. Main courses $9–$19. Mon–Sat 11am–9pm.

COFFEE, BAKERIES & DESSERTS

For other sweet treats, see the section on "Candies, Pralines & Pastries" in the "Shopping" chapter, p. 189.

Angelo Brocato's Ice Cream & Confectionery ★★★   ICE CREAM/DESSERT   Though this sweet, genuine ice cream parlor celebrated its 100th birthday under 5 feet of water, it's long since come back—and ostensibly not a thing has changed. Run by the same family since 1905, Angelo Brocato makes rich Italian ice cream and ices daily, cookies, and pastries amid a wonderful throwback atmosphere. Standards like chocolate and *stracciatella* (chocolate chip) are capital-P Perfect; the fresh lemon ice is legendary (don't try to decide between that and seasonal fresh fruit ices, like Ponchatoula strawberry and blood orange; just get both), while the panna cotta custard has brought us to our knees. After that we get a fresh cannoli. Heck yeah, we do.

214 N. Carrollton Ave. ✆ **504/486-1465.** www.angelobrocatoicecream.com. Everything under $10. Tues–Thurs 10am–10pm; Fri–Sat 10am–10:30pm; Sun 10am–9pm. Closed Mon.

Buttermilk Drop Bakery and Cafe ★★ BAKERY/DESSERT   Dear Donut People (and you know who you are): After you've done Café du Monde, you need to

bean FREAKS

If you're one of those single-source, third-wave, cold-pressed, pour-over-only people, and you know who you are, here are a few coffee joints du jour that might satisfy you. Might.

All except purist Spitfire offer some variation on pastries and light savory fare.

○ **Hi Volt** (Lower Garden District): 1829 Sophie Wright Pl. (✆ **504/123-4567**; http://hivolt coffee.com; Mon–Fri 6:30am–7pm; Sat 8am–8pm; Sun 8am–2pm).

○ **Merchant** (CBD): 800 Common St. (✆ **504/571-9580;** www. merchantneworleans.com; Mon–Fri 7am–5:30pm; Sat–Sun 8am–4:30pm).

○ **Spitfire** (French Quarter): 627 St. Peter St. (✆ **504/384-0655.** Mon–Thurs 8am–7pm; Fri–Sat 8am–8pm.

○ **Velvet** (Uptown): 5637 Magazine St. (✆ **504/450-2129;** www. throwacupcake.com; Mon–Tues 7am–2pm; Wed–Sun 7am–5pm).

see Henry the Donut Whisperer for the $20 dozen: around $6 for a dozen donuts, the rest for the cab from the Quarter and back. It's about what you'd pay for a ride to the Maple Leaf, and equally worth it. Have the cab wait, hope the line is short, stick to the drops and classic glazed. Fun fact: Dwight Henry starred in the film *Beasts of the Southern Wild*!

1718 N. Dorgenois St., 7th Ward. ✆ **504/252-04538.** www.buttermilkdrop.com. A dozen donuts around $6. Cash only. Sun–Sat 6am–6pm.

Café du Monde ★★★ COFFEE/DESSERT   Excuse us while we wax rhapsodic.

Since 1862, Café du Monde has been selling café au lait and beignets (and nothing but) on the edge of Jackson Square. A New Orleans landmark, it's a must-stop, and *the* place for people-watching, 24 hours a day. A beignet (ben-*yay*) is a square French doughnut–type object, steaming-hot and covered in powdered sugar. You might be tempted to shake off some of the sugar. Don't. Trust us. Pour more on, even. At three to an order for about $2.35, they're a hell of a deal. Wash them down with chicory café au lait (good with extra powdered sugar) or really good hot chocolate. Feeling guilty? The fresh orange juice is excellent, too, and presumably has vitamins.

In the French Market, 800 Decatur St. ✆ **504/525-4544.** www.cafedumonde.com. 3 beignets for $2.35. Cash only. Daily 24 hr. Closed Christmas.

Morning Call ★★ COFFEE/DESSERT/LIGHT FARE   The original French Quarter Morning Call was a Café du Monde rival back in the 1870s. This new outlet, in the midst of glorious, oak-filled City Park harkens back to that old style and is a very welcome addition to Mid-City. You're here for café au lait and beignets, which usually come fresh from the fryer, and you self-sprinkle powdered sugar atop them to your liking (which may mean removing the lids of the shaker bottles). They also have a few Creole standbys, jambalaya and red beans and such, which are awfully handy at 4am or if you're famished from a longer-than-expected museum visit.

3325 Severn Ave., in the Casino Building, City Park (east of the Sculpture Garden). ✆ **504/885-4068.** www.morningcallcoffeestand.com. $3–$10. Cash only. Daily 24 hr. Closed Christmas.

Café EnVie ★ COFFEE/BAKERY/LIGHT FARE   This handsome coffeehouse has a nice selection of drinks, pastries, bagels, and full breakfast. Good for folks staying in the Marigny area, or for a shot of espresso while waiting for the clubs on Frenchmen to get cranking.

1241 Decatur St. ℭ **504/524-3689.** Everything under $10. Daily 7am–midnight.

Creole Creamery ★★★ ICE CREAM/DESSERT   Shakes and malts and scoops, oh my! Thick, luscious ice cream with a rotating list of standard and exotic flavors, from lavender-honey and absinthe to red velvet cake and tiramisu. Refreshing, maybe even mandatory in summer, and open late enough for a scoop on the way to or from an Uptown club or bar.

4924 Prytania St. ℭ **504/894-8680.** www.creolecreamery.com. Everything under $10 except 8 scoop "Eating Challenge" and whole cakes. No credit cards. Sun–Thurs noon–10pm; Fri–Sat noon–11pm.

Croissant D'Or ★★ COFFEE/BAKERY   A quiet and calm place with the same snacks you might find in a French-leaning coffeehouse, and you can almost always find an open table inside or in the pretty courtyard. Are the croissants made of gold? The prices feel like it sometimes, but they are credibly French.

617 Ursulines St. ℭ **504/524-4663.** www.croissantdornola.com. Sandwiches & pastries under $6. Wed–Mon 6am–3pm.

La Boulangerie ★★★ BAKERY   This bakery would be a jewel even if it were in a major bread city. It sells perhaps the only authentic, crusty baguettes in the city (the owners are from France, so they are particular about their bread, as you might guess). But still, we often opt for the heavily studded olive bread, just slightly greasy (in a good way) with olive oil. Heaven. They also do marvelous croissants, chocolate-filled croissants, and other pastries, and even have savory sandwiches. No coffee, though.

4600 Magazine St. (Uptown). ℭ **504/269-3777.** Breads, pastries, sandwiches $3–$8. Mon, Wed–Sat 6am–6pm (closed Tue); Sun 6:30am–4pm.

La Divina Gelateria ★★ ICE CREAM/DESSERT   This superb gelato place has a great selection of standard and exotic ice cream flavors, and a few tables inside and in the alleyway outside. Look for seasonal fruits and flavors and daily options like dark chocolate with cayenne gelato, sorbets of fruit, herbs, or local Abita Turbo dog beer— and the dairy is from Louisiana cows. They also have nice light lunches and excellent coffee.

621 St. Peter St. (French Quarter). ℭ **504/302-2692.** www.ladivinagelateria.com. Scoops $2–$6. Mon–Wed 11am–10pm; Thurs 8:30am–10pm; Fri–Sat 8:30am–11pm; Sun 8:30am–10pm. Also at 3005 Magazine St. ℭ **504/342-2634.** Sun–Thurs 11am–9pm; Fri–Sat 11am–10pm.

Meltdown Ice Pops ★★ DESSERT/ICE CREAM   If you're exploring the Marigny or Bywater, Meltdown ice pops come in standard and exotic flavors made from local ingredients (hand-picked berries, even). Daily flavors range from Vietnamese coffee and salted caramel (our personal favorites) to herb-inflected concoctions like pineapple basil and Ponchatoula strawberry basil, some with chunks of fruit. The straightforward fudgsicles (watermelon or peanut butter) are kid-pleasers.

4011 St. Claude St. ℭ **504/301-0905.** www.meltdownpops.com. $3 each. Cash only. Wed–Mon 1pm–6pm.

A snoball's CHANCE

We all scream for ice cream (New Orleans is no exception), but New Orleans has another popular iced dessert: the snoball. Lest you think it's just a snow cone or shaved ice clone, let us assure you: It's no such thing. These mouthwatering concoctions are made with only the best-quality shaved ice, ice so fine that skiers envy the powder. And the flavors—including exotic ones such as wedding cake (almond, mostly), nectar (think cream soda, only much better), and even orchid cream vanilla (bright purple and must be seen to be believed)—are absolutely delectable (the better proprietors make their own flavored syrups). Order them with condensed or evaporated milk if you prefer your refreshing drinks on the more decadently creamy side, or go further—some shops have started spiking them with booze. At any time on a hot day, lines can be out the door, and like so many other local specialties, loyalties are fierce. You should stop in at any snoball stand you see, but these are worth seeking out. Hours vary, so call ahead; most open mid-day till 7 or 8pm; many close for winter. Go with a sweet tooth and get plenty of napkins.

Hansen's Sno-Bliz (4801 Tchoupitoulas St.; *C* **504/891-9788;** www.snobliz. com) is a city tradition after decades of service, still provided with a smile by the third-generation owner Ashley Hansen, who officially took over after her grandparents died in the months following Katrina. Hansen's grandparents invented the shaved-ice machine in use here and elsewhere, and made their own special syrups. Snoballs come in a souvenir cup. Try the bubble-gum-flavored Sno-bliz. **Plum St. Snoballs** (1300 Burdette St.; *C* **504/866-7996;** www.plumstreet snoball.com) has been cooling New Orleaneans for more than 70 years, serving favorites in Chinese food containers. Fans of **Pandora's** (901 S. Carrollton Ave.; *C* **504/289-0765**) say its ice is the softest anywhere, and the flavor list is so long it's taking over the neighborhood. You'll have to fight the hordes of school kids in line, even, it often seems, during school hours. But clearly they've learned where to get a good snoball. Bywater upstart **Peity Street Snoballs** (612 Piety St.; *C* **504/782-2569**) is attracting the foodie crowd with their fresh-fruit extracts and novel flavors, like Vietnamese coffee and hibiscus pomegranate.

P.J.'s Coffee & Tea Company ★★ COFFEE   P.J.'s is a local institution with many locations. It offers a great variety of teas, coffees, and espressos, and it roasts its town coffee beans. The iced coffee is made with a 12-hour cold-water process. The granita "slushee" is great on those hot, muggy Louisiana days.

5432 Magazine St. *C* **504/355-2202.** www.pjscoffee.com. Drinks and pastries 95¢–$4. Daily 6am–9pm (sometimes later on weekends). P.J.'s has branches at Tulane University. *C* **504/865-5705;** 644 Camp St. *C* **504/529-3658;** and 7264 Maple St. *C* **504/861-5335,** among other locations.

Royal Blend Coffee & Tea House ★ COFFEE/LIGHT FARE   This place is set back off the street; to reach it, you walk through a courtyard. Order a sandwich, quiche, or salad and take it out into the courtyard. If you're just in the mood for coffee and pastry, they have plenty of that, too, and the pastry menu changes daily.

621 Royal St. *C* **504/523-2716.** www.royalblendcoffee.com. Drinks and pastries 85¢–$3; lunch items $5–$10. Daily 8am–6pm. Royal Blend has a branch at 204 Metairie Rd. in Metairie. *C* **504/835-7779.**

Sucré ★★★ DESSERT/LIGHT FARE   See the listing for this high-end confectionery under "Candies, Pralines, & Pastries," on p. 189. A new French Quarter location (opening in early 2014 at 622 Conti St.) will offer all of Sucre's wonderful sweet stuff plus pour-over coffee, made-to-order soufflés, light savory fare, and a full bar in a second-floor salon.

3025 Magazine St. ℭ **504/520-8311.** www.shopsucre.com. All desserts under $10, except full cakes. Sun–Thurs 8am–10pm; Fri–Sat 8am–midnight.

EXPLORING NEW ORLEANS

We've made no secret of our favorite New Orleans activities: walking, eating, listening to music, dancing, and eating again. But between those activities, there's much to see, do, and experience. New Orleans is a vibrant, visual city with a rich history and gobs of culture worthy of your time—some of which is indoors and blessedly air-conditioned. That's likely to be handy when you need to escape the rain or heat.

Frankly, New Orleans itself is one big sight—it's one of the most unusual-looking cities in America. It's nice and flat, just made for exploring on foot. (See the walking tours on p. 196 if you'd like some structure.)

While the French Quarter certainly is a seductive place, going to New Orleans and never leaving the Quarter is like visiting Greenwich Village and believing you've seen New York. Stroll the lush Garden District, marvel at the oaks in City Park, ride the streetcar on St. Charles Avenue and gape at the gorgeous homes, or go visit some gators on a swamp tour. Take a walk along Bayou St. John, tour the remarkable Tremé neighborhood, or ride a bike through the Bywater. And yes, if you like, make a pilgrimage to the still-recovering Lower Ninth Ward area. You'll no longer see utter devastation, but you will see restoration—and you'll be witnessing history.

THE FRENCH QUARTER

Those who have been to Disneyland might be forgiven if they experience some déjà vu upon first seeing the French Quarter. It's somewhat more worn, of course, and, in spots, a bit smellier. But despite the fact that Walt actually did replicate a French Quarter street in Disneyland's New Orleans Square, it's an actual neighborhood—over 200 years old—and one of the most visually interesting in America. (Some of the people living in the Quarter are the fifth generation of their family to do so.) That it was spared any flooding and suffered relatively little storm damage after Hurricane Katrina was a tremendous gift to the city.

There's a great deal to the French Quarter—history, architecture, cultural oddities—and to overlook all that in favor of souvenir shops and the ubiquitous bars is a darn shame. We certainly enjoy the lure of an occasional venture to Bourbon Street—in all its tacky, outlandish glory, and we absolutely recommend it. But the operative word is "occasional"—and the key to this city is getting out and fully exploring it.

A French engineer named Adrien de Pauger laid out the Quarter in 1718, and today it's a great anomaly in America. Many other American cities have torn down or gutted their historic centers, but thanks to a strict local preservation policy, the area looks much as it always has and is still the center of town.

Jackson Square bustles with musicians, artists, fortunetellers, jugglers, and those peculiar "living statue" performance artists entertaining for change (we try to always carry a few $1 bills, to throw something in the hat of those that catch our eye or ear). Pay attention to that seemingly ad-hoc jazz band that plays right in front of the Cabildo—these talented musicians might be in jeans now but may very well be in tie and tux later, playing high-end clubs. **Royal Street** is home to stellar street musicians, numerous antiques shops, and galleries, with other interesting stores on **Chartres** and **Decatur streets** and the cross streets between.

Impressions

Yet to all men whose desire only is to live a short life, but a merry one, I have no hesitation in recommending New Orleans.

—Henry Fearon, *Sketches of America*, 1817

The closer you get to **Esplanade Avenue** and toward **Rampart Street,** the more residential the Quarter becomes, and buildings are entirely homes (in the business sections, the ground floors are commercial and the stories above apartments). Peep in through any open gate; surprises await in the form of graceful brick- and flagstone-lined courtyards filled with foliage and bubbling fountains. At the same time, be mindful that throughout the Quarter, you are walking by people's homes. Be courteous, quiet, and clean, folks.

The Vieux Carré Commission is ever vigilant about balancing contemporary economic interests in the Quarter with historical preservation. There's not a traffic light in the whole interior of the French Quarter—they're relegated to fringe streets—and streetlights are of the old gaslight style. Large city buses are banned, and during part of each day, Royal and Bourbon streets are pedestrian malls. No vehicles are *ever* allowed around Jackson Square. We also applaud the exclusion of most generic chain stores.

The Quarter streets are laid out in an almost perfect rectangular grid, so it's easily navigable. It's also so well-traveled that it is nearly always safe. Again, as you get toward the fringes (especially near Rampart) and as night falls, you should exercise caution; stay in the more bustling parts and try not to walk alone.

The French Quarter walking tour in chapter 10 will give you the best overview of the historic structures in the area and of the area's (and city's) history. Many other attractions that aren't in the walking tour are listed in this chapter (and mapped on p. 199), so make sure to cross-reference as you go along.

As mentioned elsewhere, driving in the French Quarter isn't ideal. But if you must, and you're planning on a full day of sightseeing, you can reserve a parking spot at lots owned by **Premium Parking.** It's not a bad idea to have a designated parking destination, and it's a very good idea during events and peak seasons. See www.premiumparking.com.

Major Attractions

Audubon Aquarium of the Americas ★★★

It's been a busy few years at the world-class Audubon Institute's Aquarium of the Americas. Penguin evacuees made a star-studded post-Katrina return via a chartered FedEx flight, waddling home down a (FedEx) purple carpet as news cameras rolled. Then, rescued sea turtles were

New Orleans Attractions

rehabilitated here after the Gulf oil spill; some made the Aquarium their permanent home. These instances point up just how topical and relevant an aquarium can be, besides being full of cool fishies. This one, which has a strong focus on the Mississippi and the Gulf of Mexico, is highly entertaining and painlessly educational for kids and grown-ups. There's plenty of interactivity, including a new "Geaux Fish!" exhibit that follows fish from the waters to the plate. We love the huge interior rain forest (complete with birds and piranhas) and being able to look below the surface of a swamp. Not to be missed are a fine exhibit on frogs, a rare albino gator, a manta-ray touch tank, and Parakeet Pointe, where birds alight right on you (especially if you buy the $1 feed sticks).

It's easily accessible, right on the edge of the Quarter, and a handy refuge from the heat or rain. It's also part of a complex of Audubon attractions, including an **IMAX theater ★★** next door (which screens *Hurricane on the Bayou,* an astonishing Katrina documentary); the **Insectarium** (see below) a block away; and the **Audubon Zoo** (p. 140) uptown. If you plan to visit more than one Audubon attraction, spring for one of the combination admission packages. Various options are available; they're good for 14 days, and you'll save a few dollars.

1 Canal St., at the river. ✆ **800/774-7394** or 504/581-4629. www.auduboninstitute.org. Aquarium $22.50 adults, $17 seniors, $16 children 2–12. IMAX $10.50 adults, $9.50 seniors, $8 children. Four attraction combo ticket: $44.50 adults, $31.50 for seniors, $25 for children 2–12. Aquarium and IMAX Mon 10am–5pm summers only; Tues–Sun 10am–5pm year round. Call for IMAX show times. Closed Mardi Gras and Christmas.

Audubon Insectarium ★★ This fascinating museum is dedicated to all things bug and arachnid, specifically 900,000 species of critters that creep, crawl, and flutter. Located in the old U.S. Customs House, it's the largest free-standing museum in the world dedicated to its multilegged, winged subjects.

The journey through ickiness (kidding! Bugs are great!) begins in the Prehistoric hallway with 30-inch insect replicas. A gallery that simulates the experience of being underground exposes the tiny world living in our soil. In the **Tiny Termite Café,** each glass-topped table has an insect colony living in it (watch silkworms spin their fibers while you dine), and it even serves a few creepy-crawler-based snacks. Finally, the Japanese-inspired **butterfly gallery,** full of living, fluttering beauty, is a peaceful departure from the hustle outside.

423 Canal St. ✆ **800/774-7394** or 504/581-4629. www.auduboninstitute.org. Admission $16.50 adults, $13 seniors, $12 children 2–12. Insectarium, Aquarium, and IMAX tickets $44.50 adults, $31.50 seniors, $25 children. Mon 10am–5pm summers only; Tues–Sun 10am–5pm year round. Last entry at 4pm.

The Historic French Market ★★ Legend has it that the site of the French Market was originally used by Native Americans as a bartering market. It grew into an official market in 1812. From around 1840 to 1870, it was part of Gallatin Street, an impossibly rough area full of bars, drunken sailors, and criminals. Today it's a mixed bag, and not nearly as colorful as its past, but the whole thing was recently renovated and much improved (including clean public bathrooms). The farmer's market makes a fun amble as you admire everything from fresh produce and fish to more tourist-oriented items like hot sauces and Cajun and Creole mixes. Goods are pricier than at local supermarkets, but they'll pack for air travel or ship it home. Snacks like gator on a stick will amuse the kids, while a newly installed raw bar and improved food vendors will

French Quarter Attractions

Audubon Aquarium
   of the Americas **11**
Audubon Insectarium **8**
Beauregard-Keyes House **27**
The Cabildo **15**
Café du Monde **20**
Carriage Tours **18**
Congo Square **21**
The 1850 House **19**
Entergy IMAX Theatre **10**
The French Market **29**
Gallier House Museum **26**
Germaine Wells Mardi
   Gras Museum **4**
Hermann-Grima House **3**
Historic New Orleans Collection **6**
Jean Lafitte National Park and Preserve
   Folklife and Visitor Center **12**
Madame John's Legacy **24**

New Orleans Historical
   Pharmacy Museum **13**
New Orleans Historic
   Voodoo Museum **23**
Old Absinthe House **5**
Old Ursuline Convent **28**
The Old U.S. Mint **30**
Our Lady of Guadeloupe Chapel –
   International Shrine of St. Jude **2**
Pontalba Apartments **19**
The Presbytère **17**
Preservation Hall **14**
St. Louis Cathedral **16**
St. Louis Cemetery No . 1 **1**
Williams Research Center **7**
Woldenberg
   Riverfront Park **9**
Voodoo Authentica **25**
Voodoo Spiritual Temple **22**

satisfy the grown-ups (**Meals from the Heart** and **Organic Banana** are standouts). The famed flea market section is, in reality, kind of junky, but it fits the bill for T-shirts, hats, cheap sunglasses, and so on. Still, you'll find a few original art vendors sprinkled in the mix and even some bargains (and bargaining), and the flea-market items are tax free. It's convenient for souvenir shopping and New Orleans–related jewelry, especially silver—it has a vast array of inexpensive fleur-de-lis (the city's sort of unofficial design emblem) and water-meter-shaped items. If you've outshopped your luggage, you can pick up a duffle bag or small suitcase here.

On Decatur St., toward Esplanade Ave. from Jackson Sq. www.frenchmarket.org. © **504/522-2621.** Daily 9am–6pm (tends to start shutting down about an hour before closing).

St. Louis Cathedral ★ The St. Louis Cathedral prides itself on being the oldest continuously active cathedral in the United States. What usually doesn't get mentioned is that it is not the prettiest. The outside is all right, but the rather grim interior wouldn't give even a minor European church a run for its money. Still, it's worth going inside for a look—if you're lucky, you may catch a choir practice. Volunteer docents are full of fun facts about the windows and murals and how the building nearly collapsed once from water-table sinkage. Note the sloping floor: Clever architectural design somehow keeps the building upright even as it continues to sink. Outside, a plaque marks the visit by Pope John Paul II in 1987.

The cathedral's history is impressive. It formed the center of the original settlement, and remains the French Quarter's central landmark. This is the third building to stand on this spot. A hurricane destroyed the first in 1722. On Good Friday 1788, the bells of its replacement were kept silent for religious reasons rather than ringing out the alarm for a fire—which eventually burned down more than 850 buildings, including the cathedral itself.

Rebuilt in 1794, the structure was remodeled and enlarged between 1845 and 1851 by J. N. B. de Pouilly. The brick used in its construction was taken from the original town cemetery and was covered with stucco to protect the mortar from dampness. And just when you think nothing else can go wrong, along comes Katrina. The roof leaked, ruining the $1-million organ (it's been rebuilt and returned). Outside, two magnificent, ancient live oaks fell, narrowly missing a statue of Jesus. His thumbs were amputated, however, and Archbishop Hughes, in his first post-Katrina sermon in the cathedral, vowed not to replace them until all of New Orleans is healed. The dramatically lit statue makes a resplendent, if somewhat eerie, nighttime silhouette (well, we think so; others call it "Touchdown Jesus"—do make a point to walk by at night to see why).

615 Pere Antoine Alley. © **504/525-9585.** www.stlouiscathedral.org. Free admission; guided tours and large groups by reservation only. Mon–Sat 9am–4pm; Sun 9am–2pm. Cafe and gift shop Mon–Sat 10am–3pm; Sun 1–4pm.

Historic Buildings

Beauregard-Keyes House ★ This "raised cottage," with its Doric columns and handsome twin staircases, was built as a residence by a wealthy New Orleans auctioneer, Joseph LeCarpentier, in 1826. Confederate General P. G. T. Beauregard lived in the house with several members of his family for 18 months between 1865 and 1867, and from 1944 until 1970 it was the residence of Frances Parkinson Keyes (pronounced *Cause*), who wrote many novels about the region. One of them, *Madame Castel's Lodger,* concerns the general's stay in this house. *Dinner at Antoine's,* perhaps her most famous novel, was also written here. Mrs. Keyes left her home to a foundation, and the house, rear buildings, and garden are open to the public. The gift shop has a wide selection of her novels.

1113 Chartres St., at Ursuline St. (✆ **504/523-7257.** www.bkhouse.org. Admission $10 adults (no charge for active military); $9 seniors, students, and AAA members; $4 children 6–12; free for children 5 and under. Mon–Sat 10am–4pm. Tours on the hour. Closed Sun and holidays.

The 1850 House ★ James Gallier, Sr., and his son designed the historic Pontalba Buildings for the Baroness Micaela Almonester de Pontalba (see box below and the French Quarter walking tour on p. 196), who had them built in 1849 in an effort to combat the deterioration of the older part of the city. The rows of town houses on either side of Jackson Square were the largest private buildings in the country at the time. Legend has it that the baroness, miffed that her friend Andrew Jackson wouldn't tip his hat to her, had his statue erected in the square, where to this day he continues to doff his chapeau toward her top-floor apartment. It's probably not true, but we never stand in the way of a good story.

Here, the **Louisiana State Museum** presents a demonstration of life in 1850, when the buildings opened for residential use. The self-guided tour uses a fact-filled sheet explaining the history of the interior. Period furnishings show how the rooms were typically used. It vividly illustrates the difference between the "upstairs" portion of the house, where the upper-middle-class family lived in comfort (and the children, largely confined to a nursery, were raised by servants), and the "downstairs," where the staff toiled in considerable drudgery to make their bosses comfortable. It's a surprisingly enjoyable look at life in the good, or not so good, old days.

Lower Pontalba Bldg., 523 St. Ann St., Jackson Sq. (✆ **800/568-6968** or 504/568-6968. www.crt. state.la.us/museum/properties/1850house.aspx. Admission $3; $2 students, seniors, and active military; free for children 12 and under. Tues–Sun 10am–4:30pm. Closed all legal holidays.

Old Absinthe House ★ The Old Absinthe House was built in 1806 and now houses a bar and restaurant. The drink for which the building and bar were named was once outlawed in this country (certain chemical additives, not the actual wormwood used to flavor the drink, caused blindness and madness). Now you can legally sip the infamous libation in the bar and feel at one with the famous types who came before you, listed on a plaque outside: William Thackeray, Oscar Wilde, Sarah Bernhardt, and Walt Whitman. Andrew Jackson and the Lafitte brothers plotted their desperate defense of New Orleans here in 1815.

The house was a speakeasy during Prohibition, and when federal officers closed it in 1924, the interior was mysteriously stripped of its antique fixtures—including the long marble-topped bar and the old water dripper that was used to infuse water into the absinthe. Just as mysteriously, they reappeared in another bar down the street, and then once again returned to one of the restaurants on this site. The bar is now covered with business cards (and drunks), so don't come looking to recapture some kind of old-timey classy atmosphere. But it's still a genuinely fun hangout.

240 Bourbon St., btw. Iberville and Bienville sts. (✆ **504/523-3181.** Free admission. Sun–Thurs 9am–2am; Fri–Sat 9am–4am.

Old Ursuline Convent ★★ Forget tales of America being founded by brawny, brave, tough guys in buckskin and beards. The real pioneers—at least, in Louisiana—were well-educated Frenchwomen clad in 40 pounds of black wool robes. That's right; you don't know tough until you know the Ursuline nuns, and this city would have been a very different place without them.

The Sisters of Ursula came to the mudhole that was New Orleans in 1727 after a journey that several times nearly saw them lost at sea or succumbing to pirates or disease. Here, they provided the first decent medical care (saving countless lives) and later founded the first local school and orphanage for girls. They also helped raise girls shipped over from France as marriage material for local men, teaching them everything from languages to homemaking of the most exacting sort (laying the foundation for who knows how many local families).

The convent dates from 1752 (the sisters themselves moved uptown in 1824, where they remain to this day), and it is the oldest building in the Mississippi River Valley and the only surviving building from the French colonial period in the United States. It also houses Catholic archives dating back to 1718.

The **self-guided tour** of the convent shows rooms and elements of the era, as well as religious and artistic icons (the top floor, where the ghost supposedly lives, is off-limits, unfortunately). It includes access to St. Mary's Church, original site of the Ursuline convent and a former archbishop's residence. The whole convent can be viewed in an hour or less.

1100 Chartres St., at Ursuline St. ✆ **877/529-2242** or 504-525-9585. www.oldursulineconvent.org. Admission $5 adults, $4 seniors, $3 students, children 6 and under free. Mon–Sat 10am–4pm. (Last tour begins at 4pm.)

The Old U.S. Mint ★★

This is one of the many places that got pummeled during Katrina, and came out better for it. After renovation, it reopened with a split personality, but both parts are good. It's the only building in America to have served as both a U.S. and a Confederate mint, and the first floor is now a coin museum of interest for numismatists (look! O-minted coins, struck right here!) and regular folk (oooh, so *that's* how they made those, back before computers . . .). Upstairs is an exhibit celebrating the 50th Anniversary of Preservation Hall, small but worthy, with some very significant artworks, instruments, recordings, and artifacts (including Louis Armstrong's first horn). An extensive jazz museum, waylaid since Katrina, will return here once budget permits. The third floor is a gorgeous new performance space, which has lectures, music, cooking instructions, or something equally interesting most days. Definitely check the schedule of events, which are frequently free and very cool. Swingin', in fact. This is an easy museum to throw into a day's plan; you can peruse it in 60 to 90 minutes. *Fun fact:* Ghost hunters believe William Mumford, who met the noose here in 1862, still hangs around.

400 Esplanade Ave., at N. Peters St. (enter on Esplanade Ave. or Barracks St.). ✆ **800/568-6968** or 504/568-6993. www.crt.state.la.us/museum/properties/usmint and www.musicatthemint.org. Admission $6 adults; $5 students, seniors, active military; children 6 and under free. Tues–Sun 10am–4:30pm. Closed all legal holidays.

Our Lady of Guadalupe Chapel—International Shrine of St. Jude ★

This "funeral chapel" was erected in 1826 conveniently near St. Louis Cemetery No. 1, specifically for funeral services, so as not to spread disease through the Quarter. We like it for three reasons: the catacomb-like devotional chapel with plaques thanking the Virgin Mary for favors granted; the gift shop full of religious medals including a number of obscure saints; and the statue of St. Expedite. The saint got his name, according to legend, when his crate arrived with no identification other than the word EXPEDITE stamped on the outside. Now he's the "saint" you pray to when you want things in a hurry. (We are not making this up.) Expedite has his cults in France and Spain and is

lady bountiful: BARONESS DE PONTALBA

New Orleans owes a great debt to Baroness Micaela Almonester de Pontalba and her family. Without them, Jackson Square would be a mudhole. Her father, Don Almonester, used his money and influence to have the St. Louis Cathedral, Cabildo, and Presbytère built. The baroness was responsible for the two long brick apartment buildings that flank Jackson Square and for the renovation that turned the center of the square into what it is today.

Born in 1795 into the most influential family in New Orleans, the baroness married her cousin, who subsequently stole her inheritance. When she wanted a separation at a time when such things were unheard of, her father-in-law shot her several times and then shot himself. She survived, though some of her fingers did not. In subsequent portraits, she would hide the wounded hand in her dress. In the end, she got her money back—she used it for those French Quarter improvements—and also ended up taking care of her (eventually) slightly nutty husband for the rest of his life. She died in Paris in 1874; her home there is now the residence of the American ambassador. The book *Intimate Enemies*, by Christina Vella (Louisiana State University Press, 1997), has all the details about this remarkable woman.

also popular among the Voodoo folks. He's just inside the door on the right. The chapel also has a pretty great religious gift shop in case you want to pick up an Expedite prayer card. For those interested in some extra prayer power for lost causes, the St. Jude solemn novena runs the last weeks of January, April, July, and October for 9 days at a time—call for the exact start dates.

411 N. Rampart St., at Conti St. parish office. ℂ **504/525-1551.** Gift shop Mon–Sat 9am–5pm. Masses daily starting at 7am.

Museums

In addition to the destinations listed here, you might be interested in the **Germaine Wells Mardi Gras Museum** at 813 Bienville Street, on the second floor of Arnaud's restaurant (p. 81; ℂ **504/523-5433**). It has a collection of Mardi Gras costumes and ball gowns dating from 1910 through 1960. Admission is free, and the museum is open during restaurant hours, 7 days a week (6pm–close nightly; Sun 10am–2:30pm).

The Cabildo ★★ One of two fine museums flanking St. Louis Cathedral in the heart of the French Quarter, the Cabildo houses the premier collection of artifacts regarding New Orleans and Louisiana history. It starts with the earliest explorers and covers slavery, post–Civil War reconstruction, and statehood. It is well-qualified to do so: The Cabildo is the site of the signing of the Louisiana Purchase transfer (this 1795 building was the seat of government at the time; at other times it served as a courthouse and a prison). The detailed history is covered from a multicultural perspective and touches on topics like antebellum music, mourning and burial customs (a big deal during the yellow fever epidemics), immigration and assimilation, and the role of the Southern woman. Portraits of historical figures and incidents are hung throughout, and then there's Napoleon's death mask. The item and its story (it almost ended up in a trash dump) are quite fascinating. Another exhibit, "Unsung Heroes: The Secret

History of Rock 'n Roll," highlights Louisianans, famous or unknown, who had an impact on rock music. It's got tons of cool music doodads, costumes, instruments, records, and posters from the amazing collection of Dr. Ike, founder of the Ponderosa Stomp (p. 36). It's fairly dense museum, but it's terrific.

701 Chartres St. ℂ **800/568-6968** or 504/568-6968. www.crt.state.la.us/museum/properties/cabildo. Admission $6 adults; $5 students, seniors, and military; free for children 12 and under. Tues–Sun 10am–4:30pm.

Gallier House Museum ★★
James Gallier, Jr. (it's pronounced *Gaul*-ee-er, by the way; he was Irish, not French), and his father were the leading architects in New Orleans in the mid 1800s. They designed the French Opera House, Municipality Hall (now Gallier Hall), and the Pontalba Buildings. The Gallier House Museum is the architect's personal residence. It's meticulously restored, with the fancy furnishings appearing much as they would have when the Gallier family lived there (some claim Gallier's ghost is still a resident). The home displays some of his innovations—such as early indoor plumbing—as well as a decided lack thereof in the slave quarters. It's made even more gorgeous for holiday season, with period décor; check the website for other special programs. ***Fun fact for Anne Rice fans:*** This house was her muse for Louis and Lestat's New Orleans residence in *Interview with the Vampire*. Combination tickets with the Hermann-Grima House are available.

1118 and 1132 Royal St., btw. Gov. Nicholls and Ursuline sts. ℂ **504/525-5661**. www.hgghh.org. Admission $12 adults; $10 seniors, students, AAA members, children. Open for hourly guided tours Mon, Thurs, Fri 10am–2pm; Sat noon–3pm. Call ahead as hours can change; usually closed 1–2 weeks in Aug for vacation and sprucing.

Hermann-Grima House ★★
The Hermann-Grima House is a symmetrical Federal-style building (perhaps the first in the Quarter) that's very different from its French-style neighbors. The knowledgeable docents who give the regular tours make this a satisfactory stop at any time, but keep an eye out for the frequent special tours. At Halloween, for example, the house is draped in typical 1800s mourning cloth, and the docents explain mourning customs. (**Historic New Orleans Tours** [p. 149] offers a year-round interactive specialty tour of the Hermann-Grima House focusing on mourning customs.) The house, which stretches from St. Louis Street to Conti Street, passed through two different families before becoming a boardinghouse in the 1920s. It has been meticulously restored and researched, and a tour of the house is one of the city's more historically accurate offerings. On Tuesdays and Thursdays from October through May, cooking demonstrations take place in the authentic 1830s kitchen, using methods of the era. (Alas, health rules prevent those on the tour from sampling the results.) The house also contains one of the Quarter's last surviving stables, complete with stalls. Combination tickets with the Gallier House are available.

820 St. Louis St. ℂ **504/525-5661**. www.hgghh.org. Admission $12 adults; $10 seniors, students, AAA members, and children 8–18; free for children 7 and under. Open for hourly guided tours Mon, Tues, Thurs, Fri 10am–2pm; Sat noon–3pm. Call ahead as hours can change; usually closed 1–2 weeks in Aug for vacation and sprucing.

Historic New Orleans Collection—Museum/Research Center ★★
This complex of historic buildings in the middle of the French Quarter is secreted away with little signage or fanfare. But a hidden treasure lies within. All were owned by the collection's founders, General and Mrs. L. Kemper Williams, and remain an excellent look at what once was. One building is a rare survivor of the great fire of 1794. Behind

a courtyard lies the elegant former residence of General and Mrs. Williams, open for tours. There are galleries with wonderful artworks, maps, and historic documents, and tours that focus on landscaping, architecture, and Mardi Gras (during Carnival season). It's all of great relevance to anyone interested in architecture or local history, and each building has a centuries-old tale to tell. Another grandly restored, Beaux-Arts style building belonging to the complex is the **Williams Research Center,** 410 Chartres Street, near Conti Street (𝒞 **504/598-7171**), which houses many of the collection's items. It presents rotating exhibits and serves as a research center for academics and members of the public (who can access research documents with librarian assistance): if you're curious about anything regarding New Orleans or Louisiana history, the answer is probably here.

533 Royal St., btw. St. Louis and Toulouse sts. 𝒞 **504/523-4662.** www.hnoc.org. Free admission; guided tours $5. Tues–Sat 9:30am–4:30pm; Sun 10:30am–4:30pm. Tours Tues–Sat 10am, 11am, 2pm, and 3pm; Sun 11am, 2pm, and 3pm. Closed major holidays and Mardi Gras.

Madame John's Legacy ★   This is the second-oldest building in the Mississippi Valley (after the Ursuline Convent) and a rare example of Creole architecture that miraculously survived the 1794 fire. Built around 1788 on the foundations of an earlier home that was destroyed in the fire of that year, the house has had a number of owners and renters (including the son of Governor Claiborne), but none of them were named John (or even Madame!). It acquired its moniker courtesy of author George Washington Cable, who used the house as a setting for his short story '*Tite Poulette.* The protagonist was a quadroon, Madame John, named after her lover, who willed this house to her.

632 Dumaine St. 𝒞 **800/568-6968** or 504/568-6968. www.crt.state.la.us/museum/properties/madame_johns_legacy/. Free admission. Tues–Sun 10am–4:30pm. Closed Mon & holidays.

New Orleans Historical Pharmacy Museum ★   Leeches. LEEEEECHES. Yeah, they're here. So are many other icky things, and fascinating potions, and instruments-of-torture-looking artifacts (actually antique surgical devices). The first licensed pharmacist in the United States, Louis J. Dufilho, Jr., opened an apothecary shop in this Creole-style town house in 1823. This bizarre and beguiling museum opened in 1950 and displays old apothecary bottles, Voodoo potions, opium products of every ilk, suppository molds, and all variant of snake oil—in exquisite wood and glass cases. Also interesting are old makeup and perfume paraphernalia, which were brewed up by pharmacists back in the day. You'll never appreciate a modern doctor's appointment more. Try to go on a Thursday or Friday when the insightful, sometimes shocking guided tour is offered.

514 Chartres St., at St. Louis St. 𝒞 **504/565-8027.** www.pharmacymuseum.org. Admission $5 adults, $4 students and seniors, children 5 and under free. Tues–Fri 10am–2pm; Sat 10am–5pm. Guided tours noon on Thurs and Fri.

New Orleans Historic Voodoo Museum ★   This small museum is packed with dusty displays of Voodoo objects from around the world and right here in New Orleans, including some that allegedly belonged to the legendary Voodoo queen, Marie Laveau. While serious practitioners might scoff at the tourist orientation of this place, it really does offer a good introduction to the truth behind the myths of this mysterious practice. You'll get the most out of your visit if you engage with the museum's founder, usually found manning the front desk. Whoever is there is usually involved in Voodoo, either as a priest or priestess or an educator, and invariably happy to discuss it with those with a sincere interest. They can even arrange a reading or custom gris-gris bag for you. Some simple objects like Voodoo dolls and herbs are also available for sale. Why not? (Don't confuse this place with the Marie Laveau House of Voodoo on Bourbon Street.)

724 Dumaine St., at Bourbon St. © **504/680-0128.** www.voodoomuseum.com. Admission $7 adults; $5.50 students, seniors, and military; $4.50 high-school students; $3.50 children 11 and under; check website for discounts. Cemetery tour $19 adults, $10 children 12 and under. Daily 10am–6pm.

The Presbytère ★★★

The Presbytère, which flanks St. Louis Cathedral to the right, was originally built to house the clergy serving in the cathedral. That never came to pass, and the clergy's loss is our gain. It's now a museum with two excellent permanent exhibits. Upstairs, the Mardi Gras exhibit walks visitors through the holiday's history—which is so much more (and so much more interesting) than cwazy kids doing cwazy kid stuff. It shows ornate Mardi Gras Indian costumes and antique Mardi Gras Queen jewels, and there's even a replica float so you can toss mock beads at mock crowds. (To see the real thing, visit Blaine Kern's Mardi Gras World; p. 131.) On the first floor, the multimedia exhibit "Living with Hurricanes: Katrina and Beyond" is an indepth look at the history and human drama of hurricanes. First-person audio, video, and interactive displays create an educational but wholly accessible experience, and an emotionally evocative one at that (but with enough optimism, humor, and science to keep it from being downcast). One man's "IN CASE OF EMERGENCY" memo hangs on a wall: his jeans, scrawled with his name, blood type, and next-of-kin. A reproduction of a small attic with a rough hole chopped through its ceiling—and the very axe one woman used to commit a similar act—accompany her voiceover describing the incident. It's powerful stuff.

751 Chartres St., Jackson Sq. © **800/568-6968** or 504/568-6968. www.crt.state.la.us/museum/properties/presbytere/. Admission $6 adults, $5 seniors and students, free for children 12 and under. Tues–Sun 10am–4:30pm.

Woldenberg Riverfront Park ★

This 20-acre park along the river serves as promenade and public art gallery, with numerous works by popular local artists amid green lawns and hundreds of trees. Seek out the kinetic Holocaust memorial sculpture by noted Israeli sculptor Yaacov Agam, and make a slow circle around it to get the full effect of its changing perspectives, which use a rainbow to unexpected symbolic effect.

The nearby **Moonwalk ★★★** is a paved pedestrian thoroughfare along the river, a wonderful walk on a pretty New Orleans day but really a must-do for any weather other than pouring rain. It has steps that allow you to get right down to Old Muddy—on foggy nights, you feel as if you are floating above the water. There are many benches from which to view the city's busy port—perhaps while enjoying a muffuletta to a street musician's song. To your right, you'll see the Greater New Orleans Bridge and the World Trade Center of New Orleans (formerly the International Trade Mart) skyscraper as well as the Toulouse Street wharf, the departure point for excursion steamboats. This is also an excellent spot to watch full moons rise over the river.

Along the Mississippi from the Moonwalk at the old Governor Nicholls St. wharf to the Aquarium of the Americas at Canal St. © **504/861-2537.** Daily dawn–dusk.

OUTSIDE THE FRENCH QUARTER

Uptown & the Garden District

If you can see just one thing outside the French Quarter, make it the Garden District. These two neighborhoods are the first places that come to mind when one hears the words "New Orleans." The Garden District has no significant historic buildings or important museums—it's simply beautiful. In some ways, even more so than the Quarter, this is New Orleans. Authors as diverse as Truman Capote and Anne Rice have been enchanted by its spell. Gorgeous homes stand quietly amid lush foliage, elegant but ever so slightly (or more) decayed. You can see why this is the setting for so many novels; it's hard to imagine that anything real actually happens here.

But it does. Like the Quarter, this is a neighborhood, so please be courteous as you wander around. To see the sights, you need only mosey around and admire the exteriors and gardens of beautiful houses. We've kindly mapped out a comprehensive **walking tour** (p. 204) to help guide you to the Garden District's treasures and explain a little of its history. Naturally it starts with a ride on the St. Charles streetcar. You might also check out the listings starting on p. 185 to find the best shops, galleries, and bookstores on **Magazine Street,** the eclectic shopping strip that bounds the Garden District.

Meanwhile, a little background: Across Canal Street from the Quarter, "American" New Orleans begins. After the Louisiana Purchase of 1803, an essentially French-Creole city came under the auspices of a government determined to develop it as an American city. Tensions between Creole society and the encroaching American newcomers began to increase. Some historians lay this tension at the feet of Creole snobbery; others blame the naive and uncultured Americans. In any case, Creole society succeeded in maintaining a relatively distinct social world, deflecting American settlement upriver of Canal Street (Uptown); the Americans in turn came to dominate the city with sheer numbers of immigrants. Newcomers bought up land in what had been the old Gravier Plantation (now the Uptown area) and began to build a parallel city. Very soon, Americans came to dominate the local business scene, centered along Canal Street. In 1833 the American enclave that we now know as the Garden District was incorporated as Lafayette City, and—thanks in large part to the New Orleans–Carrollton Railroad, which covered the route of today's St. Charles Avenue streetcar—the Americans kept right on expanding until they reached the tiny resort town of Carrollton. It wasn't until 1852 that the various sections came together officially as a united New Orleans.

Again, as with the Quarter, it was great good fortune for the crucial economy generated by tourism that the Garden District was largely undamaged by Katrina and Rita, and its beauty remains as intoxicating as ever.

Trolling St. John's Bayou, Esplanade & Lake Pontchartrain ★★★

St. John's Bayou is one of the key reasons New Orleans exists. This body of water originally extended from the outskirts of New Orleans to Lake Pontchartrain. Jean-Baptiste Le Moyne, Sieur de Bienville, was commissioned to establish a settlement in

Louisiana that would both make money and also protect French holdings in the New World from British expansion. Bienville chose the spot where New Orleans now sits because he recognized the strategic importance of the Bayou St. John's "back-door" access to the lake, and ultimately to the Gulf of Mexico. Boats could enter the lake from the Gulf and follow the Bayou to its conclusion. From there, they were within easy portage distance of the mouth of the Mississippi River. Native Americans had used this route for years.

The early path from the city to the bayou is today's Bayou Road, an extension of Governor Nicholls Street in the French Quarter. Modern-day Gentilly Boulevard, which crosses the bayou, was another Native American trail—it led around the lake and on to settlements as far as Florida.

As New Orleans grew and prospered, the bayou became a suburb as planters moved out along its shores. In the early 1800s, a canal was dug to connect the waterway with the city, reaching a basin at the edge of Congo Square (which begat today's Basin Street). The Bayou became a popular recreation area, lined with fine restaurants and dance halls (and meeting places for Voodoo practitioners, who held secret ceremonies along its shores). Gradually, New Orleans reached beyond the French Quarter and enveloped the whole area—overtaking farmland, plantation homes, and resorts.

The canal was filled in long ago, and the bayou is a meek re-creation of itself. It is no longer navigable (even if it were, bridges were built too low to permit the passage of watercraft other than kayaks), but residents still prize their waterfront sites, and kayaks, rowboats and paddleboards make use of the bayou's smooth surface. This is one of the prettiest areas of New Orleans—full of the old houses tourists love to marvel at without the hustle, bustle, and confusion of more high-profile locations. A stroll along the banks and through the nearby neighborhoods is one of our favorite things to do on a nice afternoon.

GETTING THERE The simplest way to reach St. John's Bayou from the French Quarter is to drive straight up Esplanade Avenue about 20 blocks (you can also grab the bus that says ESPLANADE at any of the bus stops along the avenue). Right before you reach the Bayou, you'll pass **St. Louis Cemetery No. 3** (just past Leda St.). It's the final resting place of many prominent New Orleaneans, among them Father Adrien Rouquette, who lived and worked among the Choctaw; Storyville photographer E. J. Bellocq; and Thomy Lafon, the black philanthropist who bought the old Orleans Ballroom as an orphanage for African-American children and put an end to its infamous "quadroon balls," where well-bred women of mixed color would socialize with and become the mistresses of white men. Walking just past the cemetery, turn left onto Moss Street, which runs along the banks of St. John's Bayou. If you want to see an example of an 18th-century West Indies–style plantation house, stop at the **Pitot House,** 1440 Moss St. (p. 137).

To continue, drive along Wisner Boulevard, on the opposite bank of St. John's Bayou from Moss Street, and you'll pass some of New Orleans's grandest modern homes—a sharp contrast to those on Moss Street. Stay on Wisner to Robert E. Lee Boulevard, turn right, drive to Elysian Fields Avenue, and then turn left. That's the **University of New Orleans campus** on your left. Turn left onto the broad concrete highway, Lake Shore Drive. It runs for 5½ miles along the lake, and normally in the summer the parkway alongside its sea wall is swarming with swimmers and picnickers. On the other side are more luxurious, modern residences. About 2 miles down the road to the west is the fishing-oriented **Bucktown** neighborhood. If you haven't already noticed some leftover Katrina desolation along this drive, you'll probably see it here. This area, home to commercial fishing since the late 1800s, was totally devastated by the 17th Street Canal breech, including the marina, where the storm piled boats atop each other. But you'll also probably see construction, and new development under way to replace the beloved Sid-Mar's restaurant, gone for good from its decades-old Lakeview home—but locals were thrilled to see it come back a few miles farther afield in Metairie. There's a thriving restaurant hub along Harrison Avenue—good to know; you may want a snack after your drive.

As you return, you can drive through the **Lakeview** neighborhood, south of Robert E. Lee, between Canal and City Park—another area that is thriving in the post-Katrina comeback.

Lake Pontchartrain is some 40 miles long and 25 miles wide. You can drive across it over the 24-mile **Greater New Orleans Causeway,** the longest bridge in the world.

Museums & Galleries

Backstreet Cultural Museum ★★★ This small cultural gem in the heart of the Faubourg Tremé is dedicated to certain wholly unique New Orleans cultural traditions, mostly those of the African-American community. The social aid and pleasure clubs, the second-line parades, brass bands, Mardi Gras Indians, and jazz funerals are all well documented and recollected here. We guarantee that the Mardi Gras Indians' ornate beaded costumes are like nothing you've ever seen, and they are best appreciated up close. But the suits are just an entree into the intriguing traditions themselves. If Sylvester Francis is in the house, know that he's the man who started this museum, and the scrupulous collection here is largely his own. He's a fount of knowledge and a true New Orleanean, so spend a few minutes with him if you can, and say thanks. *Note:* Be forewarned; the posted hours can be a little loose.

1116 Henriette Delille St. ⓒ **504/522-4806.** www.backstreetmuseum.org. Admission $8. Tues–Sat 10am–5pm.

Blaine Kern's Mardi Gras World ★★ The scandal-ridden Kerns are the first family of float-making, and this is their headquarters. The Kerns design and build some 75 percent of the floats used by the Mardi Gras krewes during Carnival Season, and you'll find floats from previous years and those in the works for the next season. Sketches, sculptures (and sculptors at work), engineers' drawings, and king cake and coffee are all included on the tour—plus you can try on some of the elaborate, sparkling costumes that float riders wear. It's pretty nifty to see the handiwork up close, and if you can't come for Mardi Gras, at least you can get a taste here and a bit more of an understanding of what goes into it.

1380 Port of New Orleans Place. ⓒ **504/361-7821.** www.mardigrasworld.com. Admission $20 adults, $16 students and seniors (65 and over), $13 children 2–11. Daily 9:30am–5:30pm. Last tour at 4:30pm. Closed Mardi Gras, Easter, Thanksgiving, Christmas.

Confederate Memorial Hall Museum ★★ This museum's next-door neighbor, the Ogden Museum of Southern Art, attempted a bold takeover of this gorgeous, circa-1891 brick facility, but like a proud, stalwart soldier it stood firm and held off the attack. In its collection of Confederate memorabilia—the second-largest in the country, including guns, swords, photographs, oil paintings, battle flags, and Confederate uniforms—are many preserved items that came into its possession right after the Civil War, and thus are in excellent condition. Civil War buffs will be in their glory (sorry), but others will also be fascinated by the personal effects of Confederate General P. G. T. Beauregard, Confederate President Jefferson Davis, and Robert E. Lee displayed here.

929 Camp St., at St. Joseph's. ℭ **504/523-4522.** www.confederatemuseum.com. Admission $8 adults; $5 children 7–14; children under 7 free. Tues–Sat 10am–4pm.

National World War II Museum ★★★ Opened in 2000 on the anniversary of D-Day, this museum has become a New Orleans highlight and a true world-class facility. Its collection of artifacts is beyond abundant, its educational materials are top of the line, and its exhibits, which emphasize personal stories (including audio and video of civilians and soldiers recounting their firsthand experiences), make for an incredibly moving experience.

This museum is the creation of the late historian and best-selling author Stephen Ambrose, with extensive support from Tom Hanks (Ambrose wrote the war film *Saving Private Ryan*, which starred Hanks). It originally opened on the anniversary of D-Day, to commemorate Normandy and the other U.S. operations of that fateful day. Since then, it has expanded tremendously, and it's now quite enormous in both size and scope. It spans three large buildings, each with a theme. In the newest, the U.S. Freedom Pavilion (opened in 2013), seven original warplanes hang from a 10-story ceiling. From the ground up, it's an imposing sight; from eye level, it provides an almost intimate perspective. Other exhibits of note are the interactive "What Would You Do?" kiosks, which pose thoughtful moral and technical questions; a short, shocking film about the atomic bomb (not for kids)—appropriately silent except for a few excerpts of classical music; a copy of Eisenhower's backup speech apologizing to the nation in the event that D-Day failed; and the amazing story of the B-17 known as "My Gal Sal": its desolate downing, the daring rescue, and its comeback decades later. Perhaps most affecting are the many artifacts and personal items from former soldiers and their loved ones, whose stories go deeper than any history book could.

The **Stage Door Canteen** lightens the mood with live, 1940s-era USO-style shows. It's a swinging, old-fashioned outing and good, clean fun for a dinner or brunch show (adults $55–$60; children $45–$52; $30 show only). Showing in the **Solomon Victory Theater,** *Beyond All Boundaries,* is a short, widescreen film with "4D" multisensory effects, such as shaking seats, flashing lights, and falling snow. It's moderately successful at interesting kids in war history, but they may not buy the video game. Tickets are $5 (and require general admission purchase). Lastly, celeb chef John Besh helms the museum's fun **American Sector** restaurant (p. 100), serving modern comfort food that harkens back to the war era.

War veterans and civilians who were involved in the war effort often volunteer at the museum. If you meet any (and you should; they're usually ready to share their personal stories—which is the best possible exhibit a museum could offer), say thanks. Allow at least 3 hours, but you could spend days here.

945 Magazine St., in the Historic Warehouse District. ℭ **504/528-1944.** www.ddaymuseum.org. Admission for museum only $22 adults, $19 seniors, $13 active or retired military with ID and children K–12th grade, WWII veterans, military in uniform, and children under 5 free. Other discounts apply for combination tickets. Daily 9am–5pm. Closed holidays.

New Orleans Museum of Art ★★★ The crown jewel of City Park, and of New Orleans art, NOMA houses a 40,000-piece collection of 16th- through 20th-century

European paintings, drawings, sculptures, and prints; early American art; Asian art; pre-Columbian and Native American ethnographic art; a gallery entirely devoted to Fabergé; and one of the largest decorative glass collections in the country. Not everything is on display, of course, and this very manageable museum does not need to take hours to visit. The visiting exhibits of the last few years have been unfailingly interesting ("King of Arms," Rashaad Newsom's astounding 2013 solo show, for example, and Hale Woodruff's murals in 2014). The building itself is of interest: From the front, the original 1911 neoclassical building is an imposing sight among the greenery of City Park. The newer rear portion is of contemporary design, all angles and curves, steel and glass. It all works to the visitor's advantage, and the interior galleries are well lit and organized.

Next door is the superb **Besthoff Sculpture Garden ★★★**, which spotlights 50 modern sculptures amid 5 serene, landscaped acres. Artists' works by George Segal, Henry Moore, Elisabeth Frink, and Gaston Lachaise and a version of Indiana's famous pop-art *LOVE* sculpture are here. It's a cultural highlight, and admission is free. We like to grab a po' boy down at **Parkway Bakery** (p. 95) and picnic amid the artwork. Alternately, **Ralph Brennan's Cafe NOMA** inside the museum has light lunch fare and wine during museum hours; and **Morning Call** (p. 112) is just a short walk away.

1 Collins Diboll Circle, at City Park and Esplanade. ✆ **504/658-4100.** www.noma.org. Admission $10 adults, $8 seniors (65 and over) and students, $6 children 7–17, kids 6 and under and local students free. Free admission Wed. Tues–Sun 10am–6pm (Fri to 9pm). Closed Mon and most major holidays. Sculpture Garden Mon–Fri 10am–6pm; Sat–Sun 10am–5pm.

The Ogden Museum of Southern Art ★★★ If NOMA is the crown jewel, this is the crown. It's the premier collection of Southern art in the United States. The artists' works are impressive, and the graphics are informative and even clever. We particularly like the permanent exhibit of self-taught and outsider art including some from the local area. Though the building itself is quite dazzling, anchored around a sky-high atrium, one can't help wondering if that soaring space could be put to better use if it were hung with even more fine Southern art (still, we appreciate the public art the Ogden installed around the CBD in 2013, like the sculptures along Poydras Street). If you're able, come on a Thursday for **Ogden After Hours,** when a live band plays in the atrium. It might be old Delta blues or the New Orleans Philharmonic, 1930s country or straight-up jazz. On the list of special little treats you'll find in New Orleans, these evenings are near the top. We're also keen on the well-curated gift shop, which has consistently covetable souvenirs with a local spin.

925 Camp St. ✆ **504/539-9600.** www.ogdenmuseum.org. Admission $10 adults, $8 seniors and students, $5 children 5–17. Wed–Mon 10am–5pm; Thurs 6–8pm for evening shows featuring live music.

Southern Food and Beverage Museum & Museum of the American Cocktail ★★ The South's first food-and-beverage museum reopened in a gleamingly brand-new and much-needed home in 2013. This informative assemblage of Southern food and drink history, from farmers to cooks and everything in between and represented by all kinds of goodies, is in an offbeat part of town, but one that has renaissance written all over it. The comprehensive collection of artifacts illustrates how different ethnic groups (the usual French, Spanish, and African suspects, but also Germans, Italians, and Irish), geography, and time have contributed to the local cuisine. Exhibits rotate, but we enjoyed one that explored the various aspects of White House

REAL GOSPEL, NO brunch

You could do the slick "Gospel Brunch" at the House of Blues, or you could experience the real thing in a real place of worship. Don't expect fancy robes or masses of choir members, just rooms and rooms full of spirit. Try **Zion Hill Missionary Baptist Church,** 1126 N. Robertson St. (© **504/525-0507**). It's humble, right, and true (and Pastor Joshua's preaching can get pretty fiery). You may well be the only non-parishioner there, but the modest congregation is welcoming; show some mutual respect when the collection plate comes 'round. Sunday services are at 10:30am to noonish; communion service on the first Sunday of the month runs longer.

For a different musical religious experience, take in the jazzy Sunday 10am Mass at historic **St. Augustine's,** 1210 Governor Nicholls St. (© **504/525-5934;** www.staugustinecatholicchurch-new orleans.org). Home church for many a famous local musician, like Sidney Bechet, the Sunday Mass now incorporates New Orleans–tinged music and cultural color. *Tip:* Right afterward (at noon), the talented **Holy Faith Baptist Temple** band seriously rocks the house of worship just up the street at 1225 Governor Nicholls St. (© **504/525-0856**).

And if you must have that brunch, get to nearby Lil Dizzy's afterward, p. 95.

culinaria and customs through photos, menus, tableware, and even a sneak peek into the refrigerator of the official capital kitchens; we also dug an installation on all things absinthe. Events and tastings can be awfully fun, so check the schedule and see what's on. Scholars and researchers will find the extensive cookbook and menu archives pretty awesome, now housed in a new, dedicated library. A new onsite café completes the circle.

The **Museum of the American Cocktail,** a stumble through 200 years of cocktail history and New Orleans's own vital role in same, is also moving to the new location. (So the Sazerac was only *one* of the first cocktails!) Curator Ted "Dr. Cocktail" Haigh is passionate about his impressive collection and offers an original and lively glimpse into the colorful history of our favorite "poison." Historical artifacts include defunct product packaging and Prohibition-era photos. (We love the bottles of commercially sold gin, rye, and bourbon flavoring that would go into whatever rotgut you made at home to make it palatable.) Like the main SOFAB, exhibits rotate, and the museum offers regular seminars, demonstrations, and tastings.

1504 Oretha Castle Haley Blvd. © **504/569-0405.** http://southernfood.org and www.museum oftheamericancocktail.org. Admission to both museums: $10 adults; $8 AAA members; $5 seniors, active military, and students with ID. Mon–Sat 10am–7pm; Sun noon–6pm. Check for changes to hours and admission.

Historic New Orleans Churches

Church and religion are not likely to be the first things that jump to mind in a city known for its debauchery. But New Orleans remains a very Catholic city—don't forget that Mardi Gras is a pre-Lenten celebration. In fact, religion of one form or another directed much of the city's early history and molded its culture in countless ways.

For a detailed review of the **St. Louis Cathedral,** see p. 122 earlier in this chapter.

St. Alphonsus Church ★ The interior of this church is probably the most beautiful of any church in the city, right up there with some of the lusher ones in Italy. The Irish built St. Alphonsus Church in 1855 because they refused to worship at St. Mary's (see below) with their German-speaking neighbors. The gallery, columns, and sharply curving staircases lead to spooky, atmospheric balconies where the paint and plaster are peeling off in chunks.

The church no longer holds Mass. Ironically, when St. Mary's was restored, St. Alphonsus was closed, and the congregation moved across the street. Hopes for similar restoration here are high, but it's no small undertaking. The downriver bell tower was blown dramatically across the street when Katrina hit, while the upriver one was moved 15 degrees. The church also lost several stained-glass windows (since repaired) and ultimately incurred over half a million dollars in damage.

Currently, the church operates an **Arts and Cultural Center,** which includes a small Irish art and history museum. You can tour the still fabulous-looking museum interior or take the free (but donations gratefully accepted and much needed) tour conducted by Anne Rice's raconteur cousin Billy Murphy, an option we highly recommend. Informal tour times are Tuesdays, Thursdays, and Saturdays 10am to 2pm or by advance arrangement; calling ahead to check is recommended.

2030 Constance St., at St. Andrew St. ⓒ **504/524-8116.** For information, call the Friends of St. Alphonsus at ⓒ **504/482-0008.**

St. Augustine Church ★★ One of the great cultural landmarks of New Orleans's black history, St. Augustine has been a center of community life in the troubled but striving Tremé neighborhood since the mid-1800s. This church was founded by free people of color, who also purchased pews to be used exclusively by slaves (frustrating their white masters!). This was a first in the history of slavery in the U.S., and resulted in one of the most integrated churches in the country. In the modern era, under the direction of its visionary and charismatic then-pastor, Father Jerome LeDoux, St. Augustine continued to celebrate its history by integrating traditional African and New Orleans elements into its services. Homer Plessy, Sidney Bechet, and Big Chief Tootie Montana all called this their home church. In late 2005 the archdiocese decided to close St. Augustine because of diminished membership, but a major public outcry bought a reprieve, and it's going strong again. Services here are remarkable, especially when the jazzy 10am **Sunday Mass** features a guest performer like Troy Andrews or John Boutté—this can be one of the best free concerts in town.

Frequent art exhibits celebrating the neighborhood, not to mention the deeply moving Tomb of the Unknown Slave outside, make this worth a stop any time (though you should call ahead to make sure it's open). Combine it with a trip to the **Backstreet Cultural Museum** across the street. And please leave a donation; let's try to keep St. Augustine going.

1210 Governor Nicholls St. ⓒ **504/525-5934.** www.staugustinecatholicchurch-neworleans.org. Open Sunday 10am for mass and Tuesday 6pm for choir rehearsal. Otherwise, call to arrange a tour.

St. Mary's Assumption ★ Built in 1860 by the German Catholics, this is an even more baroque and grand church than its Irish neighbor across the street (see St. Alphonsus Church, above), complete with dozens of life-size saints' statues. The two churches make an interesting contrast to one another. Also inside the church is the national shrine to the hero of the 1867 yellow-fever epidemic, Blessed Father Francis

Xavier Seelos, who was beatified (one step away from sainthood) in 2000. Here you can see his original coffin, some of his personal belongings, a display containing recently discovered locks of his hair, and the centerpiece of the shrine, a reliquary containing his bodily remains. Should Father Seelos become a saint, expect this shrine to be an even bigger deal and place of pilgrimage than it already is.

2030 Constance St., at Josephine St. ℂ **504/522-6748.** Open during Mass, Mon–Sat 8am; Sat 4pm; Sun 10:30am; otherwise by appointment only.

St. Patrick's Church ★   The original St. Patrick's was a tiny wooden building founded to serve the spiritual needs of Irish Catholics. The present building, begun in 1838, was constructed around the old one, which was then dismantled. The distinguished architect James Gallier, Sr., designed much of the interior, including the altar. It opened in 1840, proudly proclaiming itself as the "American" Catholics' answer to the St. Louis Cathedral in the French Quarter (where, according to the Americans, God spoke only in French).

724 Camp St., at Girod St. ℂ **504/525-4413.** www.oldstpatricks.org.

St. Roch and the Campo Santo ★★   Saint Roch is the patron saint of plague victims; a local priest prayed to him to keep his flock safe during an epidemic in 1867. When everyone came through all right, the priest made good on his promise to build Saint Roch a chapel. The Gothic result is fine enough, but what is best is the small room just off the altar, where successful supplicants to Saint Roch leave gifts, usually in the form of plaster anatomical parts or medical supplies, to represent what the saint healed for them. The resulting collection of bizarre artifacts (everything from eyeballs and crutches to organs and false limbs) is either deeply moving or the greatest creepy spontaneous folk-art installation you've ever seen. The chapel, located on the cemetery grounds, isn't always open despite the posted hours, so hope for the best.

1725 St. Roch Ave., at N. Derbigny St. Daily 10am–5pm.

Trinity Episcopal Church ★   This is a very pretty church, outside and in: Outside, the Gothic Revival construction dates to 1853; inside, elaborate carved wood panels show off a 5,000-pipe organ. But the big attraction here is that it gets regular play. Weekly pipe organ concerts by the music director, Albinas Prizgintas, often accompanied by local singers and musicians, feature traditional repertoire by names you know, like Bach, Pachelbel, Led Zeppelin, and Michael Jackson, You could spend a worse Sunday evening, and on the list of eclectic things to do in New Orleans, this is up there.

1329 Jackson Ave. ℂ **504/522-0276.** www.trinitynola.com. Prayer service daily 7:30–9:30am; all day Sunday. Free concerts 5pm Sun.

A Few More Interesting New Orleans Buildings

Degas House ★   Legendary French Impressionist Edgar Degas had a tender spot in his heart for New Orleans. His mother and grandmother were born here, and he spent several months in 1872 and 1873 visiting his brother at this house. The trip resulted in a number of paintings, and this is the only residence or studio associated with Degas anywhere in the world that is open to the public. One of the artist's paintings showed the garden of a neighboring house. His brother liked that view, too; he later ran off with the wife of the judge who lived there. The brother's wife and children later took back her maiden name, Musson. The Musson home, as it is formally known, was erected in 1854. It has since been sliced in two, redone in an Italianate manner, and restored as a B&B. It's open to the public daily for tours (you can also reserve a combination tour/Creole breakfast); small groups can arrange painting parties. Reservations required.

2306 Esplanade Ave., north of the Quarter, before you reach N. Broad Ave. © **800/755-6730** or 504/821-5009. www.degashouse.com. Guided tours $29 per person; senior, student, and military discounts available. Breakfast, mimosas, and tour $50. Daily 10:30am–noon, or by appointment.

Gallier Hall ★   This impressive Greek Revival building was the inspiration of James Gallier, Sr. Erected between 1845 and 1853, it served as City Hall for just over a century and has been the site of many important events in the city's history—especially during the Reconstruction and Huey Long eras. Several important figures in Louisiana history lay in state in Gallier Hall, including Jefferson Davis and General Beauregard. Of late, local music legends Ernie K-Doe and Earl King were so honored. Five thousand mourners paid respects to K-Doe, who was laid out in a white costume with a silver crown and scepter before being delivered to his final resting place accompanied by a huge, brassy jazz procession. King, wearing a vivid purple suit, was also honored with a 2003 jazz funeral, with twirling umbrellas and rock royalty in attendance.

545 St. Charles Ave. Not usually open to the public.

Pitot House ★★   Set along pretty Bayou St. John (p. 209), the Pitot House is a typical West Indies–style plantation home, restored and furnished with early-19th-century Louisiana and American antiques. Dating from 1799, it originally stood where the nearby modern Catholic school now stands. In 1810 it became the home of James Pitot, the first mayor of incorporated New Orleans (he served 1804–05). Tours are usually given by a most knowledgeable docent or an equally knowledgeable architecture student and are surprisingly interesting and informative.

1440 Moss St., near Esplanade Ave. © **504/482-0312.** www.pitothouse.org. Admission $7 adults, $5 seniors and students, free for children 6 and under, parties of 10 or more $5 each. Wed–Sat 10am–3pm (last tour at 2:15pm), or by appointment.

The Mercedes-Benz Superdome ★   Completed in 1975, the Superdome is a landmark civic structure that took on a new worldwide image when it was used as a shelter during Katrina. Intended only as a locale of last resort for those who simply had no other evacuation choice (and with no adequate assistance plans in place), the Superdome quickly turned into hell on earth when tens of thousands of refugees came or were brought there. Along with the Convention Center, it became a symbol of suffering, neglect, and despair, as people were trapped without sufficient food, water, medical care, or, it seemed, hope.

As it happened, the New Orleans Saints reopened the Superdome in 2006 with much hoopla for their first home game (and a halftime show featuring U2), and went on to the playoffs. Three years later they won their first Super Bowl ever (in Miami), to rejoicing far beyond the city boundaries. Atop the team's gleaming success and the Dome's $118-million renovation (new seats, suites, and so on), the entire building was then "reskinned" in glittery gold tone, a shining beacon of what can arise from the darkest Katrina days. And what arose 2 years later was a lucrative naming-rights deal

floating ACROSS THE RIVER TO ALGIERS POINT

Algiers, annexed by New Orleans in 1870, is about a quarter-mile across the Mississippi River from New Orleans. Generally ignored because of its location, it became a sort of God's country after the hurricane because it did not flood at all, and many services, such as mail delivery, were restored quite quickly. It still has the feel of an undisturbed turn-of-the-20th-century suburb, and strolling around here is a delightfully low-key way to spend an hour or two (daytime only). It is easily accessible via the Algiers ferry that runs from the base of Canal Street. This unfancy ferry is one of New Orleans's best-kept secrets—it's a great way to get out onto the river and see the skyline (and it's perfectly timed for kids' attention spans). A ferry leaves New Orleans at 15 and 45 minutes past the hour from 7:15am to 6:30pm weekdays; weekday service starts at 10:45am and runs till 8:15pm Saturdays; 6:15 pm Sundays. The fare is $2 each way. Schedule is subject to changes; double-check at www.dotd.la.gov/ferry.

with Mercedes-Benz and the 2014 Super Bowl—capping a huge symbolic comeback. Do join the locals in a chant of "WHO DAT?!"

The stats: It's the largest fixed-dome structure in the world (680 ft. in diameter, covering 13 acres), a 27-story windowless building with a seating capacity of 76,000 and a computerized climate-control system that uses more than 9,000 tons of equipment. Inside, no posts obstruct the spectators' view of any sporting event while movable partitions and seats allow reconfigurations. Besides sports events, this flying-saucer-like building hosts conventions, balls, concerts, and other productions, as does its sister **Arena** next door. **Champions Square,** a new outdoor plaza, has become pre- and post-game central, and official Saints and Pelicans gear is available year-round in the Dome store.

1500 block of Poydras St., near Rampart St. ✆ **504/587-3663.** www.superdome.com.

PARKS, GARDENS & A ZOO

New Orleans's verdant vegetation and expansive tree canopy is one of its many charms, with greenery evident in small condo courtyards, lavish mansion landscaping, abundantly overflowing terrace pots—and wonderful public parks and gardens. Glorious live oak trees are a hallmark of the city, seen spreading across streets and over roofs everywhere (an amazing 320 million trees were lost to Hurricane Katrina, including many old oaks; thankfully, plenty also survived). The city's parks and gardens offer much more than greenery and can be an inviting respite from pounding the sightseeing pavement.

Audubon Park ★★   Across from Loyola and Tulane universities, Audubon Park and the adjacent Audubon Zoo (see listing below) sprawl over 340 acres, extending from St. Charles Avenue all the way to the Mississippi River. This tract once belonged to city founder Jean-Baptiste Le Moyne and later was part of the Etienne de Boré plantation, where sugar was granulated for the first time in 1794. Although John James

Audubon, the country's best-known ornithologist, lived only briefly in New Orleans (at what is now the Audubon Cottages hotel; p. 50), the city has honored him by naming the park, zoo, and even a golf course after him.

The huge trees with black bark are live oaks; some go back to plantation days, and more than 200 additional ones were recently planted here to replace the many that did not survive Hurricane Katrina. Other than the trees, it's not the most visually arresting park in the world—it's just pretty and a nice, wide-open place to be. Visitors can enjoy a shaded picnic among statuary, fountains, and gazebos, feed ducks in a lagoon, and pretend they're Thoreau. Or they can look with envy at the lovely old houses whose backyards abut the park. The most utilized feature of the park is the 1¾-mile paved, traffic-free walking, running, skating, and biking road that loops around the lagoon and golf course. Along the track are 18 exercise stations; tennis courts and horseback-riding facilities can be found elsewhere in the park. Audubon Zoo is toward the back of the park, across Magazine Street. Behind the zoo, check out the pavilion and green space on the riverbank; this popular area, called Riverview but nicknamed the **Fly,** has pleasant views of Frisbee players and the Mississippi.

6500 Magazine St., btw. Broadway and Exposition Blvd. (ⓒ) **504/581-4629.** www.auduboninstitute. org. Daily 5am–10pm.

Chalmette Battlefield/Jean Lafitte National Historical Park & Preserve ★★
These are the grounds where the bloody **Battle of New Orleans** was waged on January 14, 1815. Ironically, it should never have been fought: A treaty signed 2 weeks before in Ghent, Belgium, had ended the War of 1812. But word had not yet reached Congress, the commander of the British forces, or Andrew Jackson, who stood with American forces to defend New Orleans and the mouth of the Mississippi River. The battle did, however, succeed in uniting Americans and Creoles, and in making Jackson a hero in this city.

Markers on the battlefield allow you to follow the course of the battle (or you can just watch the film in the visitor center). Inside the park is a national cemetery, established in 1864. It holds only two American veterans from the Battle of New Orleans and some 14,000 Union soldiers who fell in the Civil War. For a terrific view of the Mississippi River, climb the levee in back of the Beauregard House. The drive here will take you through the Lower Ninth Ward, Arabi, and Chalmette—areas hard-hit in the federal floods.

8606 W. St. Bernard Hwy. (ⓒ) **504/589-3882.** www.nps.gov/jela. Free admission. Grounds and restrooms Tues–Sat 9am–4pm, Sun–Mon 9:30am–3:30pm. Closed Mardi Gras.

City Park ★★★
Once part of the Louis Allard plantation and named one of America's "Coolest Parks," City Park has been here a long time and has seen it all—including that favorite pastime among 18th-century New Orleans gentry: dueling. At the entrance, you'll see a statue of General P. G. T. Beauregard, whose order to fire on Fort Sumter kicked off the Civil War. The 1,300 beautifully landscaped acres provide a charming spot for a jog, bird-watching, or just gazing at the moss-dripping live oaks (the largest collection in the world!). It's also a treasure trove of culture and activity. City Park holds botanical gardens and a conservatory, picnic areas, lagoons for boating and fishing, pedal boats (p. 161), bike paths (p. 233), a brand-spanking-new tennis center, an even newer New Orleans–themed **miniature golf** course (p. 161), a bandstand with summertime concerts, two stadiums, playing fields, and a miniature train

you can ride in. That's just a start. **Carousel Gardens** is a kids' amusement area with rides; **Children's Storyland,** inside the Carousel Gardens, has fairy-tale figures for kids to scamper on and over and an antique carousel (see "Especially for Kids," later in this chapter). At Christmastime, the mighty oaks are strung with lights—quite a magical sight—and during Halloween the park hosts the massive **Voodoo Experience** music festival.

You'll also find the **New Orleans Museum of Art** (p. 132) at Collins Diboll Circle, on Lelong Avenue, in a building that is itself a work of art. Tucked away inside the **Botanical Gardens** is one of the oddest and most charming attractions in this odd and charming city, the **Train Garden.** Imagine a massive train set, the kind every 9-year-old kid (or kid at heart) would kill for. Now imagine that it's located in Dr. Seuss's basement, if Dr. Seuss was obsessed with both New Orleans and organic materials. Along 1,300 feet of track are exacting, 1/22-scale replicas of 1890s streetcars and ornately detailed, bizarrely beautiful representations of actual New Orleans neighborhoods and landmarks—all made from plant matter! In a town of weird and wonderful attractions, this is one more. The Botanical and Train Gardens are open year-round Tuesday to Sunday from 10am to 4:30pm; trains run only on Saturday and Sunday from 10am to 4pm, weather permitting.

1 Palm Dr. ⓒ **504/482-4888.** www.neworleanscitypark.com. Park open daily sunrise–11pm. Each attraction has its own hours and rates that vary by season, so call or check website. Free admission to park. Train Gardens admission $6 adults; $4 kids 5–12; 4 and under free.

Longue Vue House & Gardens ★★

Longue Vue mansion is a little pocket of the unexpected. Just 20 minutes from the city center, near the more interesting end of suburban Metairie, is a unique expression of Greek Revival architecture set on an 8-acre estate, constructed from 1939 to 1942 and listed on the National Register of Historic Places. It's like stumbling across a British country-house estate, and while it was never a plantation, it may just satisfy your Tara-esque cravings if you can't get out to River Road (p. 214)—and it's a nice place to ramble on a pretty day.

The mansion was designed to foster a close rapport between indoors and outdoors, with vistas of formal terraces and pastoral woods. The charming gardens were partly inspired by the Generalife, the former summerhouse of the sultans in Granada, Spain; look also for fountains and a colonnaded loggia. Unlike some attractions for garden enthusiasts, kids can actually have fun here in the delightful **Discovery Garden,** clever and amusing exhibits where kids can play (and maybe even learn). Keep it in mind for a family-friendly activity.

7 Bamboo Rd., New Orleans, near Metairie. ⓒ **504/488-5488.** www.longuevue.com. Admission $10 adults; $5 children 3 and over, students; $9 seniors and active military. Tues–Sat 10am–5pm; Sun 1–5pm. Hourly tours start at 10am Tues–Sat and at 1pm on Sun; last tour 4pm. Closed Jan 1, Mardi Gras, Easter Sunday, July 4th, Labor Day, Thanksgiving, and Dec 24–25.

Audubon Zoo ★★★

It's been about 30 years since a total renovation turned Audubon Zoo into one of the best in the country. It's a place of justifiable civic pride that delights even non–zoo fans—small enough to be manageable, but big enough to cover all the important zoo bases, including new elephant, leopard, and orangutan exhibits scheduled to open in 2014. Some 1,800 animals (including rare and endangered species) live in natural habitats in a setting of subtropical plants, waterfalls, lagoons, and a Louisiana swamp replica complete with rare white gators.

The funny-looking mound near the river is **Monkey Hill,** constructed so that the children of this flatlands city can see what a hill looks like. There are also some great hot-day diversions for kids: a wading pond for the young ones; the **Cool Zoo** splash park for older kids; and **Gator Run,** a new lazy river for inner-tube floating. So bring swimsuits and towels if the weather warrants. There are misters and shady oaks for humans of all ages, but hot is hot: For maximum animal action, plan your visit to avoid the hottest times of the day, when the animals are sleeping off the heat. We like taking the St. Charles Avenue streetcar to Audubon Park, where a free shuttle from the park to the zoo departs every 20 to 30 minutes.

6500 Magazine St. ℭ **504/581-4629.** www.auduboninstitute.org. Admission $15 adults, $12 seniors, $11 children 2–12. Cool Zoo and Gator Run additional $5. Aquarium/IMAX/Zoo combo tickets available. Mar through Labor Day: Tues–Sun 10am–5pm. Labor Day through 1st Tues in Mar: Tues–Sun 10am–4pm. Last ticket sold 1 hr. before closing. Closed Mardi Gras Day, 1st Fri in May, Thanksgiving, and Christmas.

NEW ORLEANS CEMETERIES

Along with Spanish moss and lacy iron balconies, the cities of the dead are part of the indelible landscape of New Orleans. Their ghostly and inscrutable presence enthralls visitors, who are used to traditional methods of burial—in the ground or in mausoleums.

New Orleans' famed cemeteries are recognized the world over for their elaborate and beautiful above-ground tombs. There are 45 cemeteries in New Orleans—31 are considered historic, and five are officially listed in the National Register of Historic Places. They are as much a tourist attraction as Jackson Square or Bourbon Street. And just like those iconic spots, the cemeteries have a fascinating backstory—one that has become twisted over time by mythology. But the truth is so fascinating that it needs little embellishment.

Sometimes called "Cities of the Dead" for their resemblance to urban centers, laid out in rows or "streets" as they are, the cemeteries have of course been a part of New Orleans nearly since its founding. For the earliest settlers, dying wasn't that big of a deal—everyone was doing it—and the dead were buried in common graves or along the riverbanks (except the hoitiest of the toity, who were buried at St. Louis Cathedral). But when the river rose or a major rain caused minor flooding, that didn't work out too well. Old Uncle Etienne had an unpleasant habit of bobbing back to the surface (doubtless no longer looking his best). This practice gave rise to some good stories (experts debate their veracity), of coffins floating downriver, bodies weighted down with rocks, and holes drilled in caskets to let the water through and prevent them from popping up from the ground like deathly balloons.

Add to that cholera and yellow-fever epidemics, which helped increase the number of bodies and also the possibility of infection. Given that the cemetery of the time was *inside* the Vieux Carré, it's all pretty disgusting to think about.

Around the late 1780s, death was getting to be a bigger deal. Well, death was getting to be more *prevalent*, what with fires and yellow fever epidemics and such; *honoring* death and the dead was indeed getting to be a bigger, more ceremonial deal. It became necessary to build new cemeteries, somany were plotted on the outskirts of town where illness and odor were less likely to be troublesome. The first, St. Peter, was begun in 1725 by the Catholic Diocese, and rests where a Superdome parking lot now sits.

Bodies were buried in the soil there. When St. Peter was full, The famed St. Louis #1 came about, in 1789 on what is now Rampart Street. The first major city of the dead—with fancy tombs and a parklike setting providing a more fitting tribute to departed loved ones. When it filled up, others soon followed, improving on the haphazard layout of St. Louis #1 to form designated "streets" in a grid pattern.

FOLLOWING OLD-WORLD STYLE

It's true that the high water table and muddy soil here influenced the popularity of the above-ground "condo crypt" look—the dead are placed in vaults that look like miniature buildings. But they are actually customary in France and Spain (and elsewhere), so it was just another tradition that the colonists brought with them to New Orleans. Some say St. Louis #1 was inspired by the famous Père Lachaise cemetery in Paris. In addition, they are an impressive sight and a sign of prestige.

The above-ground vaults are also often adorned with stunning works of sculptural art, decorations that represent the family name, occupation, or religion (which was invariably Catholic; the first Jewish cemetery was not founded until 1828). Some tombs were not owned by families, but by a group, like the firefighters, police, or a benevolent society. These were decorated thusly: Witness the enormous elk visible from the corner of Canal Street and City Park Avenue. These were helpful for families who could not afford a family tomb. The cemeteries may also have fancy ironwork in the gates and fences—and on the whole are well worth a visit.

HI HONEY, I'M HOME

So . . . all that tomb for one dead guy? Not so much. The tombs indeed host multiple bodies. The methodology is actually fairly clever. Inside the tomb are two long chambers, one above the other, separated by a shelf (sometimes two shelves). When a casket goes in, it rests on the shelf, and the vault is re-sealed with simple brick and mortar. Heat and humidity acts like a slow form of cremation. After a year and a day (by custom and rule—to accommodate the traditional year-long mourning period), another family member may be buried here. Whatever's left of the first one is moved to the bottom level, and the casket bits are removed. In some tombs, that shelf has a gap toward the back, and the remnants just get pushed back, where they fall through the gap to the vault below. Everyone eventually lies jumbled together to continue their quest to dust. And so room is made for a new casket to reside, and the exterior is closed up once again. The result is sometimes dozens of names, going back generations, on a single spot. It's an efficient, space-saving system that gives new meaning to the phrase "all in the family." If a family loses two people within the year, one of them rests in a temporary holding vault until that year-and-a-day period has passed.

UPKEEP ISSUES

By law, families must maintain their tombs. Traditionally, All Saints Day (Nov 1) is when families gather to honor their dead, and in the days leading up to it you will still see people busily tidying up and washing down the sun-bleached, whitewashed brick buildings. Some are treated with lime, leaving a yellow or green tint. Flowers, candles, photos, and memorabilia are left on and around the tombs of loved ones. Even to this day, you can go to a cemetery on November 1, and you are likely to see a tender party atmosphere, with graveside reunions and picnics.

But many graves have fallen into disrepair, when family members are no longer willing, able, or around to do the maintenance.

A tomb OF ONE'S OWN

For a singular souvenir or gift, artist **Michael Clement** sculpts miniature tombs (and shotgun houses) in rough-hewn terra cotta, finished in aged gold, bronze, and gunmetal gray. You're not going to find these in San Francisco. Not in Bali. Only in New Orleans. They're available at the **Historic New Orleans Collection gift shop** (www.hnoc.org; and p. 126) or directly from the artist (© **504/899-1804;** www.michaelj clement.com). Prices start around $95 (and remember, no tax is charged on original works of art in many parts of the city). It's not everyone who wants a gilt crypt on their coffee table, but we do.

There are laws that allow the city to take over and transfer a neglected tomb, but these are largely unenforced (and there's the creepy factor). Other laws and customs around these centuries-old tombs are murky, and responsibility for the expensive upkeep gets shifted or shunted off. So sadly, most cemeteries today face moderate to severe dishevelment. For years, crypts lay open, exposing their pitiful contents—if they weren't robbed of them—bricks, shattered marble tablets, even bones, lay strewn around. Several of the worst eyesores have been cleaned up; others still remain in deplorable shape.

For many years, New Orleans cemeteries were in shambles. Most of the restoration and cleanup efforts have been spearheaded by the nonprofit **Save Our Cemeteries** (© **504/525-3377;** www.saveourcemeteries.org). Consider throwing a few, um, bones their way, especially since cemetery access is usually free. The website accepts online donations. Save Our Cemeteries also offers tours, events, and lectures.

SURVIVORS

A faux Voodoo practice continues in some of the St. Louis cemeteries, where visitors scrawl Xs on the tombs. Please don't do this; not only is it a made-up Voodoo ritual, but it also destroys the fragile tombs.

Concerns were high for the fate of the iconic cemeteries during the Katrina disaster days, but "the system worked": The tombs survived unscathed, except for some high-water marks much like those borne by any other flooded structure.

For more information, we highly recommend Robert Florence's *New Orleans Cemeteries: Life in the Cities of the Dead* (Batture Press, 1997). It's full of photos, facts, and human-interest stories for those with a deeper interest in this fascinating aspect of New Orleans culture, and is available at bookstores throughout the city.

Three Cemeteries You Should See with a Tour

Lafayette Cemetery No. 1 ★★★   Right across the street from Commander's Palace restaurant, this is the lush uptown cemetery. Once in horrible condition, it's been mostly restored. Anne Rice's Mayfair witches have their family tomb here.
1427 Sixth St.

St. Louis Cemetery No. 1 ★★★   This is the oldest extant cemetery (1789) and the most iconic. Here lie Marie Laveau, Bernard Marigny, and assorted other New Orleans characters. Also, the acid-dropping scene from *Easy Rider* was shot here.
Basin St. btw. Conti and St. Louis sts.

Safety First

You may be warned against going to the cemeteries alone and urged to go with a scheduled tour group (see "Organized Tours," later in this chapter). Thanks to the cemeteries' location and layout—some are in dicey neighborhoods, and the crypts obscure threats to your safety—visitors have historically been prime pickings for muggers and so forth. We've heard this for years, but haven't ever heard of any actual incidents. Still, we'd avoid St. Louis #2 and Lafayette #2—and besides offering peace of mind, a good tour is totally worthwhile. If you're going to make a day of visiting the cemeteries, think about renting a car. You won't be driving through horrendous downtown traffic, you can visit tombs farther away and at your own pace, and you'll feel safer.

St. Louis Cemetery No. 2 ★   Established in 1823, the city's next-oldest cemetery, unfortunately, is in such a terrible neighborhood that regular cemetery tours don't usually bother with it, and caution is advised. **Save Our Cemeteries** (www.saveoutcemeteries.org) offers occasional tours—if one is running when you are in town, go—it's worth it. The Emperor of the Universe, R&B legend Ernie K-Doe, was laid to rest here in 2001, with bluesman extraordinaire Earl King joining him in the same tomb in 2003, and K-Doe's widow, Empress Antoinette, followed in 2009.

N. Claiborne Ave. btw. Iberville and St. Louis sts.

Some Cemeteries You Could See on Your Own

Most of these cemeteries (such as St. Louis No. 3 and Metairie) have offices that can sometimes provide maps; if they run out, they will give you directions to any grave location you like. All have sort-of-regular hours—figure anytime from 9am to 4pm as a safe bet.

Cypress Grove and Greenwood Cemeteries ★★   Located across the street from one another, both were founded in the mid-1800s by the Firemen's Charitable and Benevolent Association. Each has some highly original tombs; keep your eyes open for the ones made entirely of iron. These two cemeteries are an easy streetcar ride up Canal Street from the Quarter.

120 City Park Ave. and 5242 Canal Blvd. By car, take Esplanade north to City Park Ave., turn left until it becomes Metairie Ave.

Holt Cemetery ★★★   This one is for the more intrepid. It's not so easy to reach or find, but it's worth seeking out. Dating to the mid-1800s, this former burial grounds for indigents is the rare New Orleans cemetery with nearly all in-ground graves. They are maintained by the families—or not maintained at all, in many cases—which results in its particular, folk-art appeal, with hand-drawn markers and family memorabilia scattered about.

635 City Park Ave. (turn down tiny Rosedale Ave., across City Park Ave. from the Burger King and next to Delgado College). Mon–Fri 8am–2:30pm; Sat 8am–noon.

Hurricane Katrina Memorial ★   On the former site of Charity Hospital's paupers' field, this ominous but oddly affecting circle of tombs holds the bodies of 85 unclaimed victims of the 2005 levee failures and the names of others who perished. It's an unfussy place that's easily missed, the better for contemplative solitude, perhaps. Surrounded by a storm-shaped series of pathways, the memorial does its duty in giving one enormous pause.

5056 Canal St. Take the Canal St. streetcar to City Park Ave.

Metairie Cemetery ★   Don't be fooled by the slightly more modern look—some of the most amazing tombs in New Orleans are here. Don't miss the pyramid-and-sphinx Brunswig mausoleum, the "ruined castle" Egan family tomb, and the former resting place of Storyville madam Josie Arlington. Her mortified family had the madam's body moved when her crypt became a tourist attraction, but the tomb remains exactly the same, including the statue of a young woman knocking on the door. Legend has it that the young woman is Josie herself being turned away from her father's house or a virgin being denied entrance to Josie's brothel—she claimed never to despoil anyone. The reality is that it's just a copy of a statue Josie liked. Other famous residents include Confederate General P. G. T. Beauregard, jazz greats Louis Prima and Al Hirt, and Ruth of Ruth's Chris Steakhouse (in a marble edifice that oddly resembles one of her famous pieces of beef). You'll have to drive here (or take a taxi), but you can also drive the lanes through the cemetery (a good option for a rainy day).

5100 Pontchartrain Blvd. ✆ **504/486-6331.** Daily 8:30am–5pm. By car, take Esplanade north to City Park Ave., turn left until it becomes Metairie Ave.

St. Louis Cemetery No. 3 ★★★   Conveniently located next to the Fair Grounds racetrack (home of the Jazz Fest), St. Louis No. 3 was built on top of a former graveyard for lepers. Storyville photographer E. J. Bellocq lies here. It's a scenic cemetery and neighborhood, accessible via Esplanade Avenue.

3421 Esplanade Ave. ✆ **504/482-5065.** Mon–Sat 9am–3pm; Sun 9am–noon. Holiday closings vary.

VAMPIRES & VOODOO

Voodoo's mystical presence is one of the most common motifs in New Orleans—though the presence is mostly reduced to a tourist gimmick. With kitschy Voodoo dolls for sale and exaggerated mythology surrounding Voodoo queen Marie Laveau, a very real religion with a serious past and considerable cultural importance gets lost amid all that camp.

Voodoo's roots can be traced in part back to the African **Yoruba** religion, which incorporates the worship of several different spiritual forces that include a supreme being, deities, and the spirits of ancestors. When Africans were kidnapped, enslaved, and brought to Brazil—and, ultimately, Haiti—beginning in the 1500s, they brought their religion with them.

Later, other African religions met and melded, and when slaves were forced to convert to Catholicism, they found it easy to merge and practice both religions and rituals. Rituals involved participants dancing in a frenzy to wild drumbeats and eventually falling into a trancelike state, during which a *loa* (a spirit and/or lower-level deity intermediary between humans and gods) would take possession of them.

Voodoo was banned in Louisiana until the Louisiana Purchase in 1803. The next year, the Haitian slaves overthrew their government, and new immigrants came to New Orleans, bringing along a fresh infusion of Voodoo.

Napoleonic law (which still holds sway in Louisiana) forced slave owners to give their slaves Sundays off and to provide them with a gathering place: **Congo Square** on Rampart Street, part of what is now Louis Armstrong Park. Voodoo practice there, including dancing and drumming rituals, gave slaves a way to have their own community and a certain amount of freedom. These gatherings naturally attracted white onlookers, as did the rituals held (often by free people of color) along **St. John's Bayou.** The local papers of the 1800s are full of lurid accounts of Voodoo "orgies" and of spirits possessing both whites and blacks. The Congo Square gatherings became more like performance pieces rather than religious rituals, and legend has it that nearby madams would come down to the Sunday gatherings and hire some of the performers to entertain at their houses.

During the 1800s, the famous Voodoo priestesses came to some prominence. Mostly free women of color, they were devout religious practitioners, very good businesswomen with a steady clientele of whites who secretly came to them for help in love or money matters. During the 1900s, Voodoo largely went back underground.

It is estimated that today as much as 15% of the population of New Orleans practices Voodoo, though the public perception—casting spells or sticking pins in Voodoo dolls—is largely Hollywood nonsense.

Most of the stores and places in New Orleans that advertise Voodoo are set up strictly for tourism. This is not to say that some facts can't be found there or that you shouldn't buy a mass-produced souvenir. For an introduction to Voodoo, check out the **New Orleans Historic Voodoo Museum** (p. 127) or **Voodoo Authentica** (p. 147). For true Voodoo, however, seek out real Voodoo temples or practitioners. You can find them at the temples listed below or by calling **Ava Kay,** who works on her own. She is available for readings, gris-gris bags (packets of meaning-infused herbs, stones, and other such bits), and other items of interest by appointment only; call her at ✆ **504/412-0202**. If you stumble into one of these temples and find no one about, come back or wait quietly; they are probably conducting a reading in a side room. And be sure to check out Robert Tallant's book *Voodoo in New Orleans* (Pelican Pocket, 1983).

Voodoo Temples

The city has three authentic Voodoo temples and botanicas selling everything you might need for potions and spells. The public is welcome, and employees are happy to educate the honestly inquisitive.

The **Island of Salvation Botanica** in the New Orleans Healing Center, 2372 St. Claude Ave. (in the Marigny), and the **Temple Simbi-sen Jak,** 835 Piety St. (✆ **504/948-9961**), are run by Sallie Glassman, Voodoo priestess and author of a deck of Voodoo tarot cards. The botanica is open Wednesday through Saturday from 10:30am to 5pm, but call first to make sure they are not closed for readings (or to schedule a reading).

Located right in the French Quarter, the **Voodoo Spiritual Temple,** 828 N. Rampart St. (✆ **504/522-9627,** www.voodoospiritualtemple.org), is the real McCoy—interested tourists are welcome, but please be respectful. Priestess Miriam belonged to the Spiritual Church in Chicago before setting up this spiritual house, a temple with a store attached. There are both personal and open rituals, and the sincerely interested are quite welcome. Of interest is a haunting CD of Priestess Miriam's Voodoo chants and rituals. The temple is open but keeps irregular hours; be sure to call for hours in advance.

Primarily a store, **Voodoo Authentica,** 612 Dumaine St. (ⓒ **504/522-2111**), also has working altars. Mama Lola, subject of the sociological Voodoo study *Mama Lola: Haitian Voodou Priestess in Brooklyn,* is often in attendance, reading cards and performing cleansings. In Mid-City, **F&F Botanica,** 5801 N. Broad St. (ⓒ **504/482-5400;** www.orleanscandleco.com), is one of the largest suppliers anywhere of candles, herbs, icons and elixers for the serious practitioner; go to p. 194 for more information.

Visiting Marie Laveau

Marie Laveau is the most famous New Orleans Voodoo queen. Though she was a real woman, her life has been so mythologized that it is nearly impossible to separate fact from fiction. But who really wants to? Certainly we know that she was born a free woman of color in 1794.

A hairdresser by trade, Marie became known for her psychic abilities and powerful gris-gris. Her day job allowed her into the best houses, where she heard all the good gossip and could apply it to her other clientele. In one famous story, a young woman about to be forced into a marriage with a much older, wealthy man approached Marie. She wanted to marry her young lover instead. Marie counseled patience. The marriage went forward, and the happy groom died from a heart attack while dancing with his bride at the reception. After a respectable time, the wealthy widow was free to marry her lover.

Marie wholeheartedly believed in Voodoo—and business. Her home at what is now 1020 St. Ann St. was purportedly a gift from a grateful client. A devout Catholic, Marie attended daily Mass and was well known for her charity work.

Her death in 1881 was noted by the *Times-Picayune.* Her look-alike daughter, Marie II, took over her work, leading some to believe (mistakenly) that Marie I lived a very long time, looking quite well indeed—which only added to her legend. But Marie II allegedly worked more for the darker side than her mother. Her eventual reward, the story goes, was death by poison (delivered by whom is unknown). Today visitors bring Marie tokens (candles, Mardi Gras beads, change) and ask her for favors—she's buried in **St. Louis Cemetery No. 1.**

Anne Rice's New Orleans

Long before Sookie Stackhouse or any Originals, before anyone cared whether you were Team Edward or Team Jacob, there was Lestat—and the originator of the modern vampire era, author Anne Rice. Love her or loathe her, Anne Rice has been one of New Orleans's biggest boosters. Though her popularity may have peaked, visitors still come here because they have read her books, or simply because they're obsessed Twihards mining the eerie ore. Rice writes seductive descriptions of her hometown that are actually quite accurate—minus the vampires, witches, and ghosts, of course—and cites many real locales.

Anne Rice (née O'Brien) was born on October 4, 1941, in New Orleans to Irish parents. When she was 16, her family moved to Texas, where she met her husband, the late poet Stan Rice. They married in 1961 and moved to the San Francisco area, resettling in New Orleans in the 1980s after *Interview with the Vampire* exploded (she now lives in California). Rice remains something of a legendary doyenne of fang fiction. You can find signed copies of her books at the **Garden District Book Shop,** 2727 Prytania St. (p. 189). These landmarks play a role in her books, movies, and inspirations.

Anne Rice in the French Quarter

The romance of the French Quarter seems to attract vampires, who found easy pickin's in its dark corners in the days before electricity.

St. Louis Cemetery No. 1, 400 Basin St.: A tomb (empty, of course) with Louis the vampire's name is located here in the Vampire Chronicle books, and Louis occasionally goes to sit on it and brood. Rumor has it that Rice has purchased a tomb here for her eventual use. See p. 143 for more on cemetery tours.

Gallier House, 1132 Royal St.: This famously preserved museum is said by Rice scholars to be the model for the house on Rue Royal that was home to vampires Lestat and Louis in *Interview with the Vampire.* Also see p. 126.

The stretch of 700 to 900 Royal St.: Quite a few of the exteriors for the *Interview with the Vampire* movie were filmed along this stretch—though the set decorators had to labor long to erase all traces of the 20th century, covering the streets in mud. Imagine how folks who live around here must have felt about it.

Madame John's Legacy, 632 Dumaine St.: In the *Interview with the Vampire* movie, this is the house from which the caskets are being carried as Brad Pitt's voiceover describes Lestat and the little vampire Claudia going out on the town: "An infant prodigy with a lust for killing that matched his own. Together, they finished off whole families." Also see p. 127.

Hotel Monteleone, 214 Royal St.: This was Aaron Lightner's house in *The Witching Hour.* Also see p. 54.

Rice's characters spent time dining well at **Café du Monde** (800 Decatur St.; p. 112), **Court of Two Sisters** (613 Royal St.; p. 82), and **Galatoire's,** 209 Bourbon St.; p. 75).

Anne Rice in the Garden District

Rice's books have also featured the Garden District and the area around it, where she and her family used to live in and own properties.

Coliseum Theater, 1233 Coliseum St.: In the film version of *Interview with the Vampire,* this is the theater where Louis sees *Tequila Sunrise.*

Pontchartrain Hotel, 2031 St. Charles St.: This upscale hotel and its restaurant, the Caribbean Room (now closed), appear in *The Witching Hour.*

The old Mercedes dealership (now a different property), 2001 St. Charles Ave.: This building was at the center of an amusing local dispute. The vampire Lestat disappeared from this world through an image of himself in the window of this building. Lestat (wink, wink—could it be Copeland himself?) then mysteriously returned to this realm and bought an ad of his own, congratulating Copeland for his "stroke of genius."

St. Alphonsus Church, 2030 Constance St.: This small (now deconsecrated) church with a stunning interior (p. 135) was where Anne's parents married and she was baptized and received communion. She also took Alphonsus as her confirmation name, and it is a setting in *The Witching Hour.*

Commander's Palace, 1403 Washington Ave.: Rice readers will recognize this restaurant as a favorite of the Mayfair family (p. 103).

Lafayette Cemetery No. 1: This centerpiece of the Garden District is also a frequent setting in Rice's work, especially as a roaming ground for Lestat and Claudia in *Interview with the Vampire* and as the graveyard for the Mayfairs in *The Witching Hour.*

ORGANIZED TOURS

There are great advantages to taking tours. Though many can be touristy (by definition), someone else does the planning, and it's an easy way to get to outlying areas. A good tour guide can entertain, enlighten, and even inspire. We lean toward some of the smaller companies, in hopes that they may have fewer people than the allowable 28 people per group. We like to hang close to the guide in case we have questions; they'll often continue to share knowledge while on the way to the next point of interest—and we find that these kinds of serendipitous personal interactions are easier to come by when fewer people are being herded along. We also like that, for tours to the swamps and plantation homes, say, you'll be saving the earth a bit by carpooling (well, buspooling). Finally, we like the fact that New Orleans tour guides must be licensed, which involves rigorous study and testing. So not just anyone can load you on a bus and take you for a (literal or figurative) ride.

Tours almost always run rain or shine (no refunds), but in some instances you're allowed to move your reservation to another day. Walking tours and large bus tours provide a designated meeting point; smaller van and bus tours usually provide pickup at your hotel. Before booking, check for Groupon deals on tour tickets—they come up pretty regularly on the Groupon website (www.groupon.com).

Be aware: It's fairly common practice for hotel concierges and storefront tour offices to **earn "commission" on the tours they sell or recommend** (ditto restaurants). Some may have honest opinions about the merits of one over another, and those may be perfectly good options, but for the most part, they're selling you what they get paid to sell. If you're looking for a particular type of tour, do the research yourself and cut out the middleman; no matter how you learned about it, pay the fee directly to the company, not to your concierge or a street-corner booth. No reputable firm will insist you pay someone else first.

And another thing: The relatively new phenomenon known as **"Free Tours By Foot"** is not something we can recommend, at least not at this point. It's not that the tours themselves aren't good, per se; it's mostly because, well, they're not really free. They usually come with a heavy-hitting request for tips, and by the time you tip the guide, you're not far from the cost of tours from established providers. The business model and the hiring practices are a bit murky, as well. Frankly, we're supportive of legitimate businesses that legitimately support the city we love so much. But that's just us.

Tour Companies

The following companies offer multiple tours (and will often offer discounts if you commit to more than one). Most of them have walking tours of the **French Quarter;** the **Garden District;** and the **cemeteries,** as well as van tours of the **Lower Ninth Ward (Katrina), plantations,** and **swamps** (they provide transportation and tickets to an associated swamp or airboat tour). Other specialty tours are noted, but if you have a particular interest you don't see, contact these companies—customized tours can often be arranged.

Historic New Orleans Tours ★★★ This is one of our favorite midsize tour companies, mostly because their guides are consistently good. Quite often they have higher degrees in history or other related disciplines, and they're free to bring their own perspectives and interests to the tour, therefore keeping things fresh. The company emphasizes authenticity over sensationalism, and they're particular experts in cemeteries, with a serious depth of knowledge. The French Quarter and cemetery tours are on foot, as is a terrific "Scandalous Cocktail" tour, which strings together a series of fascinating tales around local bars and cocktails. The tour delves into historic brothels, organized crime, and even the JFK assassination. The colorful bartenders, when not too busy, also tell their own tales (do pace your drinking, though!). They also offer walking and van tours of the Garden District; and a City + Katrina van tour. Other special-interest tours (available by advance arrangement only) include music, literary, Tremé, and Creole Mourning Customs Tours, the latter a particularly novel and fascinating topic.

ⓒ **800/979-3370** or 504/947-2120. www.tourneworleans.com. The majority of Historic New Orleans tours are $20 adults; $15 students; $7 seniors and children 6–12; free for 5 and under. The Scandalous Cocktail and Creole Mourning tours are $25 per person. The 3-hour Hurricane/Rebirth tour is $40 for adults; $20 children 12 and under. Swamp and Plantation tours are $49 adults; $30 children under 12.

Tours by Isabelle ★   This is a small tour company, and tours are scheduled only when a minimum number of people sign up (so if they don't hit the minimum, there's a chance you'll end up having to switch to a different tour). The upside is you'll get much more personalized attention, and van tours are maxed out at 13 people. Isabelle's tours (available in English and French) include: a New Orleans overview; plantations; swamps and airboats; and good combination tours—like a 3½-hour City Overview with Katrina Recovery tour, which shows the French Quarter, City Park, and post-Katrina damage and sights. The City and Estate tour adds Longue Vue House and Gardens (p. 140) to a tour of the French Quarter, St. Louis Cemetery No. 3, Bayou St. John, Lake Pontchartrain, and the Uptown and Downtown neighborhoods—a very extensive overview tour with a broad reach. Note that Tours by Isabelle offers no Garden District tours.

ⓒ **504/398-0365.** www.toursbyisabelle.com. City and Katrina combination tour $65; City and Estate tour $75.

Gray Line ★★   This well-known, well-established national company also runs combination city and post-Katrina disaster tours, among many others. They were one of the first to do so, back when it was controversial and seen as exploitative, but it's here handled with the proper respect. Gray Line also offers city, swamp, and plantation tours in comfortable coaches; a 2-hour cruise on the steamboat *Natchez* (www.steamboatnatchez.com); plus French Quarter walking tours for those who wish to see ghosts and gardens or explore the city's cocktail heritage. This is the big kahuna of tour companies, with large groups and full-size buses, so it's a slicker presentation but also a slicker, glitch-free operation, from the call center to the deep bench of back-p tour guides to the very heavy schedule of tours.

2 Canal St., Ste. 1300. ⓒ **800/535-7786** or 504/569-1401. www.graylineneworleans.com. Walking tours start at $25 adults; $13 children; swamp tour with transportation $45 adults; $25 children; steamboat *Natchez* dinner and jazz cruise $72.50 adults; $34 children. Check website for other tour prices and full schedule.

Cajun Encounters ★★   This is also a larger, slicker company, but unlike Gray Line, it is locally owned. That's a point of pride and also a bit of a hallmark, as they like to hire local guides. It's been around for 15 years, and tours are on a 33-seat bus.

The City Tour is a hop on/hop off bus tour, with stops in the French Quarter, St. Louis #3 Cemetery, City Park, the Garden District, and so on. It also offers transportation and ticketing to a wonderfully eerie nighttime swamp tour.

901 Decatur St. © **866/928-6877** or 504/834-1770. www.cajunencounters.com. City + Cemetery Tour $43 adults; $32.50 children. Daytime swamp tour (with hotel pickup) $49 adult; $32.50 children. Check website for other costs, schedules, and discount offers.

Additional Tours of the French Quarter

Besides Historic New Orleans Tours and the other van or bus city tours listed above, the following tours will also introduce you to the French Quarter. Needless to say, you might want to start with the free, self-guided walking tour of the French Quarter that we've developed for you in this book in chapter 10. See p. 196.

The nonprofit volunteer group **Friends of the Cabildo ★★** (© **504/524-9118;** www.friendsofthecabildo.org) offers an excellent 2-hour walking tour of the Quarter. It leaves from in front of the 1850 House Museum Store, at 523 St. Ann St., on Jackson Square. The fee is $15 per adult; it's free for children 12 and under accompanied by an adult. Tours leave Tuesday through Sunday at 10:30am and 1:30pm, except holidays. No reservations—just show up about 15 minutes early.

The **Jean Lafitte National Park and Preserve's Folklife and Visitor Center** at 419 Decatur St., near Conti Street (© **504/589-2636;** http://www.nps.gov/jela/french quarter-site.htm), offers an excellent, free "Riverfront History Stroll" conducted by National Park Service rangers. The walking tour covers about a mile along the riverfront and brings to life the city's history and the ethnic roots of its unique cultural mix. No reservations, and only 25 people are taken in a group. The tour starts at 9:30am daily (except for Mardi Gras and Christmas); the office opens at 9am—it's strongly suggested that you get there then to ensure you get a ticket.

Le Monde Creole ★ (© **504/568-1801;** www.mondecreole.com) offers a unique spin on a French Quarter tour, using the dramatic lives of one classic Creole family as a microcosm of the Creole world of the 19th century. It's an interesting through-line for a tour of the usual spots. This tour (also available in French on request) is cash only. Tours depart daily at 10:30am, and advance reservations are required. Prices are $24 adults; $16 children 10 to 18, students, and active military; and free for kids 9 and under. Cash only.

Each Monday at 10am, the **French Market ★** (© **504/522-2621;** www.frenchmarket. org/events/upcoming) offers a free, hourlong walking tour. It focuses on their properties, and while it's not comprehensive, it includes plenty of history and anecdotes about the surrounding areas. The tour starts at the entrance to the French Market at Ursuline and N. Peters (under the arch) streets, and heads upriver past Café du Monde. It ends at the Upper Pontalba apartments on Jackson Square (on St. Peters Street). The free Wednesday tour focuses on food and music, starting at 1:30pm at the Jazz National Historical Park (916 N. Peters, tucked back from the street near Dumaine and Decatur streets, below Galvez Restaurant) and ending at the U.S. Mint building at Decatur Street and Esplanade Avenue. Both tours are first-come, first served and fill up quickly, so arrive early.

Beyond the Quarter

A walking tour of the Garden District is offered by **Historic New Orleans Tours** (see above) daily at 11am and 1:45pm. It meets at the corner of Washington and

TREMÉ, true & false

In 2010, HBO launched the drama *Tremé* to stellar reviews, intense local curiosity, and a predictable dollop of cynicism. But mostly (given the producers' widely publicized intent to "get it right"), New Orleans collectively tuned in to see itself portrayed to the nation and debate whether the show in fact nailed the authenticity.

Not surprisingly, opinions differed. But all agreed on two things: 1) It did a better job than *The Big Easy;* and 2) the show's location manager had been awfully busy.

Tremé revolves around a collection of musicians and others finding their footing in the gritty months following Katrina. Many of them are from the historic Faubourg Tremé neighborhood. This complex community just north of the French Quarter, considered the oldest African-American neighborhood in America, was the 19th-century home to the city's free people of color and has for generations been a massively productive musical enclave. It remains a leading incubator of talent and a remarkable keeper of cultural flames. The show was filmed in many locations both in and outside the real Tremé. These are a few worth visiting:

TREMÉ, THE NEIGHBORHOOD

○ **St. Augustine Church** Considered the first Catholic church to integrate African-Americans and whites, it was and remains the beating heart of the Tremé neighborhood. See p. 135.

○ **Backstreet Cultural Museum** A modest but essential collection of the cultural traditions unique to its neighborhood: brass bands, Mardi Gras Indians, jazz funerals, social aid and pleasure clubs, and so on. See p. 131.

○ **New Orleans African American Museum** Protecting and promoting African-American history, it's set in a lovely 1820s Creole

Prytania, which is 2 blocks from the St. Charles Streetcar line (Washington stop). Reserve in advance or just show up (cash only for walk-ups; $20 adult; $15 seniors and students; $7 kids 6–12). **Gray Line** (see above) also offers a Garden District walking tour, but theirs transports you via bus from their French Quarter "Lighthouse" depot (Toulouse St. at the Mississippi River), then lets you off in the Garden District where the tour begins. $26 adult, $15 child. From March 1 through October 31 it departs 9:30am daily; between November 1 and December 31 it departs at 9:30am on Monday, Wednesday, Friday, and Saturday only.

Tours of the Lower Ninth Ward focusing on Katrina devastation and restoration are offered by the operators listed under "Tour Companies," above. If observed through the right lens, touring the still-recovering areas is witnessing history, and it's important to remember.

Plantation tours of the **River Road plantation homes** are offered by the operators listed under "Tour Companies," above. See p. 214 for detailed information on the River Road plantation homes.

Tours of the Faubourg Tremé focusing on African-American history and the incredible cultural and musical legacy of this historic neighborhood are offered by **Historic New Orleans Tours** (see "Tour Companies," above; this tour is available by

villa (1418 Governor Nicholls St.;
ⓒ **504/566-1136;** www.noaam.
org; Wed–Sat 11am–4pm [subject
to change; call ahead]; $7 adults,
$5 students and seniors $3 children 2–12).

o **Lil' Dizzy's** This local diner is a
gathering place for movers, shak-
ers, neighbors, and nobodies, as
much for the neighborhood lowdown as for the divine trout
Baquet. See p. 95.

o **Congo Square** Slaves and free
people of color gathered here to
drum, dance, and practice Voodoo
rituals and eventually, many
believe, give birth to jazz. See
p. 47.

TREMÉ, THE SHOW

o **Bayona** The show's Jeanette
Desautel is roughly modeled on
Bayona's famed chef/owner Susan
Spicer. Restaurant Patois is the
actual stand-in for the fictional
"Desautel's." See p. 81.

o **Vaughan's** Already a character,
Kermit Ruffins plays himself on the
series. He plays his trumpet at
Vaughan's most Thursdays (4229
Dauphine St.; ⓒ **504/947-5562**).

o **Angelo Brocato's Ice Cream
Parlor** Creighton Bernette,
played by John Goodman,
expresses his longing for the
post-storm return of the lemon
ice at this beloved 100-year-old
institution. See p. 111.

o **Bacchanal** Jeannette's pop-up
restaurant at Bacchanal gets
rained out, but the scruffy wine
bar with the killer food and
lushly unkempt garden lives on,
thankfully (600 Poland Ave.,
Bywater; ⓒ **504/948-9111;** www.
bacchanalwine.com).

o **Tee-Eva's** The pie and praline
queen whose shop has been a fixture
on Magazine Street for years had a
cameo on Tremé as a bus passenger
(5201 Magazine St.; ⓒ **504/899-
8350;** www.tee-evapralines.com).

advance reservation only and costs $20 adults; $15 students; $7 seniors and children
6–12; free for 5 and under). The **New Orleans African American Museum,** in the
Tremé at 1418 Governor Nicholls St. at N. Villere, an easy walk from the French
Quarter (ⓒ **504/566-1136;** www.noaam.org), also offers an excellent walking tour
each Saturday at 10 a.m. It meets at the museum; advance reservations are required.
The tour only goes out if at least 5 people reserve, but that usually happens. Needless
to say, given their immersion in the area, the guides are inevitably knowledgeable. It's
$23 adults, $19 students and seniors, $12 children 2 to 12 and includes museum
admission.

Other Special-Interest Tours

Hop On, Hop Off City Sightseeing Tours—these big red double-decker buses, seen
in London, New York, and gobs of other cities, made it to the Big Easy in 2012. We're
not crazy about the sight of these garish eyesores splayed across the city's historic
streets, but conceptually it's a good way to see the city at your own pace. The buses
stop at 14 locations—from the French Market to the World War II Museum in the
Central Business District to Magazine Street in Uptown. Enough buses circulate so
that you'll be picked up within 30 minutes at any of the stops. While you're on the bus,

you can sit inside, or in the open air on top (bring sunscreen), and an onboard narrator explains the sights along the way. It's scripted, but functional. A single day pass is $29 adults and $10 kids; a 7-day pass is $39 adults and $10 kids and comes with a lagniappe of two free walking tours. You can purchase your tickets online, print out your tickets, and show up at any stop; or buy a ticket at one of two stops at 700 Decatur St. or 501 Basin St (the Basin St. Station Visitor and Information Center). The buses run continuously from 9:30am to 5pm.

Swamp Tours

A **swamp tour** can be a hoot, particularly if you get a guide who calls alligators to your boat for a little marshmallow snack (please keep your hands inside the boat—they can look a lot like a snack to a gator). On all the following tours, you're likely to see alligators and waterfowl such as egrets, owls, herons, bald eagles and ospreys. You might also spot a feral hog, otter, beaver, frog, turtle, raccoon, deer, or nutria (maybe even a black bear or a mink). But a morning spent floating on the bayou can be mighty pleasant, and learning about how this unique ecosystem contributes to the local culture and economy is quite interesting. Plus, the swamps are simply spookily beautiful.

The tour operators listed earlier in this chapter under "Tour Companies" (p. 149) all provide swamp tours, but they really just coordinate your transportation, narrate the drive, and deliver you to one of the following knowledgeable swamp-tour folks. You can also drive to one of these tours, or work through them to arrange your transportation from the city.

Dr. Wagner's Honey Island Swamp Tours ★★ (© 985/641-1769 or 504/242-5877; www.honeyislandswamp.com), at 41490 Crawford Landing Rd. in Slidell about 30 miles outside of New Orleans, takes you by boat into the interior of Honey Island Swamp to view wildlife with native professional naturalist guides (captains Charlie and Brian both grew up plying these waters). The guides provide a solid educational experience to go with the purer swamp excitement. Tours last approximately 2 hours. Prices are $23 for adults and $15 for children 11 and under if you drive to the launch site yourself; rates are $45 for adults and $32 for children if you want a hotel pickup in New Orleans.

Jean Lafitte Swamp Tours ★ (© 800/445-4109 or 504/689-4186; www.jeanlafitte swamptour.com) in Marerro offers "native Cajun" tour guides replete with lore about the flora, fauna, and legends on a swamp boat cruise through their privately owned bayou area—as well as proximity to New Orleans. Speedy airboat tours are also available for the more adventurous. Tours last 1 hour, 45 minutes and include transportation from most downtown hotels for an additional fee. Prices are $25 for adults and $12 for children 3 to 12 for drive-ups; with transportation, prices are $49 for adults and $24 for children. Kids 2 and under are free with paid adult. Check website for $10 discount.

Pearl River Eco-Tours ★★, 55050 Hwy. 90, Slidell (© 866/59-SWAMP [597-9267], 504/581-3395, or 985/649-4200; www.pearlriverecotours.com), is built on Southern hospitality. Captain Neil has been doing tours of Honey Island Swamp for over 10 years, and the other captains also know their stuff. The swamp is beautiful, even during the cooler months when the gators are less frisky. These guys also offer a small six-passenger skiff ($70 per person) and night tours, which are supremely cool even if they do freak us out a little bit ($39 adults; $29 kids 4–12). If you have a car, you can drive there and tour for $23 ($15 children 4–12). If transportation is provided from New Orleans, the cost is $49 for adults and $33 for children ages 4 to 12. Tours run at 10am and 2:30pm.

They're a little farther out and you'll need to provide your own transportation, but we'd be remiss if we didn't add two other excellent guides: **Annie Miller's Son's Swamp and Marsh Tours** ★★, 3718 Southdown Mandalay Rd., Houma (✆ **800/341-5441** or 985/868-4758; www.annie-miller.com) and **A Cajun Man's Swamp Cruise** ★, 3109 Southdown Mandalay Rd., Houma (✆ **985/868-4625;** www.cajunman.com). These neighbors are both so utterly authentic you'd swear that swamp water runs in their veins. Jimmy Miller, son of the legendary Alligator Annie, is carrying on in her down-home tradition but knows every inch of these swamps. Self-proclaimed Cajun Man Ron "Black" Guidry is an equally well-informed naturalist and usually brings his guitar and accordion along on the boat. Both require reservations, call for schedules. **Annie Miller's Sons:** $15 adults, $10 children 4 to 12, free 3 and under. Tours run 2 to 2½ hours. **A Cajun Man:** $25 adults and $15 children 12 and younger; tours run about 2 hours.

Mystical & Mysterious Tours

Interest in the ghostly, supernatural side of New Orleans has always been part of its appeal. But let's blame author Anne Rice's tales and subsequent stories of sparkly vampires for increasing the interest in tours catering to the vampire set. It has also resulted in some rather humorous infighting as rival tour operators steal each others' guides, shtick, and customers. We enjoy a good nighttime ghost tour of the Quarter as much as anyone, but we also have to admit that what's available is really hit-or-miss in presentation (it depends on who conducts your particular tour) and more miss than hit with regard to facts. Go for the entertainment value, not for the education. All the tours stop outside locations where horrifying things supposedly (or actually) happened, or inexplicable sights have supposedly been observed. Just be aware that this isn't a haunted-house tour (you don't enter any buildings other than a bar for a mid-tour break), and no shocking ghouls jump out from around dark corners. If you do see any spectral action, it'll most likely be after that bar stop.

We can send you with a clear conscience on the Cemetery and Voodoo Tour offered by **Historic New Orleans Tours** ★★★ (✆ **800/979-3370** or 504/947-2120; www.tourneworleans.com). It is consistently fact-based and not sensation-based, though no less entertaining. The trip goes through St. Louis Cemetery No. 1 and Congo Square and visits an active Voodoo temple. It leaves Monday through Saturday at 10am and 1pm (Sun at 10am only) from the courtyard at 334-B Royal St. Rates are $20 adults, $15 students and seniors, $7 children 6 to 12, and free children 5 and under. They also offer a nighttime haunted tour, perhaps the only one in town where well-researched guides provide genuine thrills and chills. It leaves at 7:30pm from Bourbon-Oh! Bar at the corner of Bourbon and Orleans streets.

As for those vampire tours . . . let's be perfectly clear. Vampires—they're not real. But if they were real, they'd hang out in the French Quarter. Both are spooky. Both are centuries old. Both are sexy. It makes sense. Personally, we prefer our history with a bit of, well, history—but if tales of bloodsuckery and high drama are what you seek, the current reigning kings are at **French Quarter Phantoms** (✆ **504/666-8300;** www.frenchquarterphantoms.com). Costumes, fake blood, Dickensian delivery—the whole magilla (but not all the guides do it). Tours cost $16 to $18, free for kids 7 and under.

The 1½-hour New Orleans Vampire tour given by **Haunted History Tours** ★, 97 Fontainebleau Dr. (📞 **888/644-6787** or 504/861-2727; www.hauntedhistorytours.com) is a step down on the drama ladder. It departs daily at 8:30pm from outside St. Louis Cathedral and costs $25 for adults, $18 students/seniors, $14 kids under 12, free kids under 6. Haunted History Tours also offers cemetery and nighttime French Quarter tours.

Whether it's high drama or serious erudition you're after, it's a good idea to call these companies and ask whether there's a guide working on your selected day who will best fulfill your interests.

Both of these companies are popular, and these tours usually go out with large groups. Try to stay near the front, so you can see and hear your guide. Even the ones with the most booming voices have to regulate their delivery out of respect for the French Quarter residents.

Food & Beverage Tours & Classes

Visitors can take can take their New Orleans culinary experience one tasty step further with a food and beverage tour or class. **Drink and Learn** ★★★ (📞 **504/578-8280;** www.drinkandlearn.com) is the aptly named walking tour given by noted cocktail impresario Elizabeth Pearce. She supplies the knowledge and the smart beverages (just tastes, not full pours) and manages to connect booze to local customs and history in an utterly different way than our high school history teacher did. It's hella fun, and she knows her stuff. It meets most nights (but not all) at 6 or 6:30 at Vacherie Restaurant (p. 87), 827 Toulouse St., and costs $50 per person, 21 and over only. Advance reservations required. Book in advance; the small groups fill up fast.

Langlois Culinary Crossroads ★★★, 1710 Pauger St. (📞 **504/934-1010;** www. langloinola.com), has upped the ante for all other cooking classes in the city. Its gorgeous Bywater facility, custom-built and opened in 2013, is spiffy sleek and smart, with monitors that allow everyone a view of the action (but all seats are good ones; classes max out at 16 students). The big differences here are that these classes are hands-on and the menus high-end. A recent menu included oyster artichoke soup, boudin cakes with apple pepper jelly, and bananas Foster crepes. Participants are invited to help stir, sear, mix, chop . . . and then dig in when the tasty, multicourse meal is served. The menus focus on local ingredients and influences and change often to help keep the instructors as interested as the students. It's a giant up from the traditional jambalaya and gumbo that some other cooking classes offer (with prices to match—classes range from $79–$129). Wines by the glass or bottle are available, and Chef Amy and the rest of the crew are fun, funny, and full of useful tips. It's an exceptional experience. Advance reservations required.

Celebrated New Orleans Chef Frank Brigtsen (see p. 103) created the yummy course curriculum at the **New Orleans Cooking Experience** ★★ (📞 **504/430-5274;** www.thenoce.com), which offers half-day cooking courses taught in a beautifully restored home near the Southern Food and Beverage Museum (p. 133). Here classic New Orleans Creole dishes are given a gourmet kick. Brigsten and other high-profile local chefs teach, and then you all dine together. It's fun, informative, and likely to be fattening. *C'est la vie.* Half-day classes cost $165 per person and include recipes, a multicourse meal, and wines. They also offer **complete culinary vacations,** which include classes, dining out, and most meals. Call for more info.

Tastebud Tours ★ (© 219/929-6648; http://tastebudtours.com/tours/new-orleans tours) provides walking and tasting tours, a fun way to make your way through a few blocks of the Quarter (and a block of the CBD). It's a Chicago-based company new to New Orleans, but the guides are local residents. They do a good job weaving together culinary traditions and the city's melting-pot history (since the different ethnic groups that have settled here over the years have all influenced the cuisine—among other things). The stops you make aren't at the finest of restaurants, but you'll sample a good cross section of some iconic New Orleans dishes, like a muffuletta, a beignet, a po'boy, and a sip of gumbo. The tastes are small- to medium-size (but a small taste of muffuletta alone is pretty filling), so you won't go hungry. The daily 1pm tours are $44 (kids 2 and under are free; others pay full rate) and last 3 to 3½ hours; reservations are required. vegetarians can be accommodated with advance notice.

Boat & Kayak Tours

For those interested in doing the Mark Twain thing, a few operators offer ways to get out on the rolling Mississippi. They're touristy but fun if you're in the right mood, and a a good family activity. Docks are at the foot of Toulouse and Canal streets, and there's ample parking. Call for reservations (required) and to confirm prices and schedules. We think it best to skip the food—too much time spent at the buffet is time better spent enjoying the river, and besides, you can find better food all over town.

The steamboat *Natchez,* 2 Canal St., Ste. 1300 (© **800/233-BOAT** [233-2628] or 504/569-1401; www.steamboatnatchez.com), a marvelous three-deck stern-wheeler docked at the wharf behind the Jackson Brewery, offers at least two 2-hour daytime cruises Monday through Saturday, and a jazz dinner cruise seven days a week. The narration is by professional guides, and the boat has a cocktail bar, live jazz, an engine room tour, an optional lunch on the first cruise of the day ($11 extra for ages 5 and up; the meal is $8 for kids 4 and under), and a gift shop. Daytime fares are $27.50 for adults, $12.25 children; evening cruises without dinner are $43 adults and $21.50 children; kids 6 and under ride free with paid adult. Dinner cruises cost $72.50 adults, $34 children 6 to 12, and $14 for children 2 to 5. The Sunday jazz brunch is $38.50; $20.25 kids 2 to 5 ($27.50/$12.25 for the cruise only). Times may change seasonally, so call ahead.

The smaller paddle-wheeler *Creole Queen,* Riverwalk Dock (© **800/445-4109** or 504/529-4567; www.neworleanspaddlewheels.com), departs from the Poydras Street Wharf adjacent to the Riverwalk every afternoon for a 1½-hour narrated excursion to the port and to the historic site of the Battle of New Orleans. There is also an 8pm jazz dinner cruise. The boat has a covered promenade deck and a snack bar, and its inner lounges are air-conditioned or heated as needed. Daytime fares are $27 for adults and $13 for children. The evening cruise is $40 for adults, $20 for children 6 to 12, and free for children 5 and under. Dinner adds $32 to the adult ticket and $14 to the 6- to 12-year-olds; dinner for kids 3 to 5 is $12.

Kayak-iti-Yat (© **985-778-5034** or 512-964-9499; http://kayakitiyat.com) explains city lore from the unique perspective of a kayak along Bayou St. John. When the weather's right, it's a sublime way to explore some historic neighborhoods, City Park, and even Lake Pontchartrain. Tours range from 2 to 4 hours, with increasing intensity of upper-body workouts (the better to justify last night's indulgent dinner). Guided kayak tours run daily. Times vary, and advance reservations are required. Costs range from $40 to $65. Call for reservations, times, and meeting-place directions. All equipment is provided, but bathroom stops are scant, so plan ahead. Check Groupon (www.groupon.com) for discount coupons.

Bicycle Tours

A bike tour is a terrific way to explore some lesser-seen parts of this flat city up close and in depth. Our suggested tours have an outright leisurely pace, so you needn't be a serious rider, but bike familiarity and a healthy dose of pluck will help you handle the hazards of potholes and traffic (including stretches along some busy avenues). Do opt-in to the optional helmet; bring sunscreen, a hat, rain poncho, and water (though most tours provide a small starter bottle) as conditions dictate. While a restroom stop is included, you'd be wise to take care of that before departure, too.

Confederacy of Cruisers (_C_ **504/400-5468;** www.confederacyofcruisers.com) offers a bike tour with an itinerary that hits parts of the Marigny, Bywater, 7th Ward, and Tremé on comfortable, well-maintained single-gear cruisers with baskets. The eight-person maximum, guide-led group pulls over about every 10 minutes at such diverse stops as the New Orleans Center for Creative Arts (NOCCA), St. Roch Cemetery, the Mother-in-Law Lounge, and St. Augustine Church, where guides offer up well-informed insights on history, culture, and architecture. They're full of restaurant recommendations, too—in fact, they also offer a culinary-themed bike tour (but that requires interrupting your bike ride with food, or interrupting your food with a bike ride—and we don't go there). The 3-hour tours are $49 and depart twice daily from Washington Square Park on Frenchmen and Royal streets, on the outskirts of the French Quarter.

Freewheelin' Bike Tours (_C_ **504/324-8257;** www.neworleansbiketour.com) has a similar itinerary, with stops for snoballs (during the season) and at St. Louis #3 Cemetery, where one of the guides' great-grandparents are buried. It goes out at 10am and 2pm every day except Wednesday. It also offers an Uptown tour through the Garden District and the Irish Channel that goes along St. Charles Avenue for a bit as well as the Warehouse District. This one goes out Thursdays, Saturdays, and Sundays at 9:30am and 1pm. We like the sturdy, American-made cruisers, which have been custom constructed for these streets, and the tours max out at 10 passengers. All tours depart from 325 Burgundy and cost $49. Reserve in advance.

As for other wheeled ways to see the city, consider the **French Quarter Segway Tours,** 214 Decatur St. (_C_ **504/619-4162;** http://neworleans.citysegwaytours.com). If you've never done it, it's really pretty fun, and most people get the hang of it quickly. Guides do spend some time with a lesson before sending you down the middle of the French Quarter streets, but not everyone is comfortable mastering a new skill, navigating the busy streets, _and_ trying to take in the sights all at once. One woman on our tour started out by running head-first into a building—but ended up loving the tour. The 2-hour tour is $65 and you'll probably get as many stares and you give. Tour times are January 1 to June 30 daily at 11am and 3pm; July 1 to September 15 daily at 10am; and September 16 to December 31 daily at 11am and 3pm.

Carriage Tours

Corny it may be, but there is a romantic lure to an old horse-drawn carriage tour of the Quarter or beyond. (The "horses" are actually mules—they handle the city heat and humidity better.) The mules are decked out with ribbons, flowers, and even hats, and the drivers seem to be in a fierce competition to win the "most entertaining" award. They share history and anecdotes of dubious authenticity; they'll also customize itineraries on request. Carriages wait on Decatur Street in front of Jackson Square from 8:30am to midnight (except in heavy rain). Private carriages are $90 per ½ hour for up to four people; or you can hop into one of the waiting carriages (you may be sharing with other tourists) for $15 per person per ½ hour. A 1½-hour Garden District tour runs $270 for one to four people. Contact ℭ **504/943-8820** or www.neworleanscarriages. com for custom tours and hotel pickups.

Antiquing Tours

Antiquing in New Orleans can be an exhilarating if overwhelming experience. For expert guidance, Macon Riddle of **Let's Go Antiquing!** (ℭ **504/899-3027;** www. neworleansantiquing.com) will organize and customize antiques-shopping tours to fit your needs. Hotel pickup is included, and she will even make lunch reservations for you and arrange shipping of any purchases. Prices vary.

ESPECIALLY FOR KIDS

If you plan to give the kids a lifelong complex for confining you to your hotel room when you *know* all that clubbing and fooding is going on mere blocks away, then perhaps New Orleans is better done *sans enfants.* But the truth is, despite its reputation, the Big Easy is a terrific family destination, with oodles of conventional and unconventional only-in-New-Orleans activities to entertain them (and you). **Mardi Gras** (p. 39) and **Jazz Fest** (p. 47) are both doable and enjoyable with kids, as are many of the organized tours (p. 149). *Tip:* Those above spooking age love to tour the cemeteries and haunted places, but long walking tours of historic homes and landmarks may be best left to the grown-ups.

The **French Quarter** in and of itself is fascinating to children over 7. You can while away a pleasant morning on a Quarter walkabout, seeing the architecture and peeking into shops, with a rest stop for powdery beignets at **Café du Monde** (p. 112). If you have kids of museum-going age, the Mardi Gras exhibit at the **Presbytère** (p. 128) or the Hurricane exhibit at the **Cabildo** (p. 125) will hold their attention for a while. Even self-conscious tweens fall for a **horse-and-buggy ride** (see "Carriage Tours," above) around the Quarter—and it works for all ages when it's hot and nap time is closing in (it might even rock the little ones to sleep). The **Algiers ferry** (p. 233) crosses the Mississippi River and ends just pre-boredom (and makes a great intro to reading *Huckleberry Finn* together). Add a clackety-clacking **streetcar ride** (p. 234), and you've hit the trifecta of ever-fascinating transportation options.

A number of the city's top attractions are obviously family-friendly, including the **Audubon Aquarium of the Americas** (p. 117). Only the most squeamish should skip the **Insectarium** (p. 120), because it's swell.

Outside the Quarter, the highly regarded **Audubon Zoo** (p. 140), complete with a seasonal splash park for the pool-deprived, is both lovely and a great diversion. For more animal action, a **swamp tour** (p. 154) is a sure-fire winner. While you're not guaranteed to see gators, it's a pretty good bet, and even so, hey, you're on a boat in a swamp. Many also offer speedier **airboats** for young adrenaline junkies.

get the kids JAZZED

In such a musical town, there is a sorrowful lack of music options for the younger set. Parents who might be trying to indoctrinate their kids into the joys of jazz, brass, or zydeco (or who just want to enjoy it themselves) will be hard-pressed to find options. Blame it on the booze—most music venues serve alcohol and are legally prohibited from allowing anyone younger than 21 to enter. The street performers along **Royal Street** and in **Jackson Square** are a good place to start. But fear not, we've got a few other interesting ideas.

- **Frenchmen Street Clubs** Yes—you make the Frenchmen Street scene with kids in tow. Two clubs, the **Maison** (p. 169) and **Three Muses** (p. 172) allow kids for the early shows, which usually start around 4 or 5pm (parents must be in attendance). Grab a table, order snacks, and let the little ones shake their little groove thangs. They'll be asked to leave when the tables break down and the drinking crowd moves in, around 9pm or 10pm.

- **Mid-City Lanes Rock 'n' Bowl** Hey, you got cool music in my bowling! Wait, you got bowling in my nightclub! It's two in one, and both work. It's hard to go wrong with this one,

although the music usually doesn't get started till 8:30ish, so bedtime might need to be pushed back some. Kids with parents are welcome. See p. 175.

- **Preservation Hall** The historic, inimitable traditional jazz venue is open to all ages. The earliest show starts at 8pm nightly and it's standing only; get there early so the young ones can see (if they're really young, stand by the door in case a boredom-induced quick exit becomes required. See p. 169.

- **Tipitina's** On Sundays at 1pm at the legendary Tip's, the torch gets passed. The **Youth Music Workshop** is a jam session/music lesson for aspiring players, where some of the city's best musicians give free lessons to kids (and also show off their chops). It's pretty free-form and largely attended by local kids, but anyone can come. Bring an instrument if you have one. See p. 176.

- **U.S. Mint** The gorgeous performance room upstairs in this museum has some form of free music nearly every day, and all ages are welcome. See p. 124.

And then there is the wonder known as **City Park.** We've already mentioned some of the all-ages features there (see p. 139, and pay particular attention to the **Train Garden;** we also think the **Besthoff Sculpture Garden,** p. 133, is suitable for most kids). If you happen to be in New Orleans in December, pay a visit here, when thousands of holiday lights turn the landscape and trees into fairy-tale scenery for the annual **Celebration in the Oaks.**

Here are a few more of the city's offerings for kids and parents to love.

Amusement Park and Children's Storyland ★★ The under-8 set will be delighted with this playground (rated one of the 10 best in the country by

Child magazine), where well-known children's stories and rhymes have inspired the charming decor. It offers plenty of characters to slide down and climb on and generally get juvenile ya-yas out.

Kids and adults will enjoy the carousel, Ferris wheels, bumper cars, miniature trains, tilt-a-whirl, lady-bug-shaped roller coaster, and other rides at the **Carousel Gardens,** also in City Park. Delighting local families since 1906, the carousel (or "da flying horses," as real locals call it) is one of only 100 all-wood merry-go-rounds in the country, and the only one in the state.

City Park at Victory Ave. ℂ **504/483-9432.** www.neworleanscitypark.com/in-the-park/carousel gardens. Admission $3, rides $3 each, unlimited rides with $17 armband. Carousel Gardens amusement park mid-Mar through mid-Nov Fri–Sun 11am–6pm with extended hours June–Aug. Storyland daily but hours vary by season. Check website for specifics.

Big Lake Boating and Biking ★★ Big Lake in City Park is a pretty spot for a boat ride, and the kids might spot egrets and turtles. There are **pedal boats** and **rowboats** for rent from **Wheel Fun,** which also rents **bicycles, tandems,** and **surreys** for use inside City Park. All that pedaling action can be a workout, which means you can justify a visit to nearby **Angelo Brocato's** ice cream parlor afterward (p. 111). Boats hold three people, at least one of whom must be 21 or older. Life jackets (provided) are required. Check website and Groupon for discount coupons.

Wheel Fun Rentals, Big Lake Trail in City Park. ℂ **504/300-1289.** www.wheelfunrentals.com. Pedal boats $20–$25/hr. Kayak $12/hr. single; $19/hr. double. Fishing boats $25/hr. Stand-up paddle boards $18. Surreys $20–$30/hr. Quad sport bikes $12/hr. Seven days a week. Dec–Mar Sat–Sun 10am–6pm; Apr–Nov 9am–8pm. Weather permitting.

City Putt Miniature Golf ★★ Two brand-new 18-hole miniature golf courses opened in 2013, and we're most impressed with the design: On one course, each hole is designed around a New Orleans neighborhood, with iconic statues and signage and stuff; the other course keys off of statewide themes (learning is fun!).

On Victory Drive in City Park, across from the entrance to Storyland and the Botanical Garden. ℂ **504/483-9458.** www.neworleanscitypark.com/in-the-park/city-putt. $8 adults; $6 children 4–12, children 3 and under free. Second round in same visit $4. Free parking. Jan to mid-November hours: Sun, Tues–Thurs 10am–10pm; Fri–Sat 10am–11pm. Closed Mon. Hours are slightly different from mid-Nov to New Year's Day when Celebration in the Oaks is under way in City Park. Last equipment rental an hour before closing.

French Quartour Kids Tour ★★ Believe it or not, this is the only tour in New Orleans designed specifically for kids (ideally ages 6–13). The good news is that it's super. The company's founder and regular guide is a former schoolteacher, and besides being an excellent kid-wrangler (and conducting the tour in costume), she manages to keep the enthusiasm level going for the full 2 hours. The spiel keeps it relatable, with attention to what life was like for kids in the olden days. There's definitely history being conveyed here and historic sites explored, but the lessons use props (which she totes around in a colorful wheeled cart), storytelling, play-acting, and enough gory details to hold most kids' focus. Emphasis on "most." Ask about seasonally themed specialty tours.

ℂ **504/975-5355.** www.frenchquaratourkids.com. $20 per person (includes kids and adults; an adult chaperone is required for up to 4 kids). Tours dailiy at 9:30am (sometimes adjusted for weather). Reservations required. Check for schedule of specialty tours. Tours meet at the Riverfront behind Jax Brewery in the French Quarter.

GAMBLING

Harrah's Casino is quite like a Vegas casino (115,000 sq. ft., 2,100 slot machines, more than 100 tables, Besh Steakhouse restaurant, and the Masquerade Lounge). It's located on Canal Street at the river (© **504/533-6000;** www. harrahs.com). *Tip:* Locals know the voluminous buffet can satisfy the most serious munchies for not-so-serious cash (it's a good deal for an awful lot of food). There's also riverboat gambling in the area. Outside the city, you can find the

Boomtown Casino (© **504/366-7711** for information and directions; www. boomtownneworleans.com), on the West Bank, and the **Treasure Chest Casino** (© **504/443-8000;** www.treasurechest. com) docked on Lake Pontchartrain in Kenner. **Slot machines** can be found in every imaginable locale in the city, from bars to laundromats to riverboats, often separated from the main room by a door or curtain.

Louisiana Children's Museum ★★★ This interactive museum is really a playground in disguise that will keep kids occupied for a good couple of hours. Along with changing exhibits, the museum offers an art shop with regularly scheduled projects, a mini grocery store, a chance to "build" a New Orleans–style home, and lots of activities exploring music, fitness, water, and life itself. If you belong to your local science museum, check for reciprocal entry privileges. *Note:* Children 15 and under must be accompanied by a parent.

420 Julia St., at Tchoupitoulas St. © **504/523-1357.** www.lcm.org. Admission $8, children under 1 free. Children 15 and under must be accompanied by an adult. Sept–May Tues–Sat 9:30am–4:30pm, Sun noon–4:30pm; June–Aug Mon–Sat 9:30am–5pm, Sun noon–5pm.

GETTING SPORTY

Big Easy Rollergirls ★ Okay, it's a total goof, but a hoot of a goof. By definition, roller derby is going to be a bit wild (though the athleticism can't be denied). Mix in New Orleansm and the resulting outcome is pure wack. The Big Easy babes play it up for all it's worth, and the crowd action is equally rowdy. More of a hipster scene than a family scene, it's all in fun, and worth the modest ticket price just to check out the fluff-punk outfits.

University of New Orleans's Human Performance Center, Elysian Fields and Leon C. Simon Dr. www.bigeasyrollergirls.com. Adults $10, kids $5.

New Orleans Pelicans ★★ Playing in the renovated New Orleans Arena (next door to the Superdome), the Pelicans (formerly the Hornets) now command an exclusive area on the sidelines called "Hollywood" where seats can be had for some serious green. A few years ago that was not a possibility. Then Chris Paul came along to change everything by leading the team to the semis and playoffs. Even after the Lakers snagged him and the franchise ownership saw some upheaval, the Pelicans put on a good b-ball show and remain a major attraction.

1501 Girod St. Ticket info © **504/525-HOOP** (525-4667). www.nba.com/pelicans. Season tickets $210–$1,680.

New Orleans Saints ★★   Who dat won the Super Bowl? The Saints' incredible Super Bowl XLIV victory in 2010 was the culmination of the city's 43-year collective dream (to say nothing of the end of 43 years of frustration), in which the beloved 'Aints finally won the big one, becoming a worldwide phenomenon, a metaphor for the city's own comeback, and a source of frenzied pride. The bounty scandal a few years later barely dampened the enthusiasm for this team, and if you're the least bit of a football fan, try to get yourself inside the Superdome (p. 137) for a Saints game— there's really nothing like it. Your best bet is the **NFL Ticket Exchange** (www.ticket exchangebyticketmaster.com). Otherwise, the pregame party at **Champions Square,** outside the Superdome (or any sports bar, really), is an excellent place to be on game days.

Superdome, 1500 block of Poydras St. Saints home office: 5800 Airline Dr., Metairie. ⓒ **504/733-0255.** Ticket info: ⓒ **504/731-1700.** www.neworleanssaints.com. Tickets $60–$500 and up depending on the game.

New Orleans Zephyrs ★★   There may be no better entertainment value in pro sports than minor-league baseball. An afternoon or evening at Zephyr Field out near the airport affirms that. Mascots Boudreaux D. and Clotile Nutria do their enthusiastic best to ensure that family fun is foremost, with various promotions and fan-participation activities. There's a pool area behind right field (rentable for groups or parties) and a general-admission grass "levee" behind center field.

Zephyr Field, 6000 Airline Dr., Metairie. ⓒ **504/734-5155.** www.zephyrsbaseball.com. Tickets $8–$14; a family 4-pack is just $13.

NEW ORLEANS NIGHTLIFE

I t's possible that New Orleans works her wily exotic charms most effectively after dark, when the jazz singers and cocktail slingers ply their magic. We'll help you wend your way through all the awesomeness, but don't forget that tomorrow beckons, with more of the city's enchantment to explore.

It is impossible to imagine New Orleans without a soundtrack of jazz, brass bands, R&B, hip hop, Cajun, and zydeco. After all, this is the town that sends you to your grave with music and then dances back from the cemetery. It's the city that lets the good times roll, and lets you take them to go (you can stroll the streets with a drink in hand, as long as it's in a plastic "go" cup). Some of the world's greatest musicians (we're not exaggerating) can be seen and heard with relative ease in remarkably intimate surroundings. And when the clubs get too full, no matter: The crowd spills into the street, where the talking, drinking, and dancing continue.

Now that you're ready to get your mojo on, here are a few things to know:

- **Club hopping is easy.** Since the city is small, most clubs are within easy walking or taxi distance from your hotel or dinner locale, and many are clustered together in one area so you can hop from one to another. Clusters of clubs can be found on Bourbon Street in the Quarter; Frenchmen Street in the Marigny; Tchoupitoulas Street in the Warehouse District; and around Willow Street in the Riverbend.
- **Showtimes vary.** Posted start and end times range from strict to strictly a suggestion (and sometimes indicate door times, not show times). Call if your schedule depends on it.
- **Bring your ID.** Some clubs allow 18-year-olds, and a few allow kids to early shows when accompanied by a parent (Three Muses, Maison, Rock 'n' Bowl). Preservation Hall is all ages. Mostly, though, it's 21+, so bring ID.
- **What does "no cover" mean?** It means buy drinks (bottled water counts) and tip the band (and/or buy their CDs, merch, whatever).
- **Look into early shows.** Early shows, starting anywhere from 5 to 7pm, are often no or low cover and a great way to avoid the crowds and the crazy.
- **Cover charges vary widely.** During big events and for big acts, they can be much higher than cited here. Crowd sizes also vary accordingly.
- **There's a blurry line between "clubs" and "bars."** Many bars (and restaurants, and hotel lounges, and streets and parks) also have music. Don't overlook them.

- **How to find out what's on:** Check **Offbeat.com** and sign up for "Weekly Beats" e-mails or go to **WWOZ.org** (you can also tune in to 90.7; club lineups are announced at the top of every odd hour). Both have good apps, worthy of downloading for the duration of your visit (and after).

THE RHYTHMS OF NEW ORLEANS

New Orleans R&B legend Ernie K-Doe was once quoted as saying, "I'm not sure, but I think all music came from New Orleans." What might be a more accurate account—and relatively hyperbole-free—is that all music came *to* New Orleans. Any style you can name, from African field hollers to industrial techno-rock to classical, finds its way to the Crescent City. Trent Reznor recorded here—then bought a house. Pianist James Booker, an eye-patched eccentric even by New Orleans standards, could make a Bach chorale strut like a second-line umbrella twirler. Then it gets blended, shaken, and stirred into a new, distinctive, and frothy concoction that could have come from nowhere else.

That sublime hybrid is what you'll likely find: jazz descended from Louis Armstrong and his Storyville compatriots. Bubbly R&B transmitted via Fats Domino and Professor Longhair. Hip hop incorporating the rhythmic Mardi Gras Indian chants. Brass bands of the second lines, infused with funk exuberance. Soak it in.

The Jazz Life of New Orleans

With thanks to jazz historian George Hocutt

Music was of great importance to the Louisiana settlers and their Creole offspring, and early on the city had a fascination with marching bands (records of parades go back to1787). Bands became required for occasions from baptisms to funerals ad infinitum—as they still are today.

In the early 19th century, slaves were allowed to congregate in the area known as **Congo Square** (now part of Armstrong Park) for dancing and drumming to the rhythms of their African and Caribbean homelands. Eventually these slaves and free men of color became accomplished instrumentalists. When blues, work songs, hollers, and spirituals were melded with their native-based rhythms and syncopations, the precursor to jazz was forming. The music was taking on a certain American and distinctly New Orleanean aura.

By the late 1890's, cornetist **Charles "Buddy" Bolden,** the "First Man of Jazz," and drummer **"Papa" Jack Laine** were taking the sounds to the next level, and to white audiences. Meanwhile, the Storyville brothel zone was flourishing on nearby Basin Street. The entertainment lineup at the better houses included a piano player in the parlor, and the immortal Jelly Roll Morton was among them.

By the uptight Twenties, Storyville was folding. Its players took the new sounds on the road: Kid Ory to California, King Oliver and his protégé Louis Armstrong to Chicago, Papa Jack and his Original Dixieland Jazz Band to New York. Their shows drew hordes and their records sold wildly. After World War II, Sidney Bechet and horn set up shop in France, and jazz consumed the continent. The jazz genie was officially out of the bottle and the craze was on.

20 CAN'T-MISS NEW ORLEANS musical EXPERIENCES

If you only have a night or two in New Orleans, try your best to hear some live local music. How to choose? Here's a list of guaranteed good time idea:

- **Kermit Ruffins,** anywhere he and his rowdy trumpet show up (try Blue Nile, Little Gem, Bullets, or his own Kermit's Treme Speakeasy).
- The roof-raising Thursday sets of the **Soul Rebels** brass band at Les Bon Ton Roulé.
- The soul-wrenching, party-starting early set of the sublime **John Boutte** at d.b.a.
- **Meschiya Lake,** whose sultry vocals would lead you to believe she time-traveled here from the 1930s (the tattoos will snap you back to reality).
- The mellow tones and vivid lyrics of singer/guitarist **Paul Sanchez.**
- Piano wizards **Tom McDermott** or **Jon Cleary,** solo or not.
- Getting your swank on in a **hotel lounge.** Try the **Davenport Lounge** at the Ritz Carlton, the Monteleone's **Carousel Bar,** or the **Polo Club** at the Windsor Court.
- Getting funked up with **Galactic, The Meters, Big Sam, Dumpstaphunk, or Papa Gros Funk.**
- Catching someone huge like Pearl Jam or Bonnie Raitt at **Tipitina's** (give the 'Fess Head statue an extra rub for your good fortune).
- Brilliant singer-songwriter **Alex McMurray** in any of his guises: solo, with the Tin Men, Happy Talk, Tom Paines, or if you hit the jackpot, doing sea shanties with the Valparaiso Men's Chorus.
- **Rebirth Brass Band** at the Maple Leaf on a Tuesday. Or anywhere, any day.
- Clarinetist **Aurora Nealand** and the **Royal Roses.** Try to keep your toes from tapping. Just. Try.
- Bowling and dancing at **Rock 'n' Bowl,** especially on zydeco night. It's a definite Barney Rubble, if you know what we mean.
- **Joe Krown,** tickling the organ keys during happy hour at Ralph's on the Park, or busting loose with the Krown, Washington & Batiste trio.
- Appreciating excellent modern jazz in a quality room, like **Snug Harbor** or **Irvin Mayfield's Playhouse.** Maybe even catching the **NOJO (New Orleans Jazz Orchestra).**
- Seeing the Stooges, Hot 8, Soul Rebels, TBC, or Rebirth and finally **getting what this brass band thing is all about**—and never wanting it to stop.
- **Dr. Michael White,** whose dulcet clarinet snake-charms even diehard jazz cynics.
- **DJ Soul Sister,** whose rainbow flow packs the floor so consistently that she essentially has a harem.
- Leaving the tourist zones for some serious **dive bar slumming**. See p. 182).
- **Don Vappie** on banjo, perhaps the swingingest strumming you'll ever see.

New Orleans is still producing jazz greats and pushing the form forward. Start with **Ellis Marsalis,** father to a group of jazz-playing sons, including **Branford, Jason,** and Pulitzer Prize–winning trumpeter **Wynton. Nicholas Payton, Irvin Mayfield, Terence Blanchard,** and brothers **Troy "Trombone Shorty" Andrews** and **James "Satchmo of the Ghetto" Andrews** (among many others) are blowing their horns to ever-adventurous distances. Obviously, the city still abounds with creativity.

Meanwhile, the nouveau traditional jazz movement is mad hot. On any given night in any given club, players from their 20s to their 70s share the bandstand, covering Jelly Roll or Django—or playing originals straight outta their eras. The **Jazz Vipers, Moonshiners, Cottonmouth Kings, Smokin' Time Jazz Band, Palmetto Bug Stompers,** and **Hot Club of New Orleans** start the long list.

Whether it's in the water, the air, or that good Creole cooking, jazz continues to grow in the fertile soil that settles on the curving banks of the Mississippi River.

Brass Bands

Today, there's way more to New Orleans brass bands than the post-funeral "second line" parade of "When the Saints Go Marching In." Now, brass is imbued with funk, R&B, reggae, and hip hop. Further, brass-band appearances on the HBO TV show *Tremé* brought the genre a new crop of fans. Classics like the **Tremé** and **Olympia Brass Bands** still hold court, but the revival goes back to the late 1980s, when **Dirty Dozen Brass Band** and **Rebirth Brass Band** started mixing things up. Today this horn-heavy, booty-moving, New Orleans born-and-bred style packs the clubs and the streets. Try to catch the sounds of Louis Armstrong look- and sound-alike (and reigning king) **Kermit Ruffins and his Barbecue Swingers; Hot 8; New Birth;** or the **Stooges.** Or newer arrivals like the blazing **TBC (To Be Continued) Brass Band** or the pumping **Young Fellaz.**

Cajun & Zydeco

Cajun and zydeco don't come from New Orleans at all. Both originated in the bayous of southwest Louisiana, a good 3 hours away. Their foundations lie in the arrival of two different French-speaking peoples in the swamp country: the white Acadians (French migrants who were booted out of Nova Scotia by the English in 1755) and the black Creole people (who came from the Caribbean slave trade). Both oppressed groups took to the folksy button accordion, newly introduced from Germany and France, which added a richness and power to their fiddle and guitar music. Later, drums, amplifiers, and steel guitars filled out the sound.

The styles began to separate after WWII, with the Cajuns gravitating toward country-and-western swing and Creole musicians being heavily influenced by the urban blues. **D. L. Menard** (the Cajun Hank Williams) and **Clifton Chenier** (the King of Zydeco) pioneered exciting new strains in their respective directions. During the great folk-music boom of the early 1960s, such figures as the **Balfa Brothers** and fiddler **Dennis McGee** performed at folk festivals. A turning point came when a Cajun group received a standing ovation at the 1964 Newport Festival, boosting the form and Cajun pride, bringing new energy, and spawning a new generation of Cajun musicians.

The proud new generation was led by accordion guru Marc and Ann Savoy and fiddler **Michael Doucet** and his band **Beausoleil,** with **Steve Riley,** and **Zachary Richard** in quick-step. The next generation of ambassadors, like the pioneering **Red Stick**

Ramblers, the Grammy-winning **Pine Leaf Boys, Feaufollet,** and the intoxicating **Lost Bayou Ramblers,** are mixing in new styles while venerating old-timey music.

As for zydeco, Clifton Chenier led the way from the 1950s on, with a handful of others (the late **Boozoo Chavis, John Delafose, Rockin' Sidney**) adding their own embellishments; **Nathan Williams** and the late, great, stately **Beau Jocque** did the same more recently. It's thriving today thanks to some of their musical progeny, including Chenier's son **C. J.,** Delafose's son **Geno,** and various Dopsie kin (**Dwayne and Rockin' Dopsie, Jr.**), and girl powerhouses like "Zydeco Sweetheart" **Rosie Ledet** and **Amanda Shaw. Terrance Simien** won the first zydeco Grammy in 2008, and the latest crop of players, like the riotous **Zydepunks,** are blending in the influences du jour.

For more on Cajun music, see "Side Trips: Cajun Country," p. 221.

Rhythm & Blues

The Delta isn't far, and the blues' gospel and African-Caribbean bloodlines took deep root in the Crescent City. In the 1950s, **Fats Domino** and his great producer-collaborator **Dave Bartholomew** fused those elements into the seminal hits "Blueberry Hill" and "Walkin' to New Orleans." Simultaneously, the unheralded **Professor Longhair** and **"Champion" Jack Dupree** were developing trailblazing piano sounds, contrasting mournful woe with party-time spirit. More piano genii followed, from **James Booker** to **Dr. John;** crooners **Johnny Adams** and "Soul Queen" **Irma Thomas** kept it smooth; and the still-amazing **Allen Toussaint** wrote, produced, and arranged his way into immortality.

The keepers of the flame today are the **Neville Brothers,** and the funky offshoot **Meters.** The genre has broadly evolved into funk, jam, and hip hop—with **Juvenile** and the Cash Money label driving that end, not to mention the only-in-New-Orleans, proto-twerking "bounce" trend led by transgender rapper **Big Freedia.** But we must include funksters **Galactic** and **Dumpstaphunk** and breakout superstar **Troy "Trombone Shorty" Andrews.**

The bluesy end of the spectrum is well represented by late greats like **Snooks Eaglin** and **Earl King,** and current keepers of the acclaim, axe men **Tab Benoit, Anders Osborne,** and **Sonny Landreth,** to name a few.

CLUB LISTINGS

The French Quarter

The Famous Door ★ Open since 1934, this is the oldest music club on Bourbon Street. Many luminaries have played here (including 13-year-old Harry Connick, Jr.). Great historic value, cheap drinks, and a solid cover band make the Famous Door fratty fun, plus there's no cover. 339 Bourbon St. ℭ **504/598-4334.** https://myspace.com/famous door. No cover.

Fritzel's European Jazz Pub ★★ From the wide open street front, this 1831 building looks sketchy, negligible even. The door folk will aggressively attempt to hustle you to a seat at the picnic tables and take your drink order. Let them: Some of the best traditional jazz is played on the teensy stage here, and the quasi-hofbrau atmosphere breeds community. 733 Bourbon St. ℭ **504/586-4800.** www.fritzelsjazz.net. 1-drink minimum per set.

Funky Pirate ★   The big (and we mean big) attraction here is bluesman "Big" Al Carson, who holds court Tuesday through Saturday from 8:30pm on. It's popular, packed (sometimes), and yes, pirate-y (always). *Note:* If "Drink from a plastic weapon" is on your bucket list, get the famously horrid Hand Grenade next door at sister bar **Tropical Isle.** 727 Bourbon St. ℂ **504/523-1960.** www.thefunkypirate.com. 1-drink minimum per set.

House of Blues ★   You can find this chain club elsewhere and you can find authentic (vs. ersatz) folk-art-laden roadhouses within a few miles (hello, Tipitina's). Even as a Live Nation venue, it's lost its domineering booking muscle to other venues. *But* when there is something worthy (Gaga and Gary Clark, Jr., have played here recently), the sightlines are good, and the regionalized, recently improved food is decent. We quite like the non-main rooms: The upstairs Parish Room feels inviting and real; the courtyard is lovely (and actually *is* real); and acoustic-oriented Big Mama's Lounge is cozy if a bit simulated. 225 Decatur St. ℂ **504/310-4999.** www.hob.com. Cover varies.

Irvin Mayfield's Jazz Playhouse ★★★   The über-talented trumpeter-bandleader's Bourbon Street retreat is the go-to spot for ambitious, established, and on-the-rise local jazz artists. Mondays with Gerald French and Wednesdays featuring the New Orleans Jazz Orchestra are sure bets. The draperied, midsize room is swank, and the well-prepared drinks aren't inexpensive (and service can be a bit snooty). But there's rarely a cover for the high-caliber talent and atmosphere. 300 Bourbon St. in the Royal Sonesa Hotel. ℂ **504/553-2299.** www.irvinmayfielda.com. Usually no cover except for the NOJO and burlesque shows.

Maison Bourbon ★   Despite its location and the DEDICATED TO THE PRESERVATION OF JAZZ sign (an attempt to confuse tourists into thinking this is Preservation Hall?), Maison Bourbon isn't a tourist trap. The music is authentic, often superb, Dixieland and traditional jazz, and the brick-lined room is a respite from the mayhem outside. 641 Bourbon St. ℂ **504/522-8818.** 1-drink minimum per set.

One Eyed Jacks ★★   With its bordello-flavored decor (swag curtains and red-flocked wallpaper, anyone?), Jack's strikes a funky/retro/hip balance. A busy front bar leads to a tiered main-room floor that wraps around another crowded bar. The cool room full of cool people is booked with cool, alternative-leaning local and touring bands (Surfer Blood, Ariel Pink, White Denim). On busy nights, the door policy can be off-putting, but that's the exception. Their 80's nights and Saturday burlesque shows are legendary. 615 Toulouse St. ℂ **504/569-8361.** www.oneeyedjacks.net. $10–$20 or more.

Palm Court Jazz Cafe ★★   This stylish dinner club serves up topnotch classic and traditional jazz Wednesday through Sunday, but Saturdays belong to trumpeter Lionel Ferbos—who turned 102 in 2013 (and he's still gigging!). Table seating (make reservations) with a small back bar for non-diners. 1204 Decatur St. ℂ **504/525-0200.** www.palmcourtjazzcafe.com. Wed–Sun 7–11pm. Cover $5 per person; entrees $16–$24. Cover $5.

Preservation Hall ★★★   The decaying, ancient-looking building lends just the right air of consecration to this, an essential spot for traditional jazz fans and, well, everyone (U2's Edge and Robert Plant have sat in here). With little air, terrible sightlines, and constant crowds, the awesomeness is in the hallowed atmosphere and the superb musicianship. Shows start at 8, 9, and 10pm; the line starts forming about an hour before. Eight "Big Shot" seats right next to the bandstand are sold online. Get them well in advance or prepare to stand. 726 St. Peter St. ℂ **888/946-JAZZ** (946-5299) or 504/522-2841. www.preservationhall.com. Cover $15; Big Shot $30.

New Orleans Nightlife

Information

Ferry Service to Algiers Point

•••• **Riverfront streetcar route/stops**

--•-- **St. Charles streetcar route/stops**

--•-- **Vieux Carre loop route/stops**

-•-■-- **Canal St. streetcar route/stops**

N. Broad St.

N. Dorgenois

N. Rocheblave

N. Tonti

N. Miro

N. Galvez

N. Johnson

N. Prieur

N. Roman

Derbigny

LaFitte Ave.

Orleans Ave.

St. Ann

Dumaine

St. Philip

Ursulines Ave.

Bayou Rd.

St. Bernard Ave.

TREMÉ DISTRICT

N. Claiborne Ave.

N. Villere

ST. LOUIS CEMETERY NO. 2

ST. LOUIS CEMETERY NO. 1

LOUIS ARMSTRONG PARK

Esplanade

FAUBOURG MARIGNY

10 METAIRIE

KENNER

90

Mississippi

BRIDGE CITY

WESTWEGO

Main Map

Uptown

610

10

FRENCH QUARTER

Superdome

MARRERO

Mercedes-Benz Superdome

Poydras

See "French Quarter Nightlife" map

Basin St.

Univ. Pl.

Conti

St. Louis

Toulouse

N. Rampart

Dauphine

Burgundy

St. Ann

Dumaine

Barracks

FRENCH QUARTER

Bourbon

Royal

Ursulines

Gov. Nichols

Esplanade

Touro

Frenchmen

Elysian Fields Ave.

Loyola Ave.

Rampart

Keefe St.

Gravier

Common

Union

Perdido

Iberville

Bienville

Canal

Chartres

CENTRAL BUSINESS DISTRICT

Carondelet

St. Charles Ave.

Lafayette

Poydras

Girod

Camp

Julia

Lafayette Square

Decatur

i

French Market

Chartres St.

Mandeville

Marigny

Spain

BYWATER

Magazine St.

Tchoupitoulas

Commerce

S. Peters

Fulton

Conv. Ctr. Blvd.

S. Joseph

Calliope

Howard Ave.

World Trade Center

RIVERFRONT

River

Mississippi

Canal St. Ferry (Toll)

Morgan

Delaronde

Seguin

ALGIERS

Convention Center

| 0 | | 1/4 mi |
| 0 | 0.25 km | |

Gay Nightlife

Marigny Art
  and Books **30**

Phoenix **33**

Country Club **36**

Performing Arts, Theaters, Cruises

Carver Theater **25**

Creole Queen **24**

Gasa Gasa **5**

Café Istanbul **32**

Civic Theatre **14**

Mahalia Jackson Theater
  for the Performing Arts **27**

Frenchmen Street & the Marigny

Blue Nile ★★★   This midsize club underwent a major rehab in 2013, adding a killer sound system and removing the view-obscuring pillars. Bookings feature a wide variety of locals, reggae, jam bands, plus late-night DJs upstairs. 532 Frenchmen St. ✆ **504/948-BLUE** (948-2583). www.bluenilelive.com. Cover free to $15.

d.b.a. ★★★   Among the best New Orleans bar/nightclubs and best beer selections (spirits too). Its live bookings feature an occasional, on-the-cusp national or Louisiana act and a wide variety of excellent local acts like magnificent crooner John Boutte, the tight blues of Walter Washington, or bluesy breakout rockers Honey Island Swamp Band. It's nonsmoking, and shows start on time. Mostly standing room only, and the low stage doesn't help those in the back. *Tip:* Boutte's early Saturday shows now command a small cover charge, but most other nights this well-booked slot is free. 618 Frenchmen St. ✆ **504/942-3731.** www.dbaneworleans.com. Cover $5–$15, occasionally higher.

Snug Harbor ★★★   This sit-down, concert-style club and early Frenchmen Street settler is the city's premier showcase for contemporary jazz. Two levels provide mostly good viewing (beware the pillars upstairs—try to sit along the rail). The adjoining restaurant has great burgers, and the shows screen on monitors in the low-ceilinged bar: for the budget-minded, it's the next best thing to live. Doors open at 7pm; sets start at 8 and 10pm. Advance online ticket purchase is wise. 626 Frenchmen St. ✆ **504/949-0696.** www.snugjazz.com. Cover $15–$40.

The Spotted Cat Music Club ★★★   Our aesthetic leans toward cramped rooms, little amplification, and scrappy bands with a fresh take on big-band, gypsy, hot—well, any type of swinging jazz. So we adore the oft-crowded Cat. The scarce seats are hardly comfy, but the 100-percent reliably fine music is the real deal, as are the frenetic-footed jitterbuggers squeezed in front of the teensy stage (often they're the instructors at Wednesday's free 5pm dance lessons). We love the uncrowded early hours (music starts at 4pm; 3pm on weekends) and local artworks on the walls. Cash only. 623 Frenchmen St. www.spottedcatmusicclub.com. No cover except special events. 1 drink per set. Tip the band.

Three Muses ★★★   Sophisticated modern lounge meets classic 1920s saloon, and we likey. It serves up beautifully balanced, new-timey cocktails and mouthwatering (quite) small plates to old-timey tunes, with no cover (but the food and drinks can add up; feta fries are best for value and sharing). The scant tables and stools go fast; expect a line when the street is hopping. Don't miss Luke Winslow-King, Debbie Davies, or muse Miss Sophie Lee if they're here. It's closed Tues; otherwise open 4pm, and kids welcome till 9ish. 536 Frenchmen St. ✆ **504/252-4801.** www.thethreemuses.com. A second location on Freret St. is in the works. No cover. Tip the band.

Elsewhere Around the City

Candlelight Lounge ★   One of the last still-operating clubs in the Faubourg Tremé, the big event here happens Wednesday around 10pm, when the rollicking, eponymous Tremé Brass Band takes the small stage. It has free red beans and rice, communal tables, cheap, fast-flowing beer, and super-friendly staff. Even though iconic drummer Uncle Lionel passed in 2013, no one in the mixed crowd leaves this streamer-strewn room without smiling or sweating. Cab it here. 925 N. Robertson. ✆ **504/525-4746.** Cover $15–$20.

French Quarter Nightlife

Clubs & Bars

The Abbey **35**

Aunt Tiki's **37**

Bar Tonique **24**

Bombay Club **2**

Cane & Table **36**

Carousel Bar at the
  Monteleone Hotel **7**

Cat's Meow **28**

Crescent City Brewhouse **16**

Erin Rose **13**

Famous Door **4**

French 75 Bar at Arnaud's **3**

Fritzel's European Jazz Pub **28**

Funky Pirate **27**

House of Blues **9**

Irvin Mayfield's Jazz Playhouse **6**

Kerry Irish Pub **11**

Lafitte's Blacksmith Shop **33**

Molly's at the Market **38**

Napoleon House **15**

One Eyed Jacks **21**

Palm Court Jazz Cafe **39**

Pat O'Brien's **19**

Patrick's Bar Vin **5**

Pirate's Alley Café and
  Absinthe House **23**

Preservation Hall **20**

SoBou **8**

Tico Tolteca **10**

Tujagues **31**

Gay Nightlife

700 Club **18**

Bourbon Pub—Parade Disco **29**

Café Lafitte in Exile **32**

Golden Lantern **34**

Good Friends Bar &
  Queens Head Pub **26**

LeRoundup **14**

Oz **30**

Rawhide 2010 **25**

Theaters, Performing Arts, Cruises

Creole Queen Steamboat **12**

Le Petit Théâtre du Vieux Carré **22**

Saenger Theatre **1**

Steamboat Natchez **17**

173

Chickie Wah-Wah ★★   We're ever so fond of this Mid-City club, where the best of the local roots, rock, blues, and singer-songwriter acts draw reverent crowds. The midsize, shotgun-style room is clean and smoke-free. Cool old tin signs lend ambience, and The Sammich snack bar serves darn good sammies. It's off the Canal Street streetcar at N. White Street, just past Broad. Try to catch Paul Sanchez, Tom McDermott, or John Cleary here. 2828 Canal St. ✆ **504/304-4714.** www.chickiewahwah.com. Cover $8–$20.

Circle Bar ★★   A 2012 renovation of the 1883 building maintained the quirky, elegant decay suitable to the laid-back, Marlboro-loving clientele in this tiny dive. The jukebox feeds the idiosyncratic vibe with mood-enhancing selections from the Velvet Underground, Dusty Springfield, and Curtis Mayfield. There's an alcove where up-and-comers play at happy hour, and good local musicians start thinking about playing at 10pm nightly. 1032 St. Charles Ave., in the CBD at Lee Circle. ✆ **504/588-2616.** www.circle barneworleans.com. Cover $5–$12.

The Howlin' Wolf ★★   The big (10,000 square feet), not-at-all-bad Wolf brings in leading local and midlevel national acts. Rock, funk, and jam are the mainstays (think Leftover Salmon, of Montreal; Sharon Jones & the Dap Kings; and local faves like Galactic, Rebirth, Dumpstaphunk). Good sound, good sightlines, good times. The smaller "Den" books eclectic indie locals, comedy, and acoustic stuff, plus the Hot 8 brass band on Sundays. Fun fact: The bar came from Al Capone's hotel in Chicago. Doors open at 9pm; shows start at 10pm. 907 S. Peters St., in the Warehouse District. ✆ **504/529-5844.** www.thehowlinwolf.com. Cover varies.

Kermit's Treme Speakeasy Restaurant & Bar ★   All aboard! Beloved trumpeter and Kermit Ruffins finally opened his own unofficial-mayor low-key, smallish club in 2012. When he plays (most—but not all—Sun and Mon, 6pm or whenever he decides), it gets crammed with bootyshakers. It's still fun. Come early for a seat, though standing gets you a better view. Kermit may barbecue, and the kitchen turns out acceptable Creole staples and occasional rustic specials (squirrel!?). It's not far from the French Quarter, but if you walk, stay on Basin St. 1535 Basin St., ✆ **504/309-5828.** www.facebook.com/pages/Kermits-Treme-Speakeasy-Restaurant-Bar/228489110603709. $10–$20 cover.

Jimmy's ★   Legendary club owner and impresario Jimmy Anselmo, who brought some of the best rock, R&B, and punk to New Orleans from the late 1970s through 2000 is set to reopen his namesake club in late 2013. We're listing it even without the details, because we're pretty sure Jimmy and his new partners will bring the good stuff. Check it out and let us know. 8400 Willow St. in the Riverbend area. www.facebook.com/jimmysmusicclub.

> ### Bender Mender
>
> If the aftermath of clubbing leaves you with a case of the liquid flu, consider the **Remedy Room** on your morning after. An actual M.D. hooks you up to an actual I.V. packed with vitamins and various other restoratives, to get you upright and sharp for that 1pm swamp tour or conference call. And may we suggest a glass of water with each cocktail. Next time. 1224 St Charles Ave. ✆ **504/301-1670.** From about $120.

Little Gem Saloon ★★★   For those who appreciate jazz history, this is the motherland. The record books may be sketchy, but most agree that jazz began on this block, and perhaps in this building. The first greats—including Buddy Bolden and Jelly Roll Morton—played the 1906 Little Gem,

THE ST. CLAUDE scene

The scruffy local alternative types have carved out a pretty pulsing, punk-infused scene (well, with some garage rock, bluegrass, metal, karaoke, and whatever else thrown in for good measure) along a stretch of St. Claude Avenue in the Bywater. The **Saturn Bar** falls somewhere between art project and junque-house, but the dive vibe is unfakeable. Punk, surf, DJs, and metal bands rotate (3067 St. Claude Ave.; © **504/949-7532**). At the spacious, comfortable **Hi-Ho Lounge,** we dig Monday night's BYOBanjo bluegrass jam; Saturdays when DJ Soul Sister brings her massive, multi-culti following; and the yummy menu of grilled cheesiness (2239 St. Claude Ave.; © **504/945-4446;** http://hiholounge.net). The **AllWays Lounge** (2240 St. Claude Ave.; © **504/218-5778;** www.theallwayslounge.com) and **Siberia** (2227 St. Claude Ave.; © **504/265-8855;** www.siberianola.com) round out the tatty, happening street scene. If this sounds like your thing, do take a cab and don't wander in this transitional area. Hungry? Hit **Borracho** in **Kajun's Pub** (2256 St. Claude Ave.; © **504/947-3735** or 504/267-6108; http://kajunpub.com) for genius-level bar food; at press time, the chef/mastermind was building Pidgin, a full-service spot next door.

and they'd love the thoroughly restored 2013 iteration. It's booking top local and visiting jazz acts in the brick-walled, velvet-curtained Ramp Room, and more casual acts downstairs at happy hour and brunch in the tile-floored Saloon. The menu reflects similar quality and sophistication, with the moules frîtes and hanger steak standing out. 445 S. Rampart St. © **504/267-4863.** www.littlegemsaloon.com. $10–$30 cover for Ramp Room shows.

Maple Leaf Bar ★★★   This classic New Orleans club is a locals bar by day, and a medium-size, tin-ceilinged, twinkle-light-strung club at night (that feels smaller when the crowds pack in, usually by 11). Personal space can become just a wistful memory and the drunk frat crowd can be maddening; seek temporary refuge on the back patio, at the back bar's junky pool table, or on the sidewalk where the overflow party goes. But it's got a vibe you can't manufacture, and when Rebirth rips it up on Tuesdays it's pretty much a must-do (but if you're only around on Thurs, see the Trio). 8316 Oak St. © **504/866-9359.** www.mapleleafbar.com. Cover $10–$20.

Mid City Lanes Rock 'n' Bowl ★★★   Bowling. Bands. Beer. If you can't have fun here, we give up. There's swing on Wednesdays, zydeco on Thursdays, and local blues, rockabilly, rock, who cares on other nights. It's an utter hoot and an unbeatable experience that draws all ages and types to the spacious (but well air-conditioned) dance floor. The custom-embroidered bowling shirts make splendid souvenirs. Fun fact: The wood tables are built from the lanes in the old (pre-Katrina) location. Dine next door at Ye Olde College Inn (p. 94) and take $5 off admission. Monday to Friday at 4pm and Saturday at 2pm until "the party closes down." 3000 S. Carrollton Ave. © **504/861-1700.** www.rocknbowl.com. Private parties sometimes take over, so call ahead. Bowling $24/hr. per lane and a $1 shoe-rental fee; show admission $5–$25.

Tipitina's ★★★   Dedicated to the late piano master Professor Longhair (that's him in bronze just inside the entrance; rub his head for luck), Tip's is, if not *the* New

Sunday School at Tipitina's

Besides its pedigree as one of the city's premier live-music venues, **Tipitina's** also actively supports and enhances the local scene through its foundation. At its Sunday-afternoon music workshops, held from 1 to 3:30pm, music students can play and study with such leading names as Stanton Moore, Johnny Vidacovich, Kirk Joseph, and Theresa Andersson. This low-key, free scene offers a pretty cool opportunity to participate, watch, and listen as traditions are passed on.

Orleans club, a major musical touchstone and a reliable place for top local and out-of-town roots, brass, jam, and rock bands from Wilco to Willie Nelson. If you can catch locals like Troy "Trombone Shorty" Andrews, Galactic, the Meters, the Nevilles, or especially Dr. John here, do not waver for a sec.

It's nothing fancy: four walls, buncha bars, wraparound balcony (often reserved for VIPs), and a stage (which, if you're under 6 feet, isn't easy to see from the back on busy nights). This uptown institution (location, not atmosphere) has good (loud) sound and air-con, and there's usually some food truck action. Get advance tix for the big shows and the festival bookings, including the brass-band blowout and Instruments a Comin' benefit, and plan on cabbing. 501 Napoleon Ave. ℂ **504/895-8477.** www.tipitinas.com. Cover varies.

THE BAR SCENE

You won't have any trouble finding a place to drink in New Orleans. Heck, thanks to "go" (or *geaux*) cups, you won't have to spend a minute without a drink in your hand. (It's legal to drink in public as long as it's in a plastic cup, and sometimes it almost seems illegal *not* to have such a cup in your hand). But there's more to this town than bars (much), and more to bars than Bourbon Street (ditto), so as with all things, let moderation preside.

There, much that's our sermon. Now read on for places to spend your precious cocktail budget. New Orleans provides some of the most convivial, quaint, or downright eccentric spots to do so. Also keep in mind that many restaurants also have excellent bars; see p. 72.

The French Quarter & the Faubourg Marigny

Bar Tonique ★★ If I lived in this Quarter's-edge neighborhood, this would be my bar. Except I wouldn't be an anti-hip service industry local, and I'd chat up the tourists more. Mostly I'd glow in the candlelight bouncing off the original brick walls, or cozy up with my honey in the smoochy booths in the offshoot alcove, sipping one of the prodigious punches, like the Blanche Dubois, or a superbly poured cocktail from another era. You know they're serious about the drinks, because there is nothing—nothing—to eat. 820 N. Rampart St. ℂ **504/324-6045.** www.bartonique.com.

The Bombay Club ★ This grown-up, wood-paneled jazz-and-martini bar bills itself as casually elegant—which politely means don't wear shorts—but it's not at all snooty. It's also a restaurant, and though the food is okay, the romantic, curtained booths in the back are awfully inviting. 830 Conti St., in the Prince Conti Hotel. ℂ **800/699-7711** or 504/586-0972. www.thebombayclub.com.

CAJUN & ZYDECO joints

There are surprisingly few of these in New Orleans, but it's the big city after all. (For the real thing, head out to bayou or prairie country.) You might catch the world-renowned Beausoleil, raucous Pine Leaf Boys, or Lost Bayou Ramblers at **d.b.a.** (p. 172) or **Tipitina's** (p. 175) while they're here "in town." Tip's also hosts a Fais do-do every Sunday at 5pm, with live Cajun music and dancing. Two other sure bets are Thursday Zydeco Nights at **Rock 'n' Bowl** (p. 175), where the bands and dancers vie for "hottest" title; and **Mulate's** (201 Julia St., at Convention Center Blvd. in the CBD; ℂ **800/854-9149** or 504/522-1492; www.mulates. com), a tourist-friendly dinner-dancehall where patient instructors help you become one of those aforementioned dancing hotties. The food is ordinary, but the dancing is folksy fun for all ages; Mulate's is open 7pm nightly, but call to make sure it's not closed for a private event.

Cane & Table ★★   One of the most anticipated openings of 2013, C&T has a "sophisticated faded" decor marked by distressed plaster and brick walls, sparkly chandeliers, and a gleaming white marble bar top. Rum is the star here, brought to you by some of New Orleans's most revered craft cocktail revivalists, constructed with house-made ingredients and squeezed-to-order juice. They call it proto-tiki; we call it high-culture colonialism. The complex flavors may not be for everyone, but start with the Boss Colada. Small plates follow the Caribbean tide: Share the chicharones; bogart the ropa vieja. 1113 Decatur St. ℂ 504/581-1112. www.caneandtablenola.com.

Carousel Bar at the Monteleone Hotel ★★★   No, you're not drunk (or maybe you are). The bar *is* spinning (one drink per rotation is the purported ratio—don't worry, its slo-o-o-w). A 2012 expansion added much-needed elbow room, couch seating, grand windows, and another (stationary) bar. It's a grown-up room with grown-up music and prices to match, but a classic. Try the Vieux Carré Cocktail, invented here some 70 years ago. 214 Royal St. ℂ 504/523-3341. www.hotelmonteleone.com.

Cat's Meow ★   The drinks and drink specials flow aplenty—the better to loosen the larynx at this foremost karaoke mecca. Whether or not you take the mic, the scene is entertaining and the crowds get thick. The action starts at 4pm Monday throught Thursday, 2pm Friday through Sunday. 701 Bourbon St. ℂ 504/523-2788. www.catskaraoke. com.

Crescent City Brewhouse ★   When this place opened in 1991, it was the first new brewery in New Orleans in more than 70 years. It still holds up as a decent micro-brewery, and comes with live jazz. 527 Decatur St. ℂ 888/819-9330 or 504/522-0571. www. crescentcitybrewhouse.com.

Cocktail Bar ★★   Guests and local professionals who prefer a refined hipness lounge on plush sofas and mingle amid the columned lobby of the Windsor Court Hotel (p. 63). With an updated cocktail program and superb mellow jazz (regulars Tim Laughlin and Shannon Powell are highly recommended), a stop here is an ideal component of a stylish evening out. We're awfully fond of the cushy upstairs **Polo Club** too, where a cool combo provides background for the well-heeled Sazerac-and-cigar crowd. 300 Gravier St., in the Windsor Court Hotel. ℂ 504/523-6000. www.windsorcourt hotel.com.

PAT O'BRIEN'S & THE MIGHTY hurricane

Pat O'Brien's, 718 St. Peter St. (☎ **504/525-4823;** www.patobriens.com), is world-famous for the hefty, vivid red, rum-based drink with the big-wind name. The bar's owners found the formula for the Hurricane during World War II, and serve it up in signature 28-ounce hurricane-lamp-style glasses. On weeknights it also comes in a 3-gallon magnum that's taller than many small children, served with long straws, and takes a group to finish (we profoundly hope)—all of whom must drink standing up. Naturally, this attracts tourists and collegians in droves. The line can stretch down the street, despite the plethora of nearby drinking options.

Pat O's is nonetheless worth a stop—it's a reliable, rowdy, friendly introduction to New Orleans. Some prefer the large lounge with the dual piano players (starting at 7pm), but when weather permits, the attractive, sprawling (often boisterous) tropical patio is the place to be. There's no minimum or cover, but the souvenir glass comes with a $3 surcharge (refunded if you turn it in at the register).

Erin Rose ★★★ Triple threat: unassuming Irish Pub, craft cocktail bar, and **Killer Po'boys** in the back room. That's the name of the enterprise *and* the description—a bold but accurate claim. Try the rum-marinated pork belly po'boy with citrus lime slaw. Killer. 0811 Conti St. ☎ **504/523-8619.** www.erinrosebar.com.

French 75 Bar at Arnaud's ★★★ A beautiful, intimate bar space in one of the Quarter's most venerable restaurants (p. 81). It feels like drinking in New Orleans should: classic and classy (and cigar-smoky later in the eve). Acclaimed bartender Chris Hannah and others are equally adept at vintage cocktails and original concoctions, including a perfect Ramos Gin Fizz and the namesake French 75 champagne cocktail. Order a side of Arnaud's dreamy soufflé potatoes to munch on. 813 Bienville St. ☎ **504/523-5433.** www.french75.com.

Kerry Irish Pub ★ This Irish pub has darts, pool, a proper pint of Guinness, and Beth Patterson, who mashes traditional Celtic folk, honeyed originals, metal-to-acoustic conversions, and hilariously filthy knockoffs. For that last nightcap, the Kerry specializes in very-late-night drinking. 331 Decatur St. ☎ **504/527-5954.** www.kerryirishpub.com.

Lafitte's Blacksmith Shop ★★ Even if it wasn't the oldest bar (and maybe building) in the Quarter or even a legendary pirate's lair, Lafitte's would merit a visit. It's ancient and ultra-atmospheric, so even amid the crowd chatter and blaring jukebox, sipping an ale in the crumbling, cavern-like, candlelit interior is nearly akin to time traveling. Stick with beer and ambience; the mixed drinks are mediocre. 941 Bourbon St. ☎ **504/593-9761.** www.lafittesblacksmithshop.com.

Molly's at the Market ★★ *The* hangout for bohos and literary locals, who chew over the state of their world and their city in this casual, comfortable, East Village–feeling bar, which many consider the best in the French Quarter. With the 2013 addition of **Dis Tacos** serving gourmet street tacos in the back bar, that may be accurate. It's 1107 Decatur St. ☎ **504/525-5169.** www.mollysatthemarket.net.

Napoleon House ★★   Set in a landmark building, the cave-dark barroom and romantically faded courtyard seem almost too perfectly aged. No plastic surgery here. Even locals come for the toasty muffuletta and signature Pimm's Cup, a cucumber-infused glass of summer. 500 Chartres St. ✆ **504/524-9752.** www.napoleonhouse.com.

Patrick's Bar Vin ★★   Half a block and a million miles from Bourbon Street, Patrick Van Voorhees, one of the city's premier sommeliers, serves conviviality and an excellent selection of wines by the glass (and other spirits). The bar feels like your great uncle's decorous but restful library (if his has rich wood paneling and ample club chairs); the sweet outdoor courtyard screams for something bubbly. 730 Bienville St., in the Hotel Mazarin. ✆ **504/200-3180.** www.patricksbarvin.com.

Pirates Alley Café and Absinthe House ★   Its tucked-away locale around the corner from St. Louis Cathedral has European-style outdoor alleyway tables. Purists will balk at its absinthe service, but others will have fun with it—flaming sugar cube and all. The food's nothing much, but it's there. 622 Pirate's Alley. ✆ **504/524-9332.** www.piratesalleycafe.com.

SoBou ★★   At a self-service gastropub, do you tip yourself? The fun here includes tables with their own beer taps and machines dispensing wine (think soda fountains, but grapier). It's less kitschy and more full-service than this sounds—it's by the Commander's Palace folks, after all. A second room is highlighted (literally—and strikingly) by a wall of white LED-lit bottles, and the pedigreed drinks are skillfully composed. The food is hit-or-miss; skip the disjointed tuna cones, but not the shrimp pinchos. Good happy-hour deals. 310 Chartres St., in the W Hotel. ✆ **504/522-4095.** www.sobounola.com.

Tico Tolteca ★★   Welcome (back) to Bali Ha'i, circa 1961. At this tiki temple, there's bamboo, flaming bowls of booze, and a DJ spinning Esquivel. But it's a sincere homage, and these are not your mother's rum sugarbombs: They're deftly made cocktails from original recipes and homemade ingredients. Beside zombies and daiquiris there are plenty of Latin-influenced choices—ditto for the tapas menu. We're hep to the wee pork tostones and the savory braised oxtails. 301 N. Peters St. inside Felipe's, up the back stairs. ✆ **504/267-4406.** www.facebook.com/tikitolteca. At press time, open Tues, Thurs & Fri nights only with plans to expand.

Tujague's ★★★   The attraction here is the centuries-old bar with the wall-size mirror, which was hand-carried—whole—from France to New Orleans (well, with some sailing). The bartenders will tell the tale while pouring one of the best Sazeracs in town (and we've done our research). There are no seats but usually some colorful characters worth sidling up to, and after an ownership change briefly threatened to turn the place into a T-shirt store last year, we're happier than ever to sidle. 823 Decatur St. ✆ **504/525-8676.** www.tujaguesrestaurant.com.

Elsewhere Around the City

Avenue Pub ★★   This is beer geek Heaven, what with 40+ options on tap and many more in bottles. Proper glassware and weekly cask ales show they're serious about their suds, but even the PBR crowd enjoys the upstairs balcony overlooking St. Charles Boulevard (and the jalapeno, cream cheese, and bacon poppers). 1732 St. Charles Ave. ✆ **504-586-9243.** www.theavenuepub.com.

GAME on

Pretty much every bar and club in town, no matter how unsporty, becomes a **sports bar** on Saints game days. So if you're looking for a place to watch the game, try anywhere. We'll single out **Mannings** for its wall-sized screen and fully reclining leather lounge chairs. Reserve them well in advance and expect to pay a hefty bounty (pardon the poor choice of words), from $25 in food & drink for an average Red Wings game to $100 for a Saints games (chair and beer bucket only) (519 Fulton St.; ✆ **504/593-8118;** www.facebook.com/ManningsNOLA).

BJ's Lounge ★★   All Bywater roads lead to junked-up corner bar BJ's on Mondays, when the local denizens, pool shooters, and High Life drinkers all groove to the soul-searing blues and raucous rhythms of **King James and the Special Men.** Little Freddie King hits it occasionally, and some guy named Robert Plant played a surprise set last year. Cab it. 4301 Burgundy St. ✆ **504/945-9256.** www.facebook.com/bjs.bywater.

The Bulldog ★   This local haunt has an incredible beer selection and unfancy but good bar food. Wednesday is buy a pint, keep the glass night (a great souvenir). Both locations have nice outdoor patios for quaffin' in the muggy New Orleans evenings with the coed crowd. Uptown: 3236 Magazine St. ✆ **504/891-1516;** Mid-City: 5135 Canal Blvd. ✆ **504/488-4191.** http://bulldog.draftfreak.com.

Cure ★★★   This mixologist mecca helped instigate the resurgence of both craft cocktails in New Orleans and now-booming Freret Street. The oasis of sleek boasts great small plates and some of the most knowledgeable bar chefs in town, who blend exceptional ingredients with personable chat. Beat the late crowds; go at happy hour. 4905 Freret St. ✆ **504/302-2357.** www.curenola.com.

Le Bon Temps Roulé ★   Inside this way-uptown, rundown shack is a smoky, cramped bar with a decent beer list. So? So schedule your visit to be in town on a Thursday, when the Soul Rebels brass band blows this here roof off. It's quite welcoming the other 6 nights of the week, too, and full of archetypal local characters. 4801 Magazine St. ✆ **504/895-8117.**

Sazerac Bar at the Roosevelt ★★   If the New Orleans bar scene were a monarchy, the historic Sazerac Bar in the glamorous Roosevelt Hotel might be queen. The sinuous wood walls and Deco-era murals here have borne witness to movie stars, political scandals, and we don't want to know what (check the bullet hole above the back kitchen door). You're here for all that panache as much as the namesake cocktail. 123 Baronne St. ✆ **504/529-4733.** www.therooseveltneworleans.com.

Swizzle Stick Bar at Café Adelaide ★★★   Lu Brow, high goddess and doyenne of New Orleans's craft cocktail revival, started it all here. There are cooler bars now, but for those who like a little sass with their class, this art-filled spot still serves inventive, finely-honed beverages and pre-Prohibition classics (and far-above-par bar food from adjoining Café Adelaide). 300 Poydras St., in the Loews Hotel. ✆ **504/595-3305.** www.cafeadelaide.com.

GAY NIGHTLIFE

These are just a few of the many bars that cater to New Orleans' thriving LBGTQ, etc. community. Expect late hours, welcoming crowds, and crowded crowds during Mardi Gras or Southern Decadence, p. 39.

For more information, pick up a copy of *Ambush* magazine (www.ambushmag. com) at the locations listed here or at Faubourg Marigny Art and Books (600 Frenchmen St.; ℂ **504/947-3700;** www.fabonfrenchmen.com).

Bars & Clubs

In addition to those listed below, you might also try the long-running **Golden Lantern,** 1239 Royal St. (ℂ **504/529-2860**), the Cheers of NOLA, described as "half of Noah's Ark—with one of everything, one drag queen, one leather boy, one guy in a suit." If Levi's and leather are your scene, check **Rawhide 2010,** 740 Burgundy St. (ℂ **504/ 525-8106;** www.rawhide2010.com), or the anything-goes **Phoenix,** 941 Elysian Fields Ave. (ℂ **504/945-9264;** www.neworleansphoenix.com).

700 Club ★ No, it's not *that* 700 Club. It's just a simple, chill bar where you can wander in and get a decent drink and something from the full kitchen. For those times when you're *not* looking for a scene, it's perfect. 700 Burgundy St. ℂ **504/561-1095.** www.700ClubNewOrleans.com.

The Bourbon Pub—Parade Disco ★★ Of the two (super-popular) bars, the downstairs pub is a bit calmer for most of its 24 hours. Upstairs, Parade Disco comes alive on weekends and features a high-tech dance setup. Themes most nights include GirlBar Tuesdays and retro video Sing-along Sundays. It gets going around 9pm and early Sunday evenings, when the cover includes free well drinks from 6pm till 8pm. 801 Bourbon St. ℂ **504/529-2107.** www.bourbonpub.com. Downstairs is 24/7; upstairs closed Mon & Wed.

Café Lafitte in Exile ★★ This is one the oldest gay bars in the U.S., established in 1953 and claiming Tennessee Williams as a former patron (believe what you will). There's a theme-night cruise bar downstairs (not so much for teeny-boppers or twinks); upstairs is a friendly, publike atmosphere. Although we don't really get the famous Sunday-night "Love is in the Air" napkin toss, we love it. 901 Bourbon St. ℂ **504/522-8397.** http://lafittes.com. Downstairs is 24/7; upstairs Thurs–Sun 1pm–till.

Country Club ★★ It's a bar, a pool, a restaurant, a club, and a nude beach. Sorta. Everyone's welcome at this converted Creole cottage in the Bywater, with its pretty veranda and dining room. You can sip a cocktail while soaking in a Jacuzzi or lounging by the pool (clothing optional), without having to stay in a fancy hotel or know fancy friends. 634 Louisa St. ℂ **504/945-0742.** www.thecountryclubneworleans.com. Pool access $8–$15; more for events.

Good Friends Bar & Queens Head Pub ★★ This truly is a friendly spot, drawing mixed genders, types, and ages. We like that the decor isn't generically techno'ed out and at least tries to maintain some NOLA feel, and that the local denizens will gladly chat you up. The upstairs Queens Head Pub is most fun during the Sunday singalong, from 3pm on. 740 Dauphine St. ℂ **504/566-7191.** www.goodfriendsbar. com. Open 24 hr. on weekends; till 2am weekdays. Upstairs pub open Thurs–Sun only.

diving IN

If you'd rather go bar-hopping with Tom Waits than Tom Cruise, you'll appreciate New Orleans's fine dive bars—and by fine, we mean down-and-dirty, neighborhood holes-in-the-wall with regulars straight out of a Jim Jarmusch casting call. Try the Elvis-themed **Kingpin**, where 20-something rocker types come for shuffleboard and cheap drink specials (1307 Lyons St., Uptown; ✆ **504/891-2373**; www.kingpinbar.com). **Snake & Jake's Christmas Club Lounge**'s only illumination comes from dwindling Christmas lights, which doesn't make it easier to find this crowded, sweat-soaked, off-the-beaten-path shack. It's

BYOD (dog), so you know it's friendly (7612 Oak St., Uptown; ✆ **504/861-2802**). Smoke-filled **Aunt Tiki's** in the depths of Decatur Street is laden with Halloween dreck and affable, slouching degenerates. As if that's not good enough, the drinks are strong and cheap (1207 Decatur St., French Quarter; ✆ **504/680-8454**). **The Abbey** has a few motley stained-glass windows. but everything else is the antithesis of church. Yet the David Lynchian clientele pray at their bar 24 hours a day, and a jukebox with classic country *and* the Cramps is worthy of worship (1123 Decatur St., French Quarter; ✆ **504/523-7177**).

LeRoundup ★ LeRoundup attracts the most diverse crowd around, 24 hours a day: drag queens, the trans community, working boys—even well-groomed men in khakis (now we just sound like SNL's Stefon). 819 St. Louis St. ✆ **504/561-8340.**

Oz ★★ This world-renowned, bass-heavy dance club might be overrated, but it still has an incredible light show, go-go boys atop the bar (usually), and drag on Wednesdays. It's a see-and-be-seen spot for a mostly young crowd including plenty of straights. The dance-floor view from the upstairs balcony is worth it alone. 800 Bourbon St. ✆ **504/593-9491.** www.ozneworleans.com. Cover varies.

PERFORMING ARTS, THEATERS & CONCERT HALLS

In addition to the resources below, culture vultures may want to see what's on tap at **Loyola** (www.loyno.edu/calendar) or **Tulane University** (http://tulane.edu/calendar), and at three eclectic performance spaces: The recently renovated **Carver Theater** (2101 Orleans Ave.; www.carvertheater.org); **Gasa Gasa** (4920 Freret St.; ✆ **504/304-7110;** www.gasagasa.com); and **Café Istanbul** (2372 St. Claude Ave.; ✆ **504/975-0286;** www.cafeistanbulnola.com).

Civic Theatre ★★ A couple of years ago there was nothing in here but the exquisite Deco chandelier and a flock of pigeons. But we're thrilled that this 1906 midsize theater is back. Nothing was spared on sound, lighting, or restoring the graceful, original plasterwork. The 2013 reopening lineup stretched from Russell Brand to Steve Earle to cult darlings Neutral Milk Hotel (a coup); the bar program is by the folks from Cure (coup #2). 510 O'Keefe St. ✆ **504/272-0865.** www.civicnola.com.

Le Petit Théâtre du Vieux Carré ★★★ One of the oldest community theaters in the U.S., "Le Petit" has occupied this building since 1923. The run nearly ended in 2011, but restaurateur Dickie Brennan came to the financial rescue. Building a new restaurant on the grounds (Tableau; p. 84) enabled the 350-seat Le Petit to reopen for its 2013 season and patrons to enjoy a dinner-and-a-play night out. Local productions of classic dramas, musicals, and comedies vary from very good to stellar. 616 St. Peter St. ✆ **504/522-2081.** www.lepetittheatre.com. Tickets $30–$50.

Mahalia Jackson Theater for the Performing Arts This cultural hub (located in Armstrong Park bordering the French Quarter) is home to the Louisiana Philharmonic Orchestra, the New Orleans Opera Association, and the New Orleans Ballet Association. The handsome, midcentury theater is spacious but not big, so every seat is decent. It also hosts theater, dance troupes, rock concerts, and other live acts. 1419 Basin St. ✆ **504/287-0351.** www.mahaliajacksontheater.com.

Saenger Theatre ★★★ Following an extensive, gajillion-dollar, post-Katrina renovation, this magnificent, 1927 stunner from the glory movie-house days was reopened in 2013, with Jerry Seinfeld headlining. Now technologically state of the art, the Saenger hosts concerts, comedy shows, theater, and other performances. 1111 Canal St. ✆ **504/287-0351.** www.saengernola.com.

Southern Repertory Theatre ★ Focusing (mostly) on Southern playwrights and themes, Southern Rep's productions are consistently high quality, if not always high budget. Anything written by, starring, or otherwise mentioning the hyper-talented Ricky Graham is probably worth catching. Location varies. ✆ **504/522-6545.** www.southern rep.com. Ticket prices vary by production, but usually $20–$40.

CRUISING THE MISSISSIPPI

The *Creole Queen* (✆ **800/445-4109** or 504/524-0814; www.creolequeen.com) and the slightly smaller steamboat *Natchez* riverboat cruisers both host lovely (if a bit touristy) jazz cruises nightly, with extensive, mediocre Creole buffets but much better live jazz and dancing against a backdrop of the city's sparkling skyline. For more on this nightlife option, see p. 157.

SHOPPING NEW ORLEANS

S hopping in New Orleans is a highly evolved leisure activity, with a shop for every strategy and a fix for every shopaholic— and every budget. Those endless T-shirt shops on Bourbon Street and the swanky antiques stores on Royal Street aren't all that New Orleans has to offer. The range of shopping here is as good as it gets—many a clever person has come to New Orleans just to open up a quaint boutique filled with strange items gathered from all parts of the globe or produced by local, somewhat twisted, folk artists.

There are deals to be made, or lavish riches to be spent, artworks to be admired, or outfits to wear home. But as all shoppers know, the fun is in the hunt. And New Orleans has some smashing hunting grounds.

MAJOR HUNTING GROUNDS

CANAL PLACE At the foot of Canal Street (365 Canal St.) near the Mississippi River, this sophisticated shopping mall holds more than 30 shops, many of them elegant retail chains like Brooks Brothers, Saks Fifth Avenue, Coach, and a sparkling new Tiffany & Co. There's also a two-story Anthropologie and a recently expanded branch of local jeweler **Mignon Faget** (p. 193). Open Monday to Saturday 10am to 7pm, Sunday noon to 6pm. www.theshopsatcanalplace.com.

THE FRENCH MARKET Shops within the historic market begin on Decatur Street across from Jackson Square; offerings include candy, cookware, fashion, crafts, toys, New Orleans memorabilia, and jewelry. A recent renovation has added a stage where live music or food demos may be featured, and much-improved food booths include an oyster bar, a terrific fresh juice bar, and the tasty **Meals from the Heart.** The farmers' market portion has pretty fruit and veggies, and the stalls with foodstuffs— including local seafood, meats, and spices—can pack your purchases for travel or shipping; the flea market section (near Esplanade) has lots of low-end souvenirs (good buys, if not good quality) and a smattering of actual art and craftworks. Open 10am to 6pm daily. Also see p. 120. www.frenchmarket.org.

JAX BREWERY Just across from Jackson Square at 600–620 Decatur St., the old brewery building has been transformed into a jumble of shops and cafes. It's a good stop for clothing and souvenirs, particularly the crawfish logo'd polo shirts and other preppie wear at **Perlis.** Open daily 10am to 7pm.

JULIA STREET   From Camp Street down to the river on Julia Street, you'll find some of the city's best contemporary-art galleries (many listed below under "Art Galleries"). Some of the works are a bit pricey, but there are good deals to be had if you're collecting and fine art to be seen if you're not.

MAGAZINE STREET   The Garden District's premier shopping drag: 6 miles of antiques, art galleries, boutiques, and all manner of restaurants in 19th-century brick storefronts and quaint cottage-like buildings, from Washington Street to Audubon Park. Our prime sections are, roughly, the 3700 to 4300 blocks (with the odd block or so of nothing); 1900 to 2100; and 5400 to 5700 blocks. Download or pick up a copy of "Magazine Street Shoppers' Guide" for a free store list and map. www.magazinestreet.com. A car or JazzyPass (p. 233) helps here.

RIVERBEND & OAK STREET   To reach these fetching Carrollton area shops, ride the St. Charles Avenue streetcar to stop no. 44, then walk down Maple Street one block to Dublin Park where a variety of shops inhabit several renovated old buildings. Walk 4 blocks down Dublin to the happening Oak Street shopping and dining district. Check out the excellent **Blue Cypress Books** and **Skip N' Whistle** T-shirt shop. Food options include the famous **Jacque-Imo's** (p. 105), and the **Plum Street Snoball** stand is a block away.

SHOPPING A TO Z
Antiques

Bush Antiques ★   There is serious stuff here, mostly of the European variety, and some not so serious. But the warren of rooms, some cunningly arranged according to theme, are giddy fun to browse whether or not you're in the market for a 19th-century French Empire settee or an elaborately embroidered priest's garment. 2109 Magazine St. 🕾 **504/581-3518.** www.bushantiques.com. Mon–Sat 11am–5pm.

Collectible Antiques ★★   One of our favorites of the dusty, jumbled, and eclectic antiques/junk stores on the Esplanade end of Decatur. Its stock runs from Art Deco to 1960s collectibles. 1232 Decatur St. 🕾 **504/566-0399.** Daily noon–6pm.

Greg's Antiques ★   A funky mixed bag of serious antiques, junky used furniture, salvaged windows and ironwork, and original local art on consignment—not necessarily pedigreed but at pretty decent prices—make this a personal favorite (and they're open late). Frequent shipments and sales mean goods move fast. 1209 Decatur St. 🕾 **504/202-8577.** Daily 10am–10pm.

Keil's Antiques ★★   Established in 1899 and currently run by the fourth generation of the founding family, Keil's has a considerable collection of 18th- and 19th-century French and English furniture, chandeliers, jewelry, and decorative items spanning three crowded floors and most budgets. Try to talk to one of the members of the family for tales of the doorman who worked his spot for 78 years and whatever other stories you can coax out of them. 325 Royal St. 🕾 **504/522-4552.** www.keilsantiques.com. Mon–Sat 9am–5pm.

Lucullus ★★★ A wonderful collection of culinary antiques as well as 17th-through 19th-century furnishings to "complement the grand pursuits of cooking, dining, and imbibing." You'll find all manner of china, Art Deco silverware, and even absinthe accoutrements here. 610 Chartres St. ☏ **504/528-9620.** www.lucullusantiques.com. Mon–Sat 9am–5pm (closed Mon in the summer).

Magazine Antique Mall ★ Diggers will dig the superb browsing and many good deals found among the 50-plus variegated stalls here. 3017 Magazine St. ☏ **504/896-9994.** www.facebook.com/magazineantiquemall. Mon–Sat 10:30am–5:30pm; Sun noon–5:30pm.

M.S. Rau ★★★ The sheer scale and absurdity of the inventory makes Rau a must-see for everyone and a destination for serious buyers. Every opulent item that could possibly be crafted from fine metals, gems, crystal, wood, china, and marble, plus articles made by every name known to the antique world, is here for the ogling or the investing, filling room after jaw-dropping room. We particularly like the selection of walking canes and the life-size knight and steed, both in full armor. Most every item has a story to tell, and the knowledgeable sales reps pleasantly indulge your curiosity. 630 Royal St. ☏ **866/349-0705** or 504/523-5660. www.rauantiques.com. Mon–Sat 9am–5:15pm.

Art Galleries

Galleries share the **Royal and Magazine street** landscapes with the aforementioned antiques shops, while in the Warehouse District, the blocks numbered 300 to 700 on Julia Street house some 20 contemporary fine-arts galleries, anchored by the **Contemporary Arts Center** and **Ogden Museum of Southern Art** (p. 133). For the more intrepid, explore the burgeoning lowbrow and outsider art movement around St. Claude Avenue (see www.scadnola.com).

Angela King Gallery ★★★ Angela King Gallery shows paintings and sculptures by significant contemporary artists such as Peter Max, LeRoy Neiman, Andrew Baird, Richard Currier, Steve Taylor, Raymond Douillet, Patterson & Barnes, and Michelle Gagliano . . . *and* a mini-gallery dedicated to the art of Dr. Seuss. 241 Royal St. ☏ **504/524-8211.** www.angelakinggallery.com. Mon–Sat 10am–5pm; Sun 11am–5pm.

Arthur Roger Gallery ★★ Arthur Roger helped develop the city's fine-art scene when he opened in New Orleans more than 30 years ago, tying the local community to the New York art world and pioneering the Warehouse District. Still blazing trails, Roger schedules shows that range from strongly regional to far-flung work. The gallery represents Francis Pavy, Ida Kohlmeyer, Douglas Bourgeois, Gene Koss, and George Dureau. 432 Julia St. ☏ **504/522-1999.** www.arthurrogergallery.com. Mon–Sat 10am–5pm.

Carol Robinson Gallery ★★ The grande dame of the local contemporary Southern arts scene, Robinson still shows accessible but surprisingly affordable works, including the stunning pastels of Sandra Burshell, Jere Allen's mysterious figures wafting in white, James King's haunting oils, and Christina Goodman's exquisite, minute tableaus. 840 Napoleon Ave. ☏ **504/895-6130.** Tues–Sat 10am–5pm.

Cole Pratt Gallery, Ltd. ★ This gallery showcases the work of Southern artists whose creations include abstract and realist paintings, sculptures, and ceramics. The art is of the highest quality, the prices are surprisingly reasonable, and the staff is welcoming. 3800 Magazine St. ☏ **504/891-6789.** www.coleprattgallery.com. Tues–Sat 10am–5pm.

Derby Pottery ★★ One of Mark Derby's hand-pressed tiles, glazed in gleaming single hues, makes for a lovely keepsake (particularly the New Orleans street-name tile reproductions). One hundred make for a stunning backsplash or fireplace surround. 2029 Magazine St. ✆ **504/586-9003.** www.derbypottery.com. Mon–Sat 10am–5pm.

A Gallery for Fine Photography ★★★ Do not skip this incredibly well-stocked photography gallery, even if you aren't in the market. It emphasizes New Orleans and Southern history and contemporary culture, including music and black culture. You can buy Ernest Bellocq's legendary Storyville photos, Herman Leonard's jazz images, or something from just about every period, style, or noted photographer. 241 Chartres St. ✆ **504/568-1313.** www.agallery.com. Tues noon–5pm; Thurs–Mon 10:30am–5:30pm; Wed by appointment.

Hemmerling Gallery ★ Bill Hemmerling's paintings of spirituals, jazz musicians, and his muse, "Sweet Olive," have charmed collectors and curators alike with their dignified naiveté. His second career as a painter spanned just 7 years, following his retirement from Sears and until his death in 2009. The gallery features giclees and a few rare originals, as well as works by several protégés. 733 Royal St. ✆ **504/524-0909.** www.hemmerlingart.com. Daily 11am–5pm (closed Wed).

Jonathan Ferrara Gallery ★★★ Since 1998, Ferrara has been showing emerging cross-media artists. Exhibitions are typically accessible yet thought provoking, with an eye toward playfulness and irony. Skylar Fein's pop pundit pieces are both hilarious and horrifying in their truth; the G.A.S. Caravaggio photobombs are equally stunning and silly. 400a Julia St. ✆ **504/522-5471.** www.jonathanferraragallery.com. Mon–Sat 11am–5pm.

Kurt E. Schon, Ltd. ★★ Here you'll find the country's largest inventory of 19th-century European paintings. Works include French and British Impressionist and post-Impressionist paintings as well as art from the Royal Academy and the French Salon. 510 St. Louis St. ✆ **504/524-5462.** www.kurteschonltd.com. Mon–Fri 10am–5pm; Sat 10am–3pm.

Martine Chaisson Gallery ★ Based on recent shows at Martine's stark gallery, we can't wait to see where she flings us next. The sweeping space screams for high-impact, highly saturated imagery, and so far she's delivered, particularly with Herman Mhire's manipulated portraiture and JT Blatty's striking photography of nudes with fossils. 727 Camp St. ✆ **504/302-7942.** www.martinechaissongallery.com. Wed–Sat 11am–5pm, Mon & Tues by appointment.

New Orleans School of GlassWorks & Printmaking Studio ★★★ This institution, with 25,000 square feet of studio space, houses a 550-pound tank of hot molten glass and a pre–Civil War press.

At this sister school to the Louvre Museum of Decorative Arts, established glasswork artists, bookbinders, and master printmakers display their work in the on-site gallery, demonstrate glass-blowing, and teach classes in their many crafts, including the popular "Wine & Design" gatherings. 727 Magazine St. ✆ **504/529-7279.** www.neworleansglassworks.com. Mon–Sat 10am–5pm.

> **Tax-Free Art**
>
> Many original works of visual art in New Orleans are exempt from sales tax, thanks to a statewide program promoting cultural activity in designated districts. Be sure to ask about sales tax where you buy.

OMG!★   Well-curated religious art, new and reclaimed, anchored by wonderful statuary and Jan Keels' stirring, gossamer, oil-on-wood angels. They also carry the fab Virgins Saints & Angels jewelry. 912B Decatur St. ✆ **504/522-8443.** www.omg-nola.com. Daily 10am–6pm.

Photo Works ★★   Photographer Louis Sahuc's family has been in New Orleans "since day one," and his life's work has been photo-documenting iconic New Orleans imagery, such as Jackson Square swathed in fog, or fragments of ironwork. 521 St. Ann St. ✆ **877/593-4130** or 504/593-9090. www.photoworksneworleans.com. Thurs–Tues 10am–5:30pm, and by appointment.

Red Truck Gallery★★★   For years, we've followed the work of Red Truck conceptual artists, including Jason D'Aquino's minute masterpieces on matchbooks; Bryan Cunningham's whack folk assemblages; and Adam Wallacavage's sea-creature chandeliers. Finally, Noah Antieau brings them under one roof. (His mad, sharp sensibility may be genetic: his mother, the supremely clever **Chris Roberts-Antieau,** creates the whimsical sewn works in her own gallery across the street). Some of it is bizarre. Most of it is brilliant, All of it we'd gladly own. Red Truck Gallery: 938 Royal St. ✆ **504/522-3630.** www.redtruckgallery.com. Daily 10am–10pm. Antieau Gallery: 927 Royal St. ✆**504/304-0849.** www.antieaugallery.com. Thurs–Mon 10am–8pm.

Rodrigue Studio New Orleans ★   Blue Dog is the Freddy Krueger of New Orleans; once you've seen Cajun artist George Rodrigue's creation, it invades your consciousness and torments your life. The ubiquitous, glaring, bordering-on-kitsch canine, shown in every imaginable pose or setting, has its fans, and this gallery is their headquarters. 730 Royal St. ✆ **504/581-4244.** www.georgerodrigue.com. Mon–Sat 10am–6pm; Sun 10am–5pm.

Books

Arcadian Books ★★   Bibliophiles will bask in these wondrous, dusty stacks, especially lovers of the classics (in English and Latin); the history (local and far beyond) inquisitive; and seekers of literature in French, German, or Russian. Proprietor Russell Desmond is ridiculously knowledgeable and nearly as personable, and knows every item in this gloriously decrepit grotto. 714 Orleans Ave. ✆ **504/523-4138.** Mon 10:30am–5:30pm; Tues–Sat 9:30am–5:30pm; Sun 11am–4pm.

Books a Million ★   We've got to give it to the chains that are still committed to bookselling, and it stocks a good selection of local titles. If you're passing through, this is a good place to pick up New Orleans–related books on your way to or from the city. 150 Northshore Blvd. in North Shore Square, Slidell. ✆ **985/641-4813.** www.booksamillion.com. Mon–Sat 10am–9pm; Sun noon–6pm.

Crescent City Books ★★   Explore two floors of dusty treasures of serious literature for the seriously literate (the emphasis is on history, local interest, literary criticism, philosophy, and art); it's also home to the excellent Black Widow Salon, and a general hub of info about literary events. 230 Chartres St. ✆**800/546-4013** or 504/524-4997. www.crescentcitybooks.com. Mon–Sat 10am–7pm; Sun 10am–5pm.

Faulkner House Books ★★★   Nobel prize–winner William Faulkner lived here while he was writing his early works, but beyond that invaluable literary morsel it also has tremendous value today as a remarkable small bookshop. Shelf after high shelf is occupied by highly collectible or desirable books, from stunning first editions to current best-sellers. Just one room and a hallway, Faulkner House feels like somebody's private home (it is)—but the gracious advice and selection here shows the art that is in bookselling. 624 Pirate's Alley. (© **504/524-2940.** www.faulknerhouse.net. Daily 10am–6pm year-round (closed Christmas and Mardi Gras Day).

Garden District Book Shop ★★★   Owner Britton Trice has stocked his sweet, medium-size shop with just about every New Orleans– or Louisiana-themed book you can think of, no matter what the focus: interiors, exteriors, food, Creoles, fiction, poetry, you name it—including many signed copies. 2727 Prytania St. (in the Rink). (© **504/895-2266.** www.gardendistrictbookshop.com. Mon–Sat 10am–6pm; Sun 10am–5pm.

Kitchen Witch ★★   In a town of foodies, chefs, cooks, and eaters of all interests and proficiency, this quirky used cookbook store is the rainbow's end. It stocks nearly 10,000 volumes, from the ultra-rare to the just-released—and if they don't have it, they'll find it. Set the egg timer or you could spend way too much time browsing and chatting here. 631 Toulouse St. (© **504/528-8382.** www.kwcookbooks.com. Wed–Mon 10am–6pm. (closed Tues).

Maple Street Book Shop ★★   Celebrating its 50th anniversary, this is an unmissable uptown destination for bookworms seeking new, used, or children's books. A perfect, beloved bookstore. 7523 and 7529 Maple St. (© **504/866-4916.** www.maplestreet bookshop.com. Mon–Sat 10am–6pm; Sun 11am–5pm.

Octavia Books ★★★   For those who, like us, adore independent bookstores, this far-uptown beauty with its sweet, tiny patio (complete with waterfall) is worth the detour. There is much more to savor here, in the extensive, well-selected stock and in the frequent signings and other literary events. 513 Octavia St. (at Laurel St.). (© **504/899-7323.** www.octaviabooks.com. Mon–Sat 10am–6pm; Sun noon–5pm.

Candies, Pralines & Pastries

Blue Frog Chocolates ★★   Perhaps the finest chocolate and candy collection in the city. Just for starters, it carries Nancy's truffles, Norman Love chocolates, Michel Cluizel fresh butter creams from France, and Jordan almonds (good ones are difficult to find). 5707 Magazine St. (© **504/269-5707.** www.bluefrogchocolates.com. Mon–Fri 10am–6pm, Sat 10am–5pm.

Laura's Candies ★   Laura's is said to be the city's oldest candy store, established in 1913. It has fabulous pralines, but it also has rich, delectable golf ball–size truffles— our personal favorite indulgence, although they've gotten a bit pricey as of late. 331 Chartres St. (© **800/992-9699** or 504/525-3880. www.laurascandies.com. Daily 10am–9pm.

Southern Candymakers ★★★   The pralines here include the usual suspects and the nontraditional (coconut and sweet potato!), but they're all creamylicious. They're made fresh right in front of you (if the display doesn't reel you in, the aroma will). We swoon for the pecan-laden *tortues*, and the boxed chocolate crawfish and gator pops make fine little gifts. 334 Decatur St. (© **800/344-9773** or 504/523-5544. www. southerncandymakers.com. Daily 10am–7pm. Also at 1010 Decatur St. (© **504/525-6170.** Daily 9am–6pm.

Sucré ★★★   *Ultimate Cake Off* winner Tariq Hanna's high-end confections and gorgeous chocolates are ideal for gifts, or for an afternoon indulgence in this stylish cafe. They're not overly sweet, so opinions vary from bland to brilliant. The sherbet-hued macaroons are awfully pretty, and the boozy "Big Kid Shakes" are great fun, but we're partial to the minicakes, like the luscious "Tiffany." Gotta love that they do "a month of éclairs" of every variety, and we're excited about the promise of tableside coffee service and made-to-order soufflés at the French Quarter location (622 Conti St.), opening mid-2014. 3025 Magazine St. ✆ **504/520-8311.** www.shopsucre.com. Sun–Thurs 7am–10pm; Fri–Sat 7am–midnight.

Costumes & Masks

Costumery is big business in New Orleans, and not just for Mardi Gras. Playing dress-up needs no event, and nothing is too elaborate. In addition to these shops, try thrift stores, where slightly used outfits can sometimes be found at a fraction of their original cost. Also check **Uptown Costume & Dance Company** (4326 Magazine St.; ✆ **504/895-7969;** www.uptowncostume.com; Mon–Tues 11am–6pm; Wed–Fri 11am–7pm; Sat 10am–6pm).

Carl Mack Presents ★★ The doyen of Mardi Gras entertainment now has a French Quarter shop that rents or creates ornate costumes for Fat Tuesday or any day. This is high-production-value stuff—no naughty nurses here. 223 Dauphine St. ✆ **504/949-4009.** www.carlmack.com. Mon–Fri 11am–5pm or by appt.

Fifi Mahony's ★★ Wig wackiness, why not? Cutesy or crazy, have the hair you've always wanted (even if just for the day),. Worth visiting just to see (or get) their outrageous custom pieces. Salon & make-up services too. 934 Royal St. ✆ **504/525-4343.** www.fifimahoneys.com. Sun–Wed noon–6pm; Thurs–Sat 11am–7pm.

Fashion, Vintage Clothing, Hats & Accessories

Fleur de Paris ★★★ The 1920s and 1930s elegance on display here brings us to our knees with covetousness. The experts here can take one look at any head and face and find the right hand-blocked, stylishly trimmed hat to fit it. Expensive, but works of art often are. They also have luscious stockings and an ever-changing collection of vintage gowns. 523 Royal St. ✆ **800/229-1899** or 504/525-1899. www.fleurdeparis.net. Daily 10am–6pm.

House of Lounge ★★ For the well-dressed couch potato or the boudoir hostess, House of Lounge offers all sorts of silky robes, glamorous gowns, and slinky lingerie. 2044 Magazine St. ✆ **504/671-8300.** www.houseoflounge.com. Mon–Sat 11am–6pm.

Love It ★★ It's easy to walk right by this exquisite, tiny jewel box of a shop, where Danna Lea crafts stunning purses and accessories from found leather and adornments; and restyles vintage clothes. Not inexpensive, but one-of-a-kind and worth the splurge. 713 Bienville St. ✆ **504/523-7888.** www.loveitnola.com. Wed–Sun 10am–6pm (expanded hours during special events).

Meyer the Hatter ★★★ Meyer's opened more than 100 years ago and has been in the same family ever since. Today the haberdashery has one of the largest selections of fine hats and caps in the South. Men will find distinguished international labels such as Bailey, Stetson, Kangol, Dobbs, and Borsalino (the women's collection is smaller). Let the owner and his son fuss over you and pick out the proper feather for your new chapeau. 120 St. Charles Ave. ✆ **800/882-4287** or 504/525-1048. www.meyerthehatter.com. Mon–Sat 10am–5:45pm.

Muse ★★ Gentlemen, should the city and the spirit move you so that only the emergency infusion of a seersucker sport jacket will suffice, Muse will fix you right up in your choice of colorful stripes (seasonally, and for about $150). 532 St. Peter St. (on Jackson Sq.). © 504/522-8738. www.museinspiredfashion.com. Daily 10am–6pm.

Oh! ★★ Whether or not you need a cocktail dress or ball gown, Sandy Thigpen's collection of vintage new and gently used finery is nonetheless an utter scream—from Halston disco pants to last year's perfect Chanel suit to an authentic fringed flapper get-up to, well, you get the idea. Exquisite, high-end lingerie as well. Buy now and figure out the occasion later. 829 Royal St. © **504/524-8807.** www.ohfinelingerie.com. Mon, Thurs–Sun 10:30am–5:30pm (closed Tues–Wed).

Trashy Diva ★★★ There's actually nothing trashy about the 1940s and '50s vintage-inspired clothes here. The flirty, curve-flattering numbers in silks and velvets will please both Bettys and Goths, not to mention the similar-era shoes and va-voom corsets and lingerie. Check the sales rack in the back for good bargains. 829 Chartres St. © **888/818-3482** or 504/581-4555 and 2048 Magazine St. © **504/299-8777.** www.trashydiva.com. Sun–Fri noon–6pm; Sat 11am–6pm (Chartres St.). Sun 1pm–5pm; Mon–Fri noon–6pm; Sat 11am–6pm (Magazine St.).

UAL ★ Destination One for local and visiting fashionistas, UAL offers incredible deals on discontinued and leftover designer goods (Alaia, Jason Wu, Lanvin, Chanel, Sanctuary). The ridiculous markdowns and sparse stock can lead to fiercely competitive (but utterly satisfying) hit-or-miss guerilla shopping. 518 Chartres St. © **504/301-4437.** Mon–Wed 10am–7pm; Thurs–Sat 10am–8pm; Sun 10am–6pm.

Violet's ★ This is a great temptation among French Quarter shops, given our adoration of romantic, Edwardian, and '20s-inspired clothes in lush velvets and satins. The dazzling creations here come with appropriate accessories (jewelry, hats, scarves). Contemporary wear as well, with an emphasis on bling. 808 Chartres St. © **504/569-0088.** Mon–Thurs 11am–7pm; Fri–Sat 10am–8pm; Sun 10am–7pm.

Voluptuous Vixen ★ Catering to real-size women (sizes 12–24), this shop has cute and/or elegant dresses, pants, fancy T-shirts, and intimate apparel. 818 Chartres St. © **504/529-3588.** www.thevoluptuousvixen.com. Daily 10am–6pm (closed Tues & Wed during summer).

Yvonne LaFleur—New Orleans ★ Yvonne LaFleur, a confessed incurable romantic, creates beautifully feminine, surprisingly affordable millinery, silk dresses, evening gowns, lingerie, and sportswear—all custom—at her Riverbend district store. 8131 Hampson St. © **800/749-9666** or 504/866-9666. www.yvonnelafleur.com. Mon–Wed & Fri–Sat 10am–6pm; Thurs 10am–8pm.

Food & Drink

Every souvenir shop in town stocks spices, hot sauce, coffee, and beignet mix. The French Market vendors do too, along with meats and seafoods, and they're set up to ship it home or pack it for travel. If you get a hankering from home, try www.cajun grocer.com.

Keife & Co ★★ If you just can't get out the door, Keife & Co. will deliver a basket with gourmet meats, cheeses, and wine to your Central Business District hotel room. If you *can* get out, stop in to grab a bottle on your way to the restaurant. 801 Howard Ave. © **504/523-7272.** www.keifeandco.com. Tues–Sat 10am–8pm.

Martin Wine Cellar ★★ Martin carries an eye-popping selection of wines, beers, and spirits for the connoisseur, the casual imbiber, or the BYOWer, many at surprisingly reasonable prices. Good selection of imported teas, cookies, cheeses, and such for in-room picnicking. We're excited that they're rebuilding in their original 1946 location at 3827 Baronne, scheduled to open in 2014. 3500 Magazine St. ℂ **855/560-9463** or 504/894-7420. www.martinwine.com. Tues–Sat 10am–7pm.

Vieux Carré Wine and Spirits ★★ If you're looking for Herbsaint, absinthe, or Sazerac rye, are a serious wine buyer, or just want a bottle for your hotel room or dinner, this densely packed French Quarter shop will fit the bill. 422 Chartres St. ℂ **504/568-9463.** Mon–Sat 8am–9pm.

W.I.NO. ★ It's try before you buy with the Wine Institute of New Orleans's Enomatic system. Top up a debit card (do this first; it's easy to run up a jolt of a tab) and set to dispensing 1-, 2-, or 3-ounce pours of some 120 wines, covering many regions and varietals. See if you don't end up with a bottle or case in your hotel room. 610 Tchoupitoulas St. ℂ **504/324-8000.** www.winoschool.com. Mon–Tues 1pm–10pm; Wed–Thurs 1pm–midnight; Fri–Sat 1pm–2am; Sun 2–10pm (closed summer).

Gifts, Home Decor & Bath

If you're in town on the last Saturday of any month, consider a trip to the **Palmer Park Arts Market** (S. Carrollton and S. Claiborne aves.; ℂ **504/523-1465;** www.artscouncil ofneworleans.org; 10am–4pm). It's got paintings, pottery, glass mosaic, jewelry, handmade frames from old wood, and more, with the quality assured, as only juried artists are permitted to participate. It's free, all original, all local and regional, and much of it is surprisingly affordable. Last stop on the St. Charles streetcar line.

Aidan Gill for Men ★★★ To be a sharp-dressed man, start here, for fine accessories and old-fashioned men's grooming implements brought thoroughly up to date, not to mention superb grooming services. Look for old-fashioned shaving brushes and hand-held razors, add a hot towel and some cigar smoke, and you've got the blissful experience called "The Shave at the End of the Galaxy" (no less authority than *Playboy* called it the "best shave in America"). 2026 Magazine St. ℂ **504/587-9090.** www.aidan gillformen.com. Mon–Fri 10am–6pm; Sat 9am–5pm; Sun 10am–6pm. Also at 550 Fulton St. ℂ **504/566-4903.** Mon, Tues, Wed, Fri, Sat 10am–6pm; Thurs 10am–7pm; Sun 10am–6pm.

The Black Butterfly ★★ The Black Butterfly is a place for any collector or admirer of miniatures. This fourth-generation shop (in business since 1894) is filled with porcelain, brass, wood, and pewter figures as well as dollhouse furniture and accessories. 727 Royal St. ℂ **504/524-6464.** www.blackbutterfly.com. Mon–Sat 11:30am–5pm; call ahead as hours can be irregular.

Hazelnut ★ Most of the housewares and gifts here are cute but unremarkable, with one notable exception: the line of toile items with a customized pattern of iconic New Orleans scenes—the St. Charles streetcar, a live oak tree, St. Louis Cathedral, and such. It's desperately darling and we want it all—the bedding, tote bag, and picture frame. Sigh. *Fun fact: Mad Men*'s Bryan Batt is part owner. 5515 Magazine St. ℂ **504/891-2424.** www.hazelnutneworleans.com. Mon–Sat 10am–6pm (10am–5pm in summer).

Hové ★★★   The oldest perfumery in the city, Hove features a fabulous selection of all-natural scents for men and women. Original creations ("Kiss in the Dark") and Southern smells such as vetiver and tea olive, available in many forms, make lovely presents, even for you. Literature buffs will be amused by the letter from author Tom Robbins, confirming that the shop in his *Jitterbug Perfume* was roughly based on Hové. 434 Chartres St. ✆ **504/525-7827.** www.hoveparfumeur.com. Mon–Sat 10am–6pm; Sun 11am–6pm.

Simon of New Orleans/Antiques on Jackson ★★   Folk artist Simon, whose brightly painted signs are seen throughout New Orleans in homes and businesses, will paint to order your own personal sign and ship it to you. There's also a particularly good collection of primitive furniture, antiques, and hodgepodgery. 1028 Jackson Ave. ✆ **504/524-8201.** Mon by appointment only; Mon–Sat 10am–5pm; Sun 11am–4pm.

Jewelry

Marion Cage ★★★   Cage's ultrafine, exquisitely wrought work is popular with collectors in Paris and New York, where she worked before opening this gallery in her native New Orleans. Clean lines of matte rose and yellow gold, rhodium, and hardwoods start around $90, like the tiny, perfectly detailed Chinese zodiac charms. 3719 Magazine St. ✆ **504/891-8848.** www.marioncage.com. Tues–Sat 10am–5pm.

Mignon Faget, Ltd. ★★   Faget, a New Orleans native, lends her signature style to New Orleans–specific designs in gold, silver, and bronze d'oré (and housewares)—all superb souvenirs or gifts. Canal Place, Level 1. ✆ **800/375-7557** or 504/524-2973. Also at 3801 Magazine St. ✆ **504/891-2005.** www.mignonfaget.com. Mon–Sat 10am–6pm.

Thomas Mann Designs/Gallery I/O ★   Local jewelry designer Thomas Mann is known for his "techno-romantic" work with metal and found objects, creating curious pieces of highly original jewelry and homewares that straddle a line between classic and contemporary. 1810 Magazine St. ✆ **800/875-2113** or 504/581-2111. www.thomasmann.com. Mon–Sat 11am–5pm.

Music

Euclid Records ★★   If you love the smell of vinyl in the morning, or any time, Euclid will fire your pheromones. This younger-than-it-feels Bywater record store (sistah of the iconic St. Louis shop) stocks vintage platters from every era and gobs of local goods. There are nominal CDs and occasional in-store performances. Look for the Pepto pink building, and let the bin diving begin. 3401 Chartres St. ✆ **504/947-4348.** www.euclidnola.com. Mon–Thurs 10am–8pm; Fri–Sat 10am–9pm; Sun 10am–5pm.

Jim Russell Records ★   A classic, packed-to-the-rafters, musty, messy, record shop. Vinyl-digger crack. 1837 Magazine St. ✆ **504/522-2602.** www.jimrussellrecords.com. Mon–Sat 11am–5pm.

Louisiana Music Factory ★★★   This is *the* place to get yourself informed about and stocked with New Orleans music, with helpful staff and a large selection of regional music—including Cajun, zydeco, R&B, jazz, blues, and gospel—plus books, posters, and T-shirts. Vinyl miners, your quarry is upstairs. Live performances most Saturdays (and beer coupons for a nearby bar). 210 Decatur St. ✆ **504/586-1094.** www.louisianamusicfactory.com. Mon–Sat 10am–7pm; Sun noon–6pm.

Peaches Records★ This family-owned indie shop moved boldly into the French Quarter space vacated by Tower Records and stocked the place with a broad swath of locally focused CDs, vinyl, books, DVDs, T-shirts, and art (plus a coffee bar). Peaches' first store (circa 1975) was a stop-off for R&B royalty (Stevie Wonder!) and later helped launch local hip-hop artists like Juvenile and Lil Wayne. 408 N. Peters St. ✆ **504/282-3322.** www.peachesrecordsneworleans.com. Mon–Sat 10am–8pm; Sun 11am–7pm.

The Occult

Bottom of the Cup Tearoom ★ This place has been open since 1929 and bills itself as the "oldest tearoom in the United States." You can have a psychic consultation and also purchase teas, books, jewelry, crystal balls, tarot cards, crystals, and healing wands. 327 Chartres St. ✆ **800/729-7148** or 504/524-1997. www.bottomofthecup.com. Daily 10am–6pm.

F&F Botanica ★★ This unassuming, jam-packed Mid-City shop is among the largest suppliers anywhere of candles, herbs, icons and elixers for the serious practitioner (and that's who shops here). Mr. Felix (Figueroa) and son will kindly assist new or non-believers. By taxi only. 5801 N. Broad St. ✆ **504/482-5400.** www.orleanscandleco.com. Mon, Tues & Thurs–Sun 8am–6pm (closed Wed & Sun).

Marie Laveau's House of Voodoo★ This is tourist voodoo, to be sure, but the voodoo dolls and gris-gris bags make great souvenirs for the right friends, and it's a fun store to poke around in. 739 Bourbon St. ✆ **504/581-3751.** www.voodooneworleans.com Sun–Thurs 10am–11:30pm; Fri–Sat 10am–1:30am (sometimes slightly earlier or later).

Voodoo Authentica ★ This shop specializing in voodoo paraphernalia feels like a real retail establishment, not someone's dusty shack. Two big rooms are filled with locally made voodoo dolls, from cheap to costly, and items ranging from an easy souvenir to serious works of art, plus a similar array of potions, spell candles, and daubs. 612 Dumaine St. ✆ **504/522-2111.** www.voodooshop.com. Daily 11am–7pm.

T-Shirts & More

If crass suits your style, by all means buy up the Bourbon Street goods. But for a garment with local flavor that's also clever and maybe even has a decent design aesthetic, there are a plethora of superior options. Shirts (and hats, hoodies, and so forth) in these shops will probably run $5 to $10 more than your average show-me-your-whatever tops, but they're softer as well as smarter.

Dirty Coast ★★ It's waaay uptown, but their eye-catching and original T-shirt designs (painted in the city) are utterly witty, like the "Crawfish Pi," with the Greek symbol composed of a tasty pile of mudbugs, and "504Ever." 5631 Magazine St. and 329 Julia St. ✆ **504/324-3745.** www.dirtycoast.com. Mon–Sun 10am–6pm.

Fleurty Girl ★★ It's hard to leave without here without one (or more) of its pithy and near-perfect NOLA-centric T-shirts, even if some need a NOLA-to-English translation. We love the cocktail-related tees, like "Call Me Old-Fashioned" and "Keep Calm and Carry a Go-Cup." Good jewelry, accessories, and fleur de lis cookie cutters, too. 632 St. Peter St. ✆ **504/304-5529.** Also 3117 Magazine St. ✆ **504/301-2557.** www.fleurtygirl.net.com. Mon–Thurs 10am–6pm; Fri–Sat 10am–7pm; Sun 10am–6pm (11am–5pm Magazine St.).

Storyville ★★ You've heard it, now wear it: Plenty of water-meter, "Who Dat," and other good Saints designs ("Believe"), but we seriously love the four seasons tee (carnival, crawfish, snoball, football). 3029 Magazine St. ℗ **504/304-6209.** www.storyville apparel.com. Daily 10am–7pm.

WALKING TOURS

We've said it before, and we will keep saying it: This town was made for walking. Except maybe at the height of the humid summer months, when one's greatest motivation is just to laze in the shade and sip cool drinks. Even then, one can do fine by flitting between air-conditioned restaurant and air-conditioned museum.

Undeniably unique New Orleans is made to stroll through and marvel at. Each gorgeous building is more interesting than the last. Colorful characters abound. The French Quarter and the Garden District have their own distinct appearances, and both are easily manageable on foot.

So put on some good walking shoes, breathe in that tropical breeze, and mosey. Go slow, take it (big) easy. Admire the lacy ironwork. Peek through French Quarter gateways, where simple facades hide exquisite courtyards with fountains, brickwork, and thick foliage. Gawk at the mighty oaks, some dripping with swaying Spanish moss.

Stroll along St. John's Bayou, turning at any corner that strikes your fancy. If you're lucky you might have a street to yourself (or share it with a fleeting ghost?). Imagine it 100 years ago; it would have looked almost as it does now.

Our personalized walking tours of the French Quarter and Garden District will give you a nice overview and answer some "That looks interesting—what the heck *is* it?" kinds of queries. Formal professional walking tours cover more ground and considerably more detail (see p. 149), if you prefer, but these tours provide a solid introduction to what is simply one of the most beautiful cities anywhere.

WALKING TOUR 1: **THE FRENCH QUARTER**

START:	**The intersection of Royal and Bienville streets.**
FINISH:	**Jackson Square.**
TIME:	**Allow approximately 2 hours, not including time spent in shops or historic homes.**
BEST TIMES:	**Any day between 8am and 10am (the quiet hours).**
WORST TIME:	**At night. Some attractions won't be open, and you won't be able to get a good look at the architecture.**

If you only spend a few hours in New Orleans, do it in the exquisitely picturesque French Quarter. In these 80 city blocks, the colonial empires of France, Spain, and, to a lesser extent, Britain, intersected with the emerging American nation. It's called the Vieux Carré or "old square," but somehow it's timeless—recognizably old while vibrantly alive. Today's residents and merchants are stewards of a rich tradition of individuality, creativity, and disregard for many of the concerns of the world beyond. This tour will introduce you to its style, history, and landmarks.

Start at the corner of Royal and Bienville streets, heading into the Quarter (away from Canal St.). That streetcar named Desire rattled along Royal Street until 1948 (then came the bus named Desire. Really). Imagine how noisy these narrow streets were when the streetcars ran here. Your first stop is:

1 339–343 Royal St., Rillieux-Waldhorn House

Now the home of Waldhorn and Adler Antiques (est. 1881), the building was built between 1795 and 1800 for Vincent Rillieux, the great-grandfather of the French Impressionist artist Edgar Degas. The wrought-iron balconies are an example of excellent Spanish colonial workmanship.

2 333 Royal St., Bank of Louisiana (Police Station)

Across the street, this old bank was erected in 1826, and its Greek Revival edifice followed in the early 1860s. The building suffered fires in 1840, 1861, and 1931, and has served as the Louisiana State Capitol, an auction exchange, a criminal court, a juvenile court, and an American Legion social hall. It now houses the Vieux Carré police station.

Cross Conti Street to:

3 403 Royal St., Latrobe's

Benjamin H. B. Latrobe died of yellow fever shortly after completing designs for the Louisiana State Bank, which opened here in 1821. He was one of the nation's most eminent architects, having contributed to the design of the U.S. Capitol and White House. Note the monogram "LSB" on the Creole-style railing. It's now a banquet hall named for the architect.

4 417 Royal St., Brennan's Restaurant

Brennan's opened in this building, also built by Vincent Rillieux, in 1855. (And at press time, the restaurant was shuttered and embroiled in a sad financial, legal, and family squabble.) One of 200 buildings destroyed in the 1794 fire, it has been home to the Banque de la Louisiane, the world-famous chess champion Paul Charles Morphy, and the parents of Edgar Degas.

5 437 Royal St., Peychaud's Drug Store

When Masons held lodge meetings here in the early 1800s, proprietor and druggist Antoine A. Peychaud served after-meeting drinks of bitters and cognac to lodge members in small egg cups, called *coquetier*—later Americanized to "cocktails." And so it began (the cocktail and the legend).

6 400 Royal St., New Orleans Court Building

Built in 1909, this was and still is a courthouse, covering the length of the block. The baroque edifice made of Georgia marble seems out of place in the French Quarter—especially considering that many Spanish-era structures were demolished to make way for it.

Cross St. Louis Street to:

7 520 Royal St., The Brulatour Court

This 1816 structure was home to François Seignouret, a furniture maker and wine importer from Bordeaux—his furniture, with a signature "S" carved into each piece, is still collected. Ask to walk into the exotic courtyard—it's one of the few four-walled courtyards in the French Quarter. From the street, notice the elaborate, fan-shaped guard screen *(garde de frise)* on the right end of the third-floor balcony, with Seignouret's "S" carved into it.

8 533 Royal St., The Merieult House

Built for the merchant Jean François Merieult in 1792, this house was the only building in the area left standing after the fire of 1794. Legend has it that Napoleon offered Madame Merieult great riches in exchange for her hair, to create a wig to present to a Turkish sultan (she refused). Nowadays, it's home to the excellent **Historic New Orleans Collection** museum and research center. (See p. 126 for tour times and details.)

Cross Toulouse Street to:

9 613 Royal St., The Court of Two Sisters

This structure was built in 1832 for a local bank president on the site of the 18th-century home of a French governor. The two sisters were Emma and Bertha Camors, whose father owned the building; from 1886 to 1906, they ran a curio store here.

10 627 Royal St., Horizon Gallery

Walk through to the magnificent courtyard in back. Seventeen-year-old opera singer Adelina Patti visited and later lived in this 1777 building after becoming a local heroine in 1860. As a last-minute stand-in lead soprano, she saved the local opera company from financial ruin.

11 640 Royal St., Le Monnier Mansion

No one thought the 1811 building would survive a fourth-floor addition in 1876, creating the city's first "skyscraper." 'Sieur George, fictional hero of George W. Cable's *Old Creole Days,* "lived" here.

Cross St. Peter Street to:

12 700 Royal St., The LaBranche House

The lacy cast-iron grillwork, with its delicate oak leaf and acorn design, makes this one of the most photographed buildings in the Quarter. This is one of 11 three-story brick row houses built from 1835 to 1840 for the widow of wealthy sugar planter Jean Baptiste LaBranche.

Walking Tour 1: The French Quarter

1 Rillieux-Waldhorn House	**18** Le Pretre Mansion
2 Bank of Louisiana	**19** Spanish Colonial Cottage
(Police Station)	**20** Madame John's Legacy
3 Latrobe's	**21** Lafitte's Blacksmith Shop
4 Brennan's Restaurant	**22** The Lalaurie Home
5 Peychaud's Drug Store	**23** Gallier House Museum
6 New Orleans Court Building	**24** Croissant D'Or
7 The Brulatour Court	**25** Beauregard-Keyes House
8 The Merieult House	**26** The Old U.S. Mint
9 The Court of Two Sisters	**27** The Historic French Market
10 Horizon Gallery	**28** Central Grocery
11 Le Monnier Mansion	**29** The Pontalba Buildings
12 The LaBranche House	**30** The Presbytère
13 Lacoul House	**31** St. Louis Cathedral
14 Pat O'Brien's	**32** The Cabildo
15 Preservation Hall	**33** Faulkner House Books
16 Lindy Boggs Home	**34** Tennessee Williams House
17 Bourbon Orleans Hotel	**35** Café du Monde

Turn left at St. Peter Street and continue to:

13 714 St. Peter St., Lacoul House

Built in 1829 by prominent physician Dr. Yves LeMonnier, this was a boarding-house run by Antoine Alciatore during the 1860s. His cooking became so popular with the locals that he eventually gave up catering to open the famous Antoine's restaurant (p. 80), still operated today by his descendants.

14 718 St. Peter St., Pat O'Brien's

Now the de facto home to the famed Hurricane cocktail (p. 178), this building was completed in 1790. Later, Louis Tabary put on popular plays here including, purportedly, the first grand opera in America. The popular courtyard is well worth a look, maybe even a refreshment.

15 726 St. Peter St., Preservation Hall

Scores of people descend on this spot nightly to hear traditional New Orleans jazz (p. 169). A daytime stop affords a glimpse, through the big, ornate iron gate, of a lush tropical courtyard in back. Erle Stanley Gardner, the author who brought us Perry Mason, lived upstairs.

Continue up St. Peter Street until you reach Bourbon Street. Turn left onto Bourbon Street.

16 623 Bourbon St., Lindy Boggs Home

Tennessee Williams and Truman Capote stayed in this house (no, not together), home until recently to Lindy Boggs, much-beloved local politician, ambassador, philanthropist (and mother of journalist Cokie Roberts), who took over husband Hale Boggs' congressional seat after his death in a plane crash. She passed away in 2013.

Turn around and head the other way down Bourbon Street. At the corner of Bourbon and Orleans streets, look down Orleans Street, toward the river, at:

17 717 Orleans St., Bourbon Orleans Hotel

Site of the famous quadroon balls, where wealthy white men met possible mistresses, free women of color who were one-fourth black (quadroon) or one-eighth (octoroon). They entered into carefully negotiated *placage*, arrangements, at these balls, which often included financial, educational, housing, and child support. Imagine the discussions on those balconies . . . . The building later became a convent for the Sisters of the Holy Family, the second-oldest order of black nuns in the country. Their founder (whose mother was a quadroon mistress!), Henriette Delille, has been presented to the Vatican for consideration for sainthood.

Turn left onto Orleans and follow it a block to Dauphine (pronounced Daw-*feen*) Street. On the corner is:

18 716 Dauphine St., Le Pretre Mansion

In 1839 Jean Baptiste Le Pretre bought this 1836 Greek Revival house and added the romantic cast-iron galleries. The house is the subject of a real-life horror story: In the 19th century, a conspicuously wealthy Turk, supposedly the brother of a sultan, rented the house. He brought an entourage of servants and beautiful young girls—all thought to have been stolen from the sultan—and threw lavish high-society parties. One night screams came from inside; the next morning, neighbors found the tenant and the young beauties lying dead in a pool of blood. The mystery remains unsolved. Local ghost experts say you can sometimes hear exotic music and piercing shrieks.

Turn right on Dauphine Street and go 2 blocks to Dumaine Street and then turn right. You'll find an interesting little cottage at:

19 707 Dumaine St., Spanish Colonial Cottage

After the 1794 fire, all houses in the French Quarter were required by law to have flat tile roofs. Most have since been covered with conventional roofs, but this Spanish colonial cottage is still in compliance with the flat-roof rule.

20 632 Dumaine St., Madame John's Legacy

This structure was once thought to be the oldest building on the Mississippi River, originally erected in 1726, 8 years after the founding of New Orleans. Recent research suggests, however, that only a few parts of the original building survived the 1788 fire. Its first owner was a ship captain who died in the 1729 *Natchez* Massacre; upon his death, the house passed to the captain of a Lafitte-era smuggling ship—and 21 owners subsequently. The present structure is a fine example of a French "raised cottage." The above-ground basement is of brick-between-posts construction (locally made bricks were too soft to be the primary building material). The hipped, dormered roof extends out over the veranda. Its name comes from George W. Cable's fictional character who was bequeathed the house in the short story *'Tite Poulette*. Part of the Louisiana State Museum complex, it is currently not open for tours.

21 941 Bourbon St., Lafitte's Blacksmith Shop

This National Historic Landmark claims to be the oldest continually operating bar in the country (see p. 178), but legend is that it was the headquarters of Jean Lafitte and his pirates, who posed as blacksmiths and used it to fence goods they'd plundered on the high seas. It still reflects the architectural influence of late-1700s French colonists. It may also be the oldest building in the Mississippi Valley, but that has not been documented. An unfortunate exterior renovation trying to replicate the original brick and plaster makes it look fake (it's actually not), but the dim interior is still an excellent place to imagine 19th-century Quarter life.

Turn right onto Bourbon Street and follow it 2 blocks to Governor Nicholls Street. Turn right and go one block to the corner of Royal Street:

22 1140 Royal St., The Lalaurie Home

Two-time widow Madame Delphine Macarty de Lopez Blanque wed Dr. Louis Lalaurie, moved into this residence in 1832, and were soon impressing the city with extravagant parties. One night in 1834 fire broke out. Neighbors crashed through a locked door to find seven starving slaves chained in painful positions, unable to move. The sight, combined with Delphine's stories of past slaves having "committed suicide" and rumors of hideous live-subject medical experiments conducted within, enraged her neighbors. Madame Lalaurie and her family escaped a mob's wrath and fled to Paris. Several years later she died in Europe. Her body was returned to New Orleans—and even then she had to be buried in secrecy. Tales of hauntings persist, especially that of one young slave child who fell from the roof trying to escape Delphine's cruelties.

The building was a Union headquarters during the Civil War, a gambling house, and home to actor Nicolas Cage. Haunted by financial difficulties, Cage returned the house to the bank in 2009, which converted it to condos.

23 1132 Royal St., Gallier House Museum

James Gallier, Jr., built this house in 1857 as his residence. He and his father were two of the city's leading architects (p. 126). Novelist Anne Rice based Lestat and Louis's home in *Interview with the Vampire* on this house.

Turn left onto Ursulines Street, toward the river.

24 617 Ursulines Ave., Croissant D'Or 🍴

For a little rest or sustenance, stop in the popular **Croissant D'Or,** 617 Ursulines St. (**📞 504/524-4663;** p. 113). The pastries here are very good, as is the ambience—inside or out.

At the corner of Ursulines and Chartres streets is the:

25 1113 Chartres St., Beauregard-Keyes House

This raised cottage was built as a residence in 1826 by Joseph Le Carpentier, though it has several other claims to fame (p. 122). Notice the Doric columns and handsome twin staircases.

Turn left onto Chartres Street and continue walking until you get to Esplanade (pronounced Es-pla-*nade*) Avenue, one of the city's most picturesque historic thoroughfares. Some of the grandest townhouses built in the late 1800s grace this wide, tree-lined avenue, once the parade ground for troops quartered on Barracks Street. The entire 400 block of Esplanade is occupied by:

26 The Old U.S. Mint

This was once the site of Fort St. Charles, built to protect New Orleans in 1792. Andrew Jackson reviewed the "troops" here—pirates, volunteers, and a nucleus of trained soldiers—whom he later led in the Battle of New Orleans. It's now a Louisiana State Museum housing coin and jazz collections (p. 124).

Follow Esplanade toward the river and turn right at the corner of North Peters Street. Follow North Peters until it intersects with Decatur Street. This is the back end of:

27 The Historic French Market

This European-style market (p. 120) has been here for well over 200 years, and today it has a farmers' market, food booths, arty-crafty goods, and flea market stalls with souvenirs.

When you leave the French Market, exit on the side away from the river onto Decatur Street toward St. Ann Street. You'll pass 923 and 919 Decatur St., where the Café de Refugies and Hôtel de la Marine, respectively, were located in the 1700s and early 1800s. These were reputed to be gathering places for pirates, smugglers, European refugees, and outlaws.

923 Decatur St., Central Grocery 🍴

If you're walking in the area of 923 Decatur St. around lunchtime, pop into **Central Grocery** (☎ **504/523-1620;** p. 90), and pick up a famed muffuletta sandwich. Eat inside at the little tables, or take your food and sit outside, maybe right on the riverbank.

Decatur Street will take you to Jackson Square. Turn right onto St. Ann Street; the twin four-story, redbrick buildings here and on the St. Peter Street side of the square are:

29 The Pontalba Buildings

These highly coveted buildings sport some of the most impressive cast-iron balcony railings in the French Quarter. They also represent early French Quarter urban revitalization—and early girl power. In the mid-1800s, Baroness Micaela Almonester de Pontalba inherited rows of buildings along both sides of the Place d'Armes from her father, Don Almonester (who rebuilt St. Louis Cathedral; p. 122). In an effort to counteract the emerging American sector across Canal Street, she razed the structures and built high-end apartments and commercial space.

The Pontalba Buildings were begun in 1849 under her direct supervision; you can see her mark today in the entwined initials "A.P." in the ironwork. They are traditional Creole-European style, with commercial space at street level, housing above, and courtyards in the rear.

Baroness De Pontalba also had Jackson Square built, including the cast-iron fence and the equestrian statue of Andrew Jackson. Her scandalous personal story (see p. 123) is equally fascinating.

At the corner of St. Ann and Chartres streets, turn left and continue around Jackson Square; you will see:

30 751 Chartres St., The Presbytère

This, the Cabildo, and the St. Louis Cathedral—all designed by Gilberto Guillemard—were the first major public buildings in the Louisiana Territory. The Presbytère was originally designed as the cathedral's rectory. Baroness Pontalba's father financed the building's beginnings, but he died in 1798, leaving only the first floor done. It was finally completed in 1813. Never used as a rectory, it became a city courthouse and now houses the excellent Louisiana State Museum (p. 123).

Next you'll come to:

31 St. Louis Cathedral

Although it is the oldest Catholic cathedral in the U.S., this is actually the third building erected on this spot—the first was destroyed by a hurricane in 1722, the second by fire in 1788. The cathedral was rebuilt in 1794; the central tower was later designed by Henry S. Boneval Latrobe, again remodeled and enlarged between 1845 and 1851 under Baroness Pontalba. The bell and stately clock (note the nonstandard Roman numeral four), were imported from France (p. 122).

On the other side of the cathedral, you'll come to Pirate's Alley. Go right down Pirate's Alley to:

32 The Cabildo

In the 1750s, this was the site of a French police station and guardhouse. Part of that building was incorporated into the Spanish government statehouse (known as the "Very Illustrious Cabildo"). It was still under reconstruction when the transfer papers for the Louisiana Purchase were signed in a room on the second floor in 1803. Since then, it has served as New Orleans's City Hall, the Louisiana State Supreme Court, and, since 1911, a Louisiana State Museum (p. 123).

Think those old Civil War cannons out front look pitifully obsolete? Think again. In 1921, in a near-deadly prank, one was loaded and fired. That missile traveled across the wide expanse of the Mississippi and 6 blocks inland, landing in a house in Algiers and narrowly missing its occupants.

33 624 Pirate's Alley, Faulkner House Books

In 1925, William Faulkner lived here. He contributed to the *Times-Picayune* and worked on his first novels, *Mosquitoes* and *Soldiers' Pay*, making this lovely store a requisite stop for literature lovers and book buyers of any persuasion (p. 188).

To the left of the bookstore is a small alley that takes you to St. Peter Street, which is behind and parallel to Pirate's Alley.

34 632 St. Peter St., Tennessee Williams House

Have a sudden urge to scream "Stella!!!" at that second-story wrought-iron balcony at 632 St. Peter St.? No wonder. This is where Tennessee Williams wrote *A Streetcar Named Desire,* one of the greatest pieces of American theater. He said he could hear "that rattle-trap streetcar named Desire running along Royal and the one named Cemeteries running along Canal and it seemed the perfect metaphor for the human condition."

Return to Jackson Square. On the left side of the cathedral on the corner of Chartres and St. Peter streets (with your back to the Mississippi River and Jackson Square) is:

35 813 Decatur St., Café du Monde ☕

You've finished! Now go back across Jackson Square and Decatur Street to **Café du Monde** (📞 **504/525-4544;** p. 112) for beignets and coffee. Do climb the stairs up to the levee and relax on a bench, and watch the river roll.

The Garden District

WALKING TOURS

WALKING TOUR 2: **THE GARDEN DISTRICT**

START:	**Prytania Street and Washington Avenue.**
FINISH:	**Lafayette Cemetery.**
TIME:	**45 minutes to 2 hours.**
BEST TIME:	**Daylight.**
WORST TIME:	**Night, when you won't be able to get a good look at the architecture.**

Walking through the architecturally astounding Garden District, you could get the impression that you've entered an entirely separate city—or time period—from the French Quarter of New Orleans. Although the Garden District was indeed once a separate city (Lafayette) from the Vieux Carré and was established later, their development by two different groups most profoundly distinguishes the two.

The French Quarter was settled by Creoles during the French and Spanish colonial periods, and the Garden District was created by Americans after the 1803 Louisiana Purchase. The lucrative combination of Mississippi River commerce, regional

Walking Tour 2: The Garden District

1 The Garden District
  Book Shop
2 Colonel Short's Villa
3 Briggs-Staub House
4 Our Mother of Perpetual Help
5 Women's Opera Guild Home
6 Toby's Corner
7 Bradish Johnson House
  & Louise S. McGehee School
8 Pritchard-Pigott House
9 Morris-Israel House
10 The Seven Sisters
11 Brevard-Mahat-Rice House

12 Payne-Strachan House
13 1137 Second St.
14 Joseph Merrick
  Jones House
15 Musson-Bell House
16 Robinson House
17 Koch-Mays House
18 Commander's Palace
19 Lafayette Cemetery
20c Still Perkin' ☕
20a Tracey's ☕
20b Coquette ☕
20d Sucré ☕

abundance of cash crops, slave trade, and national banks fueled the local economy, resulting in the remarkable antebellum building boom you still see here.

Thousands of Americans moved here after the Louisiana Purchase. Friction arose between the new residents and the Creoles around language barriers, religious division, competition over burgeoning commerce, and mutual snobbery. With inferior business experience, education, and organizational skills, the Creoles worried that *les Americains* would drive them out of business. Americans were thus barred from the already overcrowded French Quarter. The snubbed Americans moved upriver and created a residential district of astounding opulence: the Garden District. It is, therefore, a cultural clash reflected through architecture, with Americans creating an identity by boldly introducing styles.

Note: Houses on this tour are not open to the public. Several are owned by celebrities (names are omitted for privacy). Please be respectful of the residents.

To reach the Garden District, take the St. Charles streetcar to Washington Avenue (stop no. 16) and walk 1 block toward the river to:

1 2727 Prytania St., The Garden District Book Shop

A stellar collection of national and regional titles, with many signed editions, makes this bookshop (p. 189) an appropriate kickoff for a Garden District tour. The historic property was built in 1884 as the Crescent City Skating Rink, and subsequently acted as a livery stable, mortuary, grocery store, and gas station. Today "the Rink" also offers a coffee shop, restrooms, and air-conditioning (crucial in the summer).

Across Prytania Street, you'll find:

2 1448 Fourth St., Colonel Short's Villa

This house was built by architect Henry Howard for Kentucky Colonel Robert Short. The story goes that Short's wife missed the cornfields in her native Iowa, so he bought her the cornstalk fence. But a revised explanation has the wife requesting it because it was the most expensive fence in the building catalog. Second Civil War occupational governor Nathaniel Banks was quartered here.

Continuing down Prytania, you'll find the:

3 2605 Prytania St., Briggs-Staub House

This is the Garden District's only example of Gothic Revival architecture (unpopular among Protestant Americans because it reminded them of their Roman Catholic Creole antagonists). Original owner Charles Briggs built the relatively large adjacent servant quarters for his Irish slaves. Irish immigrants were starting to create the nearby Irish Channel neighborhood across Magazine Street from the Garden District.

4 2523 Prytania St., Our Mother of Perpetual Help

Once an active Catholic chapel, this site was one of several in the area owned by Anne Rice and the setting for her novel *Violin.* The author's childhood home is down the street at 2301 St. Charles Avenue.

5 2504 Prytania St., Women's Opera Guild Home

Some of the Garden District's most memorable homes incorporate more than one style. Designed by William Freret in 1858, this one combines Greek Revival and Queen Anne styles. It's now owned by the Women's Opera Guild. Tours are offered on Mondays from 10am to 12pm and 1 to 4pm; $7 or by appointment for groups (✆ **504/899-1945**).

6 2340 Prytania St., Toby's Corner

The Garden District's oldest known home was built in 1838 for Philadelphia wheelwright Thomas Toby in the then-popular Greek Revival style. The "non-Creole" style still followed Creole building techniques, such as raising the house up on brick piers to combat flooding and encourage air circulation.

7 2343 Prytania St., Bradish Johnson House & Louise S. McGehee School

Paris-trained architect James Freret designed this French Second Empire–style mansion for sugar factor Bradish Johnson in 1872 at a cost of $100,000 ($1.6-plus million today). Contrast the house's awesome detail with the stark classical simplicity of Toby's Corner (see above) across the street—a visual indication of the effect that one generation of outrageous fortune had on Garden District architecture. Since 1929 it has been the private Louise S. McGehee School for girls.

Turn down First Street (away from St. Charles) and it's a short block to:

8 1407 First St., Pritchard-Pigott House

This grand, Greek Revival double-galleried town house shows how, as fortunes grew, so did Garden District home sizes.

9 1331 First St., Morris-Israel House

As time passed, the simplicity of the Greek Revival style moved toward more playful design styles. By the 1860s, Italianate was popular, as seen in this (reputedly haunted) double-galleried town house. Architect Samuel Jamison designed this house and the **Carroll-Crawford House** on the next corner (1315 First St.); note the identical ornate cast-iron galleries.

Follow Coliseum Street to the left, less than half a block to:

10 2329–2305 Coliseum St., The Seven Sisters

This row of "shotgun" houses gets its nickname from a (false) story that a 19th-century Garden District resident built these homes as wedding gifts for his seven daughters. Actually, there are eight "Seven Sisters," and they were built on speculation.

"Shotgun"-style homes are so named because, theoretically, if one fired a gun through the front door, the bullet would pass unhindered out the back. (Also, a West African word for this native African house form sounds like "shotgun.") The shotgun house effectively circulates air and is common in hot climates. The relatively small shotguns are popular throughout much of Orleans, but rare along the imposing Garden District streets.

Now turn around and go back to First Street and turn left. At the corner of First and Chestnut, you'll see:

11 1239 First St., Brevard-Mahat-Rice House

The 1857 Greek Revival town house was later augmented with an Italianate bay, in a fine example of "transitional" architecture. The fence's rosettes begat the house's name, "Rosegate," and its woven diamond pattern is believed to be the precursor to the chain-link fence. This was novelist Anne Rice's home and a setting in her *Witching Hour* novels.

12 1134 First St., Payne-Strachan House

As the stone marker out front notes, Jefferson Davis, president of the Confederate States of America, died in this classic Greek Revival antebellum home, that of his friend Judge Charles Fenner. The sky-blue ceiling of the gallery is believed to keep winged insects from nesting there and to ward off evil spirits. Many local homes adhere to this tradition.

Turn right on Camp and go less than a block to:

13 1137 Second St.

This house exemplifies the Victorian architecture popularized in uptown New Orleans toward the end of the 19th century. Many who built such homes were from the Northeast and left New Orleans in the summer; otherwise, it would be odd to see this claustrophobic, "cool climate"–style house. Note the exquisite stained glass and rounded railing on the gallery.

Turn right onto Second Street and go 2 blocks to the corner of Coliseum, where you'll see:

14 2425 Coliseum St., Joseph Merrick Jones House

When previous owner Trent Reznor of the band Nine Inch Nails moved in, more anti-noise ordinances were introduced at city council. His next-door neighbor was Councilwoman Peggy Wilson. Coincidence?

Turn left onto Coliseum Street and go 1 block to Third Street. Turn left to get to:

15 1331 Third St., Musson-Bell House

This is the 1853 home of Michel Musson, one of the few French Creoles then living in the Garden District and the uncle of artist Edgar Degas, who lived with Musson on Esplanade Avenue during a visit to New Orleans. On the Coliseum Street side of the house is the foundation of a cistern. These once-common water tanks (Mark Twain once commented that it looked as if everybody in the neighborhood had a private brewery) were mostly destroyed at the turn of the 20th century when mosquitoes, which breed in standing water, were found to be carriers of yellow fever and malaria.

Turn around and cross Coliseum to see:

16 1415 Third St., Robinson House

This striking and unusual home was built between 1859 and 1865 by architect Henry Howard for tobacco grower and merchant Walter Robinson. Walk past the house to appreciate its scale—the outbuildings, visible from the front, are actually connected to the side of the main house. The entire roof is a large vat that once collected water. Add gravity and water pressure, and thus begat the Garden District's earliest indoor plumbing.

Continue down Coliseum Street 2 blocks to the corner of Washington Avenue. There you'll find:

17 2627 Coliseum St., Koch-Mays House

This picturesque chalet-style dollhouse (well, for a large family of dolls) was built in 1876 by noted architect William Freret for James Eustis, a U.S. senator and ambassador to France (perhaps justifying the full-size ballroom). It and four other spec homes he built on the block were referred to as Freret's Folly. No detail was left unfrilled, from the ironwork to the gables and finials.

18 1403 Washington Ave., Commander's Palace

Established in 1883 by Emile Commander, this turreted Victorian structure (a bordello back in the 1920s) is now the pride of the Brennan family, the most respected successful restaurateurs in New Orleans, and one of the city's top restaurants (p. 103).

19 1400 Washington Ave., Lafayette Cemetery

Established in 1833, this "city of the dead" is one of New Orleans's oldest cemeteries. It has examples of all the classic above-ground, multiple-burial techniques. These tombs typically house numerous corpses—one here lists 37 entrants, while others are designated for members of specific fire departments. More on p. 143.

Walk to St. Charles Avenue to pick up the streetcar (there is a stop right there) or flag down a cab to return to the French Quarter.

20 Wind Down at Still Perkin', Tracey's, Coquette, or Sucré ☕

Now go back to your first stop, the Rink, where you can enjoy a cup of coffee and some light refreshments at **Still Perkin'.** Or head south on Washington to Magazine Street, where a po' boy at **Tracey's,** lunch at **Coquette,** or a sweet from **Sucré** (p. 189) will satisfy other appetites.

WALKING TOUR 3: ESPLANADE RIDGE & BAYOU ST. JOHN

START:	**Esplanade Avenue and Johnson Street.**
FINISH:	**City Park.**
TIME:	**Allow approximately 2 hours, not including museum, cemetery, and lunch stops.**
BEST TIMES:	**Monday through Saturday, early or late morning.**
WORST TIMES:	**Sunday, when attractions are closed. Also, you don't want to walk in this area after dark; if you decide to stay in City Park or in the upper Esplanade area until early evening, plan to return on the bus or by taxi.**

If you're heading to City Park, the New Orleans Museum of Art, or the Jazz & Heritage Festival, consider strolling this overlooked region, or leaving enough time for sightseeing from your car. We particularly enjoy the stretch along St. John's Bayou—mostly as slow and quiet as the sluggish water itself. Historically, the Esplanade Ridge area was Creole society's answer to St. Charles Avenue—it's an equally lush boulevard with stately homes and seemingly ancient trees stretching overhead. The lots are not quite as expansive as along St. Charles, so the grand front lawns are not in evidence. Originally home to the descendants of the earliest settlers, the avenue had its finest days toward the end of the 19th century, and some of the neighborhoods along its path, especially the Faubourg Tremé, are visibly suffering. Esplanade is a little worn compared to St. Charles Avenue, but it's closer to the soul of the city (read: Regular people live here, whereas St. Charles always was and still is for the well-heeled).

You can catch a bus on Esplanade Avenue at the French Quarter, headed toward the park to your starting point. Otherwise, stroll (about 15 min.) up Esplanade Avenue to:

1 2023 Esplanade Ave., Charpentier House

Originally a plantation home, this house was designed in 1861 for A. B. Charpentier and now operates as Ashtons Bed & Breakfast (p. 61).

2 2033–2035 Esplanade Ave., Widow Castanedo's House

Juan Rodriguez purchased this land in the 1780s, and his granddaughter, Widow Castanedo, lived here until her death in 1861 (when it was a smaller, Spanish colonial–style plantation home). Before Esplanade Avenue extended this far from the river, the house was located in what is now the middle of the street. The widow tried and failed to block the extension of the street. The late-Italianate house was moved to its present site and enlarged sometime around the 1890s. It is split down the middle and inhabited today by two sisters.

3 2139 Esplanade Ave.

A great example of the typical Esplanade Ridge style. Note the Ionic columns on the upper level.

On the opposite side of the street is:

4 2176 Esplanade Ave.

A simple, classic-style town house, this was the second Bayou Road home built by Hubert Gerard, who also built the 1861 at no. 2023 (see above).

After you cross North Miro Street, Esplanade Avenue crosses the diagonal Bayou Road, which was the route to the French-Canadian settlements at St. John's Bayou in the late 17th century. Veer left at the fork to stay on Esplanade Avenue and look for:

5 Goddess of History—Genius of Peace Statue

In 1886, this triangular piece of land, called Gayarre Place, was given to the city by Charles Gayarre. George H. Dunbar donated the original terra-cotta statue, a victory monument, which was destroyed in 1938. The present one, made of cement and marble, is a replacement.

6 2306 Esplanade Ave., Degas House

The Musson family rented this house for many years. Estelle Musson married René Degas, brother of Edgar Degas, the French Impressionist artist. (She and her descendants dropped his last name after he ran off with a neighbor's wife.) Degas is said to have painted the portrait of Estelle that is now in the New Orleans Museum of Art, among other works, during the brief time he spent living here. The house was built in 1854, and the Italianate decorations were added later when it was split into two buildings. It's an B&B now.

Walking Tour 3: The Esplanade Ridge

1 Charpentier House (Ashton's)
2 Widow Castanedo's House
3 2139 Esplanade Ave.
4 2176 Esplanade Ave.
5 Goddess of History—
   Genius of Peace Statue
6 Degas House
7 Reuther House
8 2337 & 2341
   Esplanade Ave.
9 2453 Esplanade Ave.
10 2623 Esplanade Ave.
11 2809 Esplanade Ave.
12 2936 Esplanade Ave.
13a Café Degas
13b Terranova's
13c Fair Grinds
14 3330 Esplanade Ave.
15 Luling Mansion
16 St. Louis Cemetery No. 3
17 Pitot House
18 City Park

7 2326 Esplanade Ave., Reuther House

The current resident of this house—a founder of the Contemporary Arts Center and a major figure in the city's arts community—has a collection of metal and cinder-block sculptures in his front yard, readily visible from the street.

In passing, take a look at nos. 2325, 2329, and 2331—all are interesting examples of Creole cottages. Then, continue to:

8 2337 & 2341 Esplanade Ave.

These houses were identical structures when they were built in 1862 for John Budd Slawson, owner of a horse-drawn-streetcar company that operated along Bayou Road in the 19th century. Back then, they were both single-story shotgun-style houses. Notice the unusual ironwork underneath the front roof overhang.

Cross North Dorgenois Street to:

9 2453 Esplanade Ave.

Until the other was demolished, this house was one of a pair at the corner of Dorgenois Street. Though its architecture has been changed extensively, it's one of the few remaining mansard-roofed homes on Esplanade Ridge.

Cross North Broad Street to:

10 2623 Esplanade Ave.

Here is a classical revival home built in 1896 by Louis A. Jung. Note the Corinthian columns. The Jungs donated the triangular piece of land at Esplanade Avenue, Broad Street, and Crete Street to the city on the condition that it remain public property. Now called DeSoto Park, it is graced by an Art Nouveau fence.

11 2809 Esplanade Ave.

This is one of the more decorative Queen Anne–style center-hall Victorian houses on Esplanade Ridge.

12 2936 Esplanade Ave.

A nice example of what's known as a Gothic villa.

13 Take a Break at Café Degas, Terranova's, or Fair Grinds 🍵

At the intersection of Mystery Street and Esplanade Avenue, you'll find a little grouping of shops and restaurants. If you're in the area at lunchtime, you might want to stop at **Café Degas** (p. 93), for a leisurely meal—if the weather is nice, the semi-outdoor setting is exceedingly pleasant. If you just want a snack or some picnic food for City Park, you can get cold cuts, ice cream, and snacks at the family-run **Terranova's Italian Grocery,** 3308 Esplanade Ave. (📞 **504/482-4131**), across the street. Or opt for a break at the quirky **Fair Grinds** coffeehouse just off Esplanade at 3133 Ponce De Leon St. (📞 **504/913-9072**).

Continue to:

14 3330 Esplanade Ave.

A galleried frame home built in the Creole-cottage style. Also note the orientation of this stretch (and many of the houses along Esplanade Avenue). The lots are on a diagonal, so houses face Esplanade at a slight angle.

Esplanade Ridge & Bayou St. John

WALKING TOURS

Continue Leda Street, and turn right for a ½ block detour off Esplanade to:

15 Luling Mansion, 1438 Leda St.

Florence Luling, a German sugar and cotton baron, purchased 80 acres and commissioned famed architect James Gallier, Jr., to build this elaborate, three-story Italianate mansion in 1865. Built with a full moat, originally its ornate formal gardens stretched all the way to Esplanade Avenue. Later it served as the Louisiana Jockey Club (it backs up to the Fair Grounds Race Track). Although unfortunate modern adjustments have taken a toll, the original magnificence is still obvious.

Return to Esplanade Ave. and turn right. On your right is:

16 3421 Esplanade Ave., St. Louis Cemetery No. 3

This was the site of the public Bayou Cemetery, established in 1835. It was purchased by the St. Louis diocese in 1856 and contains the burial monuments of many of the diocese's priests. If you've been putting off going into the cemeteries because of concerns over safety, you can explore this one on your own—though as always, you should still be alert.

From the cemetery, head back out to Esplanade Avenue and continue walking toward City Park. When you get to the bridge, go left, following the signs, along St. John's Bayou (one of the nicest and least touristy areas of the city), to:

17 1440 Moss St., Pitot House

This Creole country house overlooks historic Bayou St. John and is open for public viewing (p. 137). Knowledgeable docents offer a window onto life in the day when the Bayou was the major trade route. Years later, this was home to the first mayor of New Orleans.

Head back to Esplanade Avenue, turn left, cross the bridge, and walk straight into:

18 Esplanade & City Park aves., City Park

Explore the sculpture garden, amphitheater, museum, botanical gardens, lakes, and much more in this glorious, expansive park (p. 139).

SIDE TRIPS: CAJUN COUNTRY & PLANTATION HOMES

I f you have time (say, 3 days), you should strongly consider a sojourn into the countryside outlying New Orleans. It makes for an interesting cultural and visual contrast to the big city. This chapter starts off by following the River Road and the plantation homes that line the banks of the Mississippi, heading upriver from New Orleans; the second part takes you 150 miles west of New Orleans to the heart of Cajun Country.

On the River Road trip, you can see many of the highlights in a day trip, but it's quite possible to keep rambling north to visit the plantation homes in the St. Francisville area. That exploration calls for an overnight stay (more if you can), as does the Cajun Country trip (more if you can).

PLANTATIONS ALONG THE GREAT RIVER ROAD

If your image of plantation homes comes strictly from Tara in *Gone With the Wind,* you can see something reasonably close to that Hollywood creation by touring these parts. You'll also see far humbler, but realistic, plantation homes, and get an idea of plantation life as it was—for better and worse.

THE EARLY PLANTERS Creole plantation houses are low-slung, simple affairs; the showier American style is closer to Hollywood's antebellum grandeur (they got grander after 1850, which most of these predate). They're smaller than you might think, even cramped compared with the lavish mansions of the Gatsby-era oil barons and today's nouveau riche. If your fantasies would be dashed without pillars and porticos, stick to Destrehan, San Francisco, Oak Alley, and Madewood.

The early planters of Louisiana were rugged frontier people. As they spread out along the Mississippi from New Orleans, they cleared vast

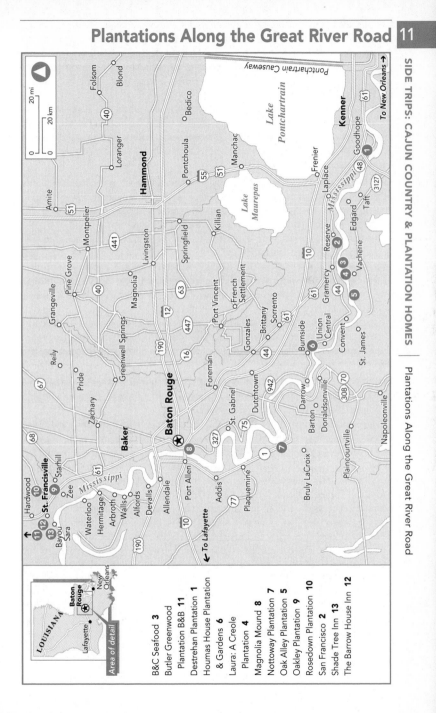

B&C Seafood **3**

Butler Greenwood Plantation B&B **11**

Destrehan Plantation **1**

Houmas House Plantation & Gardens **6**

Laura: A Creole Plantation **4**

Magnolia Mound **8**

Nottoway Plantation **7**

Oak Alley Plantation **5**

Oakley Plantation **9**

Rosedown Plantation **10**

San Francisco **2**

Shade Tree Inn **13**

The Barrow House Inn **12**

swamplands to create unhindered waterways for transporting indigo and other crops. Rough flatboats moving produce to market could be capsized by rapids, sandbars, and floating debris, or captured by river pirates. If they made it to New Orleans, these farming men (and a few extraordinary women) collected their pay and went on wild drinking, gambling, and brawling sprees—earning them a reputation as barbarians among the French Quarter Creoles.

By the 1800s, Louisiana planters (and their slaves) had introduced large-scale farming and brought more acreage under cultivation. King cotton, rice, and sugarcane were popularized around this time, bringing huge monetary returns. But natural dangers, a hurricane or a swift change in the course of the capricious Mississippi, could wipe out entire plantations and fortunes.

THE RIVERBOATS   After 1812, the planters turned to speedier and ostensibly safer new steamboats to transport their crops. When the first steamboat (the *New Orleans,* built in Pittsburgh) chugged downriver belching sooty smoke, it was so dirty and potentially explosive that it was dubbed a "floating volcano."

As vast improvements were made, moving goods to market may have (literally) floated the steamboats, but family and slaves could now travel in lavish staterooms amid ornate "grand salons" in these floating pleasure palaces. Some set up dual residences, spending the social season and winters in elegant New Orleans town houses. They shipped fine furnishings to their upriver homes, creating a more elegant lifestyle in the fields.

On the darker side, the boats were the realm of riverboat gamblers and "confidence" (or "con") men. Huge fortunes were won from, and lost to, these silver-tongued professional gamers and crooks, and no doubt a few deeds to plantations changed hands at the tables on river steamboats.

BUILDING THE PLANTATION HOUSES   During this prosperous period from the 1820s until the beginning of the Civil War, most of the impressive plantation homes were built, as were grand New Orleans town houses.

The plantation home was the focal point of a self-sustaining community and generally was located near the riverfront. Most were modest, but some had wide, oak-lined avenues leading from its entrance to a wharf. On either side of the avenue would frequently be *garçonnières* (small guesthouses, sometimes used by adolescent sons and their friends). The kitchen was often behind the main house, separated from the house because of fire danger; close by was the overseer's office. Some plantations had pigeon houses or dovecotes—and all had the inevitable slave quarters lining the lane to the crops or across the fields and out of sight. The first houses were simple "raised cottages," with long, sloping roofs, cement-covered brick walls on the ground floor, and wood-and-brick (brick between posts) construction in the living quarters on the second floor. Influenced by West Indian styles, these colonial structures suited the sultry Louisiana climate and swampy building sites and made use of native materials.

In the 1820s, they began to add Greek Revival and Georgian influences—creating a style dubbed Louisiana Classic. Large, rounded columns and wide galleries usually surrounded the main body of the house, and the roof was dormered. Inside, rooms flanked an expansive central hall They had few imported details like fireplace mantels, and were constructed of native materials, like cypress and bricks of cement-sealed river clay.

GRAND & GRANDER   By the 1850s, homes grew in tandem with prosperity. Homes became more grandiose—some with 40 rooms. Many embraced the styles of extravagant Victorian architecture, northern Italian villas, and Gothic lines (notably the fantastic San Francisco plantation, sometimes called "steamboat Gothic;" p. 220). Planters and their families brought back ornate furnishings and skilled artisans from their European travels. Glittering crystal chandeliers and *faux marbre* (false marble) mantels appeared.

Social lives, families, and egos also grew. The Madewood house on Bayou Lafourche was built explicitly to outshine Woodlawn, the beautiful home of the builder's brother (unfortunately, not open to the public).

But the enormous wealth stemmed from an economy based on human servitude. The injustice and cruelty of slavery became the seeds of its own demise. After the Civil War, large-scale farming became impossible without that labor base. During Reconstruction, lands were confiscated and turned over to people who proved unable to run them; many were subdivided. Increasing international competition began to erode the cotton and sugar markets. The culture represented by the plantation houses you'll see emerged and died in a span of less than 100 years.

THE PLANTATION HOUSES TODAY   Where dozens of grand homes once dotted the landscape along and around the river, few remain. Several that survived the Civil War fell victim to fires, floods, or industrial development. Others, too costly to be maintained, have been left to the ravages of dampness and decay. A few, however, have been saved, preserved, and upgraded with electricity and plumbing. Most are private residences, but some are open to visitors, the admission fees supplementing upkeep.

Tours of plantations are hit-or-miss—much depends on your guide. We've listed our favorite choices here. If you visit several, after a while you'll begin to hear many of the same facts about plantation life, sometimes as infill for missing or boring history. While visiting these lavish (and in some cases, lavishly restored) homes, we've also found it easy to romanticize the era, while giving short shrift to the fact that they would not exist were it not for unthinkably savage, yet unimaginably real, human cruelty.

Planning Your Trip

All the plantation homes shown on the map on p. 215 are within easy driving distance of New Orleans. How many you can tour in a day will depend on your endurance (in the car and on your feet) and time allotment. If returning late, the small highways can be a little intimidating after dark. Don't expect broad river views along the Great River Road (the roadway's name on *both* sides of the Mississippi); it's obscured by tall levees. You'll see sugarcane fields and land ravaged by oil and chemical development. But spontaneous detours through little, centuries-old towns might result in finding a choice resale shop or good road food.

If you have minimal time, we suggest touring Laura and Oak Alley. They are a mile apart, and each offers a different perspective on plantation life and the tourism industry. Laura is classic understated Creole and has a low-key but superb presentation. Tara-esque Oak Alley represents the showy Americans and is slicker and glitzier (one could even do an Oak Alley drive-by). Both are approximately an hour from New Orleans. Alternately, a day at Houmas House would also be a day well-spent.

If you're in town on **Christmas Eve,** consider driving along the River Road to see the huge bonfires residents build on the levees to light the way for the Christ child and Papa Noël (who rides in a sleigh drawn by—what else?—eight alligators!).

Organized Tours

Touring plantation houses via a bus tour is a comfortable, planning-free option. Almost every New Orleans tour company operates a plantation tour; most offer hotel pickup or at a central point in the French Quarter, and visit one or two of the houses. Costs include transportation and admission.

The reliable 4½-hour tours offered by **Gray Line** (© 800/535-7786 or 504/569-1401; www.graylineneworleans.com) visit Oak Alley or Laura Plantation. Daily tours depart Gray Line's Toulouse St. station; exact times vary during the year, so call ahead (adults $58; children 6–12 $26). Mainstay tour company **Cajun Encounters** has twice-daily combo tours of both plantations ($73 adults; $59 children), as well as a very full day outing that adds a swamp tour ($116 adults; $85 children) (© 866-928-6877 or 504/834-1770; www.cajunencounters.com). For smaller groups, we like **Tours by Isabelle** (© 877/665-8687 or 504/398-0365; www.toursbyisabelle.com). Isabelle Cossart takes groups of 6 to 13 people in a comfortable van on a daylong expedition to Oak Alley, Laura, and/or other plantations ($91). If you have fewer than 6 people, call to ask if you can join an existing tour; she'll also customize tours to other plantations.

Plantations Between New Orleans & Baton Rouge

The plantations below are listed in the order in which they appear on the map, running north along the Mississippi from New Orleans. Tours range from 1½ to 2½ hours; most people do one or two in a day (and may drive past others). Depending on which you choose to see, you may have to cross the Mississippi River by bridge a few times. The windy river makes distances deceiving; give yourself more time than you think you'll need. The plantations discussed here are roughly 1 hour from New Orleans (the most accessible for visitors to the city) and 15 minutes apart.

Destrehan Plantation ★★ Its proximity (just 30 min. from New Orleans), in-character docents (better than it sounds), and role in *Interview with the Vampire* have made Destrehan Manor a popular plantation jaunt. It's the oldest intact plantation home in the lower Mississippi Valley open to the public, built in 1787 by a free person of color for a wealthy Frenchman, and modified from its "dated" French colonial style to Greek Revival in the 1830s. Its warmly colored, graceful lines are aesthetically pleasing, and some original furnishings remain. One

River Road Pit Stop
Restaurants are in short supply along the River Road. Skip the mostly so-so cafes noted in the plantations' descriptions and stop in at **B&C Seafood,** just east of Laura Plantation. For lunch, join the locals at B&C for steaming trays of boiled shrimp and crawfish, the latter if it's in season (2155 Hwy. 18, Vacherie; © **225/265-8356;** all items $5–$24; Mon–Sat 11am–4:30pm).

ST. FRANCISVILLE & SURROUNDING
plantations

St. Francisville doesn't look like much on approach, but by the time you get to the town center, you are utterly charmed. This is not Cajun Country—this area has American plantations only and no French history, but if you're interested in plantations from an architectural, historical, or cultural perspective, you can do well by planting yourself here for an overnighter. It's 30 miles northwest of Baton Rouge and 2 hours by car from New Orleans. Contact the **St. Francisville tourism information office** for details (📞 **800/789-4221** or 225/635-4224; www.stfrancisville.us; Mon–Sat 9am–5pm, Sun 9:30am–5pm). Recommended places to stay include the **Barrow House Inn,** at 9779 Royal St., St. Francisville (📞 **225/635-4791;** www.topteninn.com; $115–$160), with beautifully restored antique-laden rooms; **Butler Greenwood Plantation B&B,** at 8345 U.S. 61, St. Francisville (📞 **225/635-6312;** www.butlergreenwood.com; doubles $135), with modest but sweet guest cottages, some with Jacuzzis or fireplaces, set on oak-laden plantation grounds; and **Shade Tree,** 9704 Royal St., St. Francisville (📞 **225/635-6116;** www.shadetreeinn.com; $145–$195), a peaceful, romantic aerie with a slight hippie bent. Attractions in St. Francisville include:

○ **Magnolia Mound** ★ This late-1700s, single-story plantation home was originally built as a small settler's house and vastly enlarged later. Costumed guides take you through the slave cabins and authentically furnished house, one of the oldest wooden structures in the state (2161 Nicholson Dr., Baton Rouge.

📞 **225/343-4955;** http://friendsofmagnoliamound.org; $10 adults, $8 seniors 65 and over and students 18–22, $4 children 5–17, free for children 4 and under; Mon–Sat 10am–4pm; Sun 1–4pm; tours begin on the hour; last tour at 3pm).

○ **Oakley Plantation at Audubon State Historic Site** ★ This simple home is where John James Audubon painted some 32 of his "Birds of America" series. A walk through the gardens and nature trails clearly illustrates why Audubon was so taken with this area; it's part of a 100-acre wildlife sanctuary (La. 965, St. Francisville. 📞 **225/635-3739;** www.crt.state.la.us/parks/iaudubon.aspx; $8 adults, $6 seniors [63 and over], $4 children 6 to 17, free for children 5 and under; daily 9am–5pm; guided tours of the house hourly 10am–4pm).

○ **Rosedown Plantation** ★★ Rosedown is by far the most impressive and historic of the more far-flung plantations, starting with its wide avenue of ancient oaks and dramatic gardens (12501 Hwy. 10, at La. 10 and U.S. 61, St. Francisville 📞 **888/376-1867** or 225/635-3332; www.lastateparks.com; house tour and historic gardens $10 adults, $8 seniors, $4 students 6–17, free for children 5 and under; daily 9am–5pm; tours begin at 10am).

room has been left un-renovated, to show the humble rawness beneath the usual public grandeur. Unlike most plantation homes, Destrehan has ramps and an elevator.

13034 River Rd., La. 48, Destrehan. ℂ **877/453-2095** or 985/764-9315. www.destrehanplantation. org. Admission $18 adults, $7 children 6–16, free for children 5 and under. Daily 9am–4pm. Closed New Year's Day, Mardi Gras, Easter, Thanksgiving, and Dec 24–25.

San Francisco ★ This brightly colored "steamboat Gothic" mansion was completed in 1856 by Edmond B. Marmillion, who died before he could occupy the home. He willed it to his two sons, one of whom married in 1855 while on a grand tour of Europe. The new wife undertook elaborate redecorations, leaving the son *sans fruscin,* or "without a cent." Thus its first name, St. Frusquin . . . later changed to San Francisco.

The fanciful, three-story house has wide galleries resembling a ship's double decks, and twin stairs leading to a broad main portal. Inside, there is beautiful carved woodwork, and cypress ceilings, and walls gloriously painted with flowers, birds, nymphs, and cherubs.

2646 Hwy. 44, Garyville. ℂ **888/509-1756** or 985/535-2341. www.sanfranciscoplantation.org. Admission $15 adults, $14 military with ID and AAA members, $10 children 7–17, free for children 6 and under. Daily Apr–Oct 9:30am–5pm, tours start at 9:40am and last tour at 4:40pm; Nov–Mar 9am–5pm, tours start at 10am and last tour at 4pm. Closed New Year's Day, Mardi Gras, Easter, Thanksgiving Day, and Dec 24–25.

Laura: A Creole Plantation ★★★ If you see only one plantation, make it Laura, simple on the outside but utterly absorbing within. It has no hoop-skirted guides, offering instead a thorough view of daily life on an 18th- and 19th-century sugar plantation, a cultural history of Louisiana's Creole population, and a mesmerizing, in-depth examination of one Creole family. Much is known about this house and its residents, thanks to extensive records (more than 5,000 documents researched in France), including the detailed memoirs of its namesake, proto-feminist head-of-the-household Laura Locoul. Many of the original artifacts on display—from cookware to jewelry—were saved by employees in a devastating 2004 fire, after which it was accurately restored to the 1805 period, including a slave cabin. *Fun fact:* The beloved B'rer Rabbit stories were first collected here by a folklorist in the 1870s. *Fun fact #2:* Fats Domino's parents lived on this plantation. Special-interest tours on Creole architecture, Creole women, children, slavery, and the "Americanization of Louisiana" are available with advance notice.

2247 La. 18, Vacherie. ℂ **888/799-7690** or 225/265-7690. www.lauraplantation.com. Admission $20 adults, $18 for military and AAA members, $6 children 6–17, free for children 5 and under. Tours run every 40 minutes. Open 10am–4pm; last tour begins at 4pm. Tours in French available Tuesdays and Saturdays. Closed Jan 1, Mardi Gras, Easter, Thanksgiving, and Dec 25.

Oak Alley Plantation ★★ This is precisely what comes to mind when most people think "plantation." A splendid white house, its porch lined with giant columns, approached by a magnificent quarter-mile drive lined with stately oak trees (the 1839 house has 28 fluted Doric columns to match the 28 trees)—yep, it's all here. Consequently, this Hollywood honey is the most famous plantation house in Louisiana. It's also the slickest operation, with an expensive lunch buffet (we say BYO picnic), hoopskirted guides, and golf carts traversing the blacktopped property.

Oak Alley lay disintegrating until 1914; new owners and restorers were responsible for its National Historic Landmark designation. Little is known about the families who lived here, so tours focus on general plantation facts. You can also stay in one of five pretty, century-old Creole cottages, now bed-and-breakfast rooms.

3645 La. 18 (60 miles from New Orleans), Vacherie. ℂ **800/44-ALLEY** (442-5539) or 225/265-2151. www.oakalleyplantation.com. Admission $20 adults, $7.50 students 13–18, $4.50 children 6–12, free for children 5 and under. Discounts for 65 and over, AAA members, and active military. Grounds open daily at 9am; tours begin every half-hour at 10am; Mon–Fri last tour at 4pm; Sat–Sun tours until 5pm. Restaurant hours 8:30-3pm. Closed Jan 1, Thanksgiving, and Dec 25.

Houmas House Plantation & Gardens ★★★ Houmas is actually two houses joined together under one roof: the original, 1775 four-room structure and the larger, Greek Revival–style house, completed in 1828 after 17 years of construction. The former sugar plantation has been restored several times since then, including by the current owner, who has invested millions in turning it into a fabulous showcase, popular event venue, and his home. It's filled with stunning art and antiques and surrounded by elegant formal gardens. What Houmas has done differently (and wisely) than most other plantations is to install a lovely cafe, a pleasant bar, and a fine-dining restaurant amid these splendid environs, so one can make a day of it (or 2 days, if one stays in the fetching, brand-new cottages, thoroughly modern in nearly every way save decor). Note that the upscale restaurant is "event" dining requiring reservations and proper dress (and a thick wallet).

40136 La. 942, Burnside (58 miles from New Orleans). ℂ **888/323-8314** or 225/473-9830. www. houmashouse.com. Admission (including guided tour) $24 adults, $15 children ages 13–18, $10 children ages 6–12, free for children 5 and under; gardens and grounds only $10. Mon–Tues 9am–5pm; Wed–Sun 9am–8pm. Closed Dec 25 and Jan 1. Take I–10 from New Orleans or Baton Rouge. Exit on La. 44 to Burnside and turn right on La. 942.

Nottoway Plantation ★★ Nottoway is everything you want in a dazzling Old South mansion. Dating from 1858, it's the largest existing plantation house in the South, a mammoth structure with 64 rooms (covering 53,000 sq. ft.) and pillars to rival the White House's. Saved from Civil War destruction by a Northern gunboat officer who had once been a guest here, the still-handsome interiors feature marvelous curlicue plasterwork, hand-carved Corinthian columns of cypress wood in the ballroom, beautiful archways, and original crystal chandeliers. You can also stay here, in rooms with period furnishings and luxurious bathrooms ($240–$320 per night including breakfast; check website for online deals).

31025 La. 1, White Castle. ℂ **866/527-6884** or 225/545-2730. www.nottoway.com. Admission $20 adults, $6 children ages 6–12, free for children 5 and under. Daily 9am–4pm, tours begin on the hour. Closed Dec 25. From New Orleans, follow I-10 west to La. 22 exit, then turn left on La. 70 across Sunshine Bridge. Exit onto La. 1 and drive 14 miles north through Donaldsonville. From Baton Rouge, take I-10 west to Plaquemine exit and then La. 1 south for 18 miles.

CAJUN COUNTRY

This area, also called Acadiana (though you won't find that on the maps) has a history and culture unique in America. It consists of a rough triangle of Louisiana made up of 22 parishes (counties), from St. Landry at the top of the triangle to the Gulf of Mexico at its base. Lafayette is the "capital" of Acadiana.

Meet the Cajuns

The Cajun's history is a sad one, but it produced a people and a culture well worth knowing. In the early 1600s, colonists from France began settling the southeastern coast of Canada in a region of Nova Scotia they named Acadia. They developed a peaceful agricultural society based on the values of a strong Catholic faith, deep love of family, and respect for their relatively small landholdings.

This pastoral existence was isolated from Europe for nearly 150 years, until Acadia became the property of the British. The king's representatives tried to force the Acadians to pledge allegiance to the British Crown, renounce Catholicism, and embrace the king's Protestantism, but for decades they steadfastly refused. Finally, the British governor of the region sent in troops. Villages were burned and families separated as ships were loaded to deport them. A 10-year diaspora began, scattering them to France, England, America's East Coast, and the West Indies. Hundreds of lives were lost to the terrible conditions onboard.

In 1765, Bernard Andry brought a band of 231 men, women, and children to reestablish a permanent home in Louisiana, a natural destination due to its strong French background. These industrious settlers worked the swampy, wildlife-infested lands, building levees, draining fields, and planting many of the farms you still see here.

Cajun Language

Much of this essay was provided by author, historian, and two-time Grammy nominee Ann Allen Savoy, who, along with her husband, Marc (an acclaimed accordion maker) are members of the Savoy-Doucet Cajun Band and several other groups. The Savoys are significant keepers of the culture, not least by having spawned a musical dynasty. All four of their talented children are carrying the cultural torch through their own music and art.

The French influence in Louisiana is one of the things that sets the state apart from the rest of the United States. Although French is spoken by most of the older Cajuns (ages 60 and up), most middle-aged Louisianans don't speak the language. This is partially because knowledge of the French language, from the 1930s on, became associated with a lack of business success or education. Cajun music was considered hokey, and Cajun culture on the whole was denigrated and stigmatized.

Today, however, Cajun culture has experienced a resurgence of popularity and respect. The young people are emphatically adopting their ancestors' language, music, recipes, and other traditions and proudly speak with the sharp, bright Cajun accent.

Cajun French is peppered with beautiful old words dating from Louis XIV, unused in France and historically intriguing. It is not a dialect of French, however; many words have been localized (a mosquito can be called a *marougouin* in one area, a *moustique* in another, a *cousin* elsewhere), and "Franglish" is common (*"On va revenir right back"*—"We'll be right back").

Additionally, the fascinating Creole language is still spoken by many black Louisianans. A compilation of French and African dialects, it is quite different from standard French, though Cajuns and black Creoles can speak and understand both languages.

ATTRACTIONS ●
Acadian Village **17**
Atchafalaya Experience **4**
Blue Moon Saloon **11**
Church of St. John the Evangelist **16**
El Sido's **6**
Evangeline Oak **5**
Festival Internationale **10**
Fred's Lounge **1**
Lafayette Visitors Center **7**
Liberty Theater **1**
Savoy Music Center **1**
Prairie Acadian Cultural Center **1**
Randol's **19**
St. Martin du Tours Church **5**
Vermilionville **14**
Whiskey River Landing **4**

Cajun Music Hot Spots

Ville Platte
Mamou
Eunice
Washington
Opelousas
Grand Coteau
Carencro
Henderson
Breaux Bridge
St. Martinville
To Baton Rouge, New Orleans

See Lafayette (below)

HOTELS ■
Aaah! T'Frere's **20**
Bois de Chenes **8**

RESTAURANTS ◆
Best Stop **3**
Borden's **13**
Charley G's **18**
French Press **9**
Johnson's Boucaniere **12**
Jolie's **15**
Ruby's **2**

Atchafalaya River

0   2 mi
0   2 km

Northgate Mall
Willow St.
SCOTT
Jay and Lionel Herbert Municipal Golf Course
Webb St.
Carmel Ave.
Cameron St.
University of Louisiana at Lafayette
LAFAYETTE
Dulles Dr.
Johnston St.
E. University Ave.
Lafayette Regional Airport
WALROY
Ridge Rd.
Acadiana Mall
PILETTE

tuning in TO CAJUN COUNTRY

Our standard soundtrack for the drive from New Orleans to Cajun Country begins with the excellent **WWOZ 90.7 FM** (to which we're assiduously tuned while in the city). After an hour on the road, static takes over, signaling the unwrapping of whatever new music we've recently purchased from **Louisiana Music Factory** (p. 193). In about half a CD's time, we can usually pull in **KBON 101.1 FM** for some rollickin' Cajun and zydeco tunes. At that point we know we've arrived, as much in geography as mood.

Cajun Music

It's hard to decide which is more important to a Cajun: food or music. In the early days when instruments were scarce, Cajuns held dances to a cappella voices. With roots probably found in medieval France, the strains usually came in the form of a brisk two-step or a waltz. Traditional groups still play mostly acoustic instruments—a fiddle, an accordion, a triangle, and maybe a guitar.

The best place to hear real Cajun music is on someone's back porch, the time-honored spot for eating some gumbo and listening to several generations of musicians jamming. If you can't wrangle an invitation, the local dance halls on any weekend will do just fine. It's quite the social scene, and there are usually willing dance coaches for newbies (don't be shy—everyone will be watching the really good dancers; you should, too). Our Cajun weekend itinerary, below, takes you on a well-rounded musical introduction to this region. For information on where to hear live Cajun music in New Orleans, see "Cajun & Zydeco Joints," in chapter 8.

Planning Your Trip

You'll see and do a lot if you follow our 3-day weekend, which includes options to customize the trip based on your own interests. A bit of adventurous wandering on your own will reward you with more finds.

The best time to visit Acadiana is during Cajun Mardi Gras (p. 46), Festival International de Louisiane (p. 34), Festivals Acadiens et Creoles (p. 36), or the Breaux Bridge Crawfish Festival—or any weekend. There always seems to be a smaller festival somewhere in the area and plenty of music throughout the year. But our tour is for a non-festival weekend.

For tons of good detailed information, contact the **Lafayette Convention and Visitors Commission** (© **800/346-1958** in the U.S.; 800/543-5340 in Canada; or 337/232-3737; www.lafayettetravel.com).

Tours

If you only have one day, **Tours by Isabelle** (© **888/223-2093** or 504/391-3544; www.toursbyisabelle.com) offers round trip van tours that will introduce you to the area ($81 and up). Plan in advance, they may not be offered every day. Each year in the 3 days between Jazz Fest weekends, **Festival Tours International** provides a stellar music-focused tour of the area (p. 49). Also see "Organized Tours," p. 149.

A CAJUN 3-DAY WEEKEND

Here is our suggested itinerary for a 3-day side trip from New Orleans to Cajun Country, designed to introduce you to this marvelous, singular culture. The drive from New Orleans is about 2½ to 3 hours, mostly via I-10 (140 miles from New Orleans). If you opt to drive back via U.S. 90, it's about 170 miles. We also take you from Lafayette to the smaller towns of Eunice, Mamou, and St. Martinville for a thorough immersion in real Cajun culture. We've provided main highway directions; a GPS will help get you to the recommended in-town destinations.

Friday, Day 1: Lafayette ★★★

Leave New Orleans early in the day and head for the River Road (Hwy. 18) plantations to tour San Francisco (p. 220), perhaps, and/or Laura Plantation (p. 220). Or head directly to Lafayette. *Tip:* Try to avoid going through Baton Rouge at afternoon rush hour.

Lafayette is a midsize city of 120,000, with a university (LSU) to boot, so you'll find plenty of hotel options. But we recommend you skip the hotels and opt for an atmospheric B&B instead. Check in at **Aaah! T'Frere's Bed & Breakfast** (1905 Verot School Rd., Lafayette; ✆ **800/984-9347** or 337/984-9347; www.tfreres.com; doubles $135) or **Bois de Chenes Bed & Breakfast** (338 N. Sterling St., Lafayette; ✆ **337/233-7816;** www.boisdechenes.com; doubles $110–$150)

Relax or take a drive around town. Visit the **Church of St. John the Evangelist** (515 Cathedral St., Lafayette; ✆ **337/232-1322;** www.saintjohncathedral. org), a splendid Dutch Romanesque edifice done in red and white brick, with fine stained glass dating to 1916.

For dinner, try **Charley G's** (3809 Ambassador Caffery Pkwy., Lafayette; ✆ **337/981-0108;** www.charleygs.com), one of Lafayette's finest seafood houses. If you have room, squeeze in a sundae from **Borden's** (1103 Jefferson St., Lafayette; ✆ **337/235-9291;** http://bordensicecreamshoppe.com), an ice cream parlor in the truest, old-timey sense. It's hardly changed since it scooped its first cone of creamy goodness back in 1940. Otherwise, head back and hit your relaxing veranda and cushy bed—Saturday is a full day.

Saturday, Day 2: Eunice & Mamou

Make the 35-minute drive to the **Savoy Music Center,** 3 miles east of Eunice (Hwy. 190 E.; ✆ **337/457-9563;** www.savoymusiccenter.com; Tues–Fri 9am–5pm, closed for lunch noon–1:30pm; Sat jam 9am–noon). On weekdays this working music store sells instruments, equipment, and Marc Savoy's exquisite, world-renowned, hand-crafted accordions (check out the folk-art aphorisms scrawled on his workshop cabinets, if you can). At the Saturday-morning jam sessions, this nondescript, faded-green building becomes the spiritual center of Cajun music, and an experience not to be missed. Local and visiting musicians young and old gather to savor this unpretentious, unparalleled music and culture. It's probably the closest thing to that back-porch experience you'll find. Bring some boudin, an instrument, or just an interest.

Stay and savor this captivating, authentic scene, or cut out (no later than 11:30 or so) to head for the alternate universe known as **Fred's Lounge** in Mamou, about 20 minutes north (west on U.S. 190; then right on LA 13; 420 6th St.; ℂ **337/468-5411;** Sat 8am–2pm; music starts at 9am). This is the other end of the Cajun music spectrum, a small-town bar that for half a century has hosted Saturday daytime dances starting at 8am. Couples waltz and two-step around the midfloor bandstand, while 80-something matriarch Tante Sue drinks shots and otherwise presides. It's pure dance-hall stuff (leaning toward the country-western side of Cajun, but much of it in French), where hardworking locals let loose. And we do mean loose (remember, they started with Coors while you were still on coffee).

Back to Eunice, sample a down-home lunch at **Ruby's** (221 W. Walnut Ave., Eunice; ℂ **337/550-7665**). Get the thick, crisp-fried pork chops if they're on the day's menu, and some stewed okra. Revise all that if the crawfish etoufée is on (or just get both; it's a long break before dinner).

Take some mellow museum time at the **Prairie Acadian Cultural Center** (250 W. Park Ave.; www.nps.gov/jela/prairie-acadian-cultural-center-eunice.htm; ℂ **337/457-8499;** free admission; donations accepted; Tues–Fri 8am–5pm; Sat 8am–6pm), a terrific small collection. Most objects on display were acquired from local families who had owned them for generations, and craft demonstrations, live music, or dance lessons may be in the offing. It's a worthy attraction on its own, and may help dispel the myths and stereotypes perpetuated by the recent rash of Louisiana-based reality shows.

When the Cultural Center shuts down, visitors—well, the entire town—migrates next door to the 1924 **Liberty Theater** (2nd St. and Park Ave.; www.eunice-la.com; ℂ **337/457-7389;** $5; doors open at 4pm; show 6–7:30pm), where the all-French show "Rendez-vous des Cajuns" kicks off with live music, dancing, and jokey storytelling. Even if you speak *non* French, you'll get it. Note that tickets go on sale at 4pm, so you may need to take a break from the Cultural Center to buy them lest they sell out. If you can't make it (big mistake), tune in to 1490 on your AM channel (locally) or krvs.org for the newfangled webcast (worldwide).

Your dinner bell is probably ringing loudly, and porky delights await you back in Lafayette at **Johnson's Boucaniere** (1111 St. John St., Lafayette; ℂ **337/269-8878;** www.johnsonsboucaniere.com; Tues–Thurs 10am–6pm, Fri 10am–9pm, Sat 7am–9pm). The Johnson family has been smoking meats since 1937, and their brisket (and that crazy grilled cheese and boudin ball sandwich) should not be missed. There are only a few tables, so if you're weary, call in your order from the road and take it to enjoy back at your B&B.

If you're not worn out, check out what's on at the **Blue Moon Saloon** (215 E. Convent St., Lafayette; ℂ **337/234-2422;** www.bluemoonpresents.com; cover $10–$20; Wed–Sat 8pm–close), the city's premier live music venue. Cajun, zydeco, and all forms of modern alternative roots music brings in the LSU student body and others. For more traditional Cajun music and dancing, two-step to **Randol's** (2320 Kaliste Saloom Rd.; ℂ **337/981-7080;** www.randols.com; Sun–Thurs 5–9:30pm, Fri–Sat 5–10:30pm). You may be joined by fellow tourists on the dance floor, but on Saturday nights you'll also find an easygoing, accessible scene (you can dine here as well, but we're more fond of the dance scene than the

boudin: GET LINKED IN

Boudin (boo-dan) is a Cajun sausage link made of pork, rice, onions, and spices and stuffed inside a chewy casing. If it's done right, it's spicy and sublime. In these parts, you can get this inexpensive (about $3 per lb.) snack at just about any grocery store or gas station. Disputes rage about whose is best (**www.boudin link.com** has digitized the argument). It's best eaten while leaning against a car, chased with a Barq's root beer.

Conducting a comparison test is great fun, but our singular choice in these parts is the **Best Stop,** 615 Hwy 93 N., Scott (exit 97 off the I-10) (© **337/233-5805;** www.beststopinscott.com). it's always busy, so the links and crunchy pig-fat cracklins (aka chicharones) are always fresh. Did we mention that they ship? Best Stop is open Monday through Saturday 6am to 8pm, Sunday 6am to 6pm.

cuisine). For the adventurous night owl, find your way to **El Sido's** (1523 N. St. Antoine St., Lafayette; © **337/235-0647;** cover $7–$15; Fri–Sat 9pm–2am, occasionally Sun–Mon during festival weekends) on the outskirts of town. It's not always easy to find out what's on at the long-standing roadhouse, but on Saturday night it's a good bet it's zydeco, often with a more bluesy or urban edge than the traditional stuff, and some astoundingly good dancers. That all gets going around 10pm.

Sunday, Day 3: Lafayette & St. Martinville ★★

After a relaxing breakfast at your B&B, visit **Vermilionville** ★★ (300 Fisher Rd., off Surrey St.; © **337/233-4077;** www.vermilionville.org; $10 adults, $8 seniors, $6 students, free for children 5 and under; Tues–Sun 10am–4pm; admission desk closes at 3pm), a Cajun-Creole settlement reconstructed on the bayou's banks, where costumed staff and craftspeople demonstrate activities of 18th- to 19th-century daily life and musicians jam. While it may sound like a kitschy "Cajunland" theme park, it's actually quite a valid operation and a good introduction to the culture.

Or take the **Atchafalaya Experience,** Lafayette (© **337/277-4726** or 337/233-7816; http://theatchafalayaexperience.com; $50 13 and up; $25 kids 8–12; free for 7 and under [1 per family]; call for times and reservations), an outstanding swamp, bird, and wildlife tour led by virtuoso naturalists who were raised on these bayous (if you're staying at Bois des Chenes B&B, it's the men of the house). If you have not yet taken to the waters of the Louisiana swamps, seeing this stunning, primeval, vital ecosystem is a must-do, and these guides are as good as it gets. Bring a hat, sunscreen, water, and insect repellent.

Lunch takes you back to downtown Lafayette to the **French Press** (214 E. Vermilion St.; © **337/233-9449;** http://thefrenchpresslafayette.com; Tues–Fri 7am–2pm; Sat–Sun 9am–2pm; Fri–Sat 5:30–9pm), a casual but refined spot on the higher end of the hipness scale. The biscuit sliders with boudin balls and sugarcane syrup are to kill for; the chicken and waffles aren't far behind. If you're ready for lighter fare by now, the winning shrimp salad boasts a kicking rémoulade.

To further experience the history, legend, and romance of this region, take a leisurely drive to the lovely, historic burg of **St. Martinville.** Get there by taking Pinhook Road to the small country route, LA 96, and driving 16 miles to reach the peaceful town square. St. Martinville dates from 1765, when it was a military station. It was once known as "la Petite Paris" for the many French aristocrats who settled here after fleeing the French Revolution.

The town centers around **St. Martin du Tours Church,** constructed in 1836—the fourth-oldest Roman Catholic church in Louisiana—and poetry. Besides its natural and historic charm, the town is the home of Evangeline Emmeline, the (debatably) fictional heroine of Longfellow's tragic poem. A statue of her next to the church was donated to the town in 1929 by a movie company that filmed the epic here; star Dolores del Rio supposedly posed for the sculptor. At Port Street and Bayou Teche is the ancient **Evangeline Oak** and commemorative mural, where self-proclaimed descendants claim Emmeline's boat landed at the end of her journey here from Nova Scotia. From St. Martinville, return to New Orleans via I-10 again, or alternately, via U.S. 90.

PLANNING YOUR TRIP TO NEW ORLEANS

N o matter what your idea of the perfect New Orleans trip is, this chapter will give you the information to make informed plans about getting here, getting around, and the essentials for an easy Big Easy vacation. We'll also point you toward additional resources, so you can let the *bons temps* begin even before you arrive.

GETTING THERE

By Plane

Most major domestic and some international airlines serve the city's **Louis Armstrong New Orleans International Airport (MSY).** The airport is 15 miles west of the city, in Kenner. You'll find information booths scattered around the airport and in the baggage claim area, as well as a branch of the **Travelers Aid Society.**

In 2013, **Southern Airways Express** (http://iflysouthern.com) began operating regional flights from Memphis, Birmingham, Destin, and other midsize Southern cities to **Lakefront Airport (NEW).** The Art Deco airport is conveniently located just 9 miles from downtown New Orleans.

Some large airlines offer transatlantic or transpacific passengers special discount tickets under the name **Visit USA,** which allows mostly one-way travel from one U.S. destination to another at very low prices. Unavailable in the U.S., these discount tickets must be purchased abroad in conjunction with your international fare. This system is the easiest, fastest, cheapest way to see the country.

GETTING INTO TOWN FROM THE AIRPORT

For $20 per person (one-way), the official **Airport Shuttle New Orleans** (© **866/596-2699** or 504/522-3500; www.airportshuttleneworleans.com) van will take you directly from the airport to your hotel in the French Quarter, Garden District, Central Business District, or Faubourg Marigny. There are Airport Shuttle information desks (staffed 24 hr.) in the airport. *Note:* If you plan to take the Airport Shuttle *to* the airport when you depart, you must call a day in advance to arrange a pickup time. You can also book and pay for a round-trip ($38) in advance, via phone or online. It's free for kids 5 and under.

A **taxi** from the airport to most hotels will cost $33 for one to two people; for three or more passengers, the fare is $14 per person. Taxi stands are outside the baggage-claim area.

To ride in style from the airport to your hotel, try **Bonomolo Limousine Service** (*©* **800/451-9258** or 504/522-0892; www.bonolimo.com). Airport transfer service in a Lincoln MKS starts at $75 plus 20% gratuity.

From the airport, you can reach the **Central Business District** by **Jefferson Transit public bus No. E-2** for $2. The bus goes to Tulane Avenue and Carrollton Avenue daily, or Tulane and Loyola Monday through Friday, where riders can transfer to the Regional Transit Authority lines for an additional $1.25. Buses run from 5:20am, departing from the upper level of the airport about every 25 minutes. The Tulane/Carrolton line runs until 9pm daily; the line to Loyola runs until 6:30pm Monday through Friday only. For more information, call **Jefferson Transit** (*©* **504/818-1077;** www.jeffersontransit.org) or the **Regional Transit Authority** (*©* **504/248-3900;** www.norta.com).

By Car

You can drive to New Orleans via **I-10, I-55, U.S. 90, U.S. 61,** or across the Lake Pontchartrain Causeway on **La. 25.** From any direction, you'll see the city's distinctive and swampy outlying regions; if possible, drive in during daylight and allow time to enjoy the scenery. U.S. 61 or La. 25 offer the best views, but the larger roads are considerably faster.

It's a good idea to call your hotel in advance for directions and parking fees and instructions. Most hotels have parking facilities or can refer you to a garage nearby. Daily fees can be hefty.

AAA (*©* **800-222-7623,** ext. 7000 or 504/837-1080; www.aaa.com) will assist members with trip planning and emergency services.

Approximate drive time to New Orleans from Atlanta is 8 hours; from Houston it's 6 hours; Chicago, 15 hours; Baton Rouge is an hour and a half away.

Driving in New Orleans can be a hassle, and parking is a nightmare. It's a great city for walking, and cabs are plentiful and not too expensive, so you really don't need a car unless you're planning several day trips. Nevertheless, most major national car-rental companies are represented at the airport.

International visitors should note that insurance and taxes are almost never included in quoted rental-car rates in the U.S. Be sure to ask your rental agency about additional fees for these, as they can be significant. See "By Car" under "Getting Around" later in this section for more on rental-car age and payment requirements.

By Train

Passenger rail lines pass through some beautiful scenery. **Amtrak** (*©* **800/USA-RAIL** [872-7245] or 504/528-1612; www.amtrak.com) trains serve the city's **Union Passenger Terminal,** 1001 Loyola Ave. in the Central Business District. The station is on the recently completed Loyola streetcar line, and plenty of taxis wait outside the passenger terminal. Hotels in the French Quarter and the Central Business District are a short ride or a healthy walk away.

International visitors can buy a **USA Rail Pass,** good for 15, 30, or 45 days of unlimited travel on **Amtrak,** as well as various regional passes. They're available online or through many overseas travel agents. See Amtrak's website for the cost of travel within the western, eastern, or northwestern United States. Reservations are generally required and should be made as early as possible.

By Boat

While not a traditional means of getting to or from New Orleans, several major cruise lines do embark from the Port of New Orleans. Many passengers add a visit to the Crescent City before or after their Caribbean cruise—a right fine vacation. Contact **Royal Caribbean** (© **866/562-7625**; www.royalcaribbean.com), **Carnival Cruises** (© **888/227-6482**; www.carnival.com), or **Norwegian Cruise Line** (© **866/234-7350;** www.ncl.com) for information. **American River Cruises** plies the Mississippi River to New Orleans (© **800/460-4618**; www.americancruiselines.com); **Blount Small Ship Adventures'** cruise hugs the Gulf Shore (© **800/556-7450**; www.blountsmall shipadventures.com).

GETTING AROUND

By Car

Unless you're planning extensive or far-flung explorations outside the major tourist zones, you really don't need to rent a car during your stay in New Orleans. The town is flat, ultra-picturesque, and made for walking; there are plenty of taxis and good public transportation. Indeed, a streetcar ride is as much entertainment as a practical means of getting around. Meanwhile, driving and parking in the French Quarter bring grief. Many streets are narrow, potholed, and crowded, and one-way. (This is among the most confusing cities we've driven around in, up there with Rome.) Street parking is minimal and lots are fiendishly expensive (hotel lots can be criminally high). That said, this book still recommends a few outlying destinations for those who can access them.

If you're visiting from abroad and plan to rent a car in the United States, foreign driver's licenses are usually recognized, but you should get an international one if your home license is not in English.

Car-rental agencies with a presence in New Orleans include Advantage, Avis, Budget, Dollar, Enterprise, Hertz, National, and Thrifty. Rental rates vary according to the time of your visit and from company to company, so do some advance comparison shopping. Try different dates and pickup points, and ask about corporate or organizational discounts (such as AAA or frequent-flier-program memberships). Rates decrease for weekly (or longer) rentals. Also, check the major online travel sites, like Expedia, Orbitz, Hotwire, Travelocity, or Priceline.

To rent a car in the United States, you need a valid driver's license and a major credit card (and a passport for foreign visitors). Some will accept a debit card with a cash deposit. The minimum age is usually 25, but Enterprise and Budget will rent to younger people for an added surcharge; they may also require proof of ability to pay (such as paycheck stubs and utility bills). It's a good idea to buy maximum insurance coverage unless you're certain your own auto or credit card insurance is sufficient. Stick to the major companies because what you might save with smaller companies might not be worth the headache if you have mechanical troubles on the road.

At press time in New Orleans, the cost of gasoline (also called gas, but never petrol), is about $3.40 a gallon, but we all know how that can fluctuate. Generally, gas costs in New Orleans tends to be at or slightly below the U.S. average. Taxes are already included in the printed price. One U.S. gallon equals 3.8 liters or .85 imperial gallons. Fill-up locations are known as gas or service stations; they are readily available on major streets (but none are located within the French Quarter). Most accept credit or debit cards right at the pump or via prepayment to the clerk (clerks will also accept cash, of course). Change is given inside if your tank fills up before you reach your prepaid amount.

When driving in New Orleans, right turns on a red light are legal except where NO RIGHT TURN ON RED signs are posted, so keep your eyes open for those. Similarly, many major intersections restrict left turns. Drive past the intersection, make a U-turn at the next allowable place, then double-back and turn right (a maneuver sometimes called the "Louisiana Left").

Streetcars run down the center of Canal Street and St. Charles, Carrollton, ad Loyola avenues, requiring motorists to cross their paths frequently. Look *both* ways for streetcars, yield the right of way to them, and allow ample time to complete track crossings. They'll brake between stops if you're in their way, of course, but it's best not to get stuck on the tracks and impede their progress.

It is illegal to have an open container of alcohol, including "go cups," in a moving car, and, of course, driving while under the influence of alcohol is a serious offense.

Keep doors locked and never leave belongings, packages, or gadgets (GPS, iPods, and the like) visible in parked cars.

By Taxi

Taxis are plentiful in New Orleans, and except during the busiest times (we're looking at you, Mardi Gras and Jazz Fest) they can be hailed easily on the street in the French Quarter and in some parts of the Central Business District. They are also usually lined up at taxi stands at larger hotels. Otherwise, call and expect a cab to appear in about 15 minutes. The rate is $3.50 when you enter the taxi and $2.40 per mile thereafter. During special events, the rate is $5 per person (or the meter rate if it's greater), even for short hops. From the French Quarter to an uptown restaurant or club, expect to spend $15 to $22. The fee for transfers between hotels is $10 no matter how short the ride.

The cab behemoth is **United Cabs** (© **504/524-9606;** www.unitedcabs.com). **Nawlins Cab** (a family breakaway from United) operates by smartphone app (© **504/522-9059;** www.nawlinscabl.com) as does **Carriage Cab,** the slightly upscale sister to Checker and Yellow Cabs (© **504/207-7777;** www.neworleanscarriagecab.com). As of 2013, all cabs were required to accept credit cards.

You can also hire a taxi for a few hours or day at negotiable hourly rates (usually in the mid-$30/hour rate), a hassle-free way to tour far-flung areas of the city.

On Foot

We can't stress this enough: Walking is by far the best way to see New Orleans (besides, you need to walk off all those calories!). You'll miss the many unique and sometimes glorious sights if you whiz past them. Slow down, stroll, and take it in. If it's just too hot, humid, or rainy, there's always a cab or bus nearby.

By Bike

One of the best ways to see the city is by bike. The terrain is flat, the breeze feels good, there are new bike paths and improved driver awareness, and you can cover ground pretty swiftly on two wheels. But the streets can be bumpy and potholed, so experience and comfort with city riding is helpful. **Bicycle Michael's,** 622 Frenchmen St. (✆ **504/945-9505;** www.bicyclemichaels.com), is the oldest shop and still has good-quality, multigear hybrids and mountain bikes starting at $25 for a half-day (4 hr.); $35 a day. At the other end of the French Quarter, **American Bicycle Rentals,** 317 Burgundy St. (✆ **866/293-4037;** www.amebrc.com), has super-sturdy, well-maintained, cushy-seated single-speed bikes with coaster brakes for $10 an hour; $25 for a half-day, $36 full day. At 1818 Magazine Street in the Lower Garden District, **A Musing Bicycles** (✆ **504/208-9779;** amusingbikes.com) rents single-speed cruisers by the hour ($8) or day ($30). **Joy Ride Bicycles** (✆ **504/982-1617;** www.joyridebikerentals.com) delivers lightweight, single-speed cruiser bikes to hotels; full-day rentals only (or longer) start at $35 a day. All include locks; baskets and helmets (recommended, but not required) may be additional. Credit-card deposits and waiver signatures required. Longer-term rentals are available. Also see the section on bicycle tours in chapter 7 (p. 158).

By Pedicab

New to the city in 2011, these rickshaw-like tricycles will get two people from A to B via pedal power (a driver's, not yours). They're easy to hail in the French Quarter and occasionally seen in other tourist parts, or you can call to request one—try **Bike Taxi Unlimited** (✆ **504/891-3441**) or **NOLA Pedicabs** (✆ **504/274-1300**). Rates are $5 for the first 5 blocks, $1 per block per person after that, so getting from A to G or H can add up fast.

By Ferry

The **Algiers Ferry** is one of the city's great assets, not just for transportation to the old Algiers Point neighborhood, but to get a view of the city from the Mississippi River. It's a working ferry, but it's more than that at night, when the city's glowing skyline reflects on the water. The 25-minute, round-trip ride from the foot of Canal Street costs $4 for pedestrians. The ferry runs 7:15am to 6:30pm Monday to Thursday, Friday 7:15am to 8:00pm, Saturday 10:45am to 8pm, and Sunday 10:45am to 6:00pm. Hours are currently in flux; verify them at www.dotd.la.gov/ferry.

> ### Discounted Rides with the JazzyPass
>
> If you don't have a car in New Orleans, invest in a **JazzyPass,** which allows unlimited rides on all streetcar and bus lines. It's a bargain and a convenience at $3 for 1 day or $9 for 3 days. One-day passes can be purchased when boarding; get multiday passes at Walgreens drug stores and other locations. To find the nearest one, ask at your hotel or guesthouse or contact the **Regional Transit Authority** (**RTA;** ✆ **504/248-3900;** www.norta.com).

By Bus

New Orleans has a good public bus system, so chances are there's a bus that runs exactly where you want to go. The local fare at press time is $1.25 (you must have exact change in bills or coins), transfers are an extra 25¢, and express buses are $1.25 (or you can use a **JazzyPass;** see below). For route information, contact the **RTA** (② **504/248-3900;** www.norta.com) or pick up one of the excellent city maps available at the **Visitor Information Center,** 529 St. Ann Street, in the French Quarter.

By Streetcar

Besides being a National Historic Landmark, the **St. Charles Avenue streetcar** is also a convenient, scenic, and fun way to get from downtown to Uptown and back. The iconic green cars click and clack for 6½ miles. It runs 24 hours a day at frequent intervals; the fare is $1.25 each way. All streetcars take exact change in bills or coins only, or JazzyPasses (see above). Streetcars can get crowded at school and business rush hours. Board at Canal and Carondelet streets (directly across Canal from Bourbon Street in the French Quarter).

The streetcar line winds beyond the point where St. Charles Avenue bends into Carrollton Avenue. The end of the line is at Palmer Park and Playground at Claiborne Avenue (there's decent shopping in the Riverbend shopping area; see p. 185). It will cost you another $1.25 for the ride back to Canal Street. It costs 10¢ to transfer from the streetcar to a bus.

The **Riverfront streetcar** runs the length of the French Quarter, from the Old Mint at Esplanade past the Convention Center to the Pontchartrain Expressway, with stops along the way. It runs from 7:30am to 10:30pm, and is a great foot saver as you explore the riverfront. The fare is $1.25, and there's wheelchair ramp access (but not on the St. Charles line).

The **Canal Street** line has spiffy (air-conditioned!) bright-red cars. The line services two destinations, so check the sign on the front of the car: "Cemeteries" goes to several of the older cemeteries and runs from 5am to 3am; "City Park" goes through Mid-City, to City Park/the New Orleans Museum of Art, and Jazz Fest. Be prepared for jammed streetcars during Jazz Fest, because the line runs to within a few blocks of the Fair Grounds. If your destination is strictly Canal Street/Carrollton, any of the cars will take you there. One-way fares are $1.25, and the line runs between 7am and 1:15am.

The new **Loyola line** runs along Loyola Street, connecting the Union Passenger Terminal (and Amtrak and Greyhound passengers) with the Canal Street line, and continues to the French Market on weekends (6:30am–9:30pm).

[Fast FACTS] NEW ORLEANS

African-American Travelers   New Orleans's African-American history is rich with important milestones, from the joyous nascence of jazz to the horrors of the slave trade to crucial civil rights achievements (to say nothing of the essential contributions to the city's culture, cuisine, politics, and literature). The **historic Tremé neighborhood** is a touchstone in itself, with a number of worthy sights within its bounds (see box, p. 152). The statewide **African American Heritage Trail** is an excellent network of cultural and historic points; information and maps are available at www.astorylikenoother.com. A tour of the **9th Ward** may be of interest (see "Organized Tours," p. 149). The **House of Dance and Feathers** (1317 Tupelo St.; ② **504/957-2678;** www.houseofdanceandfeathers.org) is essential for anyone interested in the Mardi Gras Indian tradition (p. 42), though it's open by appointment only. The *Essence Festival* is a huge draw (p. 35), and the restaurant and music options relevant to black heritage could fill a weeklong vacation without repetition.

Area Codes   The area code for New Orleans is 504.

Business Hours   Most stores are open 10am to 6pm; bars can stay open until the wee hours, and restaurants' hours vary depending on the types of meals they serve. Expect breakfast to start around 8am, lunch around 11am, and dinner at 6pm.

Car Rental   See "By Car" under "Getting There," earlier in this chapter.

Cellphones   See "Mobile Phones," later in this section.

Crime   See "Safety," later in this section.

Customs   For U.S. Customs details, consult your nearest U.S. embassy or consulate, or **U.S. Customs** (www.cbp.gov). For information on what you're allowed to bring home, contact one of the following agencies:

U.S. Citizens: U.S. Customs & Border Protection (CBP), 1300 Pennsylvania Ave. NW, Washington, DC 20229 (📞 **877/227-5511;** www.ct.gov/dcp.gov).

Canadian Citizens: Canada Border Services Agency, Ottawa, Ontario, K1A 0L8 (📞 **800/461-9999** in Canada, or 204/983-3500; www.cbsa-asfc.gc.ca).

U.K. Citizens: HM Revenue & Customs, Crownhill Court, Tailyour Road, Plymouth, PL6 5BZ (📞 **0300 200 3700;** www.hmrc.gov.uk).

Australian Citizens: Australian Customs Service, Customs House, 5 Constitution Ave., Canberra City, ACT 2601 (📞 **1300/363-263;** from outside Australia, +61 2 9313 3010; www.customs.gov.au).

New Zealand Citizens: New Zealand Customs, The Customhouse, 1 Hinemoa St., Harbour Quays, PO Box 2218, Wellington, 6140 (📞 **+64 4 901 4500** or 0800/428-786; www.customs.govt.nz).

Disabled Travelers   Most disabilities shouldn't stop anyone from traveling in New Orleans. Most public places are required to comply with disability-friendly regulations. Almost all public establishments (except a few National Historic Landmarks) and at least some modes of public transportation provide accessible entrances and facilities.

Still, a few places may be inaccessible, with regulatory allowances due to their historic nature or structural fragility. Before you book a reservation, call and inquire based on your needs. The city's newer hotels and restaurants are fully accommodating, but many older ones have done excellent retrofitting.

The city's bumpy and uneven sidewalks (and sometimes potholed or cobblestoned) streets can be challenging for wheelchairs and walkers (though most have curb cuts). The St. Charles streetcar requires a big step up and does not have a lift (all other streetcar lines do).

For paratransit information and reservations, call **RTA Paratransit** (📞 **504/827-7433;** www.norta.com/accessiblity).

Doctors   See "Health."

Drinking Laws   The legal age for purchase and consumption of alcoholic beverages is 21; proof of age is required and often requested at bars, nightclubs, and restaurants, so bring ID when you go out (but don't be surprised if people much younger take a seat next to you at the bar). Alcoholic beverages are available round-the-clock, 7 days a week. Bars can stay open all night in New Orleans, and liquor is sold in grocery and liquor stores. You're allowed to drink in public but not from a glass or bottle. Bars will provide a plastic "go cup" into which you can transfer your drink as you leave (and some have walk-up windows for quick and easy refills).

A warning: Although New Orleans has a reputation for tolerance, make no mistake: Public intoxication and "drunk and disorderly" are most definitely illegal, as many a jailed tourist can testify. Practice moderation and make smart decisions. And of course, don't even think about driving (car, motorcycle, or bicycle) while intoxicated: This is a zero-tolerance crime. Further, do not carry open containers of alcohol in your car or any public area that isn't zoned for alcohol consumption. The police can fine you on the spot.

Driving Rules See "Getting Around," p. 231.

Electricity Like Canada, the United States uses 110 to 120 volts AC (60 cycles), compared to 220 to 240 volts AC (50 cycles) in most of Europe, Australia, and New Zealand. Downward converters that change 220–240 volts to 110–120 volts are difficult to find in the United States, so bring one with you.

Embassies & Consulates All embassies are in the nation's capital, Washington, D.C. Some consulates are in major U.S. cities (including a few in New Orleans). If your country isn't listed below, call for directory information in Washington, D.C. (✆ **202/555-1212**), or check www.embassy.org/embassies.

Australia: 1601 Massachusetts Ave. NW, Washington, DC 20036 (✆ **202/797-3000;** www.usa.embassy.gov.au). Consulates are in New York, Honolulu, Houston, Los Angeles, and San Francisco.

Canada: 501 Pennsylvania Ave. NW, Washington, DC 20001 (✆ **202/682-1740;** www. canadianembassy.org). Other Canadian consulates are in Buffalo (New York), Detroit, Los Angeles, New York, and Seattle.

Ireland: 2234 Massachusetts Ave. NW, Washington, DC 20008 (✆ **202/462-3939;** www. embassyofireland.org). Irish consulates are in Boston, Chicago, New York, San Francisco, and other cities. See website for complete listing.

New Zealand: 37 Observatory Circle NW, Washington, DC 20008 (✆ **202/328-4800;** www.nzembassy.com). New Zealand consulates are in Los Angeles, Salt Lake City, San Francisco, and Seattle.

United Kingdom: 3100 Massachusetts Ave. NW, Washington, DC 20008 (✆ **202/588-6500;** www.gov.uk/government/world/organisations/british-embassy-washington). Other British consulates are in Atlanta, Boston, Chicago, Cleveland, Houston, Los Angeles, New York, San Francisco, and Seattle.

Emergencies For fire, ambulance, and police, dial ✆ **911** from any phone (it is a free call). Calls from landlines will route to the local emergency dispatch center. From mobile phones, immediately tell the operator your location and the nature of the emergency.

Family Travel New Orleans doesn't spring to mind as the first place to take a child, but it offers plenty of activities and sights appropriate for children, who often get a real kick out of the city (and love Mardi Gras!). Summer months bring the heat but also the bargains, so weigh your family's tolerance levels for a visit during school vacation. Also see p. 33.

Gasoline Please see "By Car" under "Getting Around," earlier in this chapter.

Health The widespread mold and floodwater-related illnesses that were feared after Katrina never materialized, and there have been no ill effects on air or water supply from the Deepwater oil spill. (Booze and butter pose greater dangers.)

If you have a medical condition that may require care, make appropriate arrangements before traveling to New Orleans. See "Hospitals" below for **hospitals, urgent-care centers,** and an **emergency number.** If you need a doctor for less urgent health concerns, try **Ochsner On Call** (✆ **504/842-3155** or 866/624-7637; www.ochsner.org) or visit **New Orleans Urgent Care,** 900 Magazine St. (✆ **504/552-2433;** www.neworleansurgentcare. com; Mon–Sat 10am–7pm, Sun 9am–1pm). Also see "Pharmacy" in this section.

Pollen, sun, uneven sidewalks, overindulgence, and mosquitoes (especially near the swamps and bayous) are the most common medical annoyances. Packing insect repellent, sunscreen, and protective clothing, digestive aids, and antihistamines may help prevent minor health annoyances.

Hospitals In an emergency, dial ☏ **911** from any phone to summon paramedics. For nonemergency injuries or illnesses, call or go to the emergency room at **Ochsner Baptist Medical Center,** 2700 Napoleon Ave. (☏ **504/899-9311**), or the **Tulane University Medical Center,** 1415 Tulane Ave. (☏ **504/588-5800**).

Insurance Travel insurance is a good "safety net" idea if you think for some reason you may need to cancel or postpone your trip. Most medical insurance policies cover you if you are on vacation, but check with your policy before you depart. For more on travel insurance, please see "Tips & Tools" at www.frommers.com.

Internet, Wi-Fi & Computer Rentals Nearly all major hotels have free Wi-Fi in their lobbies, as do many cafes, bars, and all Starbucks (there's one in the French Quarter in the Canal Place Mall, 365 Canal St.; ☏ **504/566-1223**). The vast majority of hotels also offer some form of in-room Internet access, usually high-speed, often wireless. Many now include the cost in the room charge; some add a surcharge of $10 to $20 daily. Barring that, the easiest option is simply to boot up and see what signals you get; or walk down any commercial street and look for "Free Wi-Fi" signs. It's a pretty well-wired city. Alternately, a concierge or front desk attendant should be able to direct you to nearby public Wi-Fi locations.

Most larger hotels have business centers with computers for rent. **FedEx Offices** with fully loaded rental computer stations with Internet access can be found at 555 Canal St. (☏ **504/654-1057**); 762 St. Charles Ave. (☏ **504/581-2541**); and several other locations. **Louis Armstrong Airport** has free Wi-Fi coverage in all passenger areas.

Language English is spoken everywhere, while French, Cajun French, and Spanish are heard occasionally in New Orleans.

Legal Aid If you are pulled over by the police for a minor infraction (such as speeding), never attempt to pay the fine directly to an officer; this could be construed as attempted bribery, a much more serious crime. Pay fines by mail, or directly into the hands of the clerk of the court. If accused of a more serious offense, say and do nothing before consulting a lawyer. Here in the U.S., the burden is on the state to prove a person's guilt beyond a reasonable doubt, and everyone has the right to remain silent, whether he or she is suspected of a crime or actually arrested. Once arrested, a person can make one telephone call to a party of his or her choice. The international visitor should call his or her embassy or consulate.

LGBT Travelers New Orleans is a very welcoming town with an extensive and active LGBTQ community. For resources, start with *Ambush Magazine,* 828-A Bourbon St. (www.ambushmag.com), which covers the scene; the website offers plenty of links to other interesting sites. The **Big Easy Metropolitan Community Church,** 1333 S. Carrollton Ave. (☏ **504/270-1622**); www.bigeasymcc.com), serves a primarily gay and lesbian congregation. The website **www.gayneworleans.com** provides information on hotels, restaurants, arts, and nightlife. The local **Lesbian and Gay Community Center** (www.facebook.com/lgbtccno; www.lgbtccneworleans.org) is currently staffed part-time by volunteers and not always accessible, but its sites have good info.

Mail & Shipping At press time, domestic postage rates were 33¢ for a postcard and 46¢ for a letter up to 1 ounce. For international mail, a first-class postcard or letter stamp costs $1.10. For more information, go to **www.usps.com.**

If you aren't sure what your address will be in the United States, mail can be sent to you, in your name, c/o General Delivery at the main post office of the city or region where you expect to be. (Call ☏ **800/275-8777** for information on the nearest post office.) The addressee must pick up mail in person and produce proof of identity (driver's license, passport, and so on). Most post offices will hold mail for up to 1 month and are open Monday to Friday 8am to 6pm and Saturday 9am to 3pm.

Always include ZIP codes when mailing items in the U.S. If you don't know the ZIP code, visit www.usps.com/zip4.

Medical Care   See "Health."

Medical Requirements   Unless you're arriving from an area known to be suffering from an epidemic (particularly cholera or yellow fever), inoculations or vaccinations are not required for entry into the United States.

Mobile Phones   Mobile (cell) phone and texting service in New Orleans is generally good, with AT&T/T-Mobile, Verizon, and Sprint all getting excellent coverage. Some dead zones still exist around the city and inside old brick buildings. International mobile phone service can be hit-or-miss (despite what you may have been told before you began your trip). If you plan to use your phone a lot while in New Orleans, it may be worthwhile to invest in an inexpensive "pay as you go" phone from a local outlet. There's an **AT&T** store at 201 St. Charles Ave. (© **504/581-2900**) and a **Radio Shack** at 6045 Magazine St. (© **504/895-4765**). Depending on the current offers, you may even get a generous credit for calls when you buy the phone. Various calling plans are available. Most no longer charge for roaming; some have costs for texting or data downloading. Discuss the options to determine which one best suits your needs before making a commitment, and read the agreement to make sure you're not purchasing more or longer-term services than you need.

If you have a computer and Internet service, consider using a broadband-based telephone service such as Skype (www.skype.com) or Vonage (www.vonage.com), which allow you to make free international calls from your computer. Neither service requires that the people you're calling also have the service (though there are fees if they do not).

Money & Costs   Frommer's lists prices in the local currency. The currency conversions quoted below were correct at press time. However, rates fluctuate, so before departing consult a currency exchange website such as **www.oanda.com/convert/classic.**

THE VALUE OF THE U.S. DOLLAR VS. OTHER POPULAR CURRENCIES

US$	C$	£	€	A$	NZ$
1.0	1.05	0.64	0.76	1.09	1.27

Costs in New Orleans are generally right in the middle of, and sometimes lower than, other midsize U.S. "destination" cities—less than New York, for example, but more than Phoenix. Prices have crept up over the last few years, so it's no longer the great value it once was. However, costs does vary greatly by season. You can often find superb hotel deals in the heat of summer, while prices can soar during big events. December's prix-fixe Réveillon deals can get you into restaurants for dinners that might otherwise be prohibitive.

With a few cash-only exceptions, major credit cards are accepted everywhere (some don't accept American Express, Discover, or Diner's Club). Cash is king anywhere, and ATMs are plentiful throughout the city (including inside many bars and souvenir shops). Expect a $2.50 to $4.00 charge to use an ATM outside your network. To avoid the fee, most grocery and convenience stores will allow you to get a small amount of cash back with your purchase (from $10–$100, depending on store policy).

Beware of hidden credit-card fees while traveling. Check with your credit or debit card issuer to see what fees, if any, will be charged for overseas transactions, even if those charges were made in U.S. dollars. Check with your bank before departing to avoid surprise charges on your statement.

WHAT THINGS COST IN NEW ORLEANS	US$
Taxi from airport to the Quarter	33.00 (for two people)
Shuttle from airport to the Quarter	20.00 (per person)
Cost of bus/streetcar one-way	1.25
Day pass for bus/streetcar	3.00
Standard room at Ritz-Carlton	199.00–329.00
Standard room at International House	119.00–379.00
Standard room at Drury Inn	119.00–239.00
Order of 3 beignets or cup of café au lait at Café du Monde	2.14
Dinner at Commander's Palace (3 courses)	65.00 (per person)
Dinner at Irene's Cuisine (3 courses)	44.00 (per person)
Muffuletta sandwich at Central Grocery	14.50
Ticket to a show at Tipitina's	10.00–25.00
Cost of a Hurricane at Pat O'Brien's with souvenir glass	11.00
Cost of a Pimm's Cup at Napoleon House	6.50

For help with currency conversions, tip calculations, and more, download Frommer's convenient Travel Tools app for your mobile device. Go to www.frommers.com/go/mobile and click on the Travel Tools icon.

Newspapers & Magazines   The city has two local papers: *The Advocate* (www.theneworleansadvocate.com), which publishes daily; and the *Times-Picayune* (www.nola.com), which publishes Wednesday, Friday, and Sunday editions. *Offbeat* (www.offbeat.com) and *Where Y'at* are monthly entertainment guides with live music, art, and special event listings. Both are usually found in hotels and clubs, and get scarce toward the end of the month. *Gambit Weekly* (www.bestofneworleans.com), which comes out every Sunday, is the city's free alternative paper and has a good mix of news and entertainment information.

Packing   What to pack depends largely on what you plan to do while visiting New Orleans. But comfortable walking shoes are a must year-round. A compact umbrella will often be put to use, as will other raingear during the wetter months and a sun hat for much of the year. A light sweater or jacket is needed even in the hottest weather, when the indoor air can get frigid. Casual wear is the daytime norm, but cocktail wear is appropriate in nicer restaurants, and some of the old-liners require jackets for gentlemen. Also see the suggestions under "Health" and "Safety" in this section.

Passports   Every air traveler entering the U.S. is required to show a valid passport (including U.S. citizens). Those entering by land and sea must also present a passport or other appropriate documentation. See www.dhs.gov/crossing-us-borders for more information.

Australia   Australian Passport Information Service (© **131-232;** www.passports.gov.au).
Canada   **Passport Office,** Passport Canada Program, Gatineau QC K1A 0G3 (© **800/567-6868;** www.ppt.gc.ca).
Ireland   **Passport Office,** Frederick Buildings, Molesworth Street, Dublin 2 (© **+353 1 671 1633;** www.dfa.ie).

New Zealand   Passports Office, Department of Internal Affairs, 109 Featherston St., Wellington, 6140 (📞 **0800 22 50 50** in New Zealand, or +64 (4) 463 9360; www.passports. govt.nz).

United Kingdom   Visit your nearest passport office, major post office, or travel agency, or contact the **HM Passport Office,** 4th Floor, Peel Building, 2 Marsham St., London, SW1P 4DF (📞 **0300 222 0000;** www.ips.gov.uk).

United States   To find your regional passport office, check the U.S. State Department website (travel.state.gov/passport) or call the **National Passport Information Center** (📞 **877/487-2778**) for automated information.

Pharmacy   Pharmacies (a.k.a., chemists or druggists) are easily found. Large chain pharmacies including **Rite Aid, CVS,** and **Walgreen's** operate throughout the city. There are 24-hour pharmacies at the **Walgreen's** at 1801 St. Charles Ave. in the Lower Garden District (📞 **504/561-8458**) and in Mid-City at 2418 S. Carrollton Ave. (📞 **504/861-5033**).

Petrol   Please see "By Car" under "Getting Around," earlier in this chapter.

Police   Dial 📞 **911** for emergencies. This is a free call from any phone. Calls from landlines will route to the local law emergency dispatch agency. From mobile phones, immediately tell the operator your location and the nature of the emergency.

Safety   It's true that New Orleans has a high crime rate. But most of the serious crime is drug-related and confined to areas where tourists do not go. Still, we urge you to be very cautious about where you go, what you do, and with whom—particularly at night. In short, behave with the same savvy and street smarts you would demonstrate in any big city: Travel in groups or pairs, take cabs if you're not sure of an area, stay in well-lighted areas with plenty of street and pedestrian traffic, follow your instincts if something seems "off." Stay alert and walk with confidence; avoid looking distracted, confused, or (sorry) drunk. Speaking of which, one way to ensure you will look like a tourist—and thus, a target—is to wear Mardi Gras beads at any time other than Mardi Gras season.

iPhones have become a target of grab-and-run thieves, especially since users, like those who text while walking, are frequently distracted. If you must check something on your phone, stop into a hotel lobby or bar.

When it's not in use, put that expensive camera out of sight. Use camera cases and purses with a shoulder strap, carried diagonally over the shoulder so a simple tug won't dislodge them. Consider using a money belt or other hidden travel wallet. Ditch the trendy enormous bag and invest in a cute little shoulder-strappy thing for clubbing, one you can dance with rather than leave on your seat (better yet, go purse-free). And never leave valuables in the outside pocket of a backpack. If you must store belongings in a car, store them in the trunk, Leave expensive-looking jewelry and other conspicuous valuables at home, and by all means, don't look for or buy drugs or engage in any illegal activity.

On **Bourbon Street** be careful when socializing with strangers, and be alert to distractions by potential pickpocket teams. Take cabs down Esplanade and into the **Faubourg Marigny.**

Scattered sections of the **Tremé, Bywater,** and the **Irish Channel** section of the Lower Garden District are transitional and may be considered sketchy. This shouldn't dissuade you from visiting, but it should keep you on your toes. Don't travel solo; do take cabs, even for short rides.

Single Travelers   Single travelers, both male and female, should feel comfortable in New Orleans. Many restaurants, including some of the city's finest, serve meals at the bar—a personal favorite spot when dining solo (Emeril's, Coquette, Cochon, and Acme come to mind). Still, single women travelers in particular should heed the warnings in the "Safety" section, above.

Smoking Technically, smoking is not allowed in most public places, with some exceptions such as free-standing bars. Restaurants are nonsmoking (though many bars serve some food, and thus smoking is allowed); often the nearest courtyard or street becomes an impromptu smoking section. Hotel lobbies are nonsmoking, but guest rooms can be designated as smoking or nonsmoking (be sure to make your preference clear when reserving a room; many hotels are entirely smoke-free). Historically, nightclubs have been smokers' havens, but there's a growing trend toward nonsmoking clubs (see www.letsbe totallyclear.org for a list of them).

Taxes The United States has no value-added tax (VAT) or other indirect tax at the national level. Every state, county, and city may levy its own local tax on all purchases, including hotel and restaurant checks and airline tickets. These taxes will not appear on price tags. The sales tax in New Orleans is 9%. Add 4% tax to hotel bills, for a total of 13%. There is also a nightly tax of 50¢ to $2 based on the number of rooms a hotel has.

On the upside, international travelers who purchase goods in Louisiana to take to their home countries can often get the sales tax refunded in full. When you make your purchase, keep your receipt and also request a "tax back" voucher (you'll be asked to show your passport). Before you leave the state, bring your receipts and vouchers to the Refund Center at New Orleans Airport (main lobby of Terminal C; allow time before your flight). You'll be rebated in cash up to US$500 (larger rebates are mailed; see www.louisianatax free.com for instructions and more information). Not all stores participate, so ask first.

Also, many original works of art purchased in New Orleans are tax-exempt. Do inquire, as this applies in designated cultural districts only.

Telephones Hotel costs for long-distance and local calls made from guest rooms vary widely. Local calls range from complimentary to astronomically expensive; long-distance calls typically fall into the latter category. If you intend to use the room phone, definitely inquire about phone charges. You may be better off using a mobile phone or a **prepaid calling card.** Public payphones are rare, but some (i.e., at airports) accept credit cards. Most long-distance and international calls can be dialed directly from any phone. **To make calls within the United States and to Canada,** dial 1 followed by the area code and the seven-digit number. **For other international calls,** dial 011 followed by the country code, city code, and the number you are calling. Calls to area codes **800, 888, 877,** and **866** are toll-free. For **reversed-charge (collect) calls,** dial the number 0 then the area code and number. When the operator comes on the line, specify that you are calling collect.

For **directory assistance** ("Information"), dial 411 for help finding numbers in the U.S. and Canada; for long-distance information, dial 1, the appropriate area code, plus 555-1212. This call may result in a charge.

Time New Orleans is in the Central Time Zone (CST), which is 1 hour earlier than Eastern Standard Time and 5 hours earlier than Greenwich Mean Time. The continental United States is divided into **four time zones:** Eastern Standard Time (EST), Central Standard Time (CST), Mountain Standard Time (MST), and Pacific Standard Time (PST). Alaska and Hawaii have their own zones. When it's 9am in Los Angeles (PST), it's 7am in Honolulu (HST),10am in Denver (MST), 11am in New Orleans and Chicago (CST), noon in New York City (EST), 5pm in London (GMT), and 2am the next day in Sydney.

Daylight saving time (summer time) is in effect from 1am on the second Sunday in March to 1am on the first Sunday in November, except in Arizona, Hawaii, the U.S. Virgin Islands, and Puerto Rico. Daylight saving time moves the clock 1 hour ahead of standard time.

Tipping Tips are a very important part of certain workers' income, and the standard way of showing appreciation for services provided (it's certainly not compulsory if the service is poor!). In hotels, tip **bellhops** at least $1 per bag ($2–$3 if you have a lot of luggage) and tip the **chamber staff** $1 to $2 per day (more if you've been extra messy). Tip the **doorman** or **concierge** if he or she has provided you with some specific service (for example, calling a cab for you or obtaining tickets or reservations). Tip the **valet-parking attendant** $1 every time you get your car.

In restaurants, bars, and nightclubs, tip **service staff** and **bartenders** 15% to 20% of the check, tip **checkroom attendants** $1 per garment, and tip **valet-parking attendants** $2 to $3 per vehicle. Some restaurants will automatically add a tip to the bill for larger parties (typically 18% for six or more guests, but this can vary). Check your bill or ask your server if gratuity has been included in your bill.

As for other service personnel, tip **cab drivers** 15% of the fare, tip **skycaps** at airports at least $2 per bag (more if you have a lot of luggage), and tip **hairdressers** and **barbers** 15% to 20%.

For help with tip calculations, currency conversions, translations, and more, download our convenient Travel Tools app for your mobile device. Go to www.frommers.com/go/mobile and click on the Travel Tools icon.

Toilets   You won't find public toilets or "restrooms" on the streets in most U.S. cities, but they can be found in hotel lobbies, bars, restaurants, museums, department stores, railway and bus stations, and service stations. Large hotels and fast-food restaurants are often the best bet for clean facilities. Restaurants and bars may restrict their restrooms to paying patrons.

Tours   There are tours geared toward antiquing, literature, history, gay and lesbian culture, ghosts, and voodoo, along with tours of the fabled, stunning swamps, plantation homes, cemeteries, and various areas of New Orleans. For more on tours, see chapters 7 and 11. For information on voluntourism, see p. 38. For self-guided walking tours, see chapter 10.

Festival Tours International offers group trips to the Jazz & Heritage Festival, with an optional side trip to Cajun Country (p. 221). The **New Orleans Cooking Experience** (p. 156) offers half-day and 3-day trips with on-site bed-and-breakfast lodging and hands-on classes by master chefs.

VAT   See "Taxes," earlier in this section.

Visas   The U.S. State Department has a **Visa Waiver Program (VWP)** allowing citizens of the following countries to enter the United States without a visa for stays of up to 90 days: Andorra, Australia, Austria, Belgium, Brunei, Czech Republic, Denmark, Estonia, Finland, France, Germany, Greece, Hungary, Iceland, Ireland, Italy, Japan, Latvia, Liechtenstein, Lithuania, Luxembourg, Malta, Monaco, the Netherlands, New Zealand, Norway, Portugal, San Marino, Singapore, Slovakia, Slovenia, South Korea, Spain, Sweden, Switzerland, and the United Kingdom. (**Note:** This list was accurate at press time; for the most up-to-date list of countries in the VWP, consult http://travel.state.gov/visa.) Even though a visa isn't necessary, in an effort to help U.S. officials check travelers against terror watch lists before they arrive at U.S. borders, visitors from VWP countries must register online through the Electronic System for Travel Authorization (ESTA) before boarding a plane or a boat to the U.S. Travelers must complete an electronic application providing basic personal and travel eligibility information. The Department of Homeland Security recommends filling out the form at least 3 days before traveling. Authorizations will be valid for up to 2 years or until the traveler's passport expires, whichever comes first. Currently, there is one US$14 fee for the online application. Existing ESTA registrations remain valid through their expiration dates. **Note:** Any passport issued on or after October 26, 2006, by a VWP country must be an **e-Passport** for VWP travelers to be eligible to enter the U.S. without a visa. Citizens of these nations also need to present a round-trip air or cruise ticket upon arrival. E-Passports contain computer chips capable of storing biometric information, such as the required digital photograph of the holder. If your passport doesn't have this feature, you can still travel without a visa if the valid passport was issued before October 26, 2005, and includes a machine-readable zone, or if the valid passport was issued between October 26, 2005, and October 25, 2006, and includes a digital photograph. For more information, go to **http://travel.state.gov/visa.** Canadian citizens may enter the United States without visas, but will need to show passports and proof of residence.

Citizens of all other countries must have (1) a valid passport that expires at least 6 months later than the scheduled end of their visit to the U.S., and (2) a tourist visa.

For information about U.S. Visas go to **http://travel.state.gov** and click on "Visas." Or go to one of the following websites:

Australian citizens can obtain up-to-date visa information from the **U.S. Embassy Canberra,** Moonah Place, Yarralumla, ACT 2600 (ⓒ **02/6214-5600**), or by checking the U.S. Diplomatic Mission's website at **http://canberra.usembassy.gov/visas.html.**

British subjects can obtain visa appointments the **U.S. Embassy Visa Appointment Line** (ⓒ **020-3608-6998**from within the U.K. or ⓒ **703-439-2367** from within the U.S. Also see **https://ais.usvisa-info.com/en-gb.**

Irish citizens can obtain up-to-date visa information through the **U.S. Embassy Dublin,** 42 Elgin Rd., Ballsbridge, Dublin 4 (ⓒ **(01)903-6255** from within the Republic of Ireland; **http://dublin.usembassy.gov.visas.html**).

Citizens of **New Zealand** can obtain up-to-date visa information by contacting the **U.S. Embassy New Zealand,** 29 Fitzherbert Terrace, Thorndon, Wellington (ⓒ **(04) 462 6000** from within New Zealand**; http://newzealand.usembassy.gov/visas.html**).

Visitor Information   Even a seasoned traveler should consider writing or calling ahead to the **New Orleans Convention & Visitors Bureau,** 2020 St. Charles Ave., New Orleans, LA 70130 (ⓒ **800/672-6124** or 504/566-5011; www.neworleanscvb.com). The friendly, helpful staff will help with advice and decision-making; if you have a special interest, they'll help you plan your visit around it—this is definitely one of the most helpful tourist centers in any major city.

The **New Orleans Welcome Center,** 529 St. Ann St. (ⓒ **504/568-5661;** daily Tues–Sat 9am–5pm) has walking- and driving-tour maps; booklets on restaurants, accommodations, sightseeing, special tours; and more. Note that the **tour offices** scattered around the city are for-profit offices operated by tourism businesses hawking their wares. Rather than unbiased services that will recommend the best tour for you, these are commissioned sales offices.

Water   Tap water is safe to drink in New Orleans, although bottled water is still popular.

Wi-Fi   See "Internet, Wi-Fi & Computer Rentals," earlier in this section.

Index

See also Accommodations and
Restaurant indexes, below.

General Index

A

The Abbey, 182
Accommodations, 50–69. *See
also* Accommodations Index
  alternate options, 58
  best, 4–5
  Cajun Country, 225
  Central Business District,
    62–65
  Faubourg Marigny & Bywater,
    58–60
  French Quarter & Faubourg
    Tremé, 50–58
  during Mardi Gras, 42
  Mid-City/Esplanade, 60–62
  with outstanding restaurants,
    68
  Uptown/The Garden District,
    66–69
African-American travelers, 234
Aidan Gill for Men, 192
Airboat tours, 159
Airport Shuttle New Orleans,
  229
Air travel, 229–230
Algiers Ferry, 233
Algiers Point, 18, 138
Allstate Sugar Bowl Classic, 33
AllWays Lounge, 175
Ambush magazine, 181
Americans Wetlands
  Conservation Corps, 38
Amusement Park and Children's
  Storyland, 160–161
Angela King Gallery, 186
Angelo Brocato's Ice Cream
  Parlor, 153
Angelo Brocato's ice cream
  parlor, 161
Annie Miller's Son's Swamp and
  Marsh Tours, 155
Antiques, 159, 185–186
Arcadian Books, 188
Area code, 235
Armstrong, Louis, 29
  Satchmo Summerfest, 35
Art galleries, 186–188
Arthur Roger Gallery, 186
Arts and Cultural Center, 135
Atchafalaya Experience
  (Lafayette), 227
Audubon Aquarium of the
  Americas, 117, 120
Audubon Insectarium, 120
Audubon Park, 138–139
Audubon Zoo, 140–141

Aunt Tiki's, 182
Avenue Pub, 179

B

Bacchus krewe, 46
Backstreet Cultural Museum,
  131, 135, 152
Bank of Louisiana (Police
  Station), 197
Bars, 2, 176–180
  dive bars, 182
  gay, 181–182
Bar Tonique, 176
Baseball, 163
Battle of New Orleans, 25, 139
Bayona, 153
Bayou Food Festival, 36
Beauregard-Keyes House, 122–
  123, 202
Besthoff Sculpture Garden, 133,
  160
Big Easy Rollergirls, 162
Big Lake Boating and Biking, 161
Biking, 2
  Big Lake, 161
  rentals, 233
  tours, 158
BJ's Lounge, 180
The Black Butterfly, 192
Blaine Kern's Mardi Gras World,
  131
Blue Frog Chocolates, 189
Blue Moon Saloon (Lafayette),
  226
Blue Nile, 172
Boat tours and cruises, 157–158,
  183, 231
  swamp tours, 154–155
The Bombay Club, 176
Bonomolo Limousine Service,
  230
Books, recommended, 27–29
Books a Million, 188
Bookstores, 188–189
Boomtown Casino, 162
Borracho, 175
Bosworth, Sheila, 27
Botanical Gardens, 14, 140
Bottom of the Cup Tearoom, 194
Boudin, 227
Bounce, 31
Bourbon Orleans Hotel, 200
The Bourbon Pub-Parade Disco,
  181
Bourbon Street, 9
  during Mardi Gras, 44
  sights along, 200, 201
Boutte, John, 166
Bowling, 2
BP Deepwater Horizon oil spill,
  20–21
Bradish Johnson House, 207
Brass bands, 31, 167
Brevard-Mahat-Rice House, 208

Briggs-Staub House, 206
Brite, Poppy Z., 27
Brulatour Court, 198
Bucktown, 131
The Bulldog, 180
Burke, James Lee, 27
Bush Antiques, 185
Business hours, 235
Bus tours, 149–151, 153
Bus travel, 230, 233–234
Butler, Robert Olen, 29
Bywater, 15
  accommodations, 58–60
  restaurants, 90–92

C

The Cabildo, 9, 125–126, 151,
  203–204
Cable, George Washington, 27,
  127
Café du Monde, 8–9
Café Istanbul, 182
Café Lafitte in Exile, 181
Cajun Country, 221–228
  Mardi Gras, 46
  suggested itinerary, 225–228
Cajun cuisine, 80
Cajun Encounters, 150–151
Cajun language, 222
A Cajun Man's Swamp Cruise,
  155
Cajun music, 29, 167–168, 224
Cajun Zydeco Festival, 35
Calendar of events, 33–36
Canal Place, 184
Canal Street, 15
Canal Street streetcar, 49, 234
Candies, pralines and pastries,
  189–190
Candlelight Lounge, 172
Cane & Table, 177
Carl Mack Presents, 190
Carol Robinson Gallery, 186
Carousel Bar at the Monteleone
  Hotel, 177
Carousel Gardens, 140, 161
Carriage tours, 158–159
Carroll-Crawford House, 207
Car travel, 230
Carver Theater, 182
Casinos, 162
Cat's Meow, 177
Celebration in the Oaks, 36, 160
Cellphones, 238
Cemeteries, 141–145
Central Business District (CBD),
  15, 18
  accommodations, 62–65
  restaurants, 96–102
Central Grocery, 9, 90, 203
Chalmette Battlefield/Jean
  Lafitte National Historical Park
  & Preserve, 139
Champions Square, 138

245

GENERAL INDEX

Restaurants

Before, During, or After your use of an EasyGuide... you'll want to consult

FR◀MMERS.COM

FROMMERS.COM IS KEPT UP-TO-DATE, WITH:

NEWS
The latest events (and deals) to affect your next vacation

BLOGS
Opinionated comments by our outspoken staff

FORUMS
Post your travel questions, get answers from other readers

SLIDESHOWS
On weekly-changing, practical but inspiring topics of travel

CONTES▀▀
Enabling you to wir

PODCA▀
Of our weekly, nationw

DESTINAT
Hundreds of cities, their hotels

TRIP ID▀
Valuable, offbeat suggestions

*AND MUCH ▀

Smart travelers consult ▀